CCSP: Securing Cisco IOS Networks Study Guide

Securing Cisco IOS Networks Exam (SECUR 642-501)

OBJECTIVE	CHAPTER
Basic Cisco Router Security	
Secure administrative access for Cisco routers	1, 2, 3, 4
Describe the components of a basic AAA implementation	2
Test the perimeter router AAA implementation using applicable debug commands	2
Advanced AAA Security for Cisco Router Networks	
Describe the features and architecture of CSACS 3.0 for Windows	3
Configure the perimeter router to enable AAA processes to use a TACACS remote service	3, 4
Cisco Router Threat Mitigation	
Disable unused router services and interfaces	4
Use access lists to mitigate common router security threats	4
Cisco IOS Firewall CBAC Configuration	
Define the Cisco IOS Firewall and CBAC	5
Configure CBAC	5
Cisco IOS Firewall Authentication Proxy Configuration	
Describe how authentication proxy technology works	6
Configure AAA on a Cisco IOS Firewall	6

SYBEX

OBJECTIVE	CHAPTER

Exam objectives are subject to change at any time without prior notice and at Cisco's sole discretion. Please visit Cisco's website (http://www.cisco.com) for the most current exam objectives listing.

CCSP:
Securing Cisco IOS Networks
Study Guide

CCSP™:
Securing Cisco IOS Networks

Study Guide

Todd Lammle
Carl Timm, CCIE #7149

San Francisco • London

SYBEX®

Associate Publisher: Neil Edde
Acquisitions Editor: Maureen Adams
Developmental Editor: Heather O'Connor
Production Editor: Mae Lum
Technical Editors: Craig Vazquez, Dan Aguilera, Jason T. Rohm
Copyeditor: Sarah H. Lemaire
Compositor: Judy Fung
Graphic Illustrators: Tony Jonick, Scott Benoit
CD Coordinator: Dan Mummert
CD Technician: Kevin Ly
Proofreaders: Laurie O'Connell, Nancy Riddiough, Monique van den Berg
Indexer: Nancy Guenther
Book Designers: Bill Gibson, Judy Fung
Cover Designer: Archer Design
Cover Photographer: Tony Stone

Library of Congress Card Number: 2003103564

ISBN: 0-7821-4231-1

SYBEX

To Our Valued Readers:

Thank you for looking to Sybex for your Cisco Certified Security Professional exam prep needs. Developed by Cisco to validate expertise in designing and implementing secure Cisco internetworking solutions, the CCSP certification stands to be one of the most highly sought after IT certifications available.

We at Sybex are proud of the reputation we've established for providing certification candidates with the practical knowledge and skills needed to succeed in the highly competitive IT marketplace. It has always been Sybex's mission to teach individuals how to utilize technologies in the real world, not to simply feed them answers to test questions. Just as Cisco is committed to establishing measurable standards for certifying those professionals who work in the cutting-edge field of internetworking, Sybex is committed to providing those professionals with the means of acquiring the skills and knowledge they need to meet those standards.

The authors, editors, and technical reviewers have worked hard to ensure that this Study Guide is comprehensive, in-depth, and pedagogically sound. We're confident that this book, along with the collection of cutting-edge software study tools included on the CD, will meet and exceed the demanding standards of the certification marketplace and help you, the CCSP certification exam candidate, succeed in your endeavors.

Good luck in pursuit of your CCSP certification!

Neil Edde
Associate Publisher—Certification
Sybex, Inc.

Acknowledgments

I would like to thank Neil Edde and Maureen Adams for helping me get this project off the ground and making this a really great book—one I happen to be very excited about! Thank you, Neil and Maureen!

And kudos to you too, Heather! Ms. O'Connor was instrumental in helping me develop this book's content. She and Mae Lum, the production editor, shepherded the whole project through production—no small task! I'd also like to thank Monica Lammle for helping me make this my best book to date and Carl Timm and Donald Porter, whose technical expertise was instrumental in the writing of this book—I couldn't have done it without all of you!

My thanks also to the Sybex editorial and production team: copyeditor Sarah Lemaire; compositor Judy Fung, proofreaders Laurie O'Connell, Nancy Riddiough, and Monique van den Berg; and indexer Nancy Guenther.

Contents at a Glance

Contents

Introduction

Welcome to the exciting world of Cisco security certification! You've picked up this book because you want something better/more—better skills, more opportunities, better jobs, more job security, better quality of life, more mintage in your pocket—things like that. That's no pie-in-the-sky fantasy for you, my friend—you're smart! How do I know that? Because you've made a wise decision in picking up this book, and you wouldn't have done that unless you were smart. And you're right—Cisco security certification *can* really help you do everything from getting your first networking job to realizing your dreams of more money, prestige, job security, and satisfaction if you're already in the industry. Basically, as long as you don't have some weird, unfortunate workplace habit such as, oh, let's say, shower-fasting, you're all-the-rage, serious promotion material if you're packing Cisco certifications. And only that much more so if you make the move into security and get certified there!

Cisco security certifications can give you another important edge—jumping through the hoops and learning what's required to get those certifications will thoroughly improve your understanding of *everything* related to security internetworking, which is relevant to much more than just Cisco products. You'll be totally dialed in—equipped with a solid knowledge of network security and how different topologies work together to form a secure network. This definitely can't hurt your cause! It's beneficial to every networking job—it's the reason Cisco security certification is in such high demand, even at companies with only a few Cisco devices!

These new Cisco security certifications reach beyond the popular certifications such as the CCNA/CCDA and CCNP/CCDP to provide you with an indispensable factor in understanding today's secure network—insight into the Cisco secure world of internetworking.

So really, by deciding you want to become Cisco security certified, you're saying that you want to be the best—the best at routing and the best at network security. This book will put you way ahead on the path to that goal.

You may be thinking, "Why is it that networks are so vulnerable to security breaches anyway? Why can't the operating systems provide protection?" The answer is pretty straightforward: Users want lots of features and Microsoft gives the users what they want because features sell. Capabilities such as sharing files and printers, and logging into the corporate infrastructure from the Internet are not just desired—they're expected. The new corporate battle cry is, "Hey, give us complete corporate access from the Internet and make it super fast and easy—but make sure it's really secure!" Oh yeah, we'll get right on that.

Am I saying that Microsoft is the problem? No—they're only part of it. There are just too many other security issues for any one company to be at fault. But it is true that providing any and all of the features that any user could possibly want on a network at the click of a mouse certainly creates some major security issues. And it's also true that we certainly didn't have the types of hackers we have today until Windows accidentally opened the door for them. But all of that is really just the beginning. To become truly capable of defending yourself, you must understand the vulnerabilities of a plethora of technologies and networking equipment. And trust me, there's no shortage of them!

So, the goal here is really twofold: First, I'm going to give you the information you need to understand all those vulnerabilities, and second, I'm going to show you how to create a single, network-wide security policy. But before I go there, there are two key questions behind most security issues on the Internet:

- How do you protect confidential information but still allow access for the corporate users that need to get to that information?

- How do you protect your network and its resources from unknown or unwanted users from outside your network?

If you're going to protect something, you have to know where it is, right? Where important/confidential information is stored is key for any network administrator concerned with security. You'll find the goods in two places: physical storage media (such as hard drives or RAM) and in transit across a network in the form of packets. This book's focus is mainly on the network security issues relative to the transit of confidential information across a network. But it's important to remember that both physical media and packets need to be protected from intruders within your network and outside of it. TCP/IP is used in all of the examples in this book because it's the most popular protocol suite these days and also because it has some inherent and truly ugly security weaknesses.

But you won't stop there. You'll need to look beyond TCP/IP and understand that both operating systems and network equipment come with their own vulnerabilities to address as well. If you don't have passwords and authentication properly set on your network equipment, you're in obvious trouble. If you don't understand your routing protocols and especially, how they advertise throughout your network, you might as well leave the building unlocked at night. Furthermore, how much do you know about your firewall? Do you have one? If so, where are its weak spots? Does it have any gaping holes? If you haven't covered all these bases, your equipment will be your network's Achilles heel.

What is Good Security?

So now you have a good idea of what you're up against in the battle to provide security for your network. To stay competitive in this game, you need to have a sound security policy that is both monitored and used regularly. Good intentions won't stop the bad guys from getting you. It's planning and foresight that will save your neck. All possible problems need to be considered, written down, discussed, and addressed with a solid action plan.

And you need to communicate your plan clearly and concisely to the powers that be by providing management with your solid policy so that they can make informed decisions. With knowledge and careful planning, you can balance security requirements with user-friendly access and approach. And you can accomplish all of it at an acceptable level of operational cost. But this, as with many truly valuable things, is not going to be easy to attain.

First-class security solutions should allow network managers the ability to offer improved services to their corporate clients—both internally and externally—and save the company a nice chunk of change at the same time. If you can do this, odds are good that you'll end up with a nice chunk of change too. Everybody (but not the bad guys) gets to win. Sweet!

Basically, if you can understand security well, and if you figure out how to effectively provide network services without spending the entire IT budget, you'll enjoy a long, lustrous, and lucrative career in the IT world. You must be able to

- Enable new networked applications and services.
- Reduce the costs of implementation and operations of the network.
- Make the Internet a global, low-cost access medium.

It's also good to remember that people who make really difficult, complicated things simpler and more manageable tend to be honored, respected, and generally very popular—read, in demand and employed. One way to simplify the complex is to break a large, multifaceted thing down into nice, manageable chunks. To do this, you need to classify each network into each one of the three types of network security classifications: trusted networks, untrusted networks, and unknown networks. You should know a little bit about these before you begin this book.

Trusted networks   *Trusted networks* are the networks you want to protect, and they populate the zone known as the *security perimeter*. The security perimeter is connected to a firewall server through network adapter cards. Virtual private networks (VPNs) are also considered trusted networks, only they send data across untrusted networks. So they're special—they create special circumstances and require special considerations in establishing a security policy for them. The packets transmitted on a VPN are established on a trusted network, so the firewall server needs to authenticate the origin of those packets, check for data integrity, and provide for any other security needs of the corporation.

Untrusted networks   *Untrusted networks* are those found outside the security perimeters and not controlled by you or your administrators, such as the Internet and the corporate ISP. Basically, these are the networks you are trying to protect yourself from while still allowing access to and from them.

Unknown networks   Because you can't categorize something you don't know, *unknown networks* are described as neither trusted or untrusted. This type of mystery network doesn't tell the firewall if it's an inside (trusted) network or outside (untrusted) network. Hopefully, you won't have networks such as these bothering you.

How to Use This Book

If you want a solid foundation for the serious effort of preparing for the Securing Cisco IOS Networks (SECUR 642-501) exam, then look no further. I've spent a huge amount of time putting this book together in a way that will thoroughly equip you with everything you need to pass the SECUR exam, as well as teach you how to completely configure security on Cisco routers.

This book is loaded with lots of valuable information. You'll really maximize your studying time if you understand how I put this book together.

To benefit the most from this book, I recommend you tackle it like this:

1. Take the assessment test immediately following this introduction. (The answers are at the end of the test, so no cheating.) It's okay if you don't know any of the answers—that's why you bought this book! But you do need to carefully read over the explanations for any question you do happen to get wrong and make note of which chapters the material comes from. It will help you plan your study strategy. Again, don't be too bummed out if you don't know any answers—just think instead of how much you're about to learn!

2. Study each chapter carefully, making sure that you fully understand the information and the test objectives listed at the beginning of each chapter. And really zero in on any chapter or part of a chapter that's dealing with areas where you missed questions in the assessment test.

3. Take the time to complete the written lab at the end of the chapter. Do *not* skip this—it directly relates to the SECUR exam and the relevant stuff you've got to glean from the chapter you just read. So no skimming—make sure you really, *really* understand the reason for each answer!

4. Answer all of the review questions related to that chapter. (The answers appear at the end of the chapter.) While you're going through the questions, jot down any questions that confuse you and study those sections of the book again. Don't throw away your notes—go over the questions that were difficult for you again before you take the exam. Seriously—don't just skim these questions! Make sure you completely understand the reason for each answer, because the questions were written strategically to help you master the material that you must know before taking the SECUR exam.

5. Complete all the hands-on labs in the chapter, referring to the relevant chapter material so that you understand the reason for each step you take. If you don't happen to have a bunch of Cisco equipment lying around to mess around with, be sure to study the examples extra carefully. You can also check out `www.routersim.com` for a router simulator to help you gain hands-on experience.

6. Try your hand at the bonus exams that are included on the CD provided with this book. These questions appear only on the CD, and testing yourself will give you a clear overview of what you can expect to see on the real thing.

7. Answer all the flashcard questions on the CD. The flashcard program will help you prepare completely for the SECUR exam.

 The electronic flashcards can be used on your Windows computer, Pocket PC, or Palm device.

8. Make sure you read the Exam Essentials, Key Terms, and Commands Used in This Chapter lists at the end of the chapters and are intimately familiar with the information in those three sections.

I'm not going to lie to you—learning all the material covered in this book isn't going to be a day at the beach. (Unless, of course, you study at the beach. But it's still going to take you more than a day, so… oh, never mind.) What I'm trying to say is, it's going to be hard. Things that are really worthwhile tend to be like that. So you'll just have to be good boys and girls and apply yourselves regularly. Try to set aside the same time period every day to study and select a comfortable, quiet place to do so. Not every night, all comfy and cozy in bed 15 minutes before lights out either—you really don't want to find yourself reading the same paragraph over and over again, do you? Pick a distraction-free time/place combo where you can be sharp and focused. If you work hard, you'll get it all down, probably faster than you think!

This book covers everything you need to know in order to pass the SECUR exam. But even so, taking the time to study and practice with routers or a router simulator is your real key to success.

I promise—if you follow the preceding eight steps, really study and practice the review questions, the bonus exams, the electronic flashcards, and the written and hands-on labs, and practice with routers or a router simulator, it will be diamond-hard to fail the SECUR exam!

What Does This Book Cover?

Here's the information you need to know for the SECUR exam—the goods that you'll learn in this book.

Chapter 1, "Introduction to Network Security," introduces you to network security and the basic threats you need to be aware of. Chapter 1 also describes the types of weaknesses that might exist on your network. All organizations must have a well-documented policy; this chapter explains how to develop a solid corporate network security policy and outlines what guidelines it should include.

Chapter 2, "Introduction to AAA Security," is an introduction to the Cisco NAS (network access server) and AAA security. Chapter 2 explains how to configure a Cisco NAS router for authentication, authorization, and accounting.

Chapter 3, "Configuring CiscoSecure ACS and TACACS+," explains how to install, configure, and administer the CiscoSecure ACS on Windows 2000 and Windows NT servers. (Chapter 3 also briefly describes the CiscoSecure ACS on Unix servers.) In addition, this chapter describes how the NAS can use either TACACS+ or RADIUS to communicate user access requests to the ACS.

Chapter 4, "Cisco Perimeter Router Problems and Solutions," introduces you to the Cisco perimeter router and the problems that can occur from hackers to a perimeter router on your network. This chapter also describes how you can implement solutions to these problems.

Chapter 5, "Context-Based Access Control Configuration," introduces you to the Cisco IOS Firewall and one of its main components, Context-Based Access Control (CBAC). Chapter 5 explains how CBAC is both different and better than just running static ACLs when it comes to protecting your network.

Chapter 6, "Cisco IOS Firewall Authentication and Intrusion Detection," discusses the IOS Firewall Authentication Proxy, which allows you to create and apply access control policies to individuals rather than to addresses. In addition, this chapter also explains the IOS Firewall Intrusion Detection System (IDS), which allows your IOS router to act as a CiscoSecure IDS sensor would, spotting and reacting to potentially inappropriate or malicious packets.

Chapter 7, "Understanding Cisco IOS IPSec Support," introduces the concept of virtual private networks (VPNs) and explains the solutions to meet your company's off-site network access needs. Chapter 7 also describes how VPNs use IP Security (IPSec) to provide secure communications over public networks.

Chapter 8, "Cisco IPSec Pre-Shared Keys and Certificate Authority Support," explains how to configure IPSec for pre-shared keys—the easiest of all the IPSec implementations—and how to configure site-to-site IPSec for certificate authority support.

Chapter 9, "Cisco IOS Remote Access Using Cisco Easy VPN," covers a very cool development in VPN technology—Cisco Easy VPN. Cisco Easy VPN is a new feature in IOS that allows any capable IOS router to act as a VPN server.

Appendix A, "Introduction to the PIX Firewall," describes the features and basic configuration of the Cisco PIX Firewall. Although there are no SECUR exam objectives that cover the PIX Firewall, this appendix helps you understand and configure a PIX box.

The Glossary is a handy resource for Cisco terms. It's a great reference tool for understanding some of the more obscure terms used in this book.

Most chapters include written labs, hands-on labs, and plenty of review questions to make sure you've mastered the material. Don't skip these tools—they're invaluable to your success.

What's on the CD?

We worked really hard to provide some very cool tools to help you with your certification process. All of the following gear should be loaded on your workstation when studying for the test:

The All-New Sybex Test Engine

The test preparation software, developed by the experts at Sybex, prepares you to pass the SECUR exam. In this test engine, you will find all the review and assessment questions from the book, plus two bonus exams that appear exclusively on the CD. You can take the assessment test, test yourself by chapter, or take the bonus exams. Your scores will show how well you did on each SECUR exam objective.

To find more test-simulation software for all Cisco and Microsoft exams, look for the CertSim link at www.routersim.com.

Electronic Flashcards for PC and Palm Devices

So to prepare for the exam, you do...what? Let's summarize. First, you read this book. Then you proceed to study the review questions at the end of each chapter and work through the bonus exams included on the CD. After that, you test yourself with the flashcards included on the CD. Having done these things, you're now unshakably confident because you know that if you can get through these difficult questions and understand the answers, you're truly a formidable force. You can take the worst the SECUR exam can throw at you.

That's because the flashcards include about 150 questions designed to hit you harder than Jet Li and make sure you're the Terminator of test-takers—meaning you *are* ready for the exam. Between the review questions, the practice exams, and the flashcards, you'll be ready to rock with everything you need and more to pass!

CCSP: Securing Cisco IOS Networks Study Guide in PDF

Sybex offers the *CCSP: Securing Cisco IOS Networks Study Guide* in PDF format on the CD so you can read the book on your PC or laptop if you travel and don't want to carry a book, or if you just like to read from the computer screen. Acrobat Reader 5.1 with Search is also included on the CD.

Cisco Security Certifications

There are quite a few new Cisco security certifications to be had, but the good news is that this book, which covers the SECUR exam, is the prerequisite for all Cisco security certifications! All of these new Cisco security certifications also require a valid CCNA.

Cisco Certified Security Professional (CCSP)

You have to pass five exams to get your CCSP. The pivotal one of those is the SECUR exam. So if you have passed the SECUR, you need to take only four more. Here they are—the exams you must pass to call that CCSP yours:

- Securing Cisco IOS Networks (642-501 SECUR)
- Cisco Secure PIX Firewall Advanced (642-521 CSPFA)
- Cisco Secure Intrusion Detection System (642-531 CSIDS) (new exam available 3rd quarter 2003)
- Cisco Secure Virtual Networks (642-511 CSVPN)
- Cisco SAFE Implementation (9E0-131 CSI)

Cisco Firewall Specialist   Cisco security certifications focus on the growing need for knowledgeable network professionals who can implement complete security solutions. Cisco Firewall Specialists focus on securing network access using Cisco IOS Software and Cisco PIX Firewall technologies.

The two exams you must pass to achieve the Cisco Firewall Specialist certification are Securing Cisco IOS Networks (642-501 SECUR) and Cisco Secure PIX Firewall Advanced (642-521 CSPFA).

Cisco IDS Specialist   Cisco IDS Specialists can both operate and monitor Cisco IOS Software and IDS technologies to detect and respond to intrusion activities.

The two exams you must pass to achieve the Cisco IDS Specialist certification are Securing Cisco IOS Networks (642-501 SECUR) and Cisco Secure Intrusion Detection System (642-531 CSIDS) (new exam available 3rd quarter 2003).

Cisco VPN Specialist   Cisco VPN Specialists can configure VPNs across shared public networks using Cisco IOS Software and Cisco VPN 3000 Series Concentrator technologies.

The two exams you must pass to achieve the Cisco VPN Specialist certification are Securing Cisco IOS Networks (642-501 SECUR) and Cisco Secure Virtual Networks (642-511 CSVPN).

The CCSP exams and exam numbers may change at any time. Please check the Cisco website (www.cisco.com) for the latest information.

For information about Sybex's Study Guides on the CCSP exams, go to www.sybex.com.

Cisco Network Support Certifications

Initially, to secure the coveted CCIE, you took only one test and then you were faced with a nearly impossible, extremely difficult lab—an all-or-nothing approach that made it really tough to succeed. In response, Cisco created a series of new certifications to help you acquire the coveted CCIE and aid prospective employers in measuring skill levels. With these new certifications, which definitely improved the ability of mere mortals to prepare for that almighty lab, Cisco opened doors that few were allowed through before. So, what are these stepping-stone certifications, and how do they help you get your CCIE?

Cisco Certified Network Associate (CCNA)

The CCNA certification was the first in the new line of Cisco certifications, and was the precursor to all current Cisco certifications. With the new certification programs, Cisco has created a type of stepping-stone approach to CCIE certification. Now, you can become a Cisco Certified Network Associate for the meager cost of the Sybex *CCNA Study Guide,* plus $125 for the test.

And you don't have to stop there—you can choose to continue with your studies and achieve a higher certification, called the Cisco Certified Network Professional (CCNP). Someone with a CCNP has all the skills and knowledge he or she needs to attempt the CCIE lab. However, because no textbook can take the place of practical experience, we'll discuss what else you need to be ready for the CCIE lab shortly.

How Do You Become a CCNA?

The first step to becoming a CCNA is to pass one little test and—poof!—you're a CCNA. (Don't you wish it were that easy?) True, it's just one test, but you still have to possess enough knowledge to understand (and read between the lines—trust me) what the test writers are saying.

I can't stress this enough—it's critical that you have some hands-on experience with Cisco routers. If you can get ahold of some Cisco 2500 or 2600 series routers, you're set. But if you can't, I have worked hard to provide hundreds of configuration examples throughout the Sybex *CCNA Study Guide* to help network administrators (or people who want to become network administrators) learn what they need to know to pass the CCNA exam.

One way to get the hands-on router experience you'll need in the real world is to attend one of the seminars offered by Globalnet Training Solutions, Inc., which is owned and run by me, Todd Lammle. The GlobalNet Training seminars will teach you everything you need to become a CCNA, CCNP, CCSP, and CCIE! Each student gets hands-on experience by configuring at least two routers and a switch—there's no sharing of equipment!

> For hands-on training with Todd Lammle, please see www.globalnettraining.com.

> Information about Sybex's *CCNA: Cisco Certified Network Associate Study Guide* can be found at www.sybex.com.

Cisco Certified Network Professional (CCNP)

So you're thinking, "Great, what do I do after passing the CCNA exam?" Well, if you want to become a CCIE in Routing and Switching (the most popular certification), understand that there's more than one path to that much-coveted CCIE certification. The first way is to continue studying and become a Cisco Certified Network Professional (CCNP), which means four more tests, in addition to the CCNA certification.

The CCNP program will prepare you to understand and comprehensively tackle the internetworking issues of today and beyond—and it is not limited to the Cisco world. You will undergo an immense metamorphosis, vastly increasing your knowledge and skills through the process of obtaining these certifications.

While you don't need to be a CCNP or even a CCNA to take the CCIE lab, it's extremely helpful if you already have these certifications.

How Do You Become a CCNP?

After becoming a CCNA, the four exams you must take to get your CCNP are as follows:

Exam 643-801: Building Scalable Cisco Internetworks (BSCI)   This exam continues to build on the fundamentals learned in the CCNA course. It focuses on large multiprotocol internetworks and how to manage them with access lists, queuing, tunneling, route distribution, route maps, BGP, EIGRP, OSPF, and route summarization.

Exam 643-811: Building Cisco Multilayer Switched Networks (BCMSN)   This exam tests your knowledge of the Cisco Catalyst switches.

Exam 643-821: Building Cisco Remote Access Networks (BCRAN)   This exam determines if you really understand how to install, configure, monitor, and troubleshoot Cisco ISDN and dial-up access products. You must understand PPP, ISDN, Frame Relay, and authentication.

Exam 643-831: Cisco Internetwork Troubleshooting Support (CIT)   This exam tests you extensively on the Cisco troubleshooting skills needed for Ethernet and Token Ring LANs, IP, IPX, and AppleTalk networks, as well as ISDN, PPP, and Frame Relay networks.

> For information about Sybex's Study Guides on the CCNP exams, go to www.sybex.com.

www.routersim.com has a complete Cisco router simulator for all CCNP exams.

And if you hate tests, you can take fewer of them by signing up for the CCNA exam and the CIT exam and then taking just one more long exam called the Foundations exam (640-841). Doing this also gives you your CCNP, but beware—it's a really long test that fuses all the material from the BSCI, BCMSN, and BCRAN exams into one exam. Good luck! However, by taking this exam, you get three tests for the price of two, which saves you 100 smackers (if you pass).

 Remember that test objectives and tests can change at any time without notice. Always check the Cisco website for the most up-to-date information (www.cisco.com).

Cisco Certified Internetwork Expert (CCIE)

Cool! You've become a CCNP, and now your sights are fixed on getting your Cisco Certified Internetwork Expert (CCIE). What do you do next? Cisco recommends a *minimum* of two years of on-the-job experience before taking the CCIE lab. After jumping those hurdles, you then have to pass the written CCIE Exam Qualification before taking the actual lab.

There are actually four CCIE certifications, and you must pass a written exam for each one of them before attempting the hands-on lab:

CCIE Communications and Services (Exams 350-020, 350-021, 350-022, 350-023)   The CCIE Communications and Services written exams cover IP and IP routing, optical, DSL, dial, cable, wireless, WAN switching, content networking, and voice.

CCIE Routing and Switching (Exam 350-001)   The CCIE Routing and Switching exam covers IP and IP routing, non-IP desktop protocols such as IPX, and bridge- and switch-related technologies.

CCIE Security (Exam 350-018)   The CCIE Security exam covers IP and IP routing as well as specific security components.

CCIE Voice (Exam 351-030)   The CCIE Voice exam covers those technologies and applications that make up a Cisco Enterprise VoIP solution.

How Do You Become a CCIE?

To become a CCIE, Cisco recommends you do the following:

1. Attend the GlobalNet Training CCIE hands-on lab program described at www.globalnettraining.com.

2. Pass the Drake/Prometric exam. (This costs $300 per exam, so hopefully, you'll pass it the first time.) See the upcoming "Where Do You Take the Exams?" section for more information.

3. Pass the one-day, hands-on lab at Cisco. This costs $1,250 (yikes!) per lab, and many people fail it two or more times. Some people never make it through—it's very difficult. Cisco has both added and deleted sites lately for the CCIE lab, so it's best to check the Cisco website for the most current information. Take into consideration that you might just need to add travel costs to that $1,250!

Cisco Network Design Certifications

In addition to the network support certifications, Cisco has created another certification track for network designers. The two certifications within this track are the Cisco Certified Design Associate and Cisco Certified Design Professional certifications. If you're reaching for the CCIE stars, we highly recommend the CCNP and CCDP certifications before attempting the lab (or attempting to advance your career).

This certification will give you the knowledge you need to design routed LAN, routed WAN, and switched LAN and ATM LANE networks.

Cisco Certified Design Associate (CCDA)

To become a CCDA, you must pass the Designing for Cisco Internetwork Solutions exam (640-861 DESGN). To pass this test, you must understand how to do the following:

- Identify customer business needs and their internetworking requirements.

- Assess the existing customer network and identify the potential issues.

- Design the network solution that suits the customer needs.

- Explain the network design to customer and network engineers.

- Plan the implementation of the network design.

- Verify the implementation of the network design.

The *CCDA: Cisco Certified Design Associate Study Guide*, 2nd ed. (Sybex, 2003) is the most cost-effective way to study for and pass your CCDA exam.

Cisco Certified Design Professional (CCDP)

If you're already a CCNP and want to get your CCDP, you can simply take the 640-025 CID test. But if you're not yet a CCNP, you must take the CCDA, CCNA, BSCI, Switching, Remote Access, and CID exams.

CCDP certification skills include the following:

- Designing complex routed LAN, routed WAN, and switched LAN and ATM LANE networks

- Building on the base level of the CCDA technical knowledge

CCDPs must also demonstrate proficiency in the following:

- Network-layer addressing in a hierarchical environment
- Traffic management with access lists
- Hierarchical network design
- VLAN use and propagation
- Performance considerations: required hardware and software; switching engines; memory, cost, and minimization

Where Do You Take the Exams?

You may take the exams at any of the more than 800 Thomson Prometric Authorized Testing Centers around the world (www.2test.com), or call 800-204-EXAM (3926). You can also register and take the exams at a VUE authorized center as well (www.vue.com), or call 877-404-EXAM (3926).

To register for a Cisco certification exam:

1. Determine the number of the exam you want to take. (The SECUR exam number is 642-501.)

2. Register with the nearest Thomson Prometric Registration Center or VUE testing center. You'll be asked to pay in advance for the exam. At the time of this writing, the exams are $125 each and must be taken within one year of payment. You can schedule exams up to six weeks in advance, or as late as the same day you want to take it. If you fail a Cisco exam, you must wait 72 hours before you get another shot at retaking the exam. If something comes up and you need to cancel or reschedule your exam appointment, contact Thomson Prometric or VUE at least 24 hours in advance.

3. When you schedule the exam, you'll get instructions regarding all appointment and cancellation procedures, the ID requirements, and information about the testing-center location.

Tips for Taking Your SECUR Exam

The SECUR exam contains about 70 questions to be completed in about 90 minutes. This can change per exam. You've got to score right around 82% to pass, but again, each exam can be a tad different, so aim higher.

Many questions on the exam have answer choices that at first glance look a lot alike—especially the syntax questions (I'll discuss those in a moment)! Remember to read through the choices super carefully because close doesn't cut it. If you get commands in the wrong order or forget one measly character, you'll get the question wrong. So, to practice, do the hands-on exercises in this book over and over again until they feel natural to you.

Watch that Syntax!

Unlike Microsoft or Novell tests, the SECUR exam has answer choices that are syntactically similar. Although some syntax is dead wrong, it is usually just *subtly* wrong. Some other choices may be syntactically correct, but they're shown in the wrong order. Cisco does split hairs, and they're not at all averse to giving you classic trick questions. Here's an example:

True or False: `access-list 101 deny ip any any eq 23` denies Telnet access to all systems.

This statement looks correct because most people refer to the port number (23) and think, "Yes, that's the port used for Telnet." The catch is that you can't filter IP on port numbers (only TCP and UDP).

Also, never forget that the right answer is the Cisco answer. In many cases, more than one appropriate answer is presented, but the *correct* answer is the one that Cisco recommends.

Here are some general tips for exam success:

- Arrive early at the exam center so you can relax and review your study materials.

- Read the questions *carefully*. Don't jump to conclusions. Make sure you're clear about *exactly* what each question asks.

- When answering multiple-choice questions that you're not sure about, use the process of elimination to discard the obviously incorrect answers first. Doing this greatly improves your odds if you need to make an educated guess.

- You can no longer move forward and backward through the Cisco exams, so double-check your answer before pressing Next, because you can't change your mind.

After you complete an exam, you'll get immediate, online notification of your pass or fail status—a printed Examination Score Report that indicates your pass or fail status, and your exam results by section. The test administrator will give you that report. Test scores are automatically forwarded to Cisco within five working days after you take the test, so you don't need to send in your score. If you pass the exam, you'll usually receive confirmation from Cisco within two to four weeks.

How to Contact the Authors

You can reach Todd Lammle through Globalnet Training Solutions, Inc. (www.globalnettraining.com), his training company in Dallas, or at RouterSim, LLC (www.routersim.com), his software company in Denver.

You can also contact Todd Lammle and Carl Timm by going to www.globalnettraining.com/forum. You can find information about Cisco certifications and also ask questions relating to their books.

Assessment Test

1. Which of the following commands trace AAA packets and monitor their activities? (Choose all that apply.)

   A. debug aaa authentication

   B. debug aaa authorization

   C. debug aaa all

   D. debug aaa accounting

2. What is the last header you can read in clear text when a packet has been encrypted using IPSec?

   A. Physical

   B. Data Link

   C. Network

   D. Transport

3. Which of the following is an example of a configuration weakness?

   A. Old software

   B. No written security policy

   C. Unsecured user accounts

   D. No monitoring of the security

4. Which IOS feature best prevents DoS SYN flood attacks?

   A. IPSec

   B. TCP Intercept

   C. MD5 authentication

   D. ACLs

5. RSA digital signatures and _____ are IPSec authentication types supported by the Cisco Easy VPN Server.

   A. Pre-shared keys

   B. LSA analog signatures

   C. DSS

   D. DES

   E. 3DES

6. Which of the following commands do you use to change the maximum number of half-open TCP connections per minute to 100?

   A. `ip inspect tcp synwait-time 100`

   B. `ip inspect tcp idle-time 100`

   C. `ip inspect max-incomplete high 100`

   D. `ip inspect one-minute high 100`

   E. `ip inspect tcp max-incomplete host 100`

7. IP spoofing, man-in-the-middle, and session replaying are examples of what type of security weakness?

   A. Configuration weakness

   B. TCP/IP weakness

   C. Policy weakness

   D. User password weakness

8. Alert is the _____ for attack signatures in the IOS Firewall IDS.

   A. Default action

   B. Non-default action

   C. Exclusionary rule

   D. Inclusionary rule

   E. Configured action

9. If you want to make sure you have the most secure authentication method, what should you use?

   A. Windows username/password

   B. Unix username/password

   C. Token cards/soft tokens

   D. TACACS+

10. Which of the following are considered typical weaknesses in any network implementation? (Choose all that apply.)

   A. Policy weaknesses

   B. Technology weaknesses

   C. Hardware weaknesses

   D. Configuration weaknesses

11. What are RSA-encrypted nonces?

    A. Manually generated/exchanged public keys

    B. Automatically generated/exchanged public keys

    C. Manually generated/exchanged private keys

    D. Automatically generated/exchanged private keys

12. What function does the `clear crypto isakmp *` command perform?

    A. It resets all LDPM SAs configured on a device.

    B. It resets all IKE RSAs configured on a device.

    C. It resets all IKE SAs configured on a device.

    D. It resets the crypto settings for a configured peer.

13. Which component of AAA provides for the login, password, messaging, and encryption of users?

    A. Accounting

    B. Authorization

    C. Authentication

    D. Administration

14. Which of the following commands do you use to change the maximum time CBAC waits before closing idle TCP connections to 10 minutes?

    A. `ip inspect tcp synwait-time 600`

    B. `ip inspect tcp idle-time 600`

    C. `ip inspect max-incomplete high 600`

    D. `ip inspect one-minute high 600`

    E. `ip inspect tcp max-incomplete host 600`

15. Which of the following are examples of policy weaknesses? (Choose all that apply.)

    A. Absence of a proxy server

    B. No trusted networks

    C. Misconfigured network equipment

    D. No disaster recovery plan

    E. Technical support personnel continually changing

16. The ESP protocol provides which service not provided by the AH protocol?

A. Data confidentiality

B. Authentication services

C. Tamper detection

D. Anti-replay detection

17. Which of the following are valid methods for populating the CiscoSecure User Database? (Choose all that apply.)

A. Manually

B. Novell NDS

C. Windows NT

D. Database Replication utility

E. Database Import utility

18. What does the command aaa new-model do?

A. It creates a new AAA server on the NAS.

B. It deletes the router's configuration and works the same as erase startup-config.

C. It disables AAA services on the router.

D. It enables AAA services on the router.

19. A connection that has failed to reach an established state is known as _____?

A. Full-power

B. Half-baked

C. Half-open

D. Chargen

20. Which of the following security database protocols can be used between the NAS and CSNT? (Choose all that apply.)

A. NTLM

B. SNA

C. TACACS+

D. Clear text

E. RADIUS

21. Which of the following are examples of a TCP/IP weakness? (Choose all that apply.)

   A. Trojan horse

   B. HTML attack

   C. Session replaying

   D. Application layer attack

   E. SNMP

   F. SMTP

22. You have just configured IPSec encryption. Which problem are you trying to solve?

   A. Denial-of-service (DoS) attacks

   B. Rerouting

   C. Lack of legal IP addresses

   D. Eavesdropping

23. You have just configured MD5 authentication for BGP. Which type of attack are you trying to prevent?

   A. DoS

   B. Rerouting

   C. Hijacking of legal IP addresses

   D. Eavesdropping

24. Using your web browser, which port do you go to (by default) to access the CSNT web server?

   A. 80

   B. 202

   C. 1577

   D. 2002

   E. 8000

25. To help you both set up and configure CBACs, Cisco has defined six steps for configuring CBAC. What is the correct order for the six steps?

   A. Define Port-to-Application Mapping (PAM).

   B. Set audit trails and alerts.

   C. Test and verify CBAC.

   D. Set global timeouts and thresholds.

   E. Apply inspection rules and ACLs to interfaces.

   F. Define inspection rules.

26. What port does ISAKMP use for communications?

   A. TCP 50

   B. UDP 50

   C. TCP 500

   D. UDP 500

27. Policy weaknesses, technology weaknesses, and configuration weaknesses are examples of what type of implementation weakness? (Choose all that apply.)

   A. Policy implementation

   B. Network implementation

   C. Hardware implementation

   D. Software implementation

28. The _____ implement(s) software to protect TCP server from TCP SYN flood attacks.

   A. Cisco access control lists (ACL)

   B. TCP Intercept feature

   C. Cisco queuing methods

   D. Cisco CBACS

29. Which of the following do *not* participate in the Cisco IOS Cryptosystem? (Choose all that apply.)

   A. DH

   B. MD5

   C. ESP

   D. DES

   E. BPR

30. The `ip inspect tcp max-incomplete host 100` command performs what function when invoked?

   A. It has no known effect on the router.

   B. It sets the total number of TCP connections per host to 1000.

   C. It sets the total number of TCP connections per host to 100.

   D. It changes the maximum number of half-open TCP connections per host to 1000.

   E. It changes the maximum number of half-open TCP connections per host to 100.

31. What key does Diffie-Hellman (DH) create during IKE phase 1?

  A. Xa

  B. Bx

  C. Xor

  D. NorX

32. Which of the following authentication methods is *not* supported by CiscoSecure ACS 3.0 for Windows NT/2000? (Choose all that apply.)

  A. Novell NDS

  B. Banyan StreetTalk

  C. DNS

  D. POP

  E. ODBC

  F. MS Directory Services

33. The `ip inspect max-incomplete high 1000` command changes what setting?

  A. It changes the maximum number of half-open TCP connections to 100.

  B. It changes the minimum number of half-open TCP connections to 1000.

  C. It changes the maximum number of half-open TCP connections to 1000.

  D. It changes the IP inspect idle timer to 1000 seconds.

  E. It changes the IP inspect idle timer to 100 seconds.

34. Which of the following statements about CS ACS 3.0 token-card server support are true? (Choose all that apply.)

  A. Microsoft is supported with service pack 6.0a.

  B. AXENT is natively supported.

  C. CryptoCard is natively supported.

  D. Novell NDS v4.*x* or higher is supported.

  E. ODBC with 6.0.1.1a service pack is supported.

35. IOS version 12.2(8)T is the minimum version required in order to run _____.

  A. LPDM

  B. Windows NT Terminal Services

  C. IOS Easy VPN Server

  D. sRAS (Secure RAS) or sDNS (Secure Domain Name Service)

36. Memory usage and _____ are two issues to consider when implementing the IOS Firewall IDS.

   A. User knowledge

   B. Signature coverage

   C. User address space

   D. TACACS+ server type

37. What does the `aaa authentication login default tacacs+ none` command instruct the router to do? (Choose all that apply.)

   A. No authentication is required to log in.

   B. TACACS+ is the default login method for all authentication.

   C. If the TACACS+ process is unavailable, no access is permitted.

   D. RADIUS is the default login method for all authentication.

   E. If the TACACS+ process is unavailable, no login is required.

   F. If the RADIUS process is unavailable, no login is required.

38. _____ and _____ are both supported by Cisco Easy VPN Server.

   A. Authentication using DSS

   B. DH1

   C. DH2

   D. Manual keys

   E. Perfect forward secrecy (PFS)

   F. DH5

39. What does an atomic signature trigger on?

   A. Single packet

   B. Duplex packet

   C. Atomic packet

   D. Two-way packet

40. Which of these statements are true regarding the following debug output? (Choose all that apply.)

```
01:41:50: AAA/AUTHEN: free_user (0x81420624) user='todd' ruser=''
    ↳port='tty0' rem_addr='async/' authen_type=ASCII service=LOGIN
priv=101:42:12:
AAA/AUTHEN/CONT (864264997): Method=LOCAL
```

A. This debug output shows that the user is using a remote database for authenticating the user todd.

B. This is a debug output from the authorization component of AAA.

C. This is a debug output from the authentication component of AAA.

D. The password will be checked against the local line password.

Answers to Assessment Test

1.   A, B, D.   The debug commands `debug aaa authentication`, `debug aaa authorization`, and `debug aaa accounting` can be used to help you trace AAA packets and monitor the AAA activities on the NAS. See Chapter 2 for more information.

2.   C.   IPSec encrypts all headers (including the data payload) after the Network layer header. See Chapter 7 for more information.

3.   C.   Unsecured user accounts are considered a weakness in configuration. See Chapter 1 for more information.

4.   B.   TCP Intercept can protect against DoS SYN flood attacks. See Chapter 4 for more information.

5.   A.   Pre-shared keys and RSA digital signatures are supported authentication types. DSS is not supported. DES and 3DES are encryption algorithms, not authentication types. See Chapter 9 for more information.

6.   D.   The `ip inspect one-minute high 100` command sets the maximum number of half-open TCP connections per minute to 100. See Chapter 5 for more information.

7.   B.   TCP/IP has some inherent weaknesses. IP spoofing, man-in-the-middle attacks, and session replaying are some examples of attacks that take advantage of TCP/IP weaknesses. See Chapter 1 for more information.

8.   A.   The default action for attack signatures is to alert. See Chapter 6 for more information.

9.   C.   Token cards/soft tokens are the most secure method of user authentication. See Chapter 2 for more information.

10.   A, B, D.   Policy, technology, and configuration weaknesses are the three typical weaknesses in any network implementation. See Chapter 1 for more information.

11.   A.   The first step in using RSA-encrypted nonces requires the user to manually generate the keys. The user must then manually enter the public key created on each device into the device they wish to peer with. See Chapter 7 for more information.

12.   C.   To reset all active IKE SAs on a device, use the * keyword with the `clear crypto isakmp` command. If you just want to reset a particular IKE SA, use the `clear crypto isakmp conn-id` command. See Chapter 8 for more information.

13.   C.   Authentication identifies a user, including login, password, messaging, and encryption. See Chapter 2 for more information.

14.   B.   The `ip inspect tcp idle-time 600` command sets the idle time on TCP connections to 10 minutes (600 seconds). See Chapter 5 for more information.

15.   D, E.   Cisco describes the absence of a disaster recovery plan and a high turnover rate in the technical support department as policy weaknesses. See Chapter 1 for more information.

16. A.   ESP provides for data confidentiality (encryption). AH does not provide encryption. See Chapter 7 for more information.

17. A, D, E.   You can populate the CiscoSecure User Database in only three ways: manually, using the Database Replication utility, or using the Database Import utility. CSNT can authenticate to external user databases such as Novell NDS or Windows NT, but it does not import these databases. See Chapter 3 for more information.

18. D.   To start AAA on an NAS, use the global configuration command aaa new-model. The new-model keyword reflects changes from the initial implementation, which is no longer supported. See Chapter 2 for more information.

19. C.   CBAC defines a half-open connection as any connection that fails to reach an established state. See Chapter 5 for more information.

20. C, E.   CSNT supports TACACS+ and RADIUS communication with the NAS. See Chapter 3 for more information.

21. C, E, F.   There are many problems with the IP stack, especially in Microsoft products. Session replaying is a weakness that is found in TCP. Both SNMP and SMTP are identified by Cisco as inherently insecure protocols in the TCP/IP stack. See Chapter 1 for more information.

22. D.   IPSec and encryption are used to prevent eavesdropping. See Chapter 4 for more information.

23. B.   MD5 authentication can be used to secure against rerouting attacks. See Chapter 4 for more information.

24. D.   The CSNT web server listens on TCP port 2002. See Chapter 3 for more information.

25. B, D, A, F, E, C.   The six steps of CBACs configuring are as follows: set audit trails and alerts, set global timeouts and thresholds, define Port-to-Application Mapping, define inspection rules, apply inspection rules and ACLs to interfaces, and finally, test and verify CBAC. See Chapter 5 for more information.

26. D.   ISAKMP uses UDP port 500 for communications. See Chapter 7 for more information.

27. B.   Policy, technology, and configuration weaknesses are the three typical weaknesses in any network implementation. See Chapter 1 for more information.

28. B.   The TCP Intercept feature implements software to protect TCP servers from TCP SYN flood attacks, which are a type of denial-of-service attack. See Chapter 4 for more information.

29. C, E.   The Cisco IOS Cryptosystem consists of DES, MD5, DSS, and DH. See Chapter 7 for more information.

30. E.   The ip inspect tcp max-incomplete host 100 command sets the maximum number of half-open TCP connections to a single host to 100. See Chapter 5 for more information.

31. A.   During IKE phase 1, DH is used to create the private keys, Xa and Xb, and the public keys, Ya and Yb. DH then uses these keys to create the shared secret key ZZ, which is used to encrypt the DES and MD5 keys. So, answer A is correct. See Chapter 7 for more information.

32. B, C, D.   The authentication methods supported by CiscoSecure 3.0 include Windows NT/2000, Novell Directory Services (NDS), Directory Services (DS), Token Server, ACS Databases, Microsoft Commercial Internet System Lightweight Directory Access Protocol (MCIS LDAP), and Open Database Connectivity (ODBC). See Chapter 3 for more information.

33. C.   The `ip inspect max-incomplete high 1000` command sets the maximum number (regardless of the destination host) of half-open TCP connections to a single host to 1000. See Chapter 5 for more information.

34. B, C.   CS ACS supports token-card servers from CryptoCard, ActivCard, Vasco, RSA ACE/Server, Secure Computing SafeWord, and AXENT Defender. See Chapter 3 for more information.

35. C.   You must have at least 12.2(8)T to run the IOS Easy VPN Server. See Chapter 9 for more information.

36. B.   Both memory usage and signature coverage are issues to consider when planning an IOS Firewall IDS implementation. Performance impact is a third issue to consider. See Chapter 6 for more information.

37. B, E.   This command specifies to use the default list against the TACACS+ server and that TACACS+ is the default login method for all authentications. The none keyword at the end means that if the TACACS+ process is unavailable, no login is required. See Chapter 3 for more information.

38. C, F.   DH groups 2 and 5 are supported by Cisco Easy VPN Server. DSS, DH1, PFS, and manual keys are not supported. See Chapter 9 for more information.

39. A.   Atomic signatures trigger on a single packet. See Chapter 6 for more information.

40. C, D.   The text after AAA/AUTHEN means that this is from the authentication component of AAA. Method=LOCAL means that the local line will be used for authentication. See Chapter 2 for more information.

Chapter 1

Introduction to Network Security

In a perfect world, network security would be as simple as merely installing some cool hardware or software onto your network and voila! Your network is now Fort Knox. In the real world, you do this and then brace yourself so you don't make too much of a scene when the inevitable corporate security breach occurs. Frustrated, you say to yourself, "I really thought I had taken the necessary precautions—I've done everything I could have!" This chapter will help you understand that there's more to network security than technology. Real network security requires understanding the inherent people and corporate policy issues as well.

News and stories about Internet identity theft, hackers jacking sensitive corporate information, or some new virus vaporizing hard drives left and right are definitely the hot topics du jour. Countless shadowy Internet users are spreading havoc from their computers, and it's really difficult—sometimes impossible—to track them down. So how do you protect yourself? Well, to begin addressing this problem, let's take a look at what Cisco says are the three main security issues that face a corporate network today:

- Security is not just a technology problem. Administrators and users are the cause of many of the security problems that corporations face today.

- Vast quantities of security technologies exist. Too many network administrators buy technology from a random advertisement they happen to read in a networking magazine. But simply throwing money at your security problems isn't usually the best solution. Predictably, many vendors would absolutely love it if they could succeed in making you believe otherwise!

- Many organizations lack a single, well-defined network-wide security policy. Some corporations don't even have a security policy—no lie! Or worse, even if they do, each department has created their own security policy independently of the others. This is highly ineffective because it creates a myriad of security holes, leaving the network wide open to attacks in a number of places.

Anyone reading this book should be concerned with network security and interested in how a network can become truly secure using proper network policy. An effective network security policy involves a strategic combination of both hardware implementation and the proper corporate handling of information. This chapter will discuss the reasons for creating a corporate security policy. Understanding them will provide you with a solid grasp of the Cisco SECUR exam objectives.

Let's move on to discuss the specific types of threats your network may be vulnerable to.

Types of Network Security Threats

Sadly, human nature does have a nasty side. And unfortunately, its lust for power, money, and revenge is sometimes aimed straight at your data. Though most of us aren't twisted, depraved, and ethically challenged, it's our fellow humans who can and often do present serious threats to our network data. You simply must realize that you need to protect it. And you can—but before you actually begin to secure your data, you must understand the different types of threats looming out there, just waiting for the opportunity to strike. There are four primary threats to network security that define the type of attacker you could be dealing with some day:

Unstructured threats   Unstructured threats typically originate from curious people who have downloaded information from the Internet and want to feel the sense of power this provides them. Sure, some of these folks—commonly referred to as Script Kiddies—can be pretty nasty, but most of them are just doing it for the rush and for bragging rights. They're untalented, inexperienced hackers, and they're really just motivated by the thrill of seeing what they can do.

Structured threats   Hackers who create structured threats are much more sophisticated than Script Kiddies. They are technically competent and calculating in their work, they usually understand network system design, and they are well versed in how to exploit routing and network vulnerabilities. They can and often do create hacking scripts that allow them to pen-etrate deep into a network's systems at will. They tend to be repeat offenders. Both structured and unstructured threats typically come from the Internet.

External threats   External threats typically come from people on the Internet or from someone who has found a hole in your network from the outside. These serious threats have become ubiquitous in the last six to seven years, during which time most companies began to show their presence on the Internet. External threats generally make their insidious way into your network via the Internet or via a dial-up server, where they try to gain access to your computer systems or network.

Internal threats   Internal threats come from users on your network, typically employees. These are probably the scariest of all threats because they're extremely tough to both catch and stop. And because these hackers are authorized to be on the network, they can do some serious dam-age in less time because they're already in and they know their way around.

Plus, the profile of an internal threat is that of the disgruntled, angry, and vengeful former or current employee, or even a contractor who wants nothing more than to cause some real pain and suffering! Although most users know this type of activity is illegal, some users also know it's fairly easy to cause a lot of damage—fast—and that they have a shake at getting away with it. That can be a huge, irresistible temptation to those with the right modus operandi or the wrong temperament!

Types of Security Weaknesses

This is probably the most important section in this chapter because it defines what security weaknesses are and how to understand inherent weaknesses in hardware, software, and people. Generally, there are three types of security weaknesses in any network implementation:

- Technology weaknesses
- Configuration weaknesses
- Policy weaknesses

Technology Weaknesses

Cisco defines *technology weaknesses* as a protocol, operating system, or hardware weakness. By default, protocols, operating systems, and hardware are typically not secure. Understanding their weaknesses can help you secure your network before you are attacked.

Technology weakness refers to the inadequacies of electronic systems, whether it is hardware or software. Technology weaknesses create a challenge for IT people because most hardware and software used in a company were already installed when they started their job.

Let's break down this category into three specific areas.

TCP/IP Weaknesses

TCP/IP has intrinsic security weaknesses because it was designed as an open standard to facilitate network communication. The fact that TCP/IP is an open standard is the main reason for its vast popularity, but the open standard nature of TCP/IP is also a reason why network attacks happen so easily and often—many people are familiar with how TCP/IP works.

For example, the original Unix sendmail daemon allows access to the Unix root, which, in turn, allows access to the entire Unix system! By simply viewing the sendmail information, a hacker can lock, load, and launch attacks on vulnerabilities specific to the operating system version. Special torture!

Yes, TCP/IP has operating system weaknesses that truly need to be addressed, but what's worse is that TCP/IP has also created network equipment weaknesses such as password protection, lack of required authentication, its routing protocols (which advertise your entire network), and firewall holes.

The two protocols that Cisco likes to pick on in the TCP/IP stack as inherently insecure are Simple Mail Transfer Protocol (SMTP) and Simple Network Management Protocol (SNMP). IP spoofing (masquerade attack), man-in-the-middle, and session replaying are specific examples of *TCP/IP weaknesses*.

Operating System Weaknesses

While every operating system has weaknesses, Microsoft Windows' weaknesses get top billing because most people use some version of Windows. To be fair, Unix and Linux have considerably fewer *operating system weaknesses* than Windows does, but they still have security issues that must be dealt with if you're running them on your network. It all comes down to a specific network's needs.

Network Equipment Weaknesses

All network equipment, such as servers, routers, switches, and so on, has some inherent security weakness. But being armed with a well-defined policy for the configuration and installation of network equipment can help tremendously in reducing the effects of *network equipment weaknesses*.

It is recommended that the following policies be in place before any piece of network equipment is configured and installed: passwords, authentication, routing protocols, and firewalls.

Configuration Weaknesses

Here's where human error comes into the fray—it's the administrator who creates *configuration weaknesses*. You'd be surprised how often a network administrator either leaves equipment at a default setting or fails to secure the network administrator accounts. Some common "come hither and hack me" scenarios exposing your everyday corporate network include configuration flaws such as unsecured user accounts, system accounts with easily guessed passwords, misconfigured Internet services, unsecured default settings in products, and misconfigured network equipment.

Unsecured User Accounts

Using default administrator accounts with no passwords and "God-like" control over the network is definitely asking for trouble. Just don't do that! If you're running Microsoft Windows NT, make sure you rename the administrator account. Doing this ensures that any intruders will at least have a slightly harder time finding and breaking into your operating system.

Put some serious thought into which users are granted which rights and privileges, because if you don't and you instead give rights away indiscriminately, chaos will ensue. Take the time to establish the rights each user really needs, and don't give them any more rights than what they really need to do their job!

Did you know that usernames and passwords are generally transmitted insecurely across the network? Ever hear of the Reconnaissance intruder? You know, the guy or gal who likes to think they are in the "Internet Special Forces" and their job is to find your network weakness and exploit it? Funny how these people always think they are performing a public service when they steal your data and that you were just *so* lucky that it was only them who broke in and not some really bad person. They actually believe that they have helped you because now you will fix "the weakness" before a "bad guy" really breaks in. Right. Anyway, these clear passwords are the kind of cool stuff that these snoopers spy for so they can use the information to gain access to your network later. As an administrator, make sure to define password policies that will help you secure your network.

System Accounts with Easily Guessed Passwords

Another way to invite trouble is to assign system account passwords that are easy to guess. To avoid this blunder, the administrator needs to set up policies on your servers that won't allow certain kinds of passwords and that make sure each password has an expiration date.

Explicitly define a corporate policy for all users that makes it crystal clear that they can't use their name, their significant other's name, their child's name, their birth date, or any other excruciatingly obvious passwords—even if they add something to it! It's also a really great idea to have them mix lowercase and uppercase letters, numbers, and special characters into their passwords. This helps defend your network against brute-force attacks that use dictionary files to guess passwords.

Misconfigured Internet Services

I know it's hard to believe, but some companies really do still use actual routable IP addresses on their network to address their hosts and servers. With the Network Address Translation (NAT) and Port Address Translation (PAT) services that are available now, there is absolutely no reason to use real IP addresses.

But you can use *private IP addresses*. These allow corporations—and even single homes—to use an IP address range that's blocked on the Internet. This provides some security for corporations, whose real IP addresses on the border router allow routing from the Internet.

This isn't a magical cure though. Ports need to be open on the router connecting the router interface to the Internet in order to allow users access to and from the Internet. This is the very hole in a firewall that attackers can and do exploit.

Don't get me wrong. By putting up a firewall—the Cisco Secure Private Internet eXchange (PIX) Firewall is one of the best—you can provide good security for your network by using *conduits*, which are basically secure connections, to open ports from the Internet to your servers. Is this bulletproof security? No, that doesn't exist, but the PIX box is good—really good!

Another potential source of trouble and exposure is that some network administrators enable Java and JavaScript in their web browsers. Doing this makes it possible for hackers to attack you with hostile Java applets.

Unsecured Default Settings in Products

Tangling things further is the fact that many hardware products ship with either no password at all or they make the password available so that the administrator can easily configure the device. On one hand, this really does make life easier—some devices are meant to be plug-and-play. For example, Cisco switches are plug-and-play because they want you to be able to just replace your hubs and instantly make your network better. And it really works, too! But you definitely need to put a password on that switch or an attacker could easily break in.

Cisco actually gave this some thought and is a step ahead in solving this problem. Cisco routers and switches won't allow Telnet sessions into them without some type of login configuration on the device. But this cool feature does nothing to guard against other types of break-in attempts, such as what the "Internet Special Forces" are trying to "protect" you from.

This is one reason why it's such a good idea to establish a configuration security policy on each device before any new equipment is installed on your network.

Misconfigured Network Equipment

Misconfigured network equipment is another exploitable flaw—weak passwords, no security policy, and unsecured user accounts can all be part of misconfigured network equipment policies.

Hardware and the protocols that run on it can also create security holes in your network. If you don't have a policy that describes the hardware and the protocols that run on each piece of equipment, hackers could be breaking in without your ever being aware that you've been attacked until it's too late.

Here's a huge problem: If you use SNMP default settings, tons of information about your network can be deciphered simply and quickly. So make sure you either disable SNMP or change the default SNMP community strings. These strings are basically passwords for gathering SNMP data.

Policy Weaknesses

You know by now that your corporate network security policy describes how and where security will be implemented within your network. And you understand that your policy should include information on how those configuration policies will be or have been initiated—right?

Let's take a moment to really clarify solid security policy by identifying the characteristics that contaminate bad policies.

Absence of a Written Security Policy

If a network administrator—or anyone else around—doesn't understand what's expected of them from the start, they'll just make things up as they go along. This is a very bad idea, and it's a good way to create the kind of chaos that will leave your network wide open to bad guys. Start your written security policy by first describing users, passwords, and Internet access. Then describe your network's hardware configuration, including all devices—PCs, servers, routers, and switches—and the security that's required to protect them.

Organization Politics

You thought I was kidding, huh? No way. Office politics absolutely play a leading role in each and every part of the corporate security policy. Understanding the power plays that occur continuously within the annals of upper management (they *are* happening—just pay attention for about five minutes to get the dynamics right) is very important indeed. What does each member of the upper management team envision and expect for the corporation's security? Does one manager have one goal and another manager have a different goal? The answer is always yes. You'll need to find a common ground if you want to get anything done.

Lack of Business Continuity

Here's another really hard-to-believe fact: Just about every corporate network is pretty much slapped together with the thought of "doing it right later." And now you are stuck with the mess. Unless you find yourself in the enviable position of being able to just move into a new building and design the network from the ground up, you'll be hard-pressed to create a single streamlined corporate security policy that you can implement evenly throughout the organization. And even then, layoffs and constant turnovers in the IT department cause security nightmares—all passwords for the equipment, servers, and so on must be changed. Sometimes corporate restructuring makes this process nasty and overwhelming, so administrators perform tasks and configure settings hastily just to keep up. Improper and/or incomplete change control on the network can expose some really ugly policy weaknesses.

 If your technical support staff is continually changing, be sure to understand that this can create a security weakness in your policies.

Lax Security Administration

Creating a fabulous corporate security policy, including monitoring and auditing your network's security, is hard work. It can be upsetting when no one cares about it. "Why implement this? They'll just tell me to change it next week!" That's probably true, but somehow you need to try to provide a solid, well-defined security policy that is also well monitored. Think of this as a policy within the policy, because if no one is monitoring or auditing company resources, those resources can and will certainly be wasted. This has potentially catastrophic implications because that type of lax security administration could easily end up exposing the corporation to legal action!

Installation and Changes That Do Not Follow the Stated Policy

Making sure that all software and hardware installations follow the stated installation policy is part of monitoring that policy. And monitoring these installations is integral to the policy's integrity. I know this is difficult and tedious, and it seems as if I'm telling you that you don't get to have a life, but it's very important—really. If you have no installation or configuration policy to adhere to, then unauthorized changes to the network's topology or some unapproved application installation can quickly create holes in your network's security.

No Disaster Recovery Plan

Disasters? Those only happen somewhere else, right? But they might happen, and they can even happen to you. So for your network's sake, earthquakes, fires, vandalism, hardware failure, vicious cord-eating rats, and even—God forbid—Internet access failure should all be things that you have a strategy for dealing with in your disaster recovery plan. Your gleaming, brilliant disaster recovery plan will describe your every answer to each and every one of these woes. If you don't do this in times of tranquil peace before you experience a meltdown, you'll experience sheer chaos, panic, and total confusion when something really does go down. And certain types of people tend to take advantage of situations like that, don't they? 'Nuf said.

Types of Network Attacks

Okay, you know your enemy and your weaknesses. But what exactly is that enemy up to, and what are they going to do to take advantage of your vulnerabilities? This is extremely important for you to understand so you can be prepared for what an attacker may throw at you. Most network attacks fall into these three categories:

Reconnaissance attacks   Reconnaissance attacks are unauthorized familiarization sessions that a hacker might use to find out what can be attacked on your network. An attacker on reconnaissance is out for discovery—mapping the network and its resources, systems, and vulnerabilities. This is often just a preliminary task. The information gathered will frequently be used to attack the network later.

Access attacks   Access attacks are waged against networks or systems to retrieve data, gain access, or escalate their access privilege. This can be as easy as finding network shares with no passwords. It's not always serious—many access attacks are performed out of curiosity or for the intellectual challenge, but beware. Some access attacks are really done to nick stuff, while other hackers perform access attacks because they want to play with your toys or use you to camouflage their identity in order to make their dirty work look as though it came from your network!

Denial-of-service (DoS) attacks   *Denial-of-service (DoS) attacks* are always nasty. Their sole purpose is to disable or corrupt network services. A DoS attack will usually either crash a system or slow it down to the point where it's rendered useless. DoS attacks are usually aimed at web servers and are surprisingly easy to perform. (The next section discusses DoS attacks in more detail.)

But there are many ways—most of them fairly common—to gather information about a network and to compromise corporate information, even to cause the destruction of a corporate web server and services. In particular, there are the three network attacks we just discussed that can cause the most trouble in your system.

TCP/IP teams up with your operating system to provide many weak, exploitable spots (if not outright invitations) into a corporation's network. TCP/IP and operating system weaknesses are probably the two greatest technology-oriented weaknesses facing corporations today.

Here is a list of the most common attacks on your network:

- Eavesdropping
- Denial-of-service attacks
- Unauthorized access
- WareZ
- Masquerade attack (IP spoofing)
- Session replaying or hijacking
- Rerouting
- Repudiation
- Smurfing
- Password attacks
- Man-in-the-middle attacks
- Application-layer attacks
- HTML attacks

When protecting your information from these attacks, it's your job to prevent the theft, destruction, corruption, and introduction of information that can cause irreparable damage to sensitive and confidential data on your network.

Eavesdropping

Eavesdropping, also known in the industry as *network snooping* and *packet sniffing*, is the act of a hacker "listening in" to your system. You wouldn't believe it, but there's a really cool product called (surprise!) a packet sniffer that enables its user to read packets of information sent across a network. Because a network's packets are not encrypted by default, they can be processed and understood by the sniffer. You can just imagine how wonderfully helpful this capability is to the network administrator trying to optimize or troubleshoot a network! But it's not exactly a stretch to visualize an evil hacker—packet sniffer in hand—using it to break into a network to gather sensitive corporate info, now is it?

And gather they can! Did you know that some applications send all information across the network in cleartext? This is especially convenient for the hacker who's striving to snag some usernames and passwords and use them to gain access to corporate resources. Yes, my friend, all bad guys need to do is jack the right account information, and they've got the run of your network. Worse, if a hacker manages to gain admin or root access, they can even create a new user ID to use at any time as a back door into your network and its resources. Then your network belongs to the hacker—kiss it goodbye!

 Real World Scenario

Simple Eavesdropping

Here is an example of simple eavesdropping that I encountered when I was checking my e-mail. This shows how easy it can be to find usernames and passwords!

Notice in this example that the EtherPeek network analyzer I'm using shows that the first packet has the username in cleartext:

```
TCP - Transport Control Protocol
    Source Port:          3207
    Destination Port:     110  pop3
    Sequence Number:      1904801173
    Ack Number:           1883396251
    Offset:               5  (20 bytes)
    Reserved:             %000000
    Flags:                %011000
                          0. .... (No Urgent pointer)
                          .1 .... Ack
```

```
                        .. 1... Push
                        .. .0.. (No Reset)
                        .. ..0. (No SYN)
                        .. ...0 (No FIN)
  Window:               64166
  Checksum:             0x078F
  Urgent Pointer:       0
  No TCP Options
POP - Post Office Protocol
  Line  1:              USER tlammle1<CR><LF>
FCS - Frame Check Sequence
  FCS (Calculated):     0x0CFCA80E
```

This next packet has the password. Everything seen in this packet (an e-mail address and a username/password) can be used to break into the system:

```
TCP - Transport Control Protocol
  Source Port:          3207
  Destination Port:     110  pop3
  Sequence Number:      1904801188
  Ack Number:           1883396256
  Offset:               5  (20  bytes)
  Reserved:             %000000
  Flags:                %011000
                        0. .... (No Urgent pointer)
                        .1 .... Ack
                        .. 1... Push
                        .. .0.. (No Reset)
                        .. ..0. (No SYN)
                        .. ...0 (No FIN)
  Window:               64161
  Checksum:             0x078F
  Urgent Pointer:       0
  No TCP Options
POP - Post Office Protocol
  Line  1:              PASS secretpass<CR><LF>
```

The username is tlammle1 and the password is secretpass—all nice and clear for everyone's viewing pleasure.

Even more insidious, eavesdropping is also used for information theft. Imagine the intruder, hacking into some financial institution, happily sneaking credit card numbers, account information, and other personal data from one of the institution's network computers or from the data crossing its network. Voila! The hacker now has everything they need for some serious identity theft.

Is there anything you can do about this? Yes. Again, it comes down to that nice, tight network security policy. To counteract eavesdropping, you need to create a policy forbidding the use of protocols with known susceptibilities to eavesdropping, and you should make sure that all important, sensitive network traffic is encrypted.

Denial-of-Service Attacks

Denial-of-service (DoS) attacks are by far the most debilitating of attacks. Even if there was only one type of DoS attack, these attacks would still be devastating. But they come in a variety of hideous flavors! I'm not exaggerating; DoS attacks can bring a corporation to its knees by crippling its ability to conduct business. A common type of DoS attack effectively renders a corporate website useless by making it impossible for legitimate users to gain access to a web server or other available Internet service provided by the victimized corporation.

It sounds pretty complicated, but DoS attacks are alarmingly simple in design. Basically, the idea is just to keep open all the available connections supported by the main server, which, in return, locks out any valid attempts to access that server or its services. Legitimate users (customers and employees) are thereby left out in the cold—they simply can't access the site because all of the targeted site's services and its bandwidth are completely used up. Think about the kind of impact this type of attack could have: It could turn a financially stable company into one in trouble—and fast!

DoS attacks are most often implemented using common Internet protocols such as TCP and ICMP—TCP/IP weaknesses for which, at present, Cisco has some promising and effective solutions. But, if the truth be told, there really isn't anything around right now that you could call bulletproof to protect your network from DoS attacks.

TCP attacks are executed by hackers who implement their attacks by opening more sessions than the victimized server can handle. It's a very simple technique, but it's also very effective because it makes that server totally inaccessible to anyone else.

ICMP attacks are known as "The Ping of Death." They're executed by an attacker using one of two techniques. The first technique is to send millions of pings to a corporation's server, keeping it consumed by the pings instead of what it's supposed to be doing. The second technique is deployed by modifying the IP portion of a header, which makes the server believe there is more data in the packet than there really is. This can ultimately make the server crash if enough of these modified packets are sent.

Here are some other kinds of DoS attacks. Remember these when studying for the SECUR exam:

Chargen In a Chargen attack, massive amounts of UDP packets are sent to a device, resulting in tremendous congestion on the network.

SYN flood A SYN flood randomly opens up many TCP ports, tying up the network equipment with bogus requests, thereby denying sessions to real users.

Packet fragmentation and reassembly   A packet fragmentation and reassembly attack exploits the buffer overrun bug in hosts or internetwork equipment.

WinNuke   A WinNuke attack uses the infamous port 139 on Windows devices to bring systems resources to its knees.

Accidental   Accidental DoS attacks can happen by legitimate users using misconfigured network devices.

E-mail bombs   Many free programs exist that allow users to send bulk e-mail to individuals, groups, lists, or domains, taking up all their e-mail service.

Land.c   A land.c attack uses the TCP SYN packet that specifies the target host's address as both the source and destination. Land.c also uses the same port on the target host as both the source and destination, which can cause the target host to crash.

The Cisco IOS provides some firewall features that help stop DoS attacks, but at present, you can't stop them completely without cutting off legitimate users. Those firewall features include

Context-Based Access Control (CBAC)   CBAC provides advanced traffic-filtering functionality and can be used as an integral part of your network's firewall.

Java blocking   Cisco's Java-blocking capability helps stop hostile Java applet attacks.

DoS detection and monitoring   If DoS detection and monitoring is used as a strong firewall feature, you'll prevent both attackers and legitimate users from gaining access to the network. You have to weigh the pros and cons of installing a DoS-monitoring system and understand what kind of protection you need versus the capabilities and ease of use that your users can live with.

Audit trails   Audit trails work well to keep track of who is attacking you, which can be very cool because you can send the logs to the FBI. (In case you don't remember or aren't aware of it, attacking a website is against the law!)

Real-time alerts log   Keeping a log of the attacks in real time is helpful in case of DoS attacks or other preconfigured conditions.

NOTE   The Cisco TCP Intercept feature implements software to protect TCP servers from TCP SYN-flooding attacks, which is a type of DoS attack.

Unauthorized Access

I'm sure that by now you've got a clear understanding of why a network intruder would want to gain access to the root in a Unix box or to the administrator function of a Windows host. By doing so, an unauthorized guest can get to the `/etc/password` file on the Unix host to access important passwords, or even to add another user on that NT host with administrative privileges and be free to move about within the network at will. Sometimes hackers do this because their goal is to steal software and distribute it if possible—more on that in a bit.

Sometimes hackers gain access into a network so they can place unauthorized files or resources on another system for ready access by other intruders.

The Cisco IOS offers you some protection with features such as Lock-and-Key, a *Terminal Access Controller Access Control System (TACACS+)* server, a remote authentication server, and *Challenge Handshake Authentication Protocol (CHAP)*, an authentication protocol. These features provide additional security against unauthorized access attempts.

In addition to a TACACS+ server and CHAP, you can provide a mechanism that authenticates a user beyond an IP network address. It supports features such as password token cards and creates other challenges to gaining access to network resources. This mechanism also requires remote reauthorization after a period of inactivity—another safeguard!

WareZ

The term *WareZ* refers to unauthorized distribution of software. It's not an actual attack on a corporate network or website; its motivation is to sell someone else's software or to distribute the unlicensed versions of software for free on the Internet. This is sometimes initiated by a company's present or former employees, or by anyone on the Internet with a cracked version of the software. As you can imagine, WareZ is a huge problem for software companies.

There are many ways to provide free software on the Internet, and many servers in the Far East blatantly provide downloads of free software because they know there is nothing anyone can do about it. The only thing that can protect you from a WareZ is to provide some type of licensing on your software that stops illegal use.

Masquerade Attack (IP Spoofing)

Masquerading or IP spoofing is fairly easy to stop once you understand how it works. An IP spoofing attack happens when someone outside your network pretends to be a trusted computer user by using an IP address that's within the range of your network's IP addresses. The attacker's plan is to steal an IP address from a trusted source for use in gaining access to network resources. A trusted computer is either one that you have administrative control over or one that you've made a decision to trust on your network.

You can head off this attack by placing an *access control list (ACL)* on the corporate router's interface to the Internet and then denying access to your internal network IP addresses from that interface. This works effectively and easily stops IP spoofing, but only if the attacker is truly coming in from outside the network.

In order to spoof a network ID, a hacker needs to change the routing tables in your router in order to receive any packets. Once they do that, the odds are good that they'll gain access to user accounts and passwords. And if your hacker happens to understand messaging protocols, they just might add a little twist and send e-mail messages from some poor employee's company e-mail account to other users in the company. That way, it looks as if that user sent the messages, and many hackers get a real kick out of embarrassing corporate users. IP spoofing helps them achieve that goal.

Session Hijacking or Replaying

When two hosts communicate, they typically use the TCP protocol at the Transport layer to set up a reliable session. This session can be *hijacked* by making the hosts believe that they are sending packets to a valid host, when in fact, they're delivering their packets to a hijacker.

You don't see this so much anymore because it's no longer necessary. A network sniffer can gather much more information, but it still happens now and then so you should be aware of it. You can protect yourself from *session hijacking* or *replaying* by using a strongly authenticated, encrypted management protocol.

Rerouting

A *rerouting attack* is launched by a hacker who understands IP routing. The hacker breaks into the corporate router and then changes the routing table to alter the course of IP packets so they'll go to the attacker's unauthorized destination instead. Some types of cookies and Java or ActiveX scripts can also be used to manipulate routing tables on hosts.

To stop a rerouting attack, you can use access control with a PIX firewall or the Cisco IOS Firewall Feature Set.

Repudiation

Repudiation is a denial of a transaction so that no communications can be traced. Doing this can prevent a third party from being able to prove that a communication between two other parties ever took place. Non-repudiation is the opposite—a third party can prove that a communication between two other parties took place. Because you generally want the ability to trace your communications and to prove that they actually did take place, non-repudiation is the preferred transaction.

Attackers who want to create a repudiation attack can use Java or ActiveX scripts to do so. They can also use scanning tools that confirm TCP ports for specific services, the network or system architecture, and the operating system. Once information is obtained, the attacker will try to find vulnerabilities associated with those entities.

To stop repudiation, set your browser security setting to high. You can also block any corporate access to public e-mail sites. In addition, add access control and authentication on your network. Non-repudiation can be used with digital signatures, which are discussed in Chapter 7, "Understanding Cisco IOS IPSec Support."

Smurfing

The latest trend in the attacker game is the *smurf attack*. This attack sends a large amount of ICMP (Internet Control Message Protocol) echo (ping) traffic to IP broadcast addresses from a supposedly valid host that is traceable. The framed host then gets blamed for the attack.

Smurf attacks send a Layer 2 (Data Link layer) broadcast. Most hosts on the attacked IP network will reply to each ICMP echo request with an echo reply, multiplying the traffic by the number of hosts responding. This eats up tons of bandwidth and results in a denial of service to valid users because the network traffic is so high.

The smurf attack's cousin is called fraggle, which uses UDP echo packets in the same fashion as the ICMP echo packets. Fraggle is a simple rewrite of smurf to use a Layer 4 (Transport layer) broadcast.

To stop a smurf attack, all networks should perform filtering either at the edge of the network where customers connect (the Access layer) or at the edge of the network with connections to the upstream providers. Your goal is to prevent source address–spoofed packets from entering from downstream networks or leaving for upstream ones.

Password Attacks

These days, it's a rare user who isn't aware of password issues, but you can still depend on the user to pick the name of their dog, significant other, or child for their password because those strings are so easy to remember. But you are wise and have defined policies to stop these easy-to-guess passwords, so you have no worries—right?

Well, almost. You've definitely saved yourself a good bit of grief by educating your users. It's just that even if your users pick really great passwords, programs that record a username and password can still be used to gather them up. If a hacker uses a program that repeatedly attempts to identify a user account and/or password, it's called a *brute-force attack*. And if it's successful, the hacker will gain access to all the resources the stolen username and password usually provides to the now ripped-off corporate user. As you can imagine, it's an especially dark day when the bad guy manages to jack the username and password of an administrator account.

Man-in-the-Middle Attacks

A *man-in-the-middle attack* is just that—a person between you and the network you are connected to who is gathering all the data that you send and receive. For a man-in-the-middle attack to be possible, the attacker must have access to the packets traveling across the networks. This means your middleman could be an internal user, someone who spoofed, or even someone who works for an Internet service provider (ISP). Man-in-the-middle attacks are usually implemented by using network packet sniffers, routing protocols, or even Transport-layer protocols.

Your middleman attacker's goal is any or all of the following:

- Theft of information
- Hijacking of an ongoing session to gain access to your internal network resources
- Traffic analysis to derive information about your network and its users
- Denial of service
- Corruption of transmitted data
- Introduction of new information into network sessions

Application-Layer Attacks

An *Application-layer attack* involves an application with well-known weaknesses that can be easily exploited. PostScript, sendmail, and FTP are a few really good examples of these types of applications. The goal is to gain access to a computer with the permissions of the account running the application, which is usually a privileged, system-level account.

Trojan Horse Programs, Viruses, and Worms

I hate to admit this, but the Trojan horse attack is actually a very cool attack—that is, if you look at the way it's implemented and, more importantly, if it's not happening to you. The Trojan horse attack creates a substitute for a common program, duping users into thinking they are in a valid program when they are not. They're actually in the *Trojan horse*, which gives the attacker the power to monitor login attempts and to capture user account and password information. This attack can even mix it up a notch and allow the horse's rider to modify application behavior so that the attacker receives all your corporate e-mail messages instead of you. Pretty stylin', huh? I told you it was cool.

Both worms and viruses spread and infect multiple systems. The difference between the two is that viruses require some form of human intervention to spread, and worms do that on their own. Because viruses, Trojan horses, and worms are conceptually alike, they're all considered to be the same form of attack. They're all software programs created for and aimed at destroying your data. Some variants of these weapons can also deny legitimate users access to resources and consume bandwidth, memory, disk space, and CPU cycles.

So be smart—use a virus program on your network and update it regularly!

HTML Attacks

Another new attack on the Internet scene exploits several new technologies: the Hypertext Markup Language (HTML) specification, web browser functionality, and HTTP.

HTML attacks can include Java applets and ActiveX controls. Their modus operandi is to pass destructive programs across the network and load them through a user's browser.

Microsoft promotes an Authenticode technology for ActiveX only but it doesn't do much except to provide a false sense of security to users. This is because attackers can use a properly signed and totally bug-free ActiveX control to create a Trojan horse!

This particular approach is unique because it involves teamwork between the attacker and you. Part one of this attack—the attacker's part—is to modify a program and set it up so that you, the user, actually initiate the attack when you either start the program or choose a function within it. And these attacks aren't hardware dependent. They're very flexible because of the portability of the programs.

The Corporate Security Policy

Whew! You made it through the introduction to network security! Great—so now that you understand all the problems associated with equipment, networks, and people, what do you do with all this information? The first step is to begin protecting your corporate network by creating and deploying a security policy that includes each and every way that you and everyone else in the company is going to guard your oh-so-sensitive data!

RFC 2196 states that a *security policy* is a formal statement of the rules by which people who are given access to an organization's technology and information assets must abide. A corporate security policy is basically a document that summarizes how the company will use and protect its computing and network resources.

When you are creating a security policy, it is important to be ever mindful of that fine balancing act between ease of use and the level of security actually needed to adequately protect corporate network services. You do a disservice to the client by locking everything down as tightly as possible and/or spending too much money on a network that really doesn't need 007-level security.

A security policy defines the following criteria:

- What's important to the enterprise

- What the company is willing to spend (in terms of dollars, personnel, and time) to protect what it has deemed important

- What level of risk it's willing to tolerate

Sounds good, but do you really need to bother with a security policy? Is creating a security policy actually worth the time, money, and effort required? Absolutely! Here's a short list of why Cisco says doing so is such a good idea. A corporate security policy

- Provides a process to audit existing network security.

- Defines which behavior is and is not allowed.

- Provides a general security framework for implementing network security.

- Often determines which tools and procedures are needed for the organization.

- Communicates consensus among a group of key decision-makers and defines the responsibilities of users and administrators.

- Defines a process for handling network security incidents.

- Enables global security implementation and enforcement. Computer security is now an enterprise-wide issue, and computing sites are expected to conform to the network security policy.

- Creates a basis for legal action if necessary.

Now that you know the basics of creating and implementing a formal security policy in your company, where do you get the rest of the information you need so that you can implement it properly? Good question. This book will seriously strengthen your security grip by showing you how to configure Cisco hardware—a crucial capability you just can't do without today.

For an in-depth description of those all-important security policies, refer to www.sybex.com for information about Sybex's Study Guides on the CCSP exams. They will provide you with everything you need to create your own tailor-made and tight policy.

Summary

A corporate security policy is a declaration of the systems and rules needed to have a secure IT structure. Various weaknesses, holes, and chinks are typically found in the armor of security policies and in the network's security itself. These vulnerabilities fall into three major categories: technology weaknesses, configuration weaknesses, and policy weaknesses.

It's very important to understand the fundamentals and characteristics of all the different weaknesses inherent to a security policy. There are specific protocols for dealing with each special type of weakness, so you should develop solid solutions to secure your system from those vulnerabilities.

Creating a corporate security policy is not easy, and implementing one is even harder. However, a solid security policy is something your organization cannot live without. There are many different types of attacks that hackers have in their arsenal; eavesdropping and denial-of-service attacks are just two of the most popular types of attacks for people who want to steal from your network and cause problems for your organization.

You can develop and implement strategies to guard against these attacks with a PIX firewall or the Cisco IOS Firewall Feature Set, which is what the rest of this book is about. By combining this understanding with your newfound appreciation of corporate security policies, you will be empowered to create and maintain a sturdy, intelligent, and cost-effective policy that's tailor-made to meet the needs of your company and its network.

In the next chapter, you'll learn how to configure Authentication, Authorization, and Accounting (AAA) services as part of the Cisco NAS interface.

Exam Essentials

Understand the three typical types of weaknesses in any network implementation. The three typical types of weaknesses found in a network implementation are technology, configuration, and policy weaknesses.

Know which attacks can occur because of TCP/IP's weaknesses. There are many attacks that can occur because of TCP/IP's inherent weaknesses. The most important attacks to remember are IP spoofing, man-in-the-middle, and session replaying.

Remember the different problems described as configuration weaknesses.   Understand the difference between configuration weaknesses and policy weaknesses. Configuration weaknesses include problems such as unsecured user accounts, system accounts with easily guessed passwords, misconfigured Internet services, unsecured default settings in products, and misconfigured network equipment.

Understand what types of issues are considered policy weaknesses.   Policy weaknesses involve problems with the corporate security policy such as the absence of a written security policy, organization politics, lack of business continuity, lax security administration, software and hardware that's installed without following the stated installation policy, and the absence of a disaster recovery plan.

Key Terms

Before you take the exam, be certain you are familiar with the following terms:

access control list (ACL)

Application-layer attack

Challenge Handshake Authentication Protocol (CHAP)

configuration weaknesses

denial-of-service (DoS) attacks

eavesdropping

HTML attacks

man-in-the-middle attack

masquerading

network equipment weaknesses

operating system weaknesses

private IP addresses

replaying

repudiation

rerouting attack

security policy

session hijacking

smurf attack

software weaknesses

TCP/IP weaknesses

technology weaknesses

Terminal Access Controller Access Control System (TACACS+)

Trojan horse

WareZ

Written Lab

This section asks you 10 write-in-the-answer questions to help you understand the technology that you need to know in order to pass the SECUR exam.

1. What two common terms are used to describe eavesdropping?

2. Most network implementations have three typical security weaknesses. What are they?

3. Improper change control and no disaster recovery plan demonstrate what type of weakness?

4. An attacker tries to steal an IP address in which type of attack?

5. Unsecured user accounts are what type of weakness?

6. What are the three technology weaknesses that can affect security?

7. No disaster recovery plan and high turnover in the technical support department are examples of which type of weakness?

8. Session replaying, SNMP, and SMTP are examples of what type of weakness?

9. List three options for countering an unauthorized access attempt.

10. Which feature protects a server from TCP SYN-flooding attacks?

Review Questions

1. Which of the following is an example of a policy weakness? (Choose all that apply.)

   A. Absence of a proxy server

   B. No trusted networks

   C. Misconfigured network equipment

   D. No disaster recovery plan

   E. Technical support personnel continually changing

2. What are the three typical weaknesses in any network implementation? (Choose all that apply.)

   A. Policy weakness

   B. Technology weakness

   C. Hardware weakness

   D. Configuration weakness

   E. Software weakness

3. Which of the following are examples of TCP/IP weaknesses? (Choose all that apply.)

   A. Trojan horse

   B. HTML attack

   C. Session replaying

   D. Application-layer attack

   E. SNMP

   F. SMTP

4. Which Cisco IOS feature would you use to protect a TCP server from TCP SYN-flooding attacks?

   A. Rerouting

   B. TCP Intercept

   C. Access control lists

   D. Encryption

5. Which of the following can be used to counter an unauthorized access attempt? (Choose all that apply.)

   A. Encrypted data

   B. Cisco Lock-and-Key

   C. Access control lists

   D. PAP

   E. CHAP

   F. IKE

   G. TACACS+

6. What security issues face organizations today? (Choose all that apply.)

   A. Security is not just a technology problem.

   B. Too many employees need remote access.

   C. Service providers don't provide the support and security they promise.

   D. Vast quantities of security technologies exist.

   E. Adopting the latest security methods can be costly.

   F. Many organizations lack a single network-wide security policy.

7. Which of the following threats is an example of snooping and network sniffing?

   A. Repudiation

   B. Masquerade threats

   C. Eavesdropping

   D. DoS

8. You are creating your security policy. Which of the following would you consider policy weaknesses? (Choose all that apply.)

   A. Improper change control

   B. IP spoofing

   C. Masquerade attack

   D. Misconfigured network equipment

   E. Consistent security policy

   F. Absence of a disaster recovery plan

9. In a masquerade attack, what does an attacker steal when pretending to come from a trusted host?

    A. Account identification

    B. User group

    C. IP address

    D. CHAP password

10. Which statements about the creation of a security policy are true? (Choose all that apply.)

    A. It helps you determine the return on your investment in the network.

    B. It provides a process with which to audit existing network security.

    C. It defines how to track down and prosecute policy offenders.

    D. It defines which behavior is and is not allowed.

    E. It helps determine which vendor security equipment or software is better than others.

    F. It allows your network to be completely secure and safe from all attacks.

11. Which of the following would be considered configuration weaknesses? (Choose all that apply.)

    A. Old software

    B. Unsecured user accounts

    C. Misconfigured Internet services

    D. No monitoring or auditing

12. Which of the following are examples of policy weaknesses? (Choose all that apply.)

    A. Organization politics

    B. Misconfigured Internet services

    C. Improper change control

    D. No monitoring or auditing of logs

    E. System accounts with easily guessed passwords

13. What are the technology weaknesses that can affect an organization? (Choose all that apply.)

    A. Software weakness

    B. TCP/IP weakness

    C. Operating system weakness

    D. Network equipment weakness

14. What policies should be in place before any network equipment is configured and installed? (Choose all that apply.)

    A. Passwords

    B. Politics

    C. Firewalls

    D. Authentication

15. Using the default settings when installing network equipment is listed as what type of weakness?

A. Technology weakness

B. Configuration weakness

C. Policy weakness

D. Software weakness

16. Lack of business continuity is listed as what type of weakness?

A. Technology weakness

B. Configuration weakness

C. Policy weakness

D. Software weakness

17. Operating system security problems are listed as what type of weakness?

A. Technology weakness

B. Configuration weakness

C. Policy weakness

D. Software weakness

18. Lax security administration is listed as what type of weakness?

A. Technology weakness

B. Configuration weakness

C. Policy weakness

D. Software weakness

19. Software and hardware installation and changes are listed as what type of weakness?

A. Technology weakness

B. Configuration weakness

C. Policy weakness

D. Software weakness

20. Not having a disaster recovery plan is listed as what type of weakness?

A. Technology weakness

B. Configuration weakness

C. Policy weakness

D. Software weakness

Answers to Written Lab

1. Network snooping and packet sniffing are two common terms for eavesdropping.

2. Policy, technology, and configuration weaknesses are the three typical security weaknesses in a network implementation.

3. Improper change control and no disaster recovery plan demonstrate policy weaknesses.

4. A masquerade attack is when an attacker tries to steal an IP address.

5. Unsecured user accounts are an example of configuration weakness.

6. TCP/IP weaknesses, operating system weaknesses, and network equipment weaknesses are three technology weaknesses that can affect security.

7. No disaster recovery plan and high turnover in the technical support department are examples of policy weaknesses.

8. Session replaying, SNMP, and SMTP are examples of TCP/IP weaknesses.

9. Cisco Lock-and-Key, CHAP, and TACACS+ are three options for countering an unauthorized access attempt.

10. The TCP Intercept feature protects a server from TCP SYN-flooding attacks.

Answers to Review Questions

1. D, E. Cisco describes the absence of a disaster recovery plan and a high turnover rate in the technical support department as policy weaknesses.

2. A, B, D. Policy, technology, and configuration weaknesses are the three typical weaknesses in a network implementation.

3. C, E, F. There are many problems with the IP stack, especially in Microsoft products. Session replaying is a weakness that is found in TCP. Both SNMP and SMTP are identified by Cisco as inherently insecure protocols in the TCP/IP stack.

4. B. The TCP Intercept feature implements software to protect TCP servers from TCP SYN-flooding attacks, which are a type of denial-of-service attack.

5. B, E, G. By using the Cisco Lock-and-Key along with CHAP and TACACS+, you can create a more secure network and help prevent unauthorized access.

6. A, D, F. The security challenge facing enterprises today is one of sorting through a wide range of solutions and choosing the right combination. A vast quantity of security technologies exist. It is not the lack of technology that makes securing the network difficult; the problem is choosing among the many different selections available and adopting those that satisfy your unique network and business requirements.

7. C. Network snooping and packet sniffing are common terms for eavesdropping.

8. A, F. Misconfigured network equipment is a configuration weakness. However, that is the first answer most people would pick for this question. A consistent security policy is not a weakness, and IP spoofing and masquerade attacks are not security policy weaknesses.

9. C. IP spoofing is fairly easy to stop once you understand the way spoofing takes place. An IP spoofing attack occurs when an attacker outside your network pretends to be a trusted computer by using an IP address that is within the range of IP addresses for your network. The attacker wants to steal an IP address from a trusted source so they can use it to gain access to network resources.

10. B, D. Taking the time to create a security policy is worth the time, money, and effort. For this question, the proper answers are that a security policy provides a process to audit existing network security and defines which behavior is and is not allowed.

11. B, C. Possible configuration weaknesses in a corporate network include unsecured user accounts, system accounts with easily guessed passwords, misconfigured Internet services, unsecured default settings in products, and misconfigured network equipment.

12. A, C, D. Possible policy weaknesses include the absence of a security policy; organization politics; lack of business continuity; the inability of the organization to implement policy evenly; improper change controls; logical access controls not being applied; lax security administration, including monitoring and auditing; software and hardware installation and changes that don't follow the stated installation policy; and the absence of a disaster recovery plan.

13. B, C, D. TCP/IP protocol weaknesses, operating system weaknesses, and network equipment weaknesses are identified by Cisco as the three technology weaknesses.

14. A, C, D. Passwords, firewalls, and authentication, as well as routing protocols, should have policies in place before any network equipment is configured and installed.

15. B. Possible configuration weaknesses in a corporate network include unsecured user accounts, system accounts with easily guessed passwords, misconfigured Internet services, unsecured default settings in products, and misconfigured network equipment.

16. C. Possible policy weaknesses include the absence of a security policy; organization politics; lack of business continuity; inability of the organization to implement policy evenly; improper change controls; logical access controls not being applied; lax security administration, including monitoring and auditing; software and hardware installation and changes that don't follow the stated installation policy; and the absence of a disaster recovery plan.

17. A. TCP/IP protocol weaknesses, operating system weaknesses, and network equipment weaknesses are identified by Cisco as the three technology weaknesses.

18. C. Possible policy weaknesses include the absence of a security policy; organization politics; lack of business continuity; inability of the organization to implement policy evenly; improper change controls; logical access controls not being applied; lax security administration, including monitoring and auditing; software and hardware installation and changes that don't follow the stated installation policy; and the absence of a disaster recovery plan.

19. C. Possible policy weaknesses include the absence of a security policy; organization politics; lack of business continuity; inability of the organization to implement policy evenly; improper change controls; logical access controls not being applied; lax security administration, including monitoring and auditing; software and hardware installation and changes that don't follow the stated installation policy; and the absence of a disaster recovery plan.

20. C. Possible policy weaknesses include the absence of a security policy; organization politics; lack of business continuity; inability of the organization to implement policy evenly; improper change controls; logical access controls not being applied; lax security administration, including monitoring and auditing; software and hardware installation and changes that don't follow the stated installation policy; and the absence of a disaster recovery plan.

Chapter
2

Introduction to AAA Security

THE FOLLOWING SECUR EXAM TOPICS ARE COVERED IN THIS CHAPTER:

- ✓ Securing network access using AAA
- ✓ Authentication methods
- ✓ Configuring local AAA
- ✓ Verifying AAA

In only a few short years, network security has grown from a consideration into a vital and critically important essential for network administrators. In an age of increasing dependence on and use of the Internet, nearly everyone—from individuals and small businesses to huge corporations, institutions, and worldwide organizations—is now a potential victim of hackers and E-crime. Although the defense techniques continue to improve with time, so does the sophistication and weaponry used by the bad guys. Today's tightest security will be laughably transparent three years from now, making it seriously necessary for an administrator to keep current with the industry's quickly evolving security trends.

Solid security hasn't just become a valuable requirement; it's also becoming increasingly complex and multi-tiered. Cisco continues to develop and extend its features to meet these demands by providing you with sharp tools like the *Network Access Server (NAS)*. The NAS isn't a real physical server; it's actually a platform created to connect an interface between the packet world and the circuit world.

Authentication, Authorization, and Accounting (AAA) services are part of the Cisco NAS interface. This technology gives you substantial control over users and what those users are permitted to do inside of your networks. And there are more tools in the shed; RADIUS and TACACS+ security servers help you implement a centralized security plan by recording network events to the security server or to a Syslog server via logging.

I know this sounds pretty complicated, and, truthfully, it is. But that's why I'm devoting an entire chapter to explaining these things to you!

I'll start with a brief introduction to Cisco NAS and AAA security. And because it's so important to understand how to properly authenticate users on a network, I'm going to discuss the various ways—good and bad—to do that. Then I'm going to cover the ins and outs (pun intended, sorry) of granting permissions and recording activity. And finally, I'll get you into the real goods—describing the more advanced aspects of Cisco NAS and AAA, including how to configure them.

Understanding Network Access Server and Cisco AAA

Before I explain AAA, it's really important that you understand and remember that Cisco's NAS is not an actual physical server. It's actually a router with a database; the server is configured and exists within that router's database. It's this feature—this configuration—that gives you the ability to add authentication, authorization, and accounting services to your router so you can provide and apply security where and how you need it—nice! Okay, great. You're asking, "So how do you configure NAS commands on a Cisco router, and when are you going to show me?" Right now! I'll explain how to do this and show you how to provide local (AAA) security for an NAS router. Let's get started.

One of the things that's so sweet about AAA architecture is that it enables systematic access security both locally and remotely! AAA technologies work within the remote client system, the NAS, and the security server to secure dial-up access. Here's a definition of each of the As in AAA:

Authentication   *Authentication* requires users to prove that they are who they say they are in one of these three ways:

- Name and password
- Challenge and response
- Token cards

Authorization   *Authorization* takes place only after authentication has validated the user. Authorization provides the needed resources specifically allowed to the user and permits the operations that the user is allowed to perform.

Accounting   AAA's *accounting* and auditing function records what the users actually do on the network and which resources they access. It also keeps track of how much time they spend using network resources for accounting and auditing purposes.

The most common form of router authentication is known as *line authentication*, also known as *character-mode access*. Line authentication uses different passwords to authenticate users, depending on the line the user is connecting through.

You can protect character-mode access to network equipment through a Cisco router as described in Table 2.1.

TABLE 2.1   Local Line Types

Line Type	Description
AUX	Auxiliary EIA/TIA-232 DTE port on Cisco routers and Ethernet switches. Used for modem-supported remote control and asynchronous routing up to 38.4Kbps.
Console	Console EIA/TIA-232 DCE port on Cisco routers and Ethernet switches. Used for asynchronous access to device configuration modes.
TTY	Standard EIA/TIA-232 DTE asynchronous line on an NAS.
VTY	Virtual terminal line and interface terminating incoming character streams that do not have a physical connection to the access server or the router.

In practice, line authentication is actually pretty limited because all users need to know the same password to authenticate. But the commands to configure line authentication are really easy:

```
Todd(config)#line con 0
Todd(config-line)#login
Todd(config-line)#password cisco
Todd(config-line)#line vty 0 4
Todd(config-line)#password lammle
Todd(config-line)#line aux 0
Todd(config-line)#password todd
```

Okay, what do you see here? In this example, a user who directly connects to a router console port needs to submit the password cisco to be allowed access. Alternatively, a user connecting via a Telnet (vty) application needs to provide the password lammle. Finally, a user connecting to the auxiliary (aux) port (such as over a modem connection) needs to provide the password todd.

It's pretty straightforward. The only subtlety you probably noticed is the login command under the console configuration. The login command instructs the router to check for a line password, and it's enabled by default on Telnet and auxiliary lines. This means that if you don't set a password for the vty lines, the default setting won't allow users to telnet into the router.

You might be wondering why I'm showing you line authentication when I just told you its use is limited. Line authentication is most effective in environments with few administrators and routers. If one administrator leaves the group, all passwords should be changed on all routers (for obvious security reasons). All current administrators must be aware of the new passwords.

Once the passwords have been set, any administrator attaching to a line will be prompted for a user-mode password. Here's an example that demonstrates an attachment to the console line:

```
Todd con0 is now available

Press RETURN to get started.
User Access Verification

Password:(does not show in output)
Todd>enable
Todd#
```

Authentication Methods

With a terminal server configuration, a router authenticates a user coming in on it by ensuring that the person attempting to connect is valid and is truly permitted access. The most common way the router determines this is by using either a password or a username/password combination. First, the user submits the needed information to the router. Then the router checks to see if that information is correct. If so, the user is then authenticated.

But that's only one way for routers to authenticate users from outside its boundaries. There are several different authentication methods you can apply to your end that involve the operating system, the security server, PAP, and CHAP authentication. I'm going to explain all of these techniques shortly, but first, I want to go into more detail about the way authentication is achieved most often—via usernames and passwords.

Username/password methods range from weak to strong in their authentication power—it depends on how vigilant you want to be. A database of usernames and passwords is employed at the simpler and least secure end of the range, while more advanced methods utilize one-time passwords. The following list begins with the least secure authentication method progressing through to the most secure authentication method:

No username or password Obviously, this is the least secure authentication method. It provides ease of connectivity but absolutely no security for network equipment or network resources. An attacker just has to find the server or network address to gain access.

Username/password (static) This authentication method is set up by a network administrator and remains in place and unchanged until the network administrator changes it. It's better than nothing, but as we discussed in Chapter 1, "Introduction to Network Security," hackers can easily decipher usernames and passwords using snooping devices.

Aging username/password This authentication method configures passwords that expire after a set time (usually between 30 and 90 days) and must be reset—most often, by the user (the administrator configures the expiration time). This method is tighter than the static username/password method, but it's still susceptible to playback attacks, eavesdropping, theft, and password cracking.

One-time passwords (OTPs) This is the most secure username/password authentication method. Most OTP systems are based on a secret pass-phrase that is used to generate a list of passwords. They're good only for one login, so they're useless to anyone who manages to eavesdrop and capture them. A list of accessible passwords is typically generated by S/KEY server software and then distributed to users.

Token cards/soft tokens This is the most secure authentication method. An administrator passes out a token card and a personal identification number (PIN) to each user. Token cards are typically the size of a credit card and are provided by a vendor to the administrator when they buy a token card server. This type of security usually consists of a remote client computer, an NAS, and a security server running token security software. Token cards and servers generally work as follows:

- An OTP is generated by the user with the token card using a security algorithm.
- The user enters this password into the authentication screen generated on the client.
- The password is sent to the token server via the network and an NAS.
- On the token server, an algorithm is used (the same algorithm that runs on the client) to verify the password and authenticate the user.

The network security policy you create provides you with the guidelines you need to determine the kind of authentication method you choose to implement on your network.

Windows Authentication

All right, so everyone knows that Microsoft graciously includes many captivating bugs and flaws with its operating system, but at least it manages to provide an initial authentication screen. As you probably know, users need to authenticate to log in to Windows. If those users happen to be local, they log in to the device via the Windows logon dialog box. If they're remote, they log in to the Windows remote dialog box using *PPP (Point-to-Point Protocol)* and TCP/IP over the communication line to the security server. Generally, that security server is responsible for authenticating users, but it doesn't have to be. A user's identity (username and password) can also be validated using an AAA security server.

Security Server Authentication

Cisco AAA access control gives you two options for authentication by a security server—it provides either a local security database or a remote one. Your Cisco NAS runs the local database for a small group of users, and if you have a simple network with one or two NASs, you can opt for local authentication through it. All of the remote security data is on a separate server that runs the AAA security protocol, and that's what provides services for both network equipment and a large group of users.

While it's true that local authentication and line security can provide you with an adequate level of security, you're way better off going there if you have fairly small network. That's because local authentication and line security require a great deal of administration.

Picture this: a really huge network with, say, 300 routers. Okay? Every time a password needs to be changed, the entire roost of routers—that's all 300, friends—must be modified individually to reflect that change. *Individually!* By the administrator—you! This is exactly why it's so very much wiser to use security servers if your network is even somewhat large.

Security servers provide centralized management of usernames and passwords and here's how they work: When a router wants to authenticate a user, it collects the username and password information from them and submits that information to the security server. The security server then compares the information it's been given to the user database to see if the user should be allowed access to the router. All usernames and passwords are stored centrally on the single security server. With administration consolidated on a single device like this, managing millions of users is like spending a day at the beach.

There are three types of security servers supported by Cisco routers: RADIUS, TACACS+, and Kerberos. Let's take a look at each of them now.

RADIUS

Remote Authentication Dial-In User Service (RADIUS) was developed by the Internet Engineering Task Force (IETF) and is basically a security system that works to guard the network against unauthorized access. RADIUS is an open standard implemented by most major vendors, and it's one of the most popular types of security servers around.

RADIUS implements a client/server architecture, where the typical client is a router, and the typical server is a Windows or Unix device that's running RADIUS software.

The authentication process has three distinct stages:

1. The user is prompted for a username and password.

2. The username and encrypted password are sent over the network to the RADIUS server.

3. The RADIUS server replies with one of the following:

Response	Meaning
Accept	The user has been successfully authenticated.
Reject	The username and password are not valid.
Challenge	The RADIUS server requests additional information.
Change Password	The user should select a new password.

TACACS+

Terminal Access Controller Access Control System (TACACS+) is also a security server, and it's really similar in many ways to RADIUS, except that TACACS+ does all that RADIUS does and more.

TACACS+ was developed by Cisco Systems, so it's specifically designed to interact with Cisco's AAA services. If you're using TACACS+, you have the entire menu of AAA features available to you—and it handles each security aspect separately:

- Authentication includes messaging support in addition to login and password functions.

- Authorization enables explicit control over user capabilities.

- Accounting supplies detailed information about user activities.

Kerberos

Kerberos is an authentication and encryption method that can be used by Cisco routers to ensure that data cannot be "sniffed" off the network. Kerberos was developed at the Massachusetts Institute of Technology (MIT) and is designed to provide you with some pretty hefty security using the Data Encryption Standard (DES) cryptographic algorithm.

Kerberos authenticates user in a manner similar to RADIUS or TACACS+, but after a user is authenticated with Kerberos, they're granted something called an admission ticket. This ticket gives the user access to other resources on the network without having to resubmit their password across the network. These tickets are non-transferable and non-refundable and have a limited life span—they're good only for one ride. When the ticket expires, the user has to renew it to be able to access resources again.

Cisco routers also support Kerberos for Telnet, rlogin, rsh, and rcp. These "Kerberized" sessions allow encrypted communication between the end station and the router. This kind of encryption support is especially wonderful for administrators who configure routers, since Telnet data is normally sent in cleartext.

And because it's now included with Windows 2000, Kerberos will no doubt continue to gain in popularity. It's currently one of the most secure methods for authenticating a user.

PAP and CHAP Authentication

One of the key benefits of PPP is the ability to add authentication services provided by PAP or CHAP. Although you should be familiar with what PAP is and how it works, you should opt for CHAP because it's the more secure of the two protocols. If your server authenticates based on a Windows NT user database, you have to use PAP or MS-CHAP (a Microsoft proprietary version of the CHAP protocol).

PAP

PAP (Password Authentication Protocol) provides only basic security authentication for connections. It offers a simple way for the remote client to establish its identity using a two-way handshake that happens only after initial PPP link establishment.

That sounds good, but the username and password information is transmitted in cleartext, and as you know by now, that opens up a world of opportunities for a hacker to find ways into your network. The bad news is that there are a few older systems that support only PAP—not the more secure CHAP.

 WARNING   PAP usernames and passwords are transmitted in cleartext, reducing the security benefits of the protocol. Use CHAP instead whenever possible.

PAP works by first establishing a connection and then checking the username and password information. After this link-establishment phase is complete, a username/password pair is repeatedly sent by the peer system to the authenticator until authentication is acknowledged or the connection is terminated. If the username and password information matches, an OK message is returned, and the session is allowed to proceed. Figure 2.1 illustrates how PAP performs authentication.

FIGURE 2.1   PAP authentication

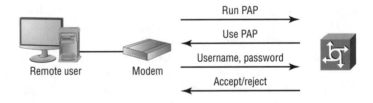

To configure PAP, you have to establish both the service and a database of usernames and passwords as follows:

```
encapsulation ppp
ppp authentication {chap | chap pap | pap chap |
   pap} [if-needed][list-name | default] [callin]
```

Usernames and passwords are addressed to the router with the `username` *name* `password` *secret* command.

That's pretty much it—there isn't much more to PAP. It works with a minimal amount of configuration mostly because of its lack of security. Be familiar with it and be aware of it, but don't use this protocol in current designs! PAP is defined in RFC 1334.

CHAP

CHAP (Challenge Handshake Authentication Protocol) is way more secure than PAP, mostly because of the mechanism it uses to transfer the username and password. CHAP periodically verifies the identity of the peer using a three-way handshake that initially occurs upon link establishment, and is repeated any time after the link has been established.

CHAP protects against *playback hacking*—resending the packet as part of an attack—by using a hash value that's valid only for that transaction. If a hacker captures the CHAP session and replays the dialogue in an attempt to access the network, the hash method will prevent the connection. In addition, the password is also hidden from the attacker because it's never sent over the circuit. The hash is valid for a relatively short period of time, and no hacker-enabling unencrypted information is sent over the link. Figure 2.2 illustrates how CHAP performs authentication.

FIGURE 2.2   CHAP authentication

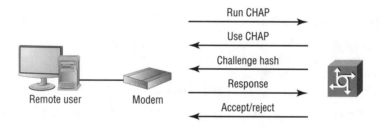

CHAP's configuration commands are a lot like PAP's configuration commands, except that instead of selecting PAP in the `ppp authentication` command, you use the `chap` keyword. The following commands are used to enable PPP (a requirement for CHAP) and to configure the router for CHAP authentication:

```
Encapsulation ppp
ppp authentication {chap | chap pap | pap chap |
   pap} [if-needed][list-name | default] [callin]
```

Did you notice that you get two additional options here: `chap pap` and `pap chap`? These keywords give you a way to select both protocols to be attempted in exactly that order; `chap pap` tries to authenticate via the CHAP protocol first. Why would you want to do this? You would use this configuration option only during a transitional phase when moving on from PAP to CHAP.

Usernames and passwords are added to the router with the `username` *name* `password` *secret* command.

And if you use the `debug ppp authentication` command to debug PPP authentication, you'll see the following output when you connect:

```
1d16h: %LINK-0-UPDOWN: Interface Serial0,
changed state to up
*Oct 17 11:22:15.297: Se0 PPP: Treating connection
as a dedicated line
*Oct 17 11:22:15.441: Se0 PPP: Phase is AUTHENTICATING,
 by this end
*Oct 17 11:22:15.445: Se0 CHAP: 0 CHALLENGE id 7
len 29 from *NASx
```

In the preceding example, you see that this connection is established on serial interface 0 and that the user is authenticating using CHAP.

In the Windows networking environment, you're given the choice to select password encryption, which works as long as you haven't set PAP to be the only authentication method on your router. Your Windows clients will try to connect with MS-CHAP, but if the box that designates that the password must be encrypted is checked, either PAP or CHAP will be used instead.

MS-CHAP Authentication

Okay, but what is *Microsoft Challenge Handshake Authentication Protocol (MS-CHAP)* anyway? It's Microsoft's version of CHAP, and it enables PPP authentication between a PC using Microsoft Windows and an NAS.

MS-CHAP differs from standard CHAP in these ways:

- MS-CHAP is enabled while the remote client and the NAS negotiate PPP parameters after link establishment.

- The MS-CHAP Response packet is in a format designed for compatibility with Microsoft's Windows networking products.

- MS-CHAP enables the network security server (authenticator) to control retry and password-changing mechanisms. MS-CHAP allows the remote client to change the MS-CHAP password.

- MS-CHAP defines a set of reason-for-failure codes returned to the remote client by the NAS.

PPP Callback

It's always great to have tricks up your sleeve for tightening up your security. With PPP, you can beef it up by using a feature called PPP callback. PPP callback commands the access server to disconnect the incoming connection and re-establish the connection via outbound dialing. In addition, PPP callback demands that the caller be in a single physical location, so if a username and password happens to get nicked by bad guys, the damage they can do is greatly diminished. You can also use the PPP callback feature to control costs because all connections appear to be from the remote-access server—read volume-based discounts! RFC 1570 documents PPP callback.

The snag here concerns your mobile users. Callback to a hotel room would require repeated configuration and a mechanism to deal with extensions. But some callback solutions allow the remote user to enter the callback number, which removes the physical location restrictions and enhances mobility.

Cisco's PPP callback feature does not permit remote users to dynamically enter the callback number.

Consider the security you get using a callback configuration:

- The remote client (the user) must connect into the remote-access server.

- Using an authentication protocol such as CHAP, the user must authenticate.

- If authentication is successful, the session will terminate and the remote-access server will call the remote client back. If the authentication fails, the connection will terminate.

- Upon callback, the client and server can again perform a password verification.

Clearly, these extra steps are worth your effort.

To configure callback, use the `ppp callback accept` command on the interface that receives the inbound call.

PPP callback will not make repeated retries to establish a return connection. This means that a busy signal or other impediment will require the client side to re-request the session.

Let's move on to look at the corporate network that you'll configure with NAS.

Configuring Your Corporate Network

This section presents the network diagram of devices that you'll be working with and configuring throughout this book. Take some time to really study it carefully. And while you're doing that, imagine that you're an expert consultant who's been hired to set up secure administrative and remote access to the NAS routers using the AAA best practices. You'll be configuring Phase 1 of the project in this chapter.

During Phase 1, you'll configure basic AAA services on the NAS using local databases. (During Phase 2, you'll migrate the local AAA database over to a CiscoSecure Access Control System. But that's going to happen in Chapter 3, "Configuring CiscoSecure ACS and TACACS+.")

The following graphic illustrates the network you've been hired to secure:

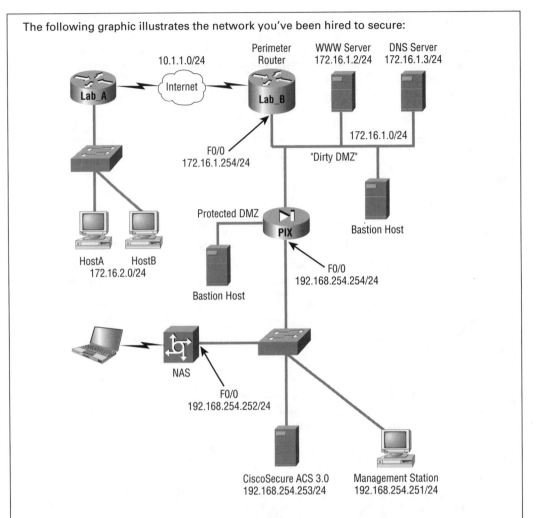

Let's go over a few terms in this diagram since you'll be using it throughout this book.

The *bastion host* is a computer that plays a crucial part in implementing your network security policy—a fact you can guess from its name. The word "bastion" refers to the well-armed defenses stationed around the perimeter of medieval castles. Think of them as the first line of defense—front-line soldiers that you have to ensure are tightly secured because of their exposed position. They are the computers between you and the untrusted or unknown networks that hackers will most often use to get to you and to break into your network. It's pretty common to find bastion hosts multitasking by providing things such as web services and public access systems.

Sometimes people call bastions *sacrificial hosts* because the odds are so good that they'll be attacked. If you're thinking that it might be a good idea to offer the bastion host a little backup, you're on the right track. Because they have only one network interface card (NIC), bastion hosts are vulnerable to IP spoofing attacks. But if you put a bastion host between two routers, you can configure it so that one router filters requests from untrusted networks, while the other router filters requests coming in from trusted networks, thus preventing spoofed packets from reaching your bastion host at all. Your routers verify that any network traffic traveling between them is addressed only to the bastion host. Most of the time, you'll find all-purpose operating systems such as Windows NT, Unix, or VMS running on a bastion host.

Here's another term—the *dirty DMZ*. Sounds really cool, huh? It's basically just a LAN inside your network that uses real Internet IP addresses. Don't confuse a dirty DMZ with a protected DMZ LAN. A DMZ LAN is connected to the inside of the Private Internet eXchange (PIX) and uses private IP addresses instead.

I know it's different, but in the example in the preceding graphic, the dirty DMZ has private IP addresses. That's only because it makes illustrating this configuration easier for the purposes of this book. Just know that your real-world dirty DMZ would have real IP addresses and would be much more vulnerable to attacks than a protected DMZ would be.

Configuring the NAS for AAA

Okay, keeping in mind all you've learned so far, it's time to show you how to configure the NAS to perform AAA using a local database. If you consider that every router is a target, then you must also understand that all interfaces on the NAS are at risk.

Here are the steps you must take to configure the NAS for AAA:

- Secure access to the exec mode with your character-mode passwords.
- Enable AAA locally on the NAS.
- Configure authentication on the NAS.
- Configure authorization on the NAS.
- Configure accounting on the NAS.
- Verify your NAS configuration.
- Troubleshoot AAA on the Cisco NAS.

Securing Access to the Exec Mode

To secure access to the exec modes, set your character-mode passwords first. Keep in mind that there are two access modes to consider when configuring the NAS: *character-mode access* and *packet-mode access*. Table 2.2 lists the different access modes, the port types, and the AAA commands.

TABLE 2.2   NAS Character and Packet Modes

Access Type	Modes	Network Access Server Port	AAA Command Element
Remote management	Character mode (line/ exec mode)	TTY, VTY, AUX, and CTY	login, exec NASI connection, ARAP, and enable
Remote network access	Packet mode (interface mode)	Async, group-async BRI, and serial (PRI)	PPP, network, and ARAP

Earlier in this chapter, you learned how to set your line passwords on the console, VTY, and AUX ports, but you still need to set your enable password. This is done using the following commands:

```
Todd#config t
Enter configuration commands, one per line.  End with CNTL/Z.
Todd(config)#enable secret globalnet
Todd(config)#enable password globalnet
The enable password you have chosen is the same as your enable secret.
This is not recommended.  Re-enter the enable password.
Todd(config)#enable password routersim
Todd(config)#
```

The best command for this task is the enable secret command because it automatically encrypts the password and supercedes the enable password. The two passwords cannot be the same.

Password Encryption

Because the enable password isn't encrypted by default, it's best to just use the enable secret command. By default, those line passwords aren't encrypted either.

So use the following command to encrypt your router passwords:

```
Todd(config)#service password-encryption
Todd(config)#^Z (Ctrl+Z)
Todd#show running-config
```

```
Current configuration:
!
hostname Todd
!
enable secret 5 $1$Qrnt$AmoVOSoe/ImPuv6jN9PeL.
enable password 7 06140034584B1B0A0C1A
!
[output cut]
line con 0
 password 7 104D000A0618
 login
 transport input none
line aux 0
 password 7 0958410D1D
 login
line vty 0 4
 password 7 082D4D43041500
 login
```

Once you've turned this command on, you need to exit from the global configuration mode and enter the show running-config command to see that the passwords are now encrypted.

At this point, turn off the service password-encryption command by using the no service-password encryption command as follows because the service password-encryption command is still running in the background, and no one needs any extra threads taking up CPU cycles:

```
Todd#config t
Enter configuration commands, one per line.  End with CNTL/Z.
Todd(config)#no service password-encryption
Todd(config)#^Z
Todd#
```

In addition to adding the character-mode passwords, you can set a username and password for each user by using the username command as follows:

```
Todd(config)#username todd password lammle
Todd(config)#line con 0
Todd(config-line)#login local
Todd(config-line)#line aux  0
Todd(config-line)#login local
```

```
Todd(config-line)#line vty 0 4
Todd(config-line)#login local
```

The router will now prompt for a username and password when a login attempt is made:

```
Todd con0 is now available
Press RETURN to get started.


User Access Verification


Username: todd
Password: (not displayed)
Todd>en
Password: (not displayed)
Todd#
```

You can now set up access for each user individually and define different levels of access for each user.

Enable AAA Locally on the NAS

You can also set up authorization, authentication, and accounting (AAA) on the router, which we'll call an NAS from here on out. After you set the character-mode passwords to secure access to the exec mode, you then need to enable AAA globally on the NAS. It's a pretty simple process:

```
Todd#config t
Enter configuration commands, one per line.  End with CNTL/Z.
Todd(config)#aaa ?
   new-model  Enable NEW access control commands and functions.(Disables OLD
              commands.)
Todd(config)#aaa new-model
Todd(config)#aaa ?
   accounting       Accounting configurations parameters.
   authentication   Authentication configurations parameters.
   authorization    Authorization configurations parameters.
   configuration    Authorization configuration parameters.
   dnis             Associate certain AAA parameters to a specific DNIS number
   nas              NAS specific configuration
   new-model        Enable NEW access control commands and functions.(Disables OLD
                    commands.)
   processes        Configure AAA background processes
   route            Static route downloading
```

And presto—that's it! Well, at least that's it for getting *started* with NAS configuration. Did you notice that once the command `aaa new-model` was entered, the accounting, authentication, and authorization parameters became available? And did you see that the `login local` command is no longer available under the line commands? I'll show you the new commands to use shortly.

While AAA was designed to centralize access control, it still demands configuration on each and every network device. The good news is that once you've configured AAA, you'll rarely find yourself having to alter it. You might need to modify your AAA configuration by changing the encryption key, but other than minor alterations like that, all changes—including those for user accounts—will be invoked at your security server. Nice, huh?

Authentication Configuration on the NAS

Now you're ready for the next step. This section will explain how to configure authentication, authorization, and accounting services on the Todd NAS router using a local database.

Authentication is configured differently on Cisco IOS-based and set-based devices, but the general parameters are similar. In broad terms, you must first instruct the device to use an authentication protocol and then provide the IP address for communications.

After you enable the NAS with AAA, you have to configure the authentication method lists and apply them to the lines and interfaces of the NAS. Here are the possible commands to be specified:

```
Todd(config)#aaa authentication ?
  arap      Set authentication lists for arap.
  banner    Message to use when starting login/authentication
  enable    Set authentication list for enable
  fail-message  Message to use for failed      login/authentication
  login     Set authentication lists for logins.
  nasi      Set authentication lists for NASI.
  password-prompt  Text to use when prompting for a password
  ppp       Set authentication lists for ppp.
  username-prompt  Text to use when prompting for a username
```

To configure authentication, first specify the service of PPP, ARAP, and NASI, or login authentication. (ARAP is AppleTalk Remote Access Protocol, and NASI is the NetWare Access Server Interface.) For now though, you're interested only in PPP.

First, you need to identify a list name or default. The list name can be any alphanumeric string you choose. Depending on your needs, you can then assign different authentication methods to each named list.

Finally, you need to specify the method used for authentication and designate how the router should handle any response for the various methods you've chosen. Once the lists have been created, you apply them to either the router lines or the interfaces.

The aaa authentication login command is used to define the type of authentication protocol you want to use. This command has two options and many variables. Here's one example:

```
Todd(config)#aaa authentication login ?
  WORD      Named authentication list.
  default   The default authentication list.
```

You can create a named list or use the default. The default argument gives you quite a few options:

```
Todd(config)#aaa authentication login default ?
  enable      Use enable password for authentication.
  line        Use line password for authentication.
  local       Use local username authentication.
  local-case  Use case-sensitive local username authentication.
  none        NO authentication.
  radius      Use RADIUS authentication.
  tacacs+     Use TACACS+ authentication.

Todd(config)#aaa authentication login default local
```

Look at the preceding command. The login default local command tells the router to authenticate using the local username and password, which can then be placed under the console, VTY, and AUX lines with the following commands:

```
Todd(config)#line console 0
Todd(config-line)#login authentication ?
  WORD      Use an authentication list with this name.
  default   Use the default authentication list.

Todd(config-line)#login authentication default
Todd(config-line)#line aux 0
Todd(config-line)#login authentication default
Todd(config-line)#line vty 0 4
Todd(config-line)#login authentication default
Todd(config-line)#
```

The following example illustrates how to use the login command with a named authentication list that I'll call "dial-in." This example puts the authentication list on the bri0/0 interface of the router:

```
Todd(config)#aaa authentication login ?
  WORD      Named authentication list.
  default   The default authentication list.
```

```
Todd(config)#aaa authentication login dial-in ?
  enable      Use enable password for authentication.
  line        Use line password for authentication.
  local       Use local username authentication.
  local-case  Use case-sensitive local username authentication.
  none        NO authentication.
  radius      Use RADIUS authentication.
  tacacs+     Use TACACS+ authentication.
```

```
Todd(config)#aaa authentication login dial-in local
```

The local keyword at the end of the command tells the router to use the local username and password for authentication.

You still need to set up PPP authentication for the list dial-in using the following command:

```
Todd(config)#aaa authentication ppp dial-in local
```

The authentication method for PPP can be a default or a named list. The preceding example uses a named list.

Now place the authentication method under the interface using the following commands:

```
Todd(config)#int bri0/0
Todd(config-if)#ppp encapsulation
Todd(config-if)#ppp authentication chap dial-in
```

Here's another example. Instead of the login command, you can use the enable default command. Doing this specifies whether a user can access the privileged level of a router. There are some options available with this command, as shown next:

```
Todd(config)#aaa authentication enable default ?
  enable   Use enable password for authentication.
  line     Use line password for authentication.
  none     NO authentication.
  radius   Use RADIUS authentication.
  tacacs+  Use TACACS+ authentication.
```

The enable keyword allows the local enable password to be used if network connectivity between the server and router is lost. You could consider this a security risk, but it's not a major one because an attacker would need to either physically access the router or compromise the internal network enough to change routes or block packets. Choosing the line command designates the local line passwords for authentication. The radius and tacacs+ commands elect a remote server for authentication. Chapter 3 describes this more completely.

Authorization Configuration on the NAS

It's undoubtedly clear to you by now that authorization is what defines the network services that are available to an individual or group. It also provides an easy means of allowing privileged mode (enable mode) access, while restricting the commands that can be executed.

This is a useful option because you might want to restrict most enable commands to be used only by a single administrator or manager and at the same time, to allow operators to perform limited diagnostic functions. You may want your more experienced operators to be granted higher levels of authorization. For example, they could be permitted to shut down an interface. The unrestricted privileged–mode is required in order for the administrator to be able to perform additional functions.

WARNING   Use care in restricting administrative rights to the router. While this is a helpful option when allocating rights to vendors and other parties, too restrictive a policy will lead to the distribution of the unrestricted account information and create an increased security risk.

Use the following parameters to restrict user access on a network:

```
Todd(config)#aaa authorization ?
  commands          For exec (shell) commands.
  config-commands   For configuration mode commands.
  configuration     For downloading configurations from AAA server
  exec              For starting an exec (shell).
  ipmobile          For Mobile IP services.
  network           For network services. (PPP, SLIP, ARAP)
  reverse-access    For reverse access connections
```

The commands command allows authorization for various levels. It's defined by the administrator, who must provide the various commands that each individual user can operate. Levels 1 and 15 are defined by default on all Cisco devices, with level 1 having only viewing access and level 15 having "God-like" access.

Here are the available levels:

```
Todd(config)#aaa authorization commands ?
  <0-15>  Enable level

Todd(config)#aaa authorization commands 1 ?
  WORD     Named authorization list.
  default  The default authorization list.
```

The preceding command sets up a level 1 access, and the command string shown next describes how that access will be authorized. I'll name it "begin":

```
Todd(config)#aaa authorization commands 1 begin ?
  if-authenticated  Succeed if user has authenticated.
  local             Use local database.
  none              No authorization (always succeeds).
  radius            Use RADIUS data for authorization.
  tacacs+           Use TACACS+.

Todd(config)#aaa authorization commands 1 begin local
```

This begin local command designates the local username database for authorizing the use of all level 1 commands.

Next, let's set a level 15 access list named "end". Remember that if you set any access other than level 1 or 15, you have to define each command that can be used at each level:

```
Todd(config)#aaa authorization commands 15 end local
```

This end local command sets the use of the local database to authorize the use of all level 15 commands.

Here's another example of how you can configure AAA authorization on your NAS. Use the following command to run authorization for all network-related service requests. The list name is "admin":

```
Todd(config)#aaa authorization network ?
  WORD     Named authorization list.
  default  The default authorization list.
Todd(config)#aaa authorization network admin local none
```

The preceding command designates the use of the local database to authorize access to all network services such as SLIP, PPP, and ARAP. But if the local server doesn't respond, the user will be able to use all network services by default.

Remember that authorization is the AAA process responsible for granting permission to access particular components in the network. You have to define these permissions based on corporate policy and user privileges.

The commands associated with authorization include parameters for the protocols you're going to use. These are the commands you use to specify what happens after the authentication phase of AAA. Table 2.3 lists and describes these commands.

TABLE 2.3   AAA Authorization Commands

Command	Description
aaa authorization commands level 15	Allows all exec commands at the specified level (0–15). In this example, this is level 15, which is regarded as full authorization and is normally associated with enable mode.
aaa authorization config-commands	Uses AAA authorization for configuration-mode commands.
aaa authorization configuration	Allows you to download the configuration from an AAA server.
aaa authorization exec	Authorizes the exec process with AAA.
aaa authorization ipmobile	Allows you to configure Mobile IP services.
aaa authorization network	Performs authorization security on all network services, including SLIP, PPP, and ARAP.
aaa authorization reverse-access	Uses AAA authorization for reverse Telnet connections.

Accounting Configuration on the NAS

AAA's accounting function records who did what and for how long. The accounting function relies on the authentication process to provide part of the audit trail. This is why it's a good idea to establish accounts with easily identified usernames—typically a last-name, first-initial configuration.

The configuration of accounting in AAA is fairly simple, but you do have a few choices to consider:

```
Todd(config)#aaa accounting ?
  commands     For exec (shell) commands.
  connection   For outbound connections. (telnet, rlogin)
  exec         For starting an exec (shell).
  nested       When starting PPP from EXEC, generate NETWORK records before
               EXEC-STOP record.
  network      For network services. (PPP, SLIP, ARAP)
  send         Send records to accounting server.
  suppress     Do not generate accounting records for a specific type of user.
  system       For System events.
  update       Enable accounting update records.
```

The preceding output lists the current AAA accounting commands available from global configuration mode. This section will focus on the network command for now.

The aaa accounting network command allows you to configure either a named list or the default:

```
Todd(config)#aaa accounting network ?
  WORD     Named Accounting list.
  default  The default accounting list.

Todd(config)#aaa accounting network default ?
  none        No accounting.
  start-stop  Record start and stop without waiting.
  stop-only   Record stop when service terminates.
  wait-start  Same as start-stop but wait for start-record commit.

Todd(config)#aaa accounting network default start-stop ?
  radius   Use RADIUS for Accounting.
  tacacs+  Use TACACS+.
```

The default keyword lets you record the start and stop times of a user's session on the network. But you've got to have a RADIUS or TACACS+ server for that, so you'll learn more about this configuration in Chapter 3.

For now, check out Table 2.4. It lists the more commonly used commands for configuring AAA accounting. The trick for deciding which command to use is to balance your need for obtaining complete accounting records against the overhead incurred by recording those records.

TABLE 2.4   AAA Accounting Commands

Command	Description
aaa accounting commands level	Audits all commands. If specified, only commands at the specified privilege level (0–15) are included.
aaa accounting connection	Audits all outbound connections, including Telnet and rlogin.
aaa accounting exec	Audits the exec process.
aaa accouting nested	Used when PPP authentication is used to record activity before the start-stop times are recorded.
aaa accounting network	Audits network service requests, including SLIP, PPP, and ARAP requests.

TABLE 2.4 AAA Accounting Commands *(continued)*

Command	Description
aaa accounting system	Audits system-level events. This includes reload, for example. Because a router reload is one of the ultimate DoS attacks, it would be useful to know the user identification that issues the command.
aaa accounting send	Documents the start and stop of a session. Audit information is sent in the background, so there is no delay for the user.
aaa accounting suppress	Sends a stop accounting notice at the end of a user process.
aaa accounting system	Similar to aaa accounting start-stop, this command documents the start of a session. However, the user is not permitted to continue until the accounting server acknowledges the log entry. This can delay user access.
aaa accounting update	Enables TACACS+ or RADIUS accounting.

One area in which AAA accounting transcends security is charge-back. If accurate start and stop times are well recorded, a company could charge users for their time spent on the system to offset the costs of running the system. ISPs have long considered this as an alternative to the flat-rate model currently used in the United States.

Verifying the NAS Configuration

The following output is from the configuration file of the Todd NAS router. It highlights the commands used for the AAA authentication and authorization configuration:

```
Todd#sh run
Building configuration...

Current configuration:
!
version 12.0
service timestamps debug uptime
service timestamps log uptime
```

```
no service password-encryption
!
hostname Todd
!
aaa new-model
aaa authentication login default local
aaa authentication login dial-in local
aaa authentication ppp dial-in local
aaa authorization commands 1 begin local
aaa authorization commands 15 end local
aaa authorization network admin local none
enable secret 5 $1$Qrnt$AmoVOSoe/ImPuv6jN9PeL.
enable password 7 06140034584B1B0A0C1A
!
username todd password 0 lammle
ip subnet-zero
!
 isdn switch-type basic-ni
!
[output cut]
```

The preceding output starts the AAA service and establishes authentication services for both the login default and the dial-in processes. The aaa authorization commands provide level 1 and level 15 access to network resources. You'll learn about the accounting commands in Chapter 3.

Troubleshooting AAA on the Cisco NAS

Everything's gone well so far, but for the darker days, let's look at some commands that help you with troubleshooting AAA configurations. These three debugging commands can be used to trace AAA packets and monitor their activities:

- debug aaa authentication
- debug aaa authorization
- debug aaa accounting

The following output results from executing the debug aaa authentication command. You can use this information to troubleshoot console logins:

```
Todd#debug aaa authentication
Todd#exit
01:41:50: AAA/AUTHEN: free_user (0x81420624) user='todd' ruser='' port='tty0'
rem_addr='async/' authen_type=ASCII service=LOGIN priv=1
```

```
01:41:51: AAA: parse name=tty0 idb type=-1 tty=-1
01:41:51: AAA: name=tty0 flags=0x11 type=4 shelf=0 slot=0 adapter=0 port=0
channel=0
01:41:51: AAA/AUTHEN: create_user (0x81420624) user='' ruser='' port='tty0' rem_
addr='async/' authen_type=ASCII service=LOGIN priv=1
01:41:51: AAA/AUTHEN/START (864264997): port='tty0' list='' action=LOGIN
service=LOGIN
01:41:51: AAA/AUTHEN/START (864264997): using "default" list
01:41:51: AAA/AUTHEN/START (864264997): Method=LOCAL
01:41:51: AAA/AUTHEN (864264997): status = GETUSER
User Access Verification
username:todd
Password: (not shown)
Todd>
01:42:12: AAA/AUTHEN/CONT (864264997): continue_login (user='(undef)')
01:42:12: AAA/AUTHEN (864264997): status = GETUSER
01:42:12: AAA/AUTHEN/CONT (864264997): Method=LOCAL
01:42:12: AAA/AUTHEN (864264997): status = GETPASS
01:42:14: AAA/AUTHEN/CONT (864264997): continue_login (user='todd')
01:42:14: AAA/AUTHEN (864264997): status = GETPASS
01:42:14: AAA/AUTHEN/CONT (864264997): Method=LOCAL
01:42:14: AAA/AUTHEN (864264997): status = PASS
```

The preceding output shows the user-mode access on the NAS (priv=1), that the username is todd, and that the method is local authentication. The following output is the enable access, which is shown as priv=15, meaning level 15 access.

```
Todd>enable
Password: (not shown)
01:42:46: AAA/AUTHEN: dup_user (0x8147DFC4) user='todd' ruser='' port='tty0' rem
_addr='async/' authen_type=ASCII service=ENABLE priv=15 source='AAA dup enable'
01:42:46: AAA/AUTHEN/START (3721425915): port='tty0' list='' action=LOGIN service
=ENABLE
01:42:46: AAA/AUTHEN/START (3721425915): console enable - default to enable pass
word (if any)
01:42:46: AAA/AUTHEN/START (3721425915): Method=ENABLE
01:42:46: AAA/AUTHEN (3721425915): status = GETPASS
Todd#
01:42:50: AAA/AUTHEN/CONT (3721425915): continue_login (user='(undef)')
01:42:50: AAA/AUTHEN (3721425915): status = GETPASS
01:42:50: AAA/AUTHEN/CONT (3721425915): Method=ENABLE
01:42:50: AAA/AUTHEN (3721425915): status = PASS
```

```
01:42:50: AAA/AUTHEN: free_user (0x8147DFC4) user='' ruser='' port='tty0' rem_
addr='async/' authen_type=ASCII service=ENABLE priv=15
```

Use the no debug aaa authentication form of the command to disable this debug mode, as follows:

Todd#**no debug aaa authentication**
```
AAA Authentication debugging is off
Todd#
```

The next output shows a successful AAA authorization:

Todd# **debug aaa authorization**
```
1:21:23: AAA/AUTHOR (0): user='Todd'
1:21:23: AAA/AUTHOR (0): send AV service=shell
1:21:23: AAA/AUTHOR (0): send AV cmd*
1:21:23: AAA/AUTHOR (342885561): Method=Local
1:21:23: AAA/AUTHOR/TAC+ (342885561): user=Todd
1:21:23: AAA/AUTHOR/TAC+ (342885561): send AV service=shell
1:21:23: AAA/AUTHOR/TAC+ (342885561): send AV cmd*
1:21:23: AAA/AUTHOR (342885561): Post authorization status = PASS
```

You can see here that the username is Todd. The second and third lines show that the attribute value (AV) pairs are authorized. The next line shows the method used for authorizing, and the final line gives you the status of the authorization.

The following output shows output from the debug aaa accounting command, which displays information on accountable events as they occur. Chapter 3 covers this topic more thoroughly.

Todd# **debug aaa accounting**
```
1:09:41: AAA/ACCT: EXEC acct start, line 10
1:09:52: AAA/ACCT: Connect start, line 10, glare
1:09:07: AAA/ACCT: Connection acct stop:
task_id=60 service=exec port=10 protocol=telnet address=172.31.3.78 cmd=glare
bytes_in=308 bytes_out=76 paks_in=45 paks_out=54 elapsed_time=14
```

Remember that the protocol used to transfer the accounting information to a server is independent of the information displayed. In addition to the debug aaa accounting command, you can use the debug tacacs and debug radius commands to examine the specific protocol information. Again, Chapter 3 provides more detail on these commands.

If you are configured for AAA accounting, you can use the show accounting command to see all the active sessions and to print accounting records. It's also useful to know that if you activate the debug aaa accounting command, the show accounting command displays additional data on the internal state of the AAA security system.

Summary

As security needs become more complex in your networking environments, Cisco continues to extend its features to meet demands. Cisco's AAA (Authentication, Authorization, and Accounting) services provide control over user access, what those users are permitted to do once they're authorized to get into your network, and records the tasks they perform during their sessions. AAA provides great techniques for network authentication, granting permissions (authorization), and keeping records of activity (accounting).

In addition, RADIUS and TACACS+ security servers allow you to implement a centralized security plan.

The configuration of AAA on the Cisco NAS (Network Access Server) using a local database is important for smaller networks. In Chapter 3, you'll learn how to move the local database to a Cisco NAS.

Exam Essentials

Remember which authentication method is the most secure.   Token cards/soft tokens are the most secure method of authentication.

Know what the AAA command wait-start radius provides.   The wait-start radius command means that a requested service cannot start until the acknowledgment has been received from the RADIUS server.

Be able to read the output of a debug aaa authentication command.   In the debug aaa authentication output, you need to find the username and the method, and see if it was successful.

Be able to read the output of a debug ppp authentication command.   In the debug ppp authentication output, you need to understand what interface the challenge is coming from.

Remember the command to enable AAA globally on the NAS.   The aaa new-model command is used to start AAA on the NAS.

Key Terms

Before you take the exam, be certain you are familiar with the following terms:

accounting	network access server (NAS)
authentication	packet-mode access
Authentication, Authorization, and Accounting (AAA)	PAP (Password Authentication Protocol)
authorization	PPP (Point-to-Point Protocol)
bastion hosts	RADIUS (Remote Authentication Dial-In User Service)
CHAP (Challenge Handshake Authentication Protocol)	sacrificial hosts
character-mode access	Syslog
dirty DMZ	TACACS+ (Terminal Access Controller Access Control System)
Kerberos	token cards/soft tokens
line authentication	

Commands Used in This Chapter

Here is the list of commands used in this chapter:

Command	Meaning
(config)#**line con 0**	Chooses the line configuration of the console port.
(config-line)#**login**	Tells the router to look in the line configuration for the password.
(config-line)#**password** *password*	Sets the line password.
(config-line)#**line vty 0 4**	Chooses the Telnet lines.
(config-line)#**line aux 0**	Chooses the AUX line.

Command	Meaning
(config)#**enable secret** *password*	Sets the enable secret password.
(config)#**enable password** *password*	Sets the enable password.
(config)#**service password-encryption**	Encrypts the enable password and the line passwords.
(config)#**username** *username* **password** *password*	Creates a username and password.
(config-line)#**login local**	Designates that the username will use the local line password for authentication.
(config)#**aaa new-model**	Enables the AAA process on the NAS.
(config)#**aaa authentication login default local**	Tells the router to authenticate using the local username and password.
(config-line)#**login authentication default**	Places the authentication login default command under the lines.
(config)#**aaa authentication login dial-in local**	Enables a command set on the BRI interface so that the local lines will be used for authentication.
(config)#**int bri0/0**	Chooses the BRI interface.
(config-if)#**ppp encapsulation**	Sets the interface encapsulation to PPP.
(config-if)#**ppp authentication chap dial-in**	Sets the interface to use CHAP authentication.
(config)#**aaa authorization commands 1 begin local**	Sets a level 1 configuration to use the local line passwords.
(config)#**aaa authorization commands 15 end local**	Sets a level 15 configuration to use the local line passwords.
(config)#**aaa #authorization network admin local none**	Performs authorization security on all network services.
#**debug aaa authentication**	Turns on debugging for AAA authentication.
#**no debug aaa authentication**	Turns off debugging for AAA authentication.
#**debug aaa authorization**	Turns on debugging for AAA authorization.
#**debug aaa accounting**	Turns on debugging for AAA accounting.

Written Lab

This section asks you 10 write-in-the-answer questions to help you understand the technology that you need to know in order to pass the SECUR exam.

1. List three packet-mode access methods.
2. List three character-mode access methods.
3. List the least secure authentication method.
4. List the most secure authentication method.
5. What is the command that enables AAA globally on the NAS?
6. What are the three AAA components?
7. Which AAA component controls user privileges?
8. True/False: Authorization servers can be used to authenticate users remotely.
9. Which AAA component identifies users?
10. Which AAA component limits a user's ability on a network?

Review Questions

1. Which of the following is the most secure authentication method?

   A. One-time passwords

   B. Token cards/soft tokens

   C. Username and password

   D. S/KEY

2. If you have a default configuration on your interface and then use the following global configuration command, which statement is true?

   ```
   aaa authorization network gns tacacs local
   ```

   A. If the TACACS+ server is not reachable, the NAS access will be enabled by default.

   B. If the TACACS+ server is not reachable, the local database will be used.

   C. The NAS will use the enable password by default.

   D. If the TACACS+ server is not reachable, the user will be denied access.

3. Which command enables AAA globally on the NAS?

   A. `aaa enable`

   B. `aaa new-model`

   C. `aaa default enable`

   D. `aaa authentication login default enable`

4. Which component of AAA provides for the identification of users?

   A. Accounting

   B. Authorization

   C. Authentication

   D. Administration

5. Which of the following can AAA use for authenticating a user? (Choose all that apply.)

   A. NDS

   B. TACACS+

   C. SQL

   D. RADIUS

6. Which component of AAA controls the privileges a user is granted?

   A. Accounting

   B. Authorization

   C. Authentication

   D. Administration

7. Which of these statements are true regarding the output of the following debug screen? (Choose all that apply.)

   ```
   1d16h: %LINK-3-UPDOWN: Interface Ethernet0, changed
   state to up
   Oct 5 12:32:12.294: BRI0/0 PPP: Treating connection as a dedicated line
   Oct 5 12:32:12.294: BRI0/0 PPP: Phase is AUTHENTICATING, by this end
   Oct 5 12:32:12.294: BRI0/0 CHAP: O CHALLENGE id 7 len 29 from *NASx
   ```

   A. The user ID is NASx.

   B. This connection is established on interface bri0/0.

   C. The user is authenticating using CHAP (Challenge Handshake Authentication Protocol).

   D. The client is attempting to set up a SLIP (Serial Line Internet Protocol) connection.

8. What does the `wait-start radius` command do when used with the `aaa accounting network` command? (Choose all that apply.)

   A. The NAS looks for the account information on a RADIUS server.

   B. Stop accounting records for network service requests are sent to the RADIUS server.

   C. Start accounting records for network service requests are sent to the local database.

   D. The requested service cannot start until the acknowledgment has been received from the RADIUS server.

9. Which of these statements are true regarding the following debug output? (Choose all that apply.)

   ```
   Dec 23 11:59:40.663: AAA/AUTHEN/CONT (1351411051):
   continue_login (user='Todd')
   Dec 23 11:59:40.663: AAA/AUTHEN (1351411051):
   status = GETPASS
   Dec 23 11:59:40.663: AAA/AUTHEN/CONT (1351411051):
   Method=LOCAL
   Dec 23 11:59:40.715: AAA/AUTHEN (1351411051):
   status = PASS
   ```

   A. The authentication was successful.

   B. The user belonged to the Todd group.

   C. The method used was local authentication.

   D. The output was generated from the `debug aaa authentication` command.

10. Which of the following are packet-mode access methods? (Choose all that apply.)

    A. BRI

    B. Async

    C. Sync

    D. Group-sync

    E. Telnet

    F. Serial

11. Which of the following are considered character-mode access methods? (Choose all that apply.)

    A. VTY

    B. Async

    C. Sync

    D. Group-async

    E. TTY

    F. Serial

    G. AUX

12. Which of the following protects against playback hacking?

    A. PPP

    B. PAP

    C. CHAP

    D. SLIP

13. Which of the following uses a three-way handshake?

    A. PPP

    B. PAP

    C. CHAP

    D. SLIP

14. Which of the following features was developed by Cisco?

    A. RADIUS

    B. TACACS+

    C. Kerberos

    D. CHAP

15. Which of the following uses the Data Encryption Standard (DES)?

   A. RADIUS

   B. TACACS+

   C. Kerberos

   D. CHAP

16. Which of the following is the most secure username/password authentication method?

   A. Static username/password

   B. Aging username/password

   C. One-time passwords (OTP)

   D. Token cards/soft tokens

17. Which of these statements are true regarding the following debug output? (Choose all that apply.)

```
1:09:41: AAA/ACCT: EXEC acct start, line 10
1:09:52: AAA/ACCT: Connect start, line 10, glare
1:09:07: AAA/ACCT: Connection acct stop:
task_id=60 service=exec port=10 protocol=telnet
```

   A. This debug output shows that the user is using the local database on the NAS.

   B. This is a debug output from the authorization component of AAA.

   C. This is a debug output from the accounting component of AAA.

   D. The user used Telnet to gain access to the NAS.

18. Which of these statements are true regarding the following debug output? (Choose all that apply.)

```
01:41:50: AAA/AUTHEN: free_user (0x81420624) user='todd' ruser='' port='tty0'
rem_addr='async/' authen_type=ASCII service=LOGIN priv=101:42:12:
AAA/AUTHEN/CONT (864264997): Method=LOCAL
```

   A. This debug output shows that the user is using a remote database for authenticating the user todd.

   B. This is a debug output from the authorization component of AAA.

   C. This is a debug output from the authentication component of AAA.

   D. The password will be checked against the local line password.

19. Which of these statements are true regarding the following debug output? (Choose all that apply.)

```
1:21:23: AAA/AUTHOR (0): user='Todd'
1:21:23: AAA/AUTHOR (0): send AV service=shell
1:21:23: AAA/AUTHOR (0): send AV cmd*
1:21:23: AAA/AUTHOR (342885561): Method=Local
```

A. The username is Todd.

B. This is a debug output from the authorization component of AAA.

C. This is a debug output from the authentication component of AAA.

D. This is using a remote database for authenticating the user Todd.

20. Which of the following commands trace AAA packets and monitor their activities? (Choose all that apply.)

A. debug aaa authentication

B. debug aaa authorization

C. debug aaa all

D. debug aaa accounting

Hands-On Labs

This section will have you configure a Cisco 2600 router with AAA. If you don't have a Cisco router, please check www.routersim.com for a SECUR router simulator.

The labs in this chapter include the following:

- Lab 2.1: Setting the Line Passwords
- Lab 2.2: Setting the Enable Passwords
- Lab 2.3: Encrypting Your Passwords
- Lab 2.4: Creating Users and Logging In
- Lab 2.5: Configuring AAA on the NAS

Lab 2.1: Setting the Line Passwords

This lab has you log in and set the character-mode passwords on your router.

1. Connect to your router and press Enter.
2. Type the command **enable**.
3. Type the command **config t**.
4. Set your hostname to "NAS" using the following command:

   Router(config)#**hostname NAS**

5. Set the console, VTY, and AUX line passwords using the following commands:

   NAS(config)#**line con 0**
   NAS(config-line)#**login**
   NAS(config-line)#**password console**
   NAS(config-line)#**line vty 0 4**
   NAS(config-line)#**password telnet**
   NAS(config-line)#**line aux 0**
   NAS(config-line)#**password todd**

6. Press Ctrl+Z and then type **copy running-config startup-config**.

Lab 2.2: Setting the Enable Passwords

This lab has you configure the enable passwords on your router.

1. Log in to the your router.
2. Type **config t** to enter global configuration mode. You should see the following output:

   NAS#**config t**
   Enter configuration commands, one per line. End with CNTL/Z.
   NAS(config)#

3. Set the enable password to "routersim" using the following command:

    NAS(config)#**enable password routersim**

4. Set the enable secret password to "globalnet" using the following command:

    NAS(config)#**enable secret globalnet**

5. Press Ctrl+Z and then type **copy running-config startup-config**.

6. Type **show running-config** and notice that the enable secret password is encrypted, but that the enable password and the line passwords are not.

Lab 2.3: Encrypting your Passwords

This lab has you configure password encryption on your router.

1. Log in to your router.

2. Go to the global configuration mode.

3. Type the following command:

    NAS(config)#**service password-encryption**
    NAS(config)#**^Z** (Ctrl+Z)

4. From the privilege mode prompt, type **show running-config** and verify that your passwords are indeed now encrypted.

5. Enter the global configuration mode and type the following commands:

    NAS#**config t**
    Enter configuration commands, one per line. End with CNTL/Z.
    NAS(config)#**no service password-encryption**
    NAS(config)#**^Z**
    NAS#

    This turns off the encryption service from running in the background on your router.

Lab 2.4: Creating Usernames and Logging In

This lab has you create a user on your router and then log in using the username and password.

1. Log in to your router.

2. Enter the global configuration mode and create a user and password. Here's an example:

    NAS#**config t**
    Enter configuration commands, one per line. End with CNTL/Z.
    NAS(config)#**username todd password lammle**

3. Under each line, add the command `login local` so that the username and password are prompted when connecting to user-mode access.

```
NAS(config)#line con 0
NAS(config-line)#login local
NAS(config-line)#line aux  0
NAS(config-line)#login local
NAS(config-line)#line vty 0 4
NAS(config-line)#login local
```

4. Press Ctrl+Z and then exit.

5. Press Enter. You should be prompted for your username and password.

Lab 2.5: Configuring AAA Authentication on the NAS

This lab has you enable AAA on the NAS and use the local database on the NAS router for authentication.

1. Log in to your router.

2. Enter the global configuration mode and enable AAA globally on the NAS with the following command:

```
NAS#config t
Enter configuration commands, one per line.  End with CNTL/Z.
NAS(config)#aaa new-model
```

3. Set the AAA authentication to authenticate with the local username and password using the following command:

```
NAS(config)#aaa authentication login default local
```

4. Set the AAA authentication under the console, VTY, and AUX lines with the following commands:

```
NAS(config)#line console 0
NAS(config-line)#login authentication ?
  WORD     Use an authentication list with this name.
  default  Use the default authentication list.
NAS(config-line)#login authentication default
NAS(config-line)#line aux 0
NAS(config-line)#login authentication default
NAS(config-line)#line vty 0 4
NAS(config-line)#login authentication default
```

5. Type the following command from the privileged mode:

   NAS#**debug aaa authentication**

6. Log out of the router.

7. Notice that the authentication takes place from the debug output.

8. Turn off debugging with the undebug all command.

Answers to Written Lab

1. Async, group-async BRI, and serial (PRI) are all considered packet-mode access methods.

2. TTY, VTY, AUX, and CTY are considered character-mode access methods.

3. The least secure authentication method is no username or password.

4. Token cards/soft tokens are the most secure type of authentication.

5. The `aaa new-model` command enables AAA globally on the NAS.

6. Authentication, authorization, and accounting are the three AAA components.

7. The authorization component controls user privileges.

8. False. Authentication servers cannot be used to authenticate users remotely.

9. The authentication component identifies users.

10. The authorization component limits a user's ability on a network.

Answers to Review Questions

1. B. Token cards/soft tokens are the most secure type of authentication.

2. B. The `tacacs local` keywords at the end of the command say to authenticate via TACACS+, and if that is not available, then use local username authentication.

3. B. To start the AAA on an NAS, use the global configuration command `aaa new-model`.

4. C. Authentication identifies a user, including login, password, messaging, and encryption.

5. B, D. TACACS+ and RADIUS provide authentication for users.

6. B. Authorization determines what a user is permitted to do after logging on.

7. B, C. Interface bri0/0 is the incoming interface being challenged by CHAP.

8. A, B, D. As in `start-stop`, the `radius` command sends both a start and a stop accounting record to the accounting server. However, if you use the `wait-start` keyword, the requested user service does not begin until the start accounting record is acknowledged. A stop accounting record is also sent.

9. A, C, D. The output shows an AAA authentication, which makes answer D correct. The third line says it is a local method of authentication, and the fourth line says it passed (successful). The user is Todd, not a member of the group Todd.

10. A, B, F. Async, group-async BRI, and serial (PRI) are all considered packet-mode access methods. TTY, VTY, AUX, and CTY are considered character-mode access methods.

11. A, E, G. Async, group-async BRI, and serial (PRI) are all considered packet-mode access methods. TTY, VTY, AUX, and CTY are considered character-mode access methods.

12. C. CHAP protects against playback hacking (resending the packet as part of an attack) by using a hash value that is valid only for that transaction.

13. C. CHAP periodically verifies the identity of the peer using a three-way handshake. The handshake is done upon initial link establishment and may be repeated any time after the link has been established.

14. B. TACACS+ was developed by Cisco and is specifically designed to interact with Cisco's AAA services.

15. C. Kerberos was developed at MIT and was designed to provide strong security using the DES cryptographic algorithm.

16. C. One-time passwords (OTP) provide the most secure username/password authentication method. Most OTP systems are based on a secret pass-phrase, which is used to generate a list of passwords. An OTP is good only for one login and is therefore not useful to anyone who manages to eavesdrop and capture it.

17. C, D. The text after AAA/ACCT means that this is from the accounting component of AAA. `protocol=telnet` means that the user has gained access via the Telnet protocol.

18. C, D. The text after AAA/AUTHEN means that this is from the authentication component of AAA. `Method=LOCAL` means that the local line will be used for authentication.

19. A, B. The text after AAA/AUTHOR means that this is from the authorization component of AAA. The username is Todd.

20. A, B, D. The debug commands `debug aaa authentication`, `debug aaa authorization`, and `debug aaa accounting` can be used to help you trace AAA packets and monitor the AAA activities on the NAS.

Chapter

3

Configuring CiscoSecure ACS and TACACS+

THE FOLLOWING SECUR EXAM TOPICS ARE COVERED IN THIS CHAPTER:

- ✓ CiscoSecure ACS for Windows NT or Windows 2000
- ✓ Installing CiscoSecure ACS 3.0 for Windows NT or Windows 2000
- ✓ Configuring CiscoSecure ACS for Windows 2000
- ✓ Administering and troubleshooting CiscoSecure ACS for Windows NT or Windows 2000
- ✓ CiscoSecure ACS 2.3 for Unix (Solaris)
- ✓ Understanding and configuring TACACS+
- ✓ Verifying TACACS+

Now that you've been introduced to the AAA (Authentication, Authorization, and Accounting) interface, and you're familiar with the configuration of an NAS (network access server) for AAA using the local database, you're ready to put these great tools to use.

And that's exactly where we're going in this chapter. I'm going to guide you through configuring AAA using a TACACS+ or RADIUS-enabled security server as a centralized database. I'm also going to explain how to use the *access control servers (ACSs)* that support this centralized security process.

This chapter begins by looking at Cisco's ACS product on the Microsoft Windows NT/ 2000 platform, zooming in on how efficient the CiscoSecure ACS 3.0 for Windows NT or Windows 2000 technology can be when it's placed between the NAS and one of several existing user databases. Doing this facilitates AAA without requiring yet another user database— one that you'll have to take the time to configure and maintain. It's a very cool strategy! Next, you'll get a quick tour through CiscoSecure ACS 2.3 for Unix (CSU), an enterprise product that runs on the Solaris platform.

This chapter wraps up by discussing the communication between the NAS and ACS. You'll see that Cisco has truly provided all that's needed for both TACACS+ and RADIUS communications between the NAS and ACS. So roll up your sleeves and let's get started!

Introduction to the CiscoSecure ACS

As is true with life, change on your network is inevitable. This is a good thing—it keeps you employed! And products that are adaptable can minimize cost while giving you the options you need to meet the changing business requirements with speed and agility. So the built-in capacity for growth and change is something you really love to see in a product. Think chameleon. And *CiscoSecure (CS) ACS 3.0 for Windows NT (CSNT) or Windows 2000* is just that product— it blends in and works well with any network access device. It can be used with dial-up NASs and firewalls, or it can be used to manage access to switches and routers. The NAS can be literally any device capable of using the TACACS+ or RADIUS protocol—a beautiful chameleon indeed.

Let's look at how CiscoSecure ACS 3.0 for Windows NT or Windows 2000 works in a simple example. Suppose that you have a network such as the one introduced in the last chapter, illustrated in the following graphic:

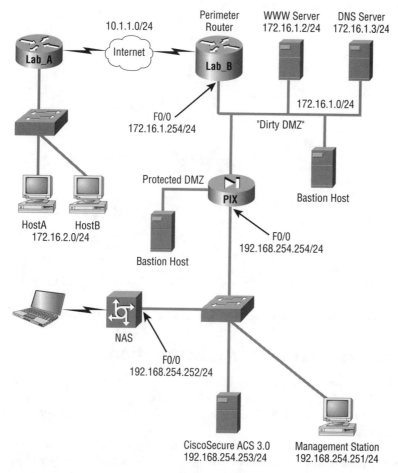

The NAS must be configured so that the user access request is redirected to CS ACS for authentication and authorization rather than checking local user databases for authentication. The NAS uses either the RADIUS or TACACS+ protocol to send the authentication request to CS ACS. CS ACS then verifies the username and password (I'll discuss that process shortly) and replies to the NAS. Once the user has been authenticated, CS ACS sends a set of authorization attributes to the NAS. Finally, if configured, the NAS accounting functions can take effect.

This can be a real advantage in situations where you have multiple NASs. Check out the network in Figure 3.1.

FIGURE 3.1 A network with multiple NAS devices

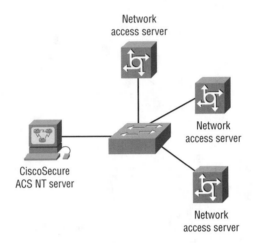

In Figure 3.1, multiple NASs are configured using TACACS+ or RADIUS to send their user access requests to a single CS ACS server.

Let's move on to discuss the database used for authentication on the CiscoSecure ACS.

Using User Databases for Authentication

CiscoSecure ACS 3.0 for Windows NT or Windows 2000 maintains its own database called the *CiscoSecure User Database*. When a user access request arrives at CiscoSecure ACS 3.0 for Windows NT or Windows 2000, it goes to that database first to check for information regarding that user.

If no matching information is found in the CiscoSecure User Database, CiscoSecure ACS 3.0 for Windows NT or Windows 2000 can be configured to check a number of additional user databases—a fine example of that wonderful flexibility—including the following options:

- Windows NT/2000
- Novell Directory Services (NDS)
- Directory Services (DS)
- Token Server
- Microsoft Commercial Internet System Lightweight Directory Access Protocol (MCIS LDAP)
- Open Database Connectivity (ODBC)

The CiscoSecure ACS 3.0 for Windows NT or Windows 2000 can use any of the following *token-card servers* (the most secure method) for authentication:

- ActivCard
- CRYPTOCard
- Vasco
- RSA ACE/Server
- Secure Computing SafeWord
- AXENT Defender

CS ACS for NT or Windows 2000 supports the following authentication protocols:

- ASCII/PAP
- CHAP
- MS-CHAP
- LEAP
- EAP-CHAP
- EAP-TLS
- EAP-MD5
- ARAP

Populating the User Database Population

And your options don't end with authentication. To provide you with even more flexibility, the CiscoSecure User Database can be populated in a number of ways:

- Manually
- With the Database Replication utility
- With the Database Import utility

Manual population really means "by hand." Unless you're really bored, you'll want to avoid all this work by using the replication and import utilities provided with the Cisco ACS.

The Database Replication utility provides fault tolerance and redundancy of your CiscoSecure User Database by allowing several independent CS ACS servers to synchronize their data. This means you can introduce a new CS ACS server that's configured for database replication to the network and can be populated with a replica of the existing CiscoSecure User Database—sweet!

If you have an existing ODBC-compliant database, you can also use the included Database Import utility `CSUtil.exe` to import user information from that database. (Refer to Cisco's documentation for formatting and import syntax.)

CS ACS supports data importing from ODBC-compliant databases such as Microsoft Access or Oracle. Importing is done with a single table to import user and group information into one or more ACS servers.

 The *CSAccupdate service* processes the ODBC import tables and updates local and remote CiscoSecure ACS installations.

New ACS Features

I've already pointed out some cool capabilities that CS ACS has to offer, but that certainly isn't the end to the goods. It has a rich set of features that allow you to customize and control the AAA process, which is exactly your goal. Being a control freak in issues concerning network security can save your bacon. And, after all, isn't the whole point of security to keep out those who have no good reason to be there in the first place? The following list of CS ACS features is by no means comprehensive, but it does include some of the highlights:

- Password aging
- User-changeable passwords
- Multi-level administration
- Group administration of users
- User and group MaxSessions
- Ability to disable an account on a specific date
- Time-of-day and day-of-week access restrictions
- Ability to disable an account after a certain number of failed attempts, as specified by the administrator
- Ability to see logged-on users and to view detailed information for each user
- Per-user TACACS+ or RADIUS attributes
- Support for Voice over IP (VoIP)
- Differing privilege levels for remote administrators
- Windows NT Performance Monitor support for real-time statistics viewing
- Configurable accounting and auditing information stored in comma-separated values (CSV) format
- Authentication forwarding
- Relational database management system (RDBMS) synchronization

- Database replication
- Scheduled ACS system backup and the ability to restore from the backup file

These and other features give you totally granular control over the AAA process, putting the matter of user access in your hands. In addition, CSNT gives you the tools you need to completely monitor the CSNT server and manipulate the user database.

And there's more! CS ACS 3.0.2 also has the following features and capabilities:

- 802.1x support
- LEAP support
- Extensible Authentication Protocol (EAP) support (EAP-MD5, EAP-TLS)
- Command authorization sets
- MS-CHAP version 2 support
- Per-user access control lists
- Shared network access restrictions (NARs)
- Wildcards in NARs
- Multiple devices per AAA client configuration
- Multiple LDAP lookups and LDAP failover
- User-defined RADIUS vendor-specific attributes (VSAs)

Installing CiscoSecure ACS 3.0

Want it short and sweet? The CS ACS installation can be condensed into the following steps:

1. Verify that the NAS and the Windows server can communicate over a LAN using TCP/IP. Ping will work just fine for this job.
2. Install the ACS 3.0 ACS on the Windows 2000 server platform. Although this supposedly works with Windows NT 4.0, it is recommended that you use a Windows 2000 server.
3. Disable IAS on the Windows 2000 server (if it's running), or the Cisco RADIUS server will not work.
4. Bring up the web browser interface of the ACS server.
5. Configure the NAS for AAA using TACACS+ and/or RADIUS.
6. Verify the installation and operation of the NAS and ACS server.

Exercise 3.1 assumes that step 1 has been completed and gets right into the installation of the ACS software.

EXERCISE 3.1

CiscoSecure ACS 3.0 Installation

After you bring up and test network connectivity between the Windows server and the NAS server, install the ACS on the Windows server using the following steps:

1. Once you click the Setup file, the ACS program displays the Before You Begin screen:

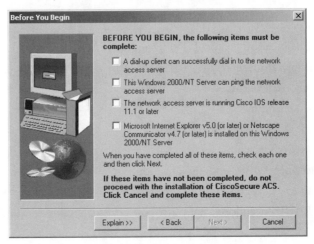

This screen asks you to verify that you have some basic configuration on the NAS before the ACS is installed. Be sure you don't miss the note about the minimum IOS Version on the NAS—especially if you're studying for your SECUR exam!

2. After you've completed the basic configuration needed to install the ACS, click Next and the Authentication Database Configuration screen appears:

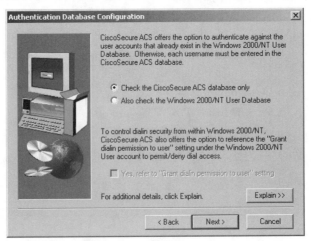

This is where you choose to use a local database on the ACS server or use the Windows server database.

3. Next, you'll be prompted to configure the ACS to talk to the NAS on the CiscoSecure ACS Network Access Server Details screen:

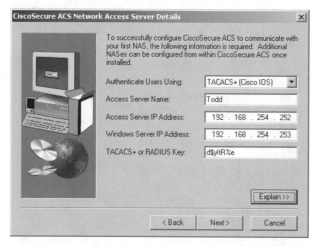

Look at the bottom right-hand corner of the screen. See that Explain button? If you click it, an Explanation of CiscoSecure ACS Network Access Server Details screen appears:

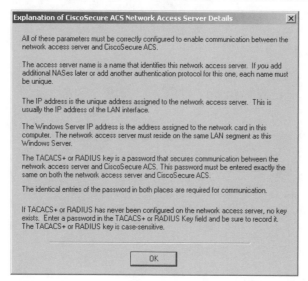

The Explanation screen can be unbelievably helpful to you. Yes! A help screen that is actually helpful—what do you know? Read through this information, and you'll learn what each file in the Details screen requires. On the CiscoSecure ACS Network Access Server Details screen, I entered the name of the NAS and the IP address of the NAS F0/0 interface. For the key, I just made up a unique and extremely hard key to break.

4. The next screen, Advanced Options, asks you to enter any advanced information to be displayed when using the ACS user interface:

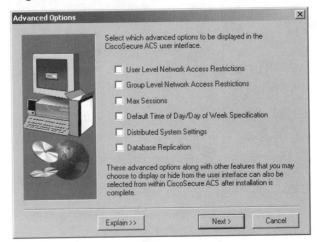

Again, to find out why you would choose each option, click the Explain button in the bottom left-hand corner. The Explanation of Advanced Options Configuration screen appears. Believe it—this is actually another helpful help screen—really!

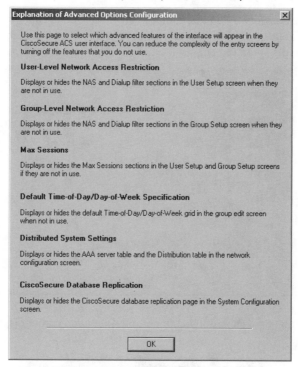

5. The next screen, Active Service Monitoring, gives you an opportunity to configure monitoring on the ACS as shown here:

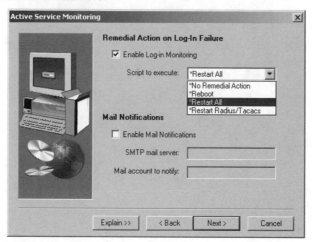

The Active Service Monitoring screen provides a great way to set up your e-mail notification in case of failure. The Explain button in the bottom left-hand corner describes what the options are, but you probably won't need to go there because they're really self-explanatory.

6. The Network Access Server Configuration screen allows you to configure the ACS so that it configures the NAS server. This is so much easier than the local authentication configuration that you did in the last chapter!

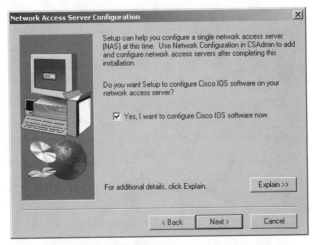

Again, clicking that Explain button in the bottom right-hand corner displays additional information:

EXERCISE 3.1 *(continued)*

7. Next you'll see the Enable Secret Password screen. It asks you for the enable secret password of the NAS and explains what the ACS installation is trying to accomplish:

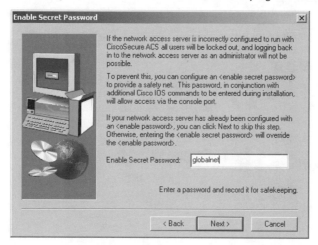

8. This next screen, Access Server Configuration, tells you that the ACS will show you how to configure the NAS, step by step. Nice!

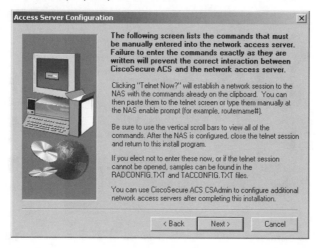

EXERCISE 3.1 *(continued)*

9. Just click Next to see the configuration you need to type into the NAS on the NAS Configuration screen:

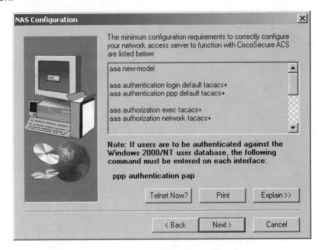

10. Keep scrolling down and you can see the entire configuration you need to configure on the
NAS. The last two configuration screens appear as follows:

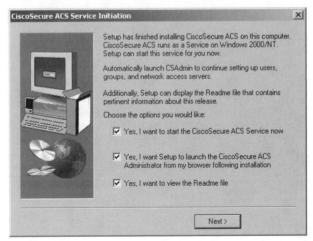

EXERCISE 3.1 *(continued)*

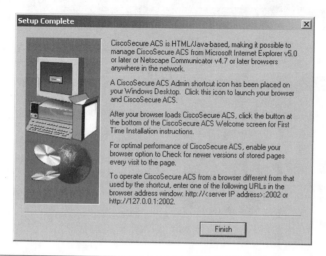

It can't get much easier than that! Did you notice that the Setup Complete screen tells you how to get into the ACS admin screen through a browser, `http://127.0.0.1:2002`? The 127.0.0.1 address is considered the loopback or diagnostic IP address of the local machine. You use this to verify that IP is running properly on a host. In this case, the IP address 127.0.0.1 also tells the browser that you mean "this host."

In a minute, I'll go through the configuration of the NAS, but first let's take a look at the ACS configuration. (If you want, this is a great time to take a short break and digest what you've just done before moving on.)

Administering CiscoSecure ACS

The CS ACS web browser interface makes the administration of AAA features pretty easy. The installation places an ACS Admin icon on the desktop of the server, and when you double-click it, you end up on the ACS Administration page, as illustrated in Figure 3.2.

FIGURE 3.2 ACS administration session

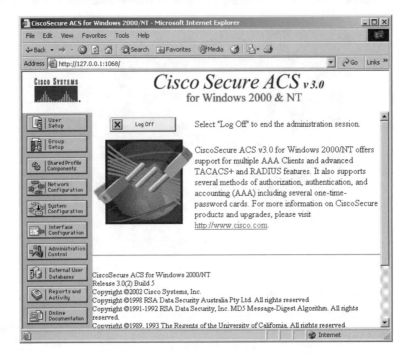

Each button on the navigation bar represents a particular area or function that you can configure. You typically don't need to configure all of the areas; nevertheless, you'll go through them all in Exercise 3.2.

 If you're studying for the exam, you don't have to memorize the fields in this area. Just use this information for documentation purposes.

In this exercise, you'll go through the ACS administration process step by step in the Windows environment. Then, I'll explain what the Unix administration is like.

EXERCISE 3.2

CiscoSecure ACS for Windows Administration

This exercise will provide you with step-by-step instructions on how to use the CiscoSecure Administration tool.

EXERCISE 3.2 *(continued)*

1. Select the User Setup button to begin configuring the CiscoSecure software. This is where you add, edit, or delete user accounts and list users in databases.

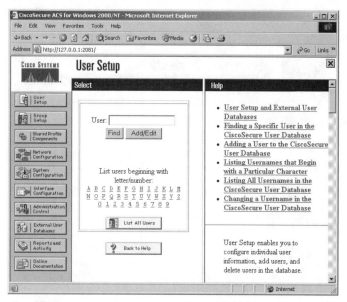

2. When you're done setting up individual users, click the Group Setup button in the left-hand margin. The Group Setup screen allows you to create, edit, and rename groups and list all users in a group.

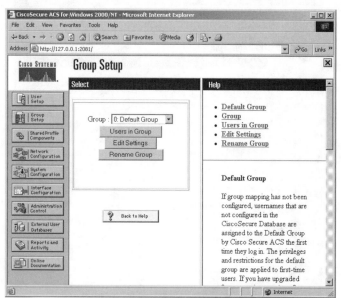

3. Next, the Shared Profile Components screen allows you to configure command authorization sets, which are configurable sets of authorization rules for device commands.

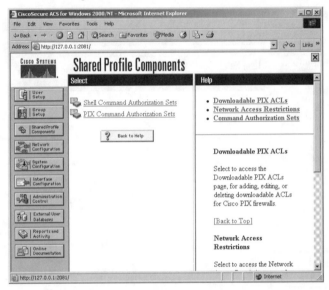

4. The Network Configuration button takes you to a screen where you configure and edit network access server parameters, add and delete network access servers, and configure AAA server distribution parameters.

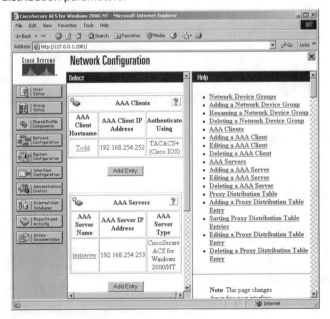

EXERCISE 3.2 *(continued)*

5. In the System Configuration screen, you can start and stop CS ACS services, configure logging, control database replication, and control RDBMS synchronization.

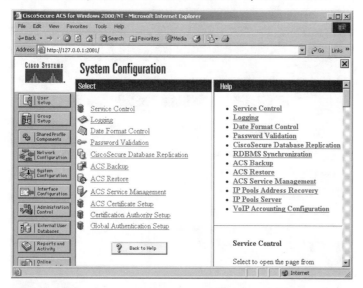

6. The Interface Configuration button takes you to a screen where you can configure user-defined fields that will be recorded in accounting logs, configure TACACS+ and RADIUS options, and control the display of options in the user interface.

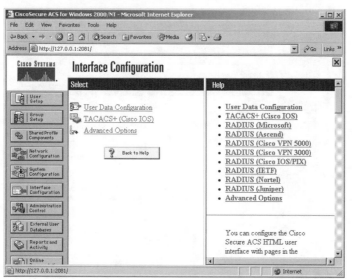

EXERCISE 3.2 *(continued)*

7. The Administration Control screen allows you to control the administration of CS ACS from any workstation on the network so you don't have to run all over the building. If you think you need the exercise, don't configure it!

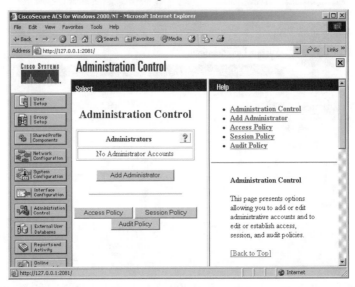

8. The External User Databases button gives you access to two screens where you configure the unknown user policy, configure authorization privileges for unknown users, and configure external database types.

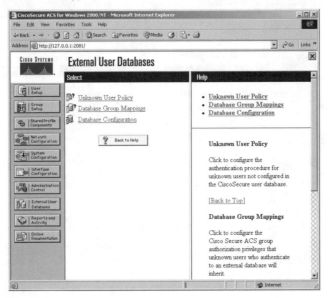

EXERCISE 3.2 *(continued)*

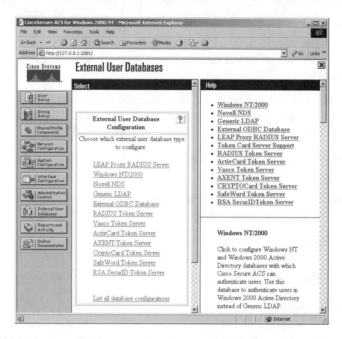

9. Clicking the Reports and Activity button displays the following screen:

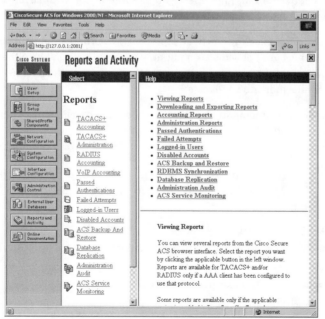

On the Reports and Activity screen, you can view the following information:

TACACS+ Accounting Reports: These reports record when sessions stop and start, record network access server messages with usernames, provide caller line identification information, and record the duration of each session.

RADIUS Accounting Reports: These reports record when sessions stop and start, record network access server messages with usernames, provide caller line identification information, and record the duration of each session.

Failed Attempts Report: This report lists authentication and authorization failures with an indication of the cause.

List Logged-in Users: This report lists all users currently receiving services for a single network access server or all network access servers with access to CS ACS.

List Disabled Accounts: This report lists all user accounts that are currently disabled.

Admin Accounting Reports: These reports list the configuration commands entered on a TACACS+ (Cisco) network access server.

You can import these files into most database and spreadsheet applications. This information is invaluable in helping you profile potentially problematic users by monitoring unusual activity. After you see these reports often enough, you'll spot potential bad guys in a snap. Of course, for that to happen, you or someone on your security team actually needs to review these reports on a regular basis.

I'm going to say this again: You can have top-of-the-line products and great people on your team, but if your security policies aren't tight, your security won't be either. If you've got the goods, make sure that policies are in place that guarantee the best use of the technology and personnel that you've invested in.

10. Lastly, the Online Documentation button provides more detailed information about the configuration, operation, and concepts of CS ACS.

Maybe you're not using Windows. Maybe you've got a Unix server set up. *CiscoSecure ACS 2.3 for Unix (CSU)* offers the same basic functions as CiscoSecure ACS for Windows discussed previously in Exercise 3.2:

- CSU accepts user access requests from an NAS using TACACS+ or RADIUS.
- CSU can be used as a centralized database for AAA, working with NASs from a variety of vendors.
- CSU has a web-based administration tool.

CSU offers relational database support for three databases: Sybase, Oracle, and SQL Anywhere (included).

Let's get right into TACACS+ and how it can be used to create a more secure network.

TACACS+ Overview

Okay, now that you've met Cisco's ACSs, let's take a second to review how the ACS and the NAS communicate. The NAS can use either TACACS+ or RADIUS to communicate user access requests to the ACS. Each of these two methods of communication has its individual strengths and purposes.

Table 3.1 summarizes the key differences between TACACS+ and RADIUS. I'll go over these in more detail shortly.

TABLE 3.1   TACACS+ and RADIUS Comparison

TACACS+	RADIUS
Transport: TCP (connection)	Transport: UDP (no connection)
CHAP is bidirectional	CHAP is unidirectional
Multiprotocol support	No ARA and no NetBEUI
Encrypts entire packet	Encrypts only passwords
Independent AAA architecture	Authentication and authorization combined
Best choice for router management	Industry standard

As you can see, TACACS+ has many advantages over RADIUS. It is for this very reason that Cisco strongly encourages the use of TACACS+. TACACS+ is really a better tool to use when you can, but you may need to use RADIUS, or both TACACS+ and RADIUS in a mixed-vendor network.

Because TACACS+ is a Cisco proprietary authentication scheme, its use in the Cisco AAA process has a number of distinct advantages. My goal here isn't to dissect TACACS+. Instead, I really want you to understand its benefits. (RFC 1492 documents Cisco's proprietary TACACS+.)

TACACS+ conforms to the AAA model—it treats authentication, authorization, and accounting as distinct and separate roles (as discussed in Chapter 2, "Introduction to AAA Security"). This means that TACACS+ has mechanisms to support each of these services, giving the security administrator much more granular control and latitude in both defining and, more importantly, implementing a security policy.

TACACS+ uses TCP as a transport protocol. I'm sure you remember that TCP opens a connection and verifies delivery of each segment. TACACS+ then encrypts the *entire contents* of each TCP segment, so anyone listening on the wire won't be able to snag information. TACACS+ supports PAP and CHAP, as well as PPP callback and per-user ACLs—all features covered in Chapter 2.

TACACS+ can be used between the NAS and ACS to control dial-in access and other access into the network. It can also be used between the network devices (routers and switches) and ACS to control authentication and authorization in the management of network devices.

Let's head right into configuring TACACS+ on your NAS.

Configuring TACACS+

Think back to Chapter 2 for a second. Remember the discussion about configuring the NAS to use the AAA process to authenticate users to a local database? Good! As you recall, you can configure authentication and authorization for local users with the username command. Let's try this out now:

```
Todd(config)#username todd password lammle
Todd(config)#line con 0
Todd(config-line)#login local
Todd(config-line)#line aux 0
Todd(config-line)#login local
Todd(config-line)#line vty 0 4
Todd(config-line)#login local
```

This configuration allows user todd to access the configured lines as long as Todd knows their passwords.

In a medium-to-large network, there are significant advantages to using TACACS+ (or other) centralized authentication services instead of local databases.

A common problem for many network administrators is the number of unsynchronized accounts a network user has. How often has a new employee been given seven, eight, or even ten separate "accounts," all with unique passwords, just to access the resources that the individual needs? Multiply that by a horde of employees, and you can just watch the stress levels build in your organization. Everyone is affected—from frustrated users trying to remember all their passwords on up to senior managers dealing with the boatload of complaints these circumstances create.

But a local database is just that—local to the NAS it resides on. If you have a single NAS, a local database may be fine. But if you have many NASs, do you really want more unsynchronized user databases?

The whole idea behind CiscoSecure ACS 3.0 for Windows NT or Windows 2000 is to allow multiple NASs to use a *single* database for AAA. That way, there is a *single* account database to be administered for each user instead of many.

Just being able to use a single database for AAA is a huge improvement over using local databases on NASs. But Cisco ACS takes it one step further. Let's assume that you have an existing network—you probably already have several user databases in existence. If you're running Microsoft Windows NT/2000 servers anywhere, you have users who have accounts in domains.

If you have any Novell NetWare servers that use Novell Directory Services (NDS), you have user accounts there as well. Maybe all of your user information is in an ODBC database.

CiscoSecure ACS 3.0 for Windows NT or Windows 2000 lets you use any of these existing user databases in AAA! This means that instead of creating a new user database exclusively for AAA, you can simply adopt an existing database from one of these other sources. Now you not only have fewer user databases to maintain, but you also bypass the work of setting up a new one—nice!

This capability to use existing user databases for AAA means that even if you have a single NAS, CiscoSecure ACS 3.0 for Windows NT or Windows 2000 is likely to be a good solution for your company or client.

Suppose that you already have more than 1,000 users in your NT domain. And let's just say (okay, this is a stretch) that each of these users needs access to your NAS. Do you really want to create a local database (as outlined in Chapter 2) with those 1,000 user accounts? I'm fairly certain you don't want to do the following:

```
Todd(config)#username user1 password pass1
Todd(config)#username user2 password pass2
Todd(config)#username user3 password pass3
Todd(config)#username user4 password pass4
Todd(config)#username user5 password pass5
Todd(config)#username user6 password pass6
Todd(config)#username user7 password pass7
Todd(config)#username user8 password pass8
Todd(config)#username user9 password pass9
Todd(config)#username user10 password pass10
Todd(config)#username user11 password pass11
Todd(config)#username user12 password pass12
Todd(config)#username user13 password pass13
Todd(config)#username user14 password pass14
Todd(config)#username user15 password pass15
Todd(config)#username user16 password pass16
```

And so on, through user1000.

Do you want to maintain those passwords? Of course not! Consider something called *employee turnover*. You can't save these tasks for a once-a-week update; new users need computer access immediately, and former employees ideally should be deleted as their shoes pass through the door for the last time due to their potential security risk. So you'd spend a part of every day maintaining passwords. Don't forget to add the time wasted with the fun and friendly HR department trying to get an accurate list of people/passwords to add and delete. And how much aggravation would occur if—because you were trying to get this done before a noon meeting—you accidentally deleted, say, a senior vice president and weren't around until after 2 P.M. (because lunch went late) to fix that problem? Scared yet? No worries— CiscoSecure ACS 3.0 for Windows NT or Windows 2000 solves your problem.

What you want to do now is use the corporate network example that you'll be configuring throughout this book and create a TACACS+ centralized database instead of using a single database on the NAS. This allows you more flexibility in your network configuration because you can create one database and use it throughout the rest of this book without having to update the database on individual NAS devices.

If you don't want to use the Cisco proprietary TACACS+, you can use the industry-standard RADIUS server. The configuration is pretty similar, and I'll show you how to perform account authorization with RADIUS right after you go through the TACACS+ configurations.

Our Corporate Network Example

Using the same network you've seen throughout this book, I'm going to walk you through changing the corporate network example from using a local AAA database residing on the NAS server to using centralized database on a CiscoSecure ACS. Here's our corporate network again:

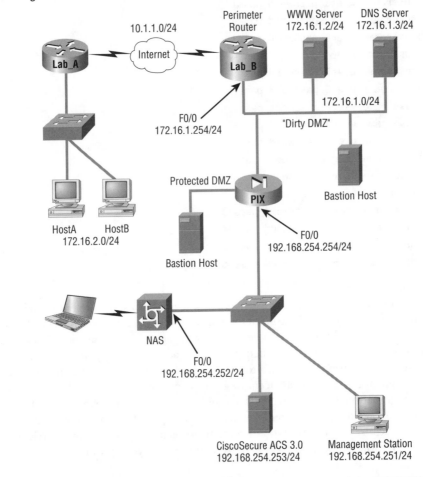

The goal here is to install and configure the CiscoSecure ACS on the NAS server to run remote RADIUS and TACACS+ authentication, authorization, and accounting features, as well as to also configure the NAS to use the ACS server for authentication.

The following example shows a configuration using TACACS+ on the Cisco 2600 Todd NAS router, configured in Chapter 2, to now authenticate against a CiscoSecure ACS user database instead:

```
User Access Verification


Username: todd
Password:


Todd>en
Password:
Todd#config t
Enter configuration commands, one per line.  End with CNTL/Z.
First, enable AAA by using the aaa new-model global configuration command.
Todd(config)#aaa new-model


The next command specifies to use the default list against the TACACS+ server and
that TACACS+ is the default login method for all authentication.
Todd(config)#aaa authentication login default tacacs+
You can add the command  none at the end of the command, which means that if the
TACACS+ process is unavailable, no login is required.
The next command sets the AAA authentication for PPP connection using the default
list against the TACACS+ database.
Todd(config)#aaa authentication ppp default tacacs+


The next authorization command determines if the user is allowed to run an EXEC
shell on the NAS against the TACTACS+ database.
Todd(config)#aaa authorization exec tacacs+


The next command sets AAA authorization for all network-related service requests,
including SLIP, PPP, PPP NCP's, and ARA protocol against the TACACS+ database.
Todd(config)#aaa authorization network tacacs+


The following AAA accounting command sets the EXEC process on the NAS to record
the start and stop time of the session against the TACACS+ database.
Todd(config)#aaa accounting network start-stop tacacs+


This next command sets AAA accounting for EXEC processes on the NAS to record the
start and stop time of the session against the TACACS+ database.
```

```
Todd(config)#aaa accounting exec start-stop tacacs+
```

The tacacs-server host command specifies the IP address of the host name of the remote TACACS+ server host.

```
Todd(config)#tacacs-server host 192.168.254.253 single
```

The tacacs-server key command specifies a shared secret text string used between the access server and the TACACS+ server. The access server and TACACS+ server use this text string to encrypt passwords and exchange responses.

```
Todd(config)#tacacs-server key d$y!tR%e
```

The next command sets AAA authentication at login to use the enable password for authentication.

```
Todd(config)#aaa authentication login no_tacacs enable
```

Choose the console 0 line.

```
Todd(config)#line console 0
```

Finally, specify that the AAA authentication list called no-tacacs is to be used on the console line.

```
Todd(config-line)#login authentication no_tacacs
```

WARNING   Be sure to first enter the tacacs-servers IP address and key. Otherwise, you can easily lock yourself out of the router once the authorization takes over and for some reason can't reach a server.

Using RADIUS

Unlike TACACS+, which is Cisco proprietary, RADIUS is not proprietary. It's important that you understand the difference between the two remote servers.

Livingston Enterprises, now part of Lucent Technologies, developed RADIUS. Like TACACS+, it's a security database protocol designed for use between an NAS and ACS, except that RADIUS is an industry standard that's supported by many third-party devices. It uses UDP/IP for communications and supports authentication but only supports authentication through passwords. RADIUS can be used for AAA, but it treats authentication and authorization as the same process, and so it combines them—a big disadvantage over TACACS+.

CiscoSecure User Database NAS Configuration for RADIUS

The following example shows the same Cisco 2600 router used in the previous section's example configured to use RADIUS against an NAS server using the CiscoSecure User Database:

```
Todd(config)#aaa new-model
Todd(config)#aaa authentication login default radius
Todd(config)#aaa authentication ppp default radius
Todd(config)#aaa authorization exec radius
Todd(config)#aaa authorization network radius
Todd(config)#aaa accounting network start-stop radius
Todd(config)#aaa accounting exec start-stop radius
Todd(config)#aaa accounting network wait-start radius
Todd(config)#radius-server host 172.16.10.5
Todd(config)#radius-server key d$y!tR%e
Todd(config)#enable secret todd
Todd(config)#aaa authentication login no_radius enable
Todd(config)#line con 0
Todd(config-line)#login authentication no_radius
```

On each interface that services dial-in users, issue the following command to tell the interface to use PPP CHAP authentication:

```
Todd(config-if)#ppp authentication chap
```

The only command different from the TACACS+ configuration is this one:

```
Todd(config)#aaa accounting network wait-start radius
```

As when using the start-stop keyword, the preceding command sends both a start and a stop accounting record to the accounting server, a RADIUS server in this example. If you use the wait-start keyword, however, the requested service cannot start until the acknowledgment has been received from the RADIUS server. A stop accounting record for network service requests is sent to the RADIUS server.

Basically, the rest of the commands are the same as those used in the TACACS+ configuration, so no additional command explanations are necessary at this point.

Verifying TACACS+

It is imperative that you can verify your configuration, so here are two debugging commands that you can use on the NAS to trace TACACS+ packets:

- debug tacacs
- debug tacacs events

However, in addition, you can still use the debug aaa commands you learned about in Chapter 2 to see the output for a TACACS+ login attempt:

```
Todd#debug tacacs
TACACS access control debugging is on
Todd#exit
Todd con0 is now available
Press RETURN to get started.
04:56:38: TAC+: Opened 192.168.254.253 index=1
04:56:38: TAC+: 192.168.254.253 (185613193) ACCT/REQUEST/STOP queued
04:56:38: TAC+: (185613193) ACCT/REQUEST/STOP processed
04:56:38: TAC+: (185613193): received acct response status = SUCCESS
User Access Verification
Password:
Todd>
04:56:43: TAC+: Using default tacacs server list.
04:56:43: TAC+: 192.168.254.253 (2537319283) ACCT/REQUEST/START queued
04:56:43: TAC+: (2537319283) ACCT/REQUEST/START processed
04:56:43: TAC+: (2537319283): received acct response status = SUCCESS

Todd#undebug all
All possible debugging has been turned off
```

There is more information displayed with the debug tacacs events command than with just the debug tacacs command:

```
Todd#debug tacacs events
TACACS+ events debugging is on
Todd#exit
Todd con0 is now available
Press RETURN to get started.

User Access Verification
Password:
05:01:08: TAC+: periodic timer started
05:01:08: TAC+: 192.168.254.253 req=81490CCC id=3169020093 ver=192 handle=0x0
    ⮑(NONE) expire=4 ACCT/REQUEST/STOP queued
05:01:08: TAC+: 192.168.254.253 ESTAB 81490CCC wrote 156 of 156 bytes
05:01:09: TAC+: 192.168.254.253 ESTAB read=12 wanted=12 alloc=17 got=12
05:01:09: TAC+: 192.168.254.253 ESTAB read=17 wanted=17 alloc=17 got=5
05:01:09: TAC+: 192.168.254.253 received 17 byte reply for 81490CCC
05:01:09: TAC+: req=81490CCC id=3169020093 ver=192 handle=0x0 (NONE) expire=4
    ⮑ACCT/REQUEST/STOP processed
```

```
05:01:09: TAC+: periodic timer stopped (queue empty)
Todd>en
Password:
05:01:55: TAC+: periodic timer started
05:01:55: TAC+: 192.168.254.253 req=81491914 id=3481072133 ver=192 handle=0x0
   ⮑(NONE) expire=5 ACCT/REQUEST/START queued
05:01:55: TAC+: 192.168.254.253 ESTAB 81491914 wrote 68 of 68 bytes
05:01:55: TAC+: 192.168.254.253 ESTAB read=12 wanted=12 alloc=17 got=12
05:01:55: TAC+: 192.168.254.253 ESTAB read=17 wanted=17 alloc=17 got=5
05:01:55: TAC+: 192.168.254.253 received 17 byte reply for 81491914
05:01:55: TAC+: req=81491914 id=3481072133 ver=192 handle=0x0 (NONE) expire=4
   ⮑ACCT/REQUEST/START processed
05:01:55: TAC+: periodic timer stopped (queue empty)
```

The following is an example of the debug aaa authentication command:

```
Todd#un all
All possible debugging has been turned off
Todd#
Todd#debug aaa authentication
AAA Authentication debugging is on
Todd#exit

User Access Verification

Password:
05:05:35: AAA/AUTHEN: free_user (0x81420624) user='' ruser='' port='tty0'
   ⮑rem_addr='async/' authen_type=ASCII service=LOGIN priv=1
05:05:36: AAA: parse name=tty0 idb type=-1 tty=-1
05:05:36: AAA: name=tty0 flags=0x11 type=4 shelf=0 slot=0 adapter=0 port=0
   ⮑channel=0
05:05:36: AAA/AUTHEN: create_user (0x81420624) user='' ruser='' port='tty0'
   ⮑rem_addr='async/' authen_type=ASCII service=LOGIN priv=1
05:05:36: AAA/AUTHEN/START (2124362753): port='tty0' list='no_tacacs'
   ⮑action=LOGIN service=LOGIN
05:05:36: AAA/AUTHEN/START (2124362753): found list no_tacacs
05:05:36: AAA/AUTHEN/START (2124362753): Method=ENABLE
05:05:36: AAA/AUTHEN (2124362753): status = GETPASS
Todd>: AAA/AUTHEN/START (3168314283): found list no_tacacs
05:05:58: AAA/AUTHEN/START (3168314283): Method=ENABLE
05:05:58: AAA/AUTHEN (3168314283): status = GETPASS
```

```
05:06:00: AAA/AUTHEN/CONT (3168314283): continue_login (user='(undef)')
05:06:00: AAA/AUTHEN (3168314283): status = GETPASS
05:06:00: AAA/AUTHEN/CONT (3168314283): Method=ENABLE
05:06:00: AAA/AUTHEN (3168314283): status = PASS
Todd>en
Password:
05:06:06: AAA/AUTHEN: dup_user (0x814909F8) user='' ruser='' port='tty0'
  ↳rem_addr='async/' authen_type=ASCII service=ENABLE priv=15 source='AAA
  ↳dup enable'
05:06:06: AAA/AUTHEN/START (338074629): port='tty0' list='' action=LOGIN
  ↳service=ENABLE
05:06:06: AAA/AUTHEN/START (338074629): console enable - default to enable
  ↳password (if any)
05:06:06: AAA/AUTHEN/START (338074629): Method=ENABLE
05:06:06: AAA/AUTHEN (338074629): status = GETPASS
Todd#
05:06:08: AAA/AUTHEN/CONT (338074629): continue_login (user='(undef)')
05:06:08: AAA/AUTHEN (338074629): status = GETPASS
05:06:08: AAA/AUTHEN/CONT (338074629): Method=ENABLE
05:06:08: AAA/AUTHEN (338074629): status = PASS
05:06:08: AAA/AUTHEN: free_user (0x814909F8) user='' ruser='' port='tty0'
  ↳rem_addr='async/' authen_type=ASCII service=ENABLE priv=15
```

The preceding output from the debug aaa authentication command shows that the method was TACACS+, and that it was successful.

Summary

Cisco offers an excellent access control server (ACS) that's available on a number of platforms. You learned about both the CiscoSecure ACS 3.0 for Windows NT (CSNT) or Windows 2000 and CSU (CiscoSecure ACS 2.3 for Unix) products.

The ACS will be an important element in your overall network security plan, and it can greatly simplify the task of managing user accounts.

As your network grows in complexity and size and you include NASs (network access servers) from multiple vendors, the ACS will scale and continue to both simplify administration and improve security. This chapter provided the information you need to understand the role of the ACS and the communication between the NAS and ACS.

Exam Essentials

Remember the ways to get user information onto the CiscoSecure User Database. There are three ways to populate the CiscoSecure User Database: manually, through the Database Replication utility, and through the Database Import utility.

Know how to access the CS ACS web-based administration utility. To bring up the web-based administration tool using a web browser, go to the IP address of the CS ACS server, port 2002.

Remember which third-party user databases CS ACS supports. CiscoSecure ACS supports Microsoft Windows NT, Novell NDS, Directory Services, MCIS LDAP, and ODBC databases.

Remember which relational databases CSU supports. CSU (CiscoSecure ACS 2.3 for Unix) supports Sybase, Oracle, and SQL Anywhere databases.

Know the advantages of TACACS+ over RADIUS. The advantages of TACACS+ include encrypted packets versus encrypted passwords in RADIUS and the use of TCP rather than UDP. TACACS+ also treats authentication, authorization, and accounting as separate roles; RADIUS combines authentication and authorization.

Understand how to set an encryption key on the NAS. To set the encryption key on a TACACS+ server, use the following commands:

```
Todd(config)#tacacs-server host 192.168.254.253
Todd(config)#tacacs-server key d$y!tR%e
```

The `tacacs-server host` *hostname* | *ip address* command specifies the IP address or the host name of the remote TACACS+ server host. The `tacacs-server key` *key* command specifies a shared secret text string used between the access server and the TACACS+ server. You can use the same commands for a RADIUS server; just exchange the keyword `tacacs-server` for `radius-server`.

Key Terms

Before you take the exam, be certain you are familiar with the following terms:

access control server (ACS)	CiscoSecure User Database
CiscoSecure ACS 2.3 for Unix (CSU)	CSAccupdate service
CiscoSecure ACS 3.0 for Windows NT or Windows 2000	token-card servers

Commands Used in This Chapter

Here is the list of commands used in this chapter:

Command	Meaning
(config)#**username** *name* **password** *password*	Creates users on the NAS.
(config)#**line con 0**	Chooses the console line.
(config-line)#**login local**	Tells the router to look in the local line for user authentication.
(config)#**aaa new-model**	Globally enables the AAA process on the NAS.
(config)#**aaa authentication login default tacacs+**	Sets AAA authentication at login using the default list against the TACACS+ server.
(config)#**aaa authentication ppp default tacacs+**	Sets the AAA authentication for PPP to use a TACACS+ server.
(config)#**aaa authorization exec tacacs+**	Sets AAA authorization to determine if the user is allowed to run an EXEC shell on the NAS against the TACACS+ database.
(config)#**aaa authorization network tacacs+**	Sets AAA authorization for all network-related requests, including SLIP, PPP, PPP NCP, and ARA protocols, against the TACACS+ database.
(config)#**aaa accounting network start-stop tacacs+**	Sets AAA accounting for all network-related server requests, including SLIP, PPP, PPP NCP, and ARA protocols, to record the start and stop times of the session against the TACACS+ database.
(config)#**aaa accounting exec start-stop tacacs+**	Sets AAA accounting for EXEC processes on the NAS to record the start and stop times of the session against the TACACS+ database.
(config)#**tacacs-server host** *ip_address* **single**	Specifies the CS ACS server that will provide AAA services for the NAS.
(config)#**tacacs-server key** *key*	Configures the encryption key that is used to encrypt the data transfer between the NAS and the CS ACS server.
(config)#**aaa authentication login no_tacacs enable**	Sets AAA authentication at login to use the enable password for authentication.

Command	Meaning
(config-line)#**login authentication no_tacacs**	Specifies that the named AAA authentication list is to be used on the console.
(config)#**aaa accounting network wait-start radius**	Sends both a start and a stop accounting record to the RADIUS accounting server. The requested service cannot start until the acknowledgment has been received from the RADIUS server.

Written Lab

This section asks you 10 write-in-the-answer questions to help you understand the technology that you need to know in order to pass the SECUR exam.

1. True or False: The authentication methods supported by CiscoSecure 3.0 include Windows NT/2000, Novell Directory Services (NDS), and ACS Databases.

2. True or False: CS ACS supports the following token-card servers from CiscoSecure 3.0: Windows NT/2000, Novell Directory Services (NDS), and ACS Databases.

3. True or False: In the command aaa authentication login default tacacs+ none, the none keyword at the end means that if the TACACS+ process is unavailable, no login is required.

4. What are the three relational databases that CSU supports?

5. The CS ACS web server listens on TCP port 2002. What is the URL for the default CS ACS web server?

6. What command sets AAA accounting for all network-related service requests, including PPP, and records the start and stop times of the session against the TACACS+ database?

7. TACACS+ uses _____ as a transport protocol and RADIUS uses _____ as a transport protocol.

8. What command sets the AAA accounting for EXEC processes on the NAS to record the start and stop times of the session against the TACACS+ database?

9. Which service is used to process the ODBC import tables and updates the local and remote CiscoSecure ACS installations?

10. You must have an IOS of _____ or greater on the NAS to support CiscoSecure ACS 3.0.

Review Questions

1. CiscoSecure ACS 3.0 for Windows NT or Windows 2000 supports which of the following authentication methods? (Choose all that apply.)

   A. Novell Directory Services (NDS)

   B. Banyan StreetTalk

   C. DNS

   D. POP

   E. ODBC

   F. DS

2. Which of the following token-card servers can be used with CS ACS 3.0? (Choose all that apply.)

   A. Microsoft

   B. AXENT Defender

   C. CRYPTOCard

   D. Novell NDS

   E. ODBC

3. Which of the following are true with regard to the following command? (Choose all that apply.)

   `Router(config)#aaa authentication login default tacacs+ none`

   A. No authentication is required to log in.

   B. TACACS+ is the default login method for all authentication.

   C. If the TACACS+ process is unavailable, no access is permitted.

   D. RADIUS is the default login method for all authentication.

   E. If the TACACS+ process is unavailable, no login is required.

   F. If the RADIUS process is unavailable, no login is required.

4. CiscoSecure ACS for Unix (CSU) supports which of the following relational databases? (Choose all that apply.)

   A. Sybase

   B. Informix

   C. PIX

   D. Oracle

   E. SQL Anywhere

5. You have just finished installing CS ACS and are on the console of the server where you installed the package. Which of the following URLs allow you to access the web-based administration tool to configure CS ACS?

   A. `http://127.0.0.1`

   B. `http://127.0.0.1:2002`

   C. `http://127.0.0.1/80`

   D. `http://127.0.0.1:80`

6. Which of the following is true regarding the following command? (Choose all that apply.)

   `Router(config)#`**`aaa account network wait-start radius`**

   A. The accounting records are stored on a TACACS+ server.

   B. Stop accounting records for network service requests are sent to the TACACS+ server.

   C. The accounting records are stored on a RADIUS server.

   D. Start accounting records for network service requests are sent to the local database.

   E. Stop accounting records for network service requests are sent to the RADIUS server.

   F. The requested service cannot start until the acknowledgment has been received from the RADIUS server.

7. Which of the following statements are true regarding this debug output? (Choose all that apply.)

```
16:43:35: TAC+: Receiving TCP/IP packet number 415842422-6 from
    ↳192.168.254.253/24
16:43:35: TAC+: (415842422): received authen response status =FAIL
16:43:35: TAC+: Closing TCP/IP connection to 192.168.254.10
```

   A. The request used the RADIUS protocol.

   B. The authentication completed.

   C. The authentication failed.

   D. The request used the TACACS+ protocol.

   E. The address of the NAS was 192.168.254.10.

   F. The `debug tacacs` command was used.

8. Which command would you use to cause a start accounting record for PPP to be sent to a TACACS+ server?

   A. `aaa authentication pppstart tacacs+`

   B. `aaa authorization exec default tacacs+`

   C. `aaa authorization network default tacacs+`

   D. `aaa accounting network default stop-only tacacs+`

   E. `aaa accounting network default start-stop tacacs+`

9. Which of these statements are true about the following debug output? (Choose all that apply.)

```
05:06:00: AAA/AUTHEN (3168314283): status = GETPASS
05:06:00: AAA/AUTHEN/CONT (3168314283): Method=ENABLE
05:06:00: AAA/AUTHEN (3168314283): status = PASS
```

   A. The request used the RADIUS protocol.

   B. The authentication completed.

   C. The authentication failed.

   D. The request used the TACACS+ protocol.

   E. The debug `tacacs` command was used.

   F. The debug `aaa authentication` command was used.

10. Which of the following is the recommended security database protocol for use between the NAS and ACS?

   A. RADIUS

   B. Kerberos

   C. PPP

   D. TACACS+

11. What does the following command provide?

```
Router(config)#aaa accounting exec start-stop tacacs+
```

   A. It allows the executive users group to use a TACACS+ server for local authentication.

   B. It documents the start and stop of a session. Audit information is sent in the background, and TACACS+ is enabled.

   C. It allows the administration group to use a TACACS+ server for local authentication.

   D. It deletes the start and stop of a session information from the TACACS+ server.

12. Which of these statements are true regarding the following command? (Choose all that apply.)

```
Router(config)#aaa authentication login default tacacs+
```

   A. No authentication is required to log in.

   B. TACACS is the default login method for all authentication.

   C. If the TACACS process is unavailable, no access is permitted.

   D. RADIUS is the default login method for all authentication.

   E. If the TACACS process is unavailable, no login is required.

   F. If the RADIUS process is unavailable, no login is required.

13. You want to import ODBC tables and update local and remote CiscoSecure ACS installations. What service will you use?

   A. CSAdmin

   B. CSAimporter

   C. CSAccupdate

   D. CSACSupdate

14. What does the following command provide?

   Router(config)#**tacacs-server key key**

   A. It specifies a shared secret text string used between the access server and the RADIUS server.

   B. It specifies a shared secret text string used between the access server and the local ACS server database.

   C. It specifies a shared secret text string used between the access server and the TACACS+ server.

   D. It specifies an open secret text string used between the access server and the TACACS+ server.

15. Which of the following commands is used to start the AAA process on the NAS?

   A. aaa newmodel

   B. aaa new-model

   C. aaa new model

   D. aaa open

   E. aaa config

16. Which external databases are supported by CiscoSecure ACS for Windows? (Choose all that apply.)

   A. NetWare NDS

   B. Oracle

   C. Windows NT/2000

   D. Token Server

   E. SQL-Linux

   F. AAA

17. You are installing ACS 3.0. What version of IOS must be installed on the NAS?

   A. 11.0 or greater

   B. 11.1 or greater

   C. 12.0 or greater

   D. 12.2 or greater

18. Which of the following are valid types of authentication supported by CiscoSecure ACS 3.0.1? (Choose all that apply.)

   A. LEAP

   B. EAP-MD5

   C. HDLC

   D. EAP-TLS

   E. DH-1

   F. AAA

19. Which command do you use to set the key for RADIUS communications between a router and the AAA server?

   A. `radius-server host` *`ip_address`*

   B. `radius server host` *`ip_address`*

   C. `radius-server key` *`key`*

   D. `radius server key` *`key`*

20. Which of the following statements regarding the CiscoSecure ACS are true? (Choose all that apply.)

   A. Multiple NAS devices can access a single CiscoSecure ACS 3.0 for Windows.

   B. The CiscoSecure ACS for Windows server can only log on to external servers.

   C. The CiscoSecure ACS for Windows server supports only TACACS+.

   D. Database replication is supported by the CiscoSecure ACS for Windows server.

   E. The service used for authentication and authorization on a CiscoSecure ACS for Windows server is called CSAdmin.

   F. The CiscoSecure ACS for Windows servers uses the CSDBsynch service to manage the user and group accounts.

Answers to Written Lab

1. True. The authentication methods supported by CiscoSecure 3.0 include Windows NT/2000, Novell Directory Services (NDS), and ACS Databases.

2. False. CS ACS supports token-card servers from CRYPTOCard, ActivCard, Vasco, RSA ACE/Server, Secure Computing SafeWord, and AXENT Defender.

3. True. The none keyword in the command aaa authentication login default tacacs+ none means that if the TACACS+ process is unavailable, no login is required.

4. Sybase, Oracle, and SQL Anywhere are the three relational databases supported by CSU.

5. http://127.0.0.1:2002 is the URL for the default CS ACS web server.

6. To set AAA accounting for all network-related service requests, including PPP, and record the start and stop times of the session against the TACACS+ database, use the command aaa accounting network default start-stop tacacs+.

7. TACACS+ uses TCP as a transport protocol, and RADIUS uses UDP as a transport protocol.

8. The command aaa accounting exec start-stop tacacs+ sets the AAA accounting for EXEC processes on the NAS to record the start and stop times of the session against the TACACS+ database.

9. The CSAccupdate service processes the ODBC import tables and updates the local and remote CiscoSecure ACS installations.

10. An IOS of 11.1 or greater on the NAS is required to support CiscoSecure ACS 3.0.

Answers to Review Questions

1.   A, E, F.   The authentication methods supported by CiscoSecure 3.0 include Windows NT/2000, Novell Directory Services (NDS), Directory Services (DS), Token Server, ACS Databases, Microsoft Commercial Internet System Lightweight Directory Access Protocol (MCIS LDAP), and Open Database Connectivity (ODBC).

2.   B, C.   CS ACS supports token-card servers from CRYPTOCard, ActivCard, Vasco, RSA ACE/Server, Secure Computing SafeWord, and AXENT Defender.

3.   B, E.   This command specifies to use the default list against the TACACS+ server and specifies that TACACS+ is the default login method for all authentications. The none keyword at the end means that if the TACACS+ process is unavailable, no login is required.

4.   A, D, E.   CSU supports three relational databases: Sybase, Oracle, and SQL Anywhere.

5.   B.   The CS ACS web server listens on TCP port 2002. The URL listed in option B is the correct syntax to access this service, *assuming you are on the console of the machine running CSNT!*

6.   C, E, F.   As when using the start-stop keyword, this command sends both a start and a stop accounting record to the accounting server, a RADIUS server in this example. If you use the wait-start keyword, the requested service cannot start until the acknowledgment has been received from the RADIUS server. A stop accounting record for network service requests is sent to the RADIUS server.

7.   C, D, F.   The output of this question is from the debug tacacs command and shows that the TACACS+ server at 192.168.254.253 rejected the authentication request.

8.   E.   The command aaa accounting network default start-stop tacacs+ command sets AAA accounting for all network-related service requests, including PPP, and records the start and stop times of the session against the TACACS+ database.

9.   B, F.   The debug output used in this question was output from the debug aaa authentication command. The authentication passed.

10. D.   Cisco recommends the use of TACACS+ wherever possible.

11. B.   The start-stop keyword keeps audit information in the background for authentication without delay using a TACACS+ server.

12. B, C.   This command specifies to use the default list against the TACACS+ server and specifies that TACACS+ is the default login method for all authentications. Because the none keyword is not at the end of the command, this means that if the TACACS+ process is unavailable, no access will be permitted.

13. C.   The CSAccupdate service processes the ODBC import tables and updates local and remote CiscoSecure ACS installations.

14. C.   The `tacacs-server key` *key* command specifies a shared secret text string used between the access server and the TACACS+ server. The access server and the TACACS+ server use this text string to encrypt passwords and exchange responses.

15. B.   To globally enable AAA on the NAS, use the global configuration command `aaa new-model`.

16. A, C, D.   The external databases supported by CiscoSecure ACS 3.0 are LEAP Proxy RADIUS server, Windows NT/2000, NetWare NDS, LDAP, external ODBC Database, and many token servers: RADIUS, Vasco, ActivCard, AXENT Defender, CryptoCard, SafeWord, and RSA SecurID.

17. B.   The NAS should be running IOS version 11.1 or greater to be able to communicate correctly with ACS 3.0.

18. A, B, D.   ACS 3.0 supports the following authentication types: ASCII/PAP, CHAP, MS-CHAP, LEAP, EAP-CHAP, EAP-TLS, EAP-MD5, and ARAP.

19. C.   The global configuration command `radius-server key` *key* is used to set the RADIUS key between the NAS and AAA server.

20. A, D, F.   The CiscoSecure ACS 3.0 server allows multiple NAS devices to communicate and authenticate, which is a significant advantage. The ACS server provides database replication, and the CSDBsynch service is used to manage user and group accounts.

Chapter

4

Cisco Perimeter Router Problems and Solutions

THE FOLLOWING SECUR EXAM TOPICS ARE COVERED IN THIS CHAPTER:

- ✓ Identifying perimeter security problems and implementing solutions
- ✓ Identifying and overcoming eavesdropping and session replay
- ✓ Identifying and solving unauthorized access, data manipulation, and malicious destruction problems
- ✓ Solving lack of legal IP address problems
- ✓ Defending against rerouting attacks
- ✓ Defending against denial-of-service attacks

By definition, *perimeter routers* are really the boundary between your network and someone else's network—or pretty much everyone else's networks if you're talking about the Internet. This makes perimeter routers your first line of defense. If your perimeter router can prevent any nasty things from getting through in the first place, you clearly won't have to deal with them later.

As I'm sure you can imagine, Internet access into the perimeter router in your network exposes you to some serious security risks. But the *Cisco IOS Firewall* software is really a very powerful defense. It equips you with some effective security and firewall features that are needed to guard against increasingly sophisticated attacks. Even better, Cisco is working constantly to improve and enhance these features and to develop new ones.

Cisco perimeter routers provide you with your first line of defense for Internet connections. They also define the de-militarized zone (DMZ) and are used to protect the bastion hosts residing there. You can also use perimeter routers to prevent the Private Internet eXchange (PIX) from being vulnerable to a direct attack. They can even provide an alarm system for you if anyone does try to break into your network via a perimeter router.

I've listed five different types of attacks you'll experience that can and do seriously compromise your network security. Unfortunately, it seems these attacks are occurring more and more frequently with each passing day. If your defenses aren't in order to prevent their success, your network—and probably your job—can be in serious trouble for sure! Consider each of the following problems when you configure your Cisco perimeter router(s). And don't stop there—understand the solutions for them, too.

- Eavesdropping and session replay

- Unauthorized access, data manipulation, and malicious destruction

- Lack of legal IP addresses

- Rerouting attacks

- Denial-of-service (DoS) attacks

Some of these attacks should be familiar to you because we talked about them in Chapter 1, "Introduction to Network Security." But this chapter will look at them again in more detail and explain how you can use the Cisco IOS Firewall to solve these problems.

Okay, let's move on now and look at specific problems and solutions.

Solving Eavesdropping and Session Replay Problems

Remember, *eavesdropping* is when a hacker is listening in and reading your data. *Session replay* happens when a sequence of packets or application commands are captured, manipulated, and replayed by bad guys with the intent of causing harm. You obviously need a solution for these ugly problems, but first let's use the corporate network example in this book, illustrated in the following graphic, as an example of how eavesdropping and session replay can be a problem.

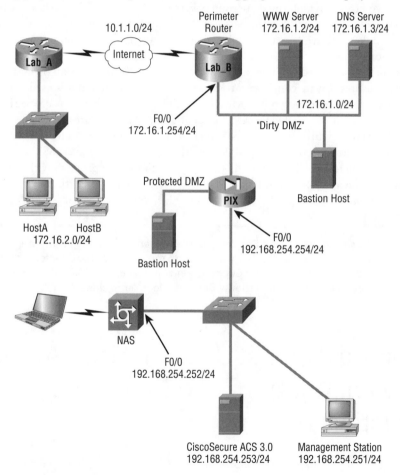

HostA needs to communicate to the bastion host in the dirty DMZ. (Recall that a dirty DMZ is defined as the part of a network that's using real Internet IP addresses.)

Okay, you have a client machine that must cross an unknown network to reach the bastion host. As you learned in Chapter 1, it's possible for someone in this unknown network who's using a protocol analyzer to capture the conversation between the client and server by eavesdropping. If successful, your data can be compromised and the session can be replayed back to the server. Your problem is that you have unencrypted data crossing an unknown network—not good. Hmm…unencrypted data—any guesses as what the solution to this problem could be?

Yes—*encryption*. Of course you'll use encryption to protect that data. In our corporate network example, you can configure the Lab_A router at the remote site to encrypt the data traveling between the client and the bastion host. The perimeter router at the corporate site would also be configured for this same operation. Those two routers will then encrypt all data passing between these two hosts. Any intermediate routers between them can still route the traffic (network headers are not encrypted). Traffic between the client and the bastion host doesn't need to be encrypted unless you really want it to be. You can control the encryption based on network, subnet, port, or protocol.

The best solution for eavesdropping and session replay is *IPSec*. IPSec is an open standards framework that ensures private communications over an IP network, and it is used and recommended by Cisco as a tool for encryption. Most of the time, the best place to use IPSec is across a public IP network. This not only ensures confidentiality, it also ensures data integrity and authenticity. IPSec is configured between two routers, and it does its work at the Network layer.

Before IPSec was introduced, lots of people used the Secure Socket Layer (SSL) to provide application encryption for web browsers and other applications. The problem with SSL is that the configuration is on an application-by-application basis, so only applications configured to use SSL were encrypted. By using IPSec, all data at the Network layer is encrypted.

Cisco suggests that IPSec encryption, VPN, and digital certificates are all viable solutions to eavesdropping and session replay problems. Chapter 7, "Understanding Cisco IOS IPSec Support," and Chapter 8, "Cisco IOS IPSec Pre-Shared Keys and Certificate Authority Support," look more closely at IPSec.

Defending Against Unauthorized Access, Data Manipulation, and Malicious Destruction

Think back and picture the perimeter router in the corporate network firewall example illustrated earlier in this chapter. It connects the DMZ to the Internet, which as you recall, is a potential source of problems. Assuming that this connection is necessary for business purposes, how can you ensure that traffic to and from the Internet is good and legitimate and not the communications equivalent of Stephen King's evil Christine?

Honestly, you can't always be sure, but you can certainly stop most of the nasty stuff using a simple tool—access control lists (ACLs). No doubt you've used these in the past, but there are a number of tasks ACLs can do for you at the perimeter to significantly beef up your security.

With your perimeter router in mind, here's a list of various packets you probably don't want to allow into your network from the Internet:

- Private address as the source IP address
- One of your internal IP addresses as the source IP address
- BOOTP, TFTP, and traceroute packets
- TCP connections to servers not in the DMZ
- DHCP reserved range
- Loopback addresses

All of these packets can be stopped with inbound ACLs on a perimeter router. Here's an example of an access list on the perimeter router stopping the dirty DMZ IP addresses from being used as source addresses from an outside intruder:

```
Lab_B(config)#access-list 110 deny ip 172.16.1.0 0.0.0.255 any
Lab_B(config)#interface s0/0
Lab_B(config-if)#access-group 110 in
```

Do you remember from your ACL studies that you also need to have a `permit` statement included in your list to make it work? It's the same here—this is just an example.

Here's another example of using a simple ACL to implement network security. These commands prevent a SYN packet from coming into the inside network from the outside network:

```
Lab_B(config)#access-list 110 deny tcp any any established
Lab_B(config)#access-list 110 permit tcp any any
Lab_B(config)#interface s0/0
Lab_B(config-if)#access-group 110 in
```

Doing this allows a SYN packet out, but it won't let anyone "SYN" in. No one from the outside network can create a session to a host on the inside network. A host on the inside network can both send out and receive an ACK so those packets are allowed to enter the DMZ.

These are two types of packets you don't want leaving your network:

- Source address not in your internal IP address space
- Source address of any machine that is not allowed Internet access by policy

And again, you can prevent that from happening by using fairly simple ACLs.

These simple examples demonstrate just how efficient ACLs can be for preventing inappropriate access. If you make the functions we've discussed off-limits to bad guys, you've denied them access to some of the most common techniques that they use to exploit networks.

 ACLs are a great weapon for guarding your network against unauthorized access, data manipulation, and malicious destruction.

Solving Lack of Legal IP Addresses Problems

Let's say you have 500 machines to connect to the Internet, and you have 254 legal IP addresses. This could definitely be a problem, but if you use Network Address Translation (NAT), you can use a pool of IP addresses to meet the needs of a large number of clients. Even better, NAT gives you some additional security benefits beyond extending IP address space.

NAT hides your internal addressing scheme from the external network. The only device that the external network will be able to see is your NAT device; everything behind it is essentially invisible. So, if you configure NAT on your perimeter router, you get to hide all of your addressing!

There's a subset of NAT called Port Address Translation (PAT) that extends NAT functionality by using TCP and UDP ports for address translation. Doing this allows a single Internet IP address to support up to 64,000 hosts, but Cisco recommends that you don't support more than 4,000 per address. Even so, that's still pretty impressive!

When your problem is the lack of legal IP addresses, your solution is to use NAT.

Fighting Rerouting Attacks

Let's suppose a bad guy could modify your routing table. Would that make you nervous? It should! The best-case scenario is that the attacker simply breaks into your network. The worst-case scenario is, well, destruction, corruption, and malfunction—Hell as your uninvited guest. Breaking your routing can cause all kinds of security problems, and there are a number of ways for the bad guys to do it. The most obvious way is to somehow gain access to a router, but that's not always necessary.

Let's take a look at the corporate network illustrated earlier in this chapter and use routers Lab_A and Lab_B, which are connected on the same network, for an example. And let's also assume that they're communicating using some routing protocol—say EIGRP. Okay, you know that if router Lab_A learns about a new path to a network, it'll dutifully inform router Lab_B using EIGRP.

Router Lab_B may change its routing table to take advantage of this new information. Router Lab_A doesn't "log in" to router Lab_B, but it is able to change router Lab_B's routing table by just sending an EIGRP update to Lab_B. This is a simple example of dynamic routing, but look again. It also demonstrates how a network can be exposed to a potential security attack.

How? Suppose you have a bad guy between routers Lab_A and Lab_B, listening to their conversations. What if that bad guy builds an EIGRP update and sends it to router Lab_B, claiming that it's from router Lab_A? Router Lab_B gets the update, processes it, and maybe even changes its routing table. This really does work sometimes—an attacker can introduce a routing update to the network that the receiving router acts upon because it has no way of knowing that the update isn't valid. This is a prime example of what's known as a *rerouting attack*.

The fundamental problem here is that the receiving router couldn't verify that the update was truly sent by the sending router. You can solve this problem by giving the receiving router the ability to verify that the source of the updates it's getting is in fact the router that the updates are supposed to be coming from. You can make this happen by enabling *MD5 authentication* on both routers.

It's possible to also use distribution lists to address the rerouting problem.

With MD5 authentication enabled, the routers receive a common key that's configured by the administrator. The routers then use that key to sign the routing updates they send and to verify the updates they receive. Any updates without matching keys won't be considered valid updates and therefore will not be acted upon. And since invaders can't extract the key from the update, they can't reproduce it to fake an update.

The following routing protocols can use MD5 authentication:

- RIPv2 (Routing Information Protocol version 2)

- OSPF (Open Shortest Path First)

- BGP (Border Gateway Protocol)

- EIGRP (Enhanced Internet Gateway Routing Protocol)

It's a good idea to deny routing protocol packets at your network's entry points because you really shouldn't see any routing protocols coming in, except for BGP. And if you're not using BGP, it's another good reason to just use static routes to and from the Internet.

Let's take a look at a configuration example of some of these technologies at work. IPSec is covered in Chapter 7 and NAT configuration isn't part of the SECUR exam, so I'm not including them here. Instead, this example focuses on enabling MD5 authentication and adding it into your routing process on the Lab_B router, whose EIGRP neighbor is out S0/0:

```
Lab_B#conf t
Lab_B(config)#router eigrp 100
Lab_B(config-router)#network 10.0.0.0
Lab_B(config-router)#network 172.16.0.0
Lab_B(config)#exit
Lab_B(config)#int s0/0
Lab_B(config-if)#ip authentication mode eigrp 100 md5
Lab_B(config-if)#ip authentication key-chain eigrp 100 toddkey
Lab_B(config-if)#exit
Lab_B(config)#key chain toddkey
```

```
Lab_B(config-key)#key 1
Lab_B(config-key)#key-string 4444444444
Lab_B(config-key)#^Z
Lab_B#
```

Of course, the neighbor router Lab_A needs to be configured as well.

 When your problem is rerouting attacks, Cisco says your solution is to use MD5 authentication.

Fighting Denial-of-Service Attacks

I first brought up *denial-of-service (DoS) attacks* back in Chapter 1, so let's take a second for a short review. These are the steps that occur in a normal TCP three-way handshake:

- The first host sends a request to speak (SYN).
- The receiving host responds by acknowledging the request and allocating resources for the conversation (SYN-ACK).
- The first host recognizes the acknowledgment (ACK).

These two hosts have established a TCP connection and can now exchange data.

One type of DoS attack is called a *SYN flood attack*. Let's say I send your server a SYN request with a make-believe source address. What do you think your server will do? It'll probably respond to my request with a SYN-ACK and allocate resources for this conversation. With nothing ever being free, a small amount of RAM on your server has now been consumed. No worries, right? But what if I send your server 100 bogus SYN requests from 100 fake addresses? Your server will send out 100 SYN-ACKs and allocate enough resources for 100 conversations. What if I send 100 more SYN requests, all from fake addresses, *per second*? How about 1000 per second? Now how is your server doing? My guess is not good. The server has probably run out of resources and either has crashed or is hanging there, overwhelmed and exhausted. And as a result, it could very well be open to exploitation.

In addition, you can't stop me from sending SYN requests to your server unless you don't want the server available for legitimate use. Even finding me is difficult, because I always lie about my origin address. But there is hope for you: *TCP Intercept*.

TCP Intercept on a perimeter router running Cisco IOS Firewall software can run in two modes: intercept and monitor. In intercept mode, the router won't immediately forward a SYN request to the server; it will proxy-answer the request (SYN-ACK) to verify that the request is valid instead. If the requesting host does not ACK back, the router never notifies the server of the connection attempt. Requests proven to be genuine are eventually handed off to the server. So if a bad guy sends hundreds or thousands of SYN requests per second, it won't matter because your server won't even see any of them. DoS attack thwarted!

When running in monitor mode, TCP Intercept will forward and monitor these TCP three-way handshakes. When it sees one that's poking along beyond an administrator-defined interval, TCP Intercept will intervene and close that connection. This means that the server won't leave resources open and hanging while waiting for the final ACK to come back.

When enabling TCP Intercept, you use an access list to define which connections TCP Intercept will be applied.

Suppose that you want to use TCP intercept to protect a server in your DMZ at IP address 172.16.10.25. The configuration commands would look like this:

```
Lab_B#config t
Lab_B(config)#access-list 151 permit tcp any host 172.16.10.25
Lab_B(config)#ip tcp intercept list 151
Lab_B(config)#ip tcp intercept mode intercept
Lab_B(config)#^Z
Lab_B#
```

 If your problem is fighting DoS attacks, your solution is to use TCP Intercept.

Turning Off and Configuring Network Services

Besides encryption, ACLs, and authorization, there are some additional commands you can configure on your perimeter router to limit access to it. By default, the Cisco IOS runs some services that are unnecessary to its normal operation, and if you don't disable them, they can be easy targets for DoS attacks and break-in attempts.

Plus, if you just use a Cisco router's default settings, it won't check routing paths to stop illegitimate traffic, and ARP traffic will be allowed to pass through its interfaces.

Blocking SNMP Packets

The Cisco IOS default configurations permit remote access from any source, so unless you're either way too trusting or insane, it should be totally obvious to you that those configurations need a bit of attention. You've got to restrict them. If you don't, the router will be a pretty easy target for an attacker who wants to log in to it. This is where access lists come into the game—they can really protect you.

If you place the following command on the serial0/0 interface of the perimeter router, it'll stop any SNMP packets from entering the router or the DMZ. (You'd also need to have a permit command along with this list to really make it work, but this is just an example.)

```
Lab_B(config)#access-list 110 deny udp any any eq snmp
Lab_B(config)#interface s0/0
Lab_B(config-if)#access-group 110 in
```

Disabling Echo

In case you don't know this already, small services are servers (daemons) running in the router that are quite useful for diagnostics. And here we go again—by default, the Cisco router has a series of diagnostic ports enabled for certain UDP and TCP services, including echo, chargen, and discard.

When a host attaches to those ports, a small amount of CPU is consumed to service these requests. All a single attacking device needs to do is send a whole slew of requests with different, random, phony source IP addresses to overwhelm the router, making it slow down or even fail. You can use the no version of these commands to stop a chargen attack:

```
Lab_B(config)#no service tcp-small-servers
Lab_B(config)#no service udp-small-servers
```

Finger is a utility program designed to allow users of Unix hosts on the Internet to get information about each other:

```
Lab_B(config)#no service finger
```

This matters because the finger command can be used to find information about all users on the network and/or the router. It's also why you should disable it. The finger command is equivalent to issuing the show users command on the router.

Here are the TCP small services:

Echo Echoes back whatever you type. Type the command telnet x.x.x.x echo ? to see the options.

Chargen Generates a stream of ASCII data. Type the command telnet x.x.x.x chargen ? to see the options.

Discard Throws away whatever you type. Type the command telnet x.x.x.x discard ? to see the options.

Daytime Returns the system date and time, if correct. It is correct if you are running NTP or have set the date and time manually from the exec level. Type the command telnet x.x.x.x daytime ? to see the options.

The UDP small services are as follows:

Echo Echoes the payload of the datagram you send.

Discard Silently pitches the datagram you send.

Chargen   Pitches the datagram you send and responds with a 72-character string of ASCII characters terminated with a CR+LF.

Turning Off BOOTP and Auto-Config

Again, by default, the Cisco router also offers async line BOOTP service as well as remote auto-configuration. To disable these functions on your Cisco router, use the following commands:

```
Lab_B(config)#no ip boot server
Lab_B(config)#no service config
```

Disabling the HTTP Interface

The `ip http server` command may be useful for configuring and monitoring the router, but the cleartext nature of HTTP can obviously be a security risk. To disable the HTTP process on your router, use the following command:

```
Lab_B(config)#no ip http server
```

To enable an HTTP server on a router for AAA, use the global configuration command `ip http server`.

Disabling IP Source Routing

The IP header source-route option allows the source IP host to set a packet's route through the IP network. With IP source routing enabled, packets containing the source-route option are forwarded to the router addresses specified in the header. Use the following command to disable any processing of packets with source-routing header options:

```
Lab_B(config)#no ip source-route
```

Disabling Proxy ARP

Proxy ARP is the technique in which one host—usually a router—answers ARP requests intended for another machine. By "faking" its identity, the router accepts responsibility for getting those packets to the "real" destination. Proxy ARP can help machines on a subnet reach remote subnets without configuring routing or a default gateway. The following command disables proxy ARP:

```
Lab_B(config)#interface s0/0
Lab_B(config-if)#no ip proxy-arp
```

Apply this command to all your router's interfaces.

Disabling Redirect Messages

ICMP redirect messages are used by routers to notify hosts on the data link that a better route is available for a particular destination. To disable the redirect messages so bad people can't draw out your network topology with this information, use the following command:

```
Lab_B(config)#interface s0/0
Lab_B(config-if)#no ip redirects
```

Apply this command to all your router's interfaces.

Disabling the Generation of ICMP Unreachable Messages

The no ip unreachables command prevents the perimeter router from divulging topology information by telling external hosts which subnets are not configured. This command is used on a router's interface that is connected to an outside network:

```
Lab_B(config)#interface s0/0
Lab_B(config-if)#no ip unreachables
```

Again, apply this to all the interfaces of your router.

Disabling Multicast Route Caching

The multicast route cache lists multicast routing cache entries. These packets can be read and so they create a security problem. To disable the multicast route caching, use the following command:

```
Lab_B(config)#interface s0/0
Lab_B(config-if)#no ip mroute-cache
```

Apply this command to all the interfaces of your router.

Disabling the Maintenance Operation Protocol (MOP)

The Maintenance Operation Protocol (MOP) works at the Data Link and Network layers in the DECnet protocol suite and is used for utility services such as uploading and downloading system software, remote testing, and problem diagnosis. So, who uses DECnet? Anyone with their hands up? I didn't think so. To disable this service, use the following command:

```
Lab_B(config)#interface s0/0
Lab_B(config-if)#no mop enabled
```

Apply this command to all the interfaces of your router.

Turning Off the X.25 PAD Service

Packet assembler/disassembler (PAD) connects asynchronous devices such as terminals, IC-card readers, and computers to public/private X.25 networks. Since every computer in the world is pretty much IP savvy, and X.25 has gone the way of the dodo bird, there is no reason to leave this service running. Use the following command to disable the PAD service:

```
Lab_B(config)#no service pad
```

Enabling the Nagle TCP Congestion Algorithm

The Nagle TCP congestion algorithm is useful for small-packet congestion, but if you're using a higher setting than the default MTU of 1500 bytes, it can create an above-average traffic load. To enable this service, use the following command:

```
Lab_B(config)#service nagle
```

It is important to understand that the Nagle congestion service can break XWindow connections to an Xserver, so don't use it if you're using XWindow.

Logging Every Event

Using the Cisco ACS server as a Syslog server can log events for you to verify. Use the `logging trap debugging` command and the `logging ip_address` command to turn this feature on:

```
Lab_B(config)#logging trap debugging
Lab_B(config)#logging 192.168.254.251
Lab_B(config)#exit
Lab_B#sh logging
Syslog logging: enabled (0 messages dropped, 0 flushes, 0 overruns)
    Console logging: level debugging, 15 messages logged
    Monitor logging: level debugging, 0 messages logged
    Buffer logging: disabled
    Trap logging: level debugging, 19 message lines logged
        Logging to 192.168.254.251, 1 message lines logged
```

The `show logging` command provides you with statistics of the log on the router.

Disabling Cisco Discovery Protocol

Cisco Discovery Protocol (CDP) does just that—it's a Cisco proprietary protocol that discovers Cisco devices on the network. But because it's a Data Link–layer protocol, it can't find Cisco devices on the other side of a router. Plus, by default, Cisco switches don't forward CDP packets, so you can't see Cisco devices attached to any other port on a switch.

When you are bringing up your network for the first time, CDP can be a really helpful protocol for verifying your network. But because you're going to be thorough and document your network, you don't need the CDP after that. And because CDP does discover Cisco routers and switches on your network, you should disable it. You do that in global configuration mode, which turns off CDP completely for your router or switch:

```
Lab_B(config)#no cdp run
```

Or you can turn off CDP on each individual interface using the following command:

```
Lab_B(config-if)#no cdp enable
```

Disabling the Default Forwarded UDP Protocols

When you use the `ip helper-address` command as follows on an interface, your router will forward UDP broadcasts to the listed server or servers:

```
Lab_B(config)#interface f0/0
Lab_B(config-if)#ip helper-address 192.168.254.251
```

You would generally use the `ip helper-address` command when you want to forward DHCP client requests to a DHCP server. The problem is that not only does this forward port 67 (BOOTP server request), it forwards seven other ports as well. To disable the unused ports, use the following commands:

```
Lab_B(config)#no ip forward-protocol udp 69
Lab_B(config)#no ip forward-protocol udp 53
Lab_B(config)#no ip forward-protocol udp 37
Lab_B(config)#no ip forward-protocol udp 137
Lab_B(config)#no ip forward-protocol udp 138
Lab_B(config)#no ip forward-protocol udp 68
Lab_B(config)#no ip forward-protocol udp 49
```

Now, only the BOOTP server request (67) will be forwarded to the DHCP server. If you want to forward a certain port, say TACACS+, use the following command:

```
Lab_B(config)#ip forward-protocol udp 49
```

Here's a list of available ports that you can opt to forward from the router, as well as the ports that are forwarded by default if you use the `ip helper-address` command:

Port or Protocol	Meaning	On by Default
<0–65535>	Port number (create your own)	
biff	Biff (mail notification, comsat, 512)	

Port or Protocol	Meaning	On by Default
bootpc	Bootstrap Protocol (BOOTP) client (68)	X
bootps	Bootstrap Protocol (BOOTP) server (67)	X
discard	Discard (9)	
dnsix	DNSIX security protocol auditing (195)	
domain	Domain Name Service (DNS) (53)	X
echo	Echo (7)	
isakmp	Internet Security Association and Key Management Protocol (500)	
mobile-ip	Mobile IP registration (434)	
nameserver	IEN116 name service (obsolete, 42)	
netbios-dgm	NetBios datagram service (138)	X
netbios-ns	NetBios name service (137)	X
netbios-ss	NetBios session service (139)	
ntp	Network Time Protocol (123)	
pim-auto-rp	PIM Auto-RP (496)	
rip	Routing Information Protocol (router, in.routed, 520)	
snmp	Simple Network Management Protocol (SNMP) (161)	
snmptrap	SNMP traps (162)	
sunrpc	Sun Remote Procedure Call (111)	
syslog	System Logger (514)	
tacacs	TAC access control system (49)	X
talk	Talk (517)	
tftp	Trivial File Transfer Protocol (TFTP) (69)	X
time	Time (37)	X
who	Who service (rwho, 513)	
xdmcp	X Display Manager Control Protocol (177)	

Summary

You're now familiar with the Cisco IOS Firewall software and some of its features, and you're aware of the dangers lurking at the perimeter of your network. You also learned about ways to keep your network and its data safe using features built into the Cisco IOS Firewall.

By matching each problem with a specific solution, you're now equipped with strategies that you can use against those attacks. Remember that the solution for eavesdropping and session replay is using encryption schemes such as IPSec. To stop unauthorized users from accessing your network, some simple access control lists work just fine. To provide relief from an IP address shortage, use NAT on the perimeter router to conserve subnets. The best solution for rerouting attacks is to configure MD5 authentication on your router. And finally, the solution for DoS attacks is to use the TCP Intercept feature.

If you brilliantly configure these features at the perimeter of your network, you're good and safe to go. And a router running the Cisco IOS Firewall software can do all of this for you.

Exam Essentials

Know the solution to eavesdropping.   To prevent eavesdropping, use IPSec encryption.

Know the commands to stop a chargen attack.   The following two commands can stop a chargen attack:

```
Lab_B(config)#no service tcp-small-servers
Lab_B(config)#no service udp-small-servers
```

Know how to prevent unauthorized access, data manipulation, and malicious destruction. To prevent certain inbound and outbound packets, use ACLs.

Know the solution to the lack of legal IP addresses problem.   If you do not have enough legal IP addresses, use NAT and PAT.

Know how to prevent rerouting attacks.   To secure your network against rerouting attacks, enable MD5 authentication.

Know how to prevent DoS attacks.   To prevent DoS attacks, enable TCP Intercept.

Key Terms

Before you take the exam, be certain you are familiar with the following terms:

Cisco IOS Firewall	perimeter routers
denial-of-service (DoS) attacks	rerouting attack
eavesdropping	session replay
encryption	SYN flood attack
IPSec	TCP Intercept
MD5 authentication	

Commands Used in This Chapter

Here is the list of commands used in this chapter:

Command	Meaning
(config)#**access-list** *number* **deny udp any any eq snmp**	Disables SNMP packets.
(config-if)#**access-group 110 in**	Configures the specified access list on your interface.
(config)#**no service tcp-small-servers**	Disables the default TCP diagnostic services.
(config)#**no service udp-small-servers**	Disables the default UDP diagnostic services.
(config)#**no service finger**	Disables the Finger service.
(config)#**no ip boot server**	Disables the boot server service.
(config)#**no service config**	Disables the auto-config feature on a router.
(config)#**no ip http server**	Disables the HTTP service.
(config)#**no ip source-route**	Disable source-route packets.
(config-if)#**no ip proxy-arp**	Disables proxy ARP on an interface.
(config-if)#**no ip redirects**	Disables IP redirects on an interface.
(config-if)#**no ip unreachables**	Disables IP unreachable messages from being sent out an interface.

Command	Meaning
(config-if)#**no ip mroute-cache**	Disables the multicast route cache.
(config-if)#**no mop enabled**	Disable the DECnet MOP service.
(config)#**no service pad**	Disables the X.25 PAD service.
(config)#**service nagle**	Enables the Nagle service.
(config)#**logging trap debugging**	Enables logging to a Syslog server.
(config)#**logging** *ip_address*	Logs messages to the specified Syslog server.
sh logging	Shows the login router memory.
(config)#**no cdp run**	Disables CDP on a Cisco device.
(config-if)#**no cdp enable**	Disables CDP on a Cisco device interface.
Lab_B(config-if)#**ip helper-address** *ip_address*	Forwards UDP packets to the specified IP address.
Lab_B(config)#**no ip forward-protocol udp** *port*	Disables forwarding a specific UDP port.
(config)#**ip forward-protocol udp** *port*	Forwards the specified UDP port.
(config)#**access-list** *number* **deny ip** *ip_address* **wildcard** **any**	Denies the specified source address to any destination.
(config)#**access-list 110 deny tcp any any established**	Sets up TCP Established on a router.
Lab_B(config)#**access-list 110 permit tcp any any**	Permits all TCP packets.
(config)#**router eigrp** *AS*	Chooses the specified EIGRP process.
(config-router)#**network** *network_number*	Configures EIGRP to advertise the specified network.
(config-if)#**ip authentication mode eigrp** *AS* **md5**	Enables MD5 authentication in IP EIGRP packets.
(config-if)#**ip authentication key-chain eigrp** *AS key_name*	Enables authentication of IP EIGRP packets.
(config)#**key chain** *key_name*	Identifies a key chain.

Command	Meaning
(config-key)#**key** *key_number*	In the key chain configuration mode, identifies the key number.
(config-key)#**key-string** *number*	In the key chain key configuration mode, identifies the key string.
(config)#**access-list** *number* **permit tcp any host ip_address**	Creates the designated access list to permit any source to the specified destination.
(config)#**ip tcp intercept list** *list_number*	Creates TCP Intercept to use the specified list.
(config)#**ip tcp intercept mode intercept**	Sets the TCP Intercept mode to intercept.

Written Lab

This section asks you 10 write-in-the-answer questions to help you understand the technology that you need to know in order to pass the MCNS exam.

1. Which TCP Intercept mode will proxy-answer incoming SYN requests and not notify the server until the originating host is verified?

2. Which command would you configure on the perimeter router if you do not want it to announce to external hosts which subnets are not configured?

3. You want to disable Finger replies on a perimeter router. Which command do you want to use?

4. Which two commands would you use on your router to prevent a chargen attack?

5. _____ can be used to encrypt data between two networks, which prevents eavesdropping.

6. In a rerouting attack, the _____ table is modified or prevented from being updated.

7. Which command disables Cisco Discovery Protocol on a perimeter router?

8. What command is used to enable an HTTP server on a router for AAA?

9. Which command disables Cisco Discovery Protocol on a perimeter router interface?

10. What command will disable proxy ARP on a perimeter router?

Review Questions

1. Which routing protocols can use MD5 authentication? (Choose all that apply.)

    A. EIGRP

    B. BGP

    C. OSPF

    D. IGRP

    E. RIPv1

2. Which IOS feature should be used when hiding multiple hosts behind a single IP address?

    A. IPX

    B. PAT

    C. BGP

    D. IPSec

    E. DHCP

3. Which IOS feature best prevents rerouting attacks?

    A. IPSec

    B. TCP Intercept

    C. MD5 authentication

    D. ACLs

4. Which IOS feature best prevents the lack of legal IP address problem?

    A. NAT

    B. TCP Intercept

    C. MD5 authentication

    D. ACLs

5. Which IOS feature best prevents unauthorized access, data manipulation, and malicious destruction problems?

    A. NAT

    B. TCP Intercept

    C. MD5 authentication

    D. ACLs

6. You have just configured TCP Intercept. Which type of problem are you trying to solve?

   A. DoS attacks

   B. Rerouting attacks

   C. Lack of legal IP addresses

   D. Eavesdropping

7. Which IOS feature best prevents eavesdropping?

   A. NAT

   B. TCP Intercept

   C. MD5 authentication

   D. ACLs

   E. IPSec

8. You have just configured ACLs at the perimeter router of your network. Which problem are you trying to solve?

   A. DoS

   B. Rerouting

   C. Lack of legal IP addresses

   D. Unauthorized access, data manipulation, and malicious destruction problems

   E. Eavesdropping

9. Which of the following can use a single IP address to address up to 64,000 internal hosts?

   A. NAT

   B. PAT

   C. IPSec

   D. TCP Intercept

10. Which TCP Intercept mode will proxy-answer incoming SYN requests and not notify the server until the originating host is verified?

   A. Intercept mode

   B. Secure mode

   C. Monitor mode

   D. None of the above

11. Which command would you configure on the perimeter router if you do not want it to announce to external hosts which subnets are not configured?

   A. `no source-route`

   B. `no ip unreachables`

   C. `no ip route-cache`

   D. `no service udp-small-servers`

12. You want to disable Finger replies on a perimeter router. Which command do you want to use?

   A. `no finger`

   B. `no finger reply`

   C. `no service finger`

   D. `disable finger`

13. Which commands would you use on your router to prevent a chargen attack? (Choose all that apply.)

   A. `no ip redirects`

   B. `no tcp-small-servers`

   C. `no ip-source route`

   D. `no chargen enable`

   E. `no udp-small-servers`

   F. `no service finger`

14. _____ can be used to encrypt data between two networks, which prevents eavesdropping.

   A. CBAC

   B. Lock and Key

   C. IPSec

   D. TCP Intercept

15. In a rerouting attack, the _____ table is modified or prevented from being updated.

   A. ARP

   B. Address

   C. Routing

   D. Bridging

16. Which command disables Cisco Discovery Protocol on a perimeter router?

    A. `no cdp enable`

    B. `no cdp forwards`

    C. `no cdp redirects`

    D. `no cdp run`

17. What command is used to enable an HTTP server on a router for AAA?

    A. `http server`

    B. `http-server`

    C. `ip http server`

    D. `ip http-server`

18. Which command disables Cisco Discovery Protocol on a perimeter router interface?

    A. `no cdp enable`

    B. `no cdp forwards`

    C. `no cdp redirects`

    D. `no cdp run`

19. What command will disable proxy ARP on a perimeter router?

    A. `disable proxy-arp`

    B. `disable ip proxy-arp`

    C. `no proxy-arp`

    D. `no ip proxy-arp`

    E. `no ip proxy arp`

20. What command is used to disable the sending of redirect messages?

    A. `no redirects`

    B. `no ip redirects`

    C. `no interface redirects`

    D. `disable ip redirects`

Hands-On Lab

The lab in this section will have you configure the perimeter router in your network with security using the Cisco IOS. You will need to have at least a 2600 router or RouterSim software to complete this lab.

Lab 4.1: Controlling TCP/IP Services

This lab will have you control TCP/IP services on the perimeter router. This lab protects exposed services with Cisco IOS software commands.

1. Log in to your perimeter router.

2. Go to global configuration mode, then to interface configuration mode for every interface (one at a time, of course!).

3. On each interface, enter the following command:

    Lab_B(config-if)#**no ip proxy-arp**

    This command disables the proxy ARP on an interface. Typically, you need to do this only on a LAN interface, not on a serial interface.

4. Enter the no ip redirects command on each interface:

    Lab_B(config-if)#**no ip redirects**

    This command disables the sending of redirect messages if the router is forced to resend a packet through the same interface on which it was received.

5. Now, on each interface, use the no ip route-cache command:

    Lab_B(config-if)#**no ip route-cache**

    This command disables the use of a high-speed switching cache for IP routing and the use of autonomous switching.

6. Enter the no ip unreachables command on each interface as follows:

    Lab_B(config-if)#**no ip unreachables**

    This command disables the generation of ICMP unreachable messages on a specified interface.

7. Turn off the TCP small servers:

    Lab_B(config-if)#**no service tcp-small-servers**

    This command disables the rarely used TCP diagnostic services.

8. Turn off the UDP small servers:

    Lab_B(config-if)#**no service udp-small-servers**

    This command disables the rarely used UDP diagnostic services.

9. Turn off the multicast route cache on each interface:

    Lab_B(config-if)#**no ip mroute-cache**

10. Turn off the Finger service. This is done in global configuration mode, not at the interface level:

    Lab_B(config)#**no service finger**

    This command disallows the Finger protocol requests made to the network server.

11. Set the no ip source-route command from global configuration mode:

    Lab_B(config)#**no ip source-route**

    This command causes the system to discard any IP datagram containing a source-route option.

12. From the global configuration mode, turn off the BOOTP server service:

    Lab_B(config)#**no ip bootp server**

13. Verify your configuration with the show running-config command.

Answers to Written Lab

1. The Intercept mode will proxy-answer incoming SYN requests and not notify the server until the originating host is verified.

2. You configure the `no ip unreachables` command on the perimeter router to prevent the router from announcing to external hosts which subnets are not configured.

3. The command `no service finger` disables Finger replies on a perimeter router.

4. You use the `no tcp-small-servers` and `no udp-small-servers` commands on your router to prevent a chargen attack.

5. To prevent eavesdropping, IPSec can be used to encrypt data between two networks.

6. The routing table is modified or prevented from being updated in a rerouting attack.

7. The `no cdp run` command disables Cisco Discovery Protocol on a perimeter router.

8. To enable an HTTP server on a router for AAA, use the `ip http server` command.

9. The `no cdp enable` command disables Cisco Discovery Protocol on a perimeter router interface.

10. To disable proxy ARP on a perimeter router, use the `no ip proxy-arp` command.

Answers to Review Questions

1. A, B, C. EIGRP, BPG, and OSPF are three routing protocols that can be configured to support MD5 authentication. RIPv2 can also use MD5 authentication.

2. B. PAT (Port Address Translation) allows up to 64,000 hosts to share a single IP address.

3. C. By using MD5 authentication, routers can verify that received routing updates are valid.

4. A. NAT (Network Address Translation) can be used to extend the utility of available IP address space.

5. D. By using ACLs (access control lists) at the perimeter, you can deny many of these types of attacks.

6. A. TCP Intercept is used to prevent DoS (denial-of-service) attacks, specifically SYN flood attacks.

7. E. IPSec can be used to encrypt data between two networks, which prevents eavesdropping.

8. D. ACLs are used to stop unauthorized access, data manipulation, and malicious destruction problems.

9. B. PAT (Port Address Translation) can support up to 64,000 hosts using a single IP address.

10. A. The TCP Intercept function will not forward SYN requests until the originating host is verified when running in Intercept mode.

11. B. By default, a Cisco router will send an IP unreachable message when a packet is destined for a subnet that is not listed in the routing table. By using the `no ip unreachables` command, you can stop the announcements to external hosts about which subnets are not configured.

12. C. The global configuration command `no service finger` disables the Finger service on the router.

13. B, E. To prevent a chargen attack, disable the TCP and UDP small servers.

14. C. IPSec can be used to encrypt data between two networks, which prevents eavesdropping.

15. C. When your problem is rerouting attacks, your routing table is being modified or prevented from being updated.

16. D. You can turn CDP off completely on a Cisco router or switch with the global command `no cdp run`. To turn CDP off on an individual interface, use the interface command `no cdp enable`.

17. C. The command to enable an HTTP server on a router is `ip http server` in global configuration mode.

18. A.   To turn CDP off on an individual interface, use the interface command `no cdp enable`. You can turn CDP off completely on a Cisco router or switch with the global command `no cdp run`.

19. D.   Proxy ARP is the technique in which one host, usually a router, answers ARP requests intended for another machine. To disable proxy ARP on a router interface, use the command `no ip proxy-arp`.

20. B.   ICMP redirect messages are used by routers to notify the hosts on the data link that a better route is available for a particular destination. To disable the sending of redirect messages, use the interface command `no ip redirects`.

Chapter
5

Context-Based Access Control Configuration

THE FOLLOWING SECUR EXAM TOPICS ARE COVERED IN THIS CHAPTER:

- ✓ Understanding the Cisco IOS Firewall
- ✓ Configuring Context-Based Access Control
- ✓ Establishing global timeouts and thresholds
- ✓ Implementing Port-to-Application Mapping
- ✓ Defining inspection rules
- ✓ Defining inspection rules and ACLs applied to router interfaces
- ✓ Verifying the Cisco IOS Firewall

Do you have a firewall on every Internet-connected site in your organization? Tell the truth now, do you really? All right, I'm sure some of you can honestly answer yes, but I'm also sure a lot of you can't. Firewalls are expensive—expensive to buy, expensive to install, and expensive to maintain. People who configure them are expensive too!

And while it may be true that entities such as huge financial institutions and other large corporations with deep pockets are willing to pony up the kind of cash that it takes to have a firewall guarding every Internet connection in their enterprise, public school districts, non-technical businesses, small offices, and other organizations often don't or can't.

In this chapter I'm going to introduce you to the Cisco IOS Firewall. You'll learn how it is configured so that you can work with the Cisco IOS Firewall both in your home and business, and save you some cash too. This chapter also explores Context-Based Access Control (CBAC) and explains the ways it can work for you within your internetwork. I'm going to show you how CBAC is both different and better at protecting your network than just running static ACLs.

Understanding the Cisco IOS Firewall

The *Cisco IOS Firewall* is a software firewall that runs on the IOS on your Cisco router—a feature you buy that augments the standard IOS and utilizes your existing hardware. You must, of course, have sufficient flash and RAM at your disposal for the IOS Firewall image. Some of you may be thinking that you can just use *access control lists (ACLs)* on your router and mimic a lot of the functionality of a firewall, and you're right, you can—but only to a degree. The Cisco IOS Firewall consists of three main components:

- Authentication Proxy

- Intrusion Detection System (IDS)

- Context-Based Access Control (CBAC)

Although I'm going to cover each one of these components with you, this chapter's main focus will be on CBAC. Both the Authentication Proxy and Intrusion Detection System are topics you'll study thoroughly in Chapter 6, "Cisco IOS Firewall Authentication and Intrusion Detection," but for now, I'll give you an overview of each of these powerful tools and then move right into CBAC.

Authentication Proxy and IDS

Have you ever been frustrated—maybe even nervous—because you're creating access policies based on IP addresses when what you really need to control is users? Most network engineers have. You can lock down a PC based on its IP address—that'll show 'em, right? Wrong. You can't prevent someone from easily getting around that one by simply using another machine!

But armed with the Authentication Proxy, you can create policies based on users rather than IP addresses! You can actually configure specific user-based access such as HTTP access to the Internet because the policy follows the user instead of being tied to a single PC. How? No matter where your user actually is, when they attempt to access resources through the firewall, they're forced to authenticate to the firewall, and so their policy follows them. You get to give each of your users their very own personal access profile that can be stored on a CiscoSecure ACS or other TACACS+ or RADIUS server—way cool!

The IOS Firewall now offers an *Intrusion Detection System (IDS)* option on mid- to high-range router platforms. This option is particularly valuable at perimeter points within the network or at peering points between networks. The IDS includes profiles or *signatures* for 59 common attacks that run the gamut from the breach-of-security types to information-gathering attacks. When a packet matches one of these signatures, the IDS can react with an alarm (CIDS or Syslog server), it can drop the packet, or it can reset the TCP session.

Context-Based Access Control

The Cisco IOS Firewall *Context-Based Access Control (CBAC)* engine provides secure, per-application access control across network boundaries. CBAC enhances security for applications that use TCP and UDP well-known ports. It provides this service by scrutinizing source and destination addresses. I'm going to show you how CBAC is both different and better at protecting your network than just running static ACLs. To give CBAC a proper introduction, I need to make sure you're crystal clear about how different it really is from an ACL—both in its operation and its capabilities.

 Real World Scenario

CBAC in Action

The Internet can be the ultimate source of grief, pain, and destruction, but don't assume that CBAC doesn't have applications that can protect you elsewhere as well.

Lots of organizations need internal security and controls as much as they need external security. Okay, well, almost as much. Anyway, you can apply CBAC anywhere you could really use a firewall, internally or externally.

For instance, let's say your company needs a cheap and easy alternative to purchasing and maintaining a firewall. CBAC could really come to the rescue because it comes as part of the package when you purchase the Cisco IOS Firewall set.

Instead of buying separate hardware for individual security problems, the Cisco IOS Firewall provides great value for an all-in-one product. This can give you flexibility in your multiprotocol networks, as well as perimeter security, intrusion detection, and VPN connections, including IPSec, L2TP, and QoS.

And because the Cisco IOS is always being maintained and updated, the CBAC configuration that can be used with a Cisco router will provide many years of investment protection.

CBAC Compared to ACLs

There are many differences between ACLs and CBAC, but at a high level, the main distinctions are that CBAC is stateful, dynamic, and can look farther into packets.

And CBAC is application aware—ACLs are not. In terms of OSI, this means that while ACLs make their decisions based on Layers 3 and 4 data, CBAC can actually look at Application-layer information. This capability makes it possible for CBAC to detect problems such as illegal or inappropriate SMTP commands, whereas an ACL can only permit or block the Transport-layer port.

CBAC keeps state tables where session information is stored and can dynamically create and modify ACLs to control traffic. It can also recognize and help prevent certain types of DoS attacks.

To begin, let's look at how an ACL works:

1. A packet arrives at an interface with an inbound ACL configured on the router.
2. The packet is compared to successive lines of the ACL, starting with the first line, until a match is made.
3. If a match is made, the packet is acted upon based on the action defined by that line of the ACL.
4. If a match isn't made, the packet is dropped.

If we were simply discussing ACLs, we could stop here. But if we did, you would miss an important distinction between a firewall and a router. So let's continue with the next packet:

5. Another packet arrives at an interface with an inbound ACL configured on the router.
6. The packet is compared to successive lines of the ACL, starting with the first line, until a match is made.
7. If a match is made, the packet is acted upon based on the action defined by that line of the ACL.
8. If a match isn't made, the packet is dropped.

Okay, this sounds familiar to our understanding of access lists. Let's continue with one more packet:

9. Another packet arrives at an interface with an inbound ACL configured on the router.

10. The packet is compared to successive lines of the ACL, starting with the first line, until a match is made.

11. If a match is made, the packet is acted upon based on the action defined by that line of the ACL.

12. If a match isn't made, the packet is dropped.

What's up with this? Why we are doing this stupid, redundant review of how an ACL works? The answer—and a key distinction between a firewall (CBAC) and a simple ACL—lies in this question: What effect does the first packet through the ACL have on the third packet through the ACL? The answer to this question clarifies why CBAC is a much more powerful guardian for your network.

When a router runs with ACLs, every packet arrives "fresh" at the router, with each packet being subject to the exact same set of rules. A traditional ACL is static—that is, every packet is treated equally, regardless of any other packets that have preceded it through the router. That's the point I was making with the preceding steps—each packet arrives individually at the ACL, and each packet is evaluated and either permitted or denied without any regard whatsoever to any packet that preceded it. Not so with CBAC. CBAC is smarter than that.

With CBAC, the rules for packets passing through the router can change depending on what has already happened; the fate of a packet can depend on what previous packets have done. This is what I mean when I say that CBAC is *stateful*. Think *state-dependent* if it helps.

CBAC monitors the state of network connections and traffic by keeping a state table of all inspected traffic; CBAC changes the access rules based on this data. An ACL can evaluate only one measly packet at a time, whereas a firewall (or CBAC) can evaluate *trends* of packets and respond appropriately to the type of trend it has identified. So with CBAC, what happens to the third packet through the router totally depends on what the two preceding packets did.

Clearly, this means that CBAC can identify and respond to problems that ACLs could never hope to—such as DoS attacks. An ACL can permit or deny TCP SYN requests, but CBAC can count the number of half-open TCP connections and make decisions about any new SYN requests dynamically! Plus, CBAC can evaluate Application-layer information by monitoring control channels and Application-layer conversations, so it can detect inappropriate commands. It literally parses the Application-layer header to extract this information. ACLs can't do that.

Now, all this discussion is not intended to make you think that ACLs are useless and that if you use them, you might as well put your data out on a public FTP server. Just don't freak out—I'm not telling you this to convince you to dump your ACLs. I'm just explaining how very different a stateful firewall is from an ACL. ACLs certainly do have their place—they're included in standard IOS. CBAC will definitely cost you a few bucks more for IOS images.

CBAC-Supported Protocols

CBAC is a strong tool and can help you monitor and log sessions created and used with many protocols. There are several protocols you can use with CBAC to monitor and log sessions.

CBAC can be configured to inspect either all TCP or UDP conversations or to focus on specific protocols. In operation, CBAC sits behind the ACLs and lets the ACL do its work first, so if a packet is dropped by an ACL, it's never inspected by CBAC. Packets that do pass through are inspected, and CBAC makes necessary changes to the state table for TCP and UDP sessions. The information in the state table is then used to make temporary modifications to ACLs that will serve to permit return traffic, or perhaps additional connections associated with a particular protocol—for example, FTP data connections. These temporary openings in the firewall are removed when they're no longer needed and are never saved to NVRAM.

The choice is yours—you get to decide whether to have CBAC inspect specific protocols or have it examine all TCP and/or UDP traffic. You also get to pick the interface and direction where the inspection will be applied to the protocols you've selected. Once CBAC monitors a protocol, it only allows return traffic to permissible sessions already in the state table.

Some protocols such as FTP use two channels when they communicate—one for control information and one for data exchange. CBAC monitors only the control channel. It reads the actual Application-layer commands and their responses so it can protect against certain types of Application-layer attacks. CBAC also tracks TCP sequence numbers, guarding against the types of attacks that manipulate them.

You can tell CBAC to inspect all TCP or UDP sessions, or you can get really specific and configure it to act as a watchdog for any of these particular protocols:

- RPC
- Microsoft RPC
- FTP
- TFTP
- UNIX R-commands (`Rlogin`, `Rsh`)
- SMTP
- Java
- SQL*Net
- RTSP
- H.323
- Microsoft NetShow
- StreamWorks
- VDOLive

Introduction to CBAC Configuration

To help you set up and configure CBACs, Cisco has defined six steps for configuring CBAC:

1. Set audit trails and alerts.
2. Set global timeouts and thresholds.
3. Define Port-to-Application Mapping (PAM).
4. Define inspection rules.
5. Apply inspection rules and ACLs to interfaces.
6. Test and verify CBAC.

You'll learn about each of these steps in detail throughout the rest of this chapter. The following graphic illustrates the network you'll be working with and configuring:

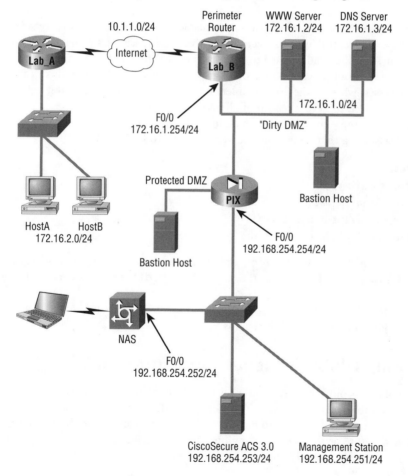

First, you need to understand the configuration and the order of the steps you'll take to build CBAC on the Lab_B router as you work through the examples in the rest of this chapter.

You'll be configuring the border router Lab_B with CBAC to protect the internal network, and you'll need to provide full access to both the web server and the DNS server from the Internet. You're also going to allow all general TCP and UDP traffic out to the Internet from your internal hosts, but not anything else.

The next section describes how to set up auditing and real-time alerts from routers running CBAC.

Using Audit Trails and Alerts

If you need it to, CBAC can generate real-time alerts and audit trails through the use of a Syslog server. This is an especially cool, useful feature if you have multiple routers running CBAC, because it allows you to monitor all enterprise alerts and even audit trails at a single, centralized location.

Alerts are triggered when CBAC discovers any suspicious activity. They're reported as Syslog error messages to the central Syslog server that you've specified. Alerts provide a record of suspected problems, and they can be used to trigger other real-time events on the Syslog server.

You can use audit trails to create a log of all inspected activities. Think of this as a record of any and all accesses, whether they're a problem or not. Audit trails are useful if your security policy identifies a need to keep a record of all network traffic.

The following example shows how both audit trails and alerts would be configured on your Lab_B router, assuming that your Syslog server is at 192.168.254.251:

```
Lab_B#conf t
Lab_B(config)#logging on
Lab_B(config)#logging 192.168.254.251
Lab_B(config)#ip inspect audit-trail
Lab_B(config)#no ip inspect alert-off
```

The no version of the ip inspect alert-off command enables alerts. Removing the no disables alerts. Likewise, the no version of the ip inspect audit-trail command disables the audit trail.

Great! You're now logging both alerts and audit trails to your Syslog server. The next step is to configure global timeouts and thresholds.

Configuring Global Timeouts and Thresholds

CBAC uses global timeouts and thresholds to determine how long to preserve state information for all sessions, established or otherwise. You can use the defaults—and you need to know what these are—or you can modify them to meet your individual needs. If you're going to change them, do it now before proceeding with any further CBAC configuration tasks.

Table 5.1 lists the commands you use to modify the default values and then describes the timeout or threshold and its default value. Once set, these values can be restored to default values by using the no form of the command, as in the following example:

Lab_B#**conf t**
Lab_B(config)#**ip inspect tcp synwait-time 60**

The default time of 30 seconds has now been changed to 60 seconds.

Lab_B(config)#**no ip inspect tcp synwait-time 60**

The default of 30 seconds has now been restored.

TABLE 5.1   Some Commands for Changing CBAC Timeouts and Thresholds

Command	Description
ip inspect tcp synwait-time	Sets how long CBAC will wait for a TCP session to be established before dropping the session. The default is 30 seconds.
ip inspect tcp finwait-time	Sets how long CBAC will wait after a TCP FIN before dropping the session. The default is 5 seconds.
ip inspect tcp idle-time	Sets how long CBAC will maintain an idle TCP connection. The default is 1 hour (3600 seconds).
ip inspect udp idle-time	Sets how long CBAC will maintain idle UDP sessions. The default is 30 seconds.
ip inspect dns-timeout	Sets how long CBAC will maintain an idle DNS name lookup session. The default is 5 seconds.
ip inspect max-incomplete high	Sets the maximum number of half-opened connections that CBAC will allow before it starts deleting them. The default is 500.
ip inspect max-incomplete low	Sets the number to go below before CBAC stops deleting half-open connections, once it starts deleting these connections. The default is 400.
ip inspect one-minute high	Sets the rate of new, half-open connections that will trigger CBAC to start deleting them. The default is 500 per minute.

TABLE 5.1 Some Commands for Changing CBAC Timeouts and Thresholds *(continued)*

Command	Description
`ip inspect one-minute low`	Sets the rate to go below before CBAC stops deleting half-open connections, once it starts deleting these connections. The default is 400 per minute.
`ip inspect tcp max-incomplete host`	Sets the maximum number of half-open connections to the same host that CBAC will allow before starting to drop them. The default is 50.

Most of these commands should be familiar to you, but a few deserve special mention.

ip inspect max-incomplete   These values can monitor both TCP and UDP sessions. *Incomplete TCP sessions* are defined as sessions where the three-way handshake hasn't been completed. *Incomplete UDP sessions* are defined as sessions where no return traffic has been detected. Once the maximum number of incomplete sessions is reached, CBAC begins deleting half-open sessions until their numbers total below the minimum value.

ip inspect one-minute   These commands are similar in operation, except instead of monitoring the total number of incomplete TCP or UDP sessions, they monitor the *rate* at which incomplete TCP or UDP sessions are being established. A sudden surge in incomplete sessions can trigger CBAC to aggressively close them, which it does until the low threshold is reached.

Let's leave the defaults on the Lab_B router and continue on to the Port-to-Application Mapping section.

Configuring PAM

You ask, and Cisco delivers! Previous versions of CBAC assumed that applications were always hosted on the same, well-known port. Live and learn. In the real world, this isn't always the case. Haven't you all set up a rogue web server on some obscure port? *Port-to-Application Mapping (PAM)* allows you to modify the default values of well-known ports, and thus teach CBAC how to recognize these familiar apps in their new homes. Check out the default PAM mappings in Table 5.2.

TABLE 5.2 Default Application Mappings

Application	Port
Cuseeme	7648
Exec	512

TABLE 5.2   Default Application Mappings *(continued)*

Application	Port
ftp	21
http	80
h323	1720
login	513
mgcp	2427
msrpc	135
netshow	1755
realmedia	7070
rtsp	554
rtsp	8554
shell	514
sip	5060
smtp	25
sql-net	1521
streamworks	1558
sunrpc	111
telnet	23
tftp	69
vdolive	7000

Okay, so these are the defaults. But what if you have an HTTP server running on port 8000? That's where PAM comes in. PAM allows you to map these applications or services to the ports that you're really using and still get to enjoy all of CBAC's capabilities. The available options in your configuration look like this:

```
Lab_B#conf t
Lab_B(config)#ip port-map ?
  cuseeme      CUSeeMe Protocol
  dns          Domain Name Server
  exec         Remote Process Execution
  finger       Finger
  ftp          File Transfer Protocol
  gopher       Gopher
  h323         H.323 Protocol (e.g, MS NetMeeting, Intel Video Phone)
  http         Hypertext Transfer Protocol
  imap         Internet Message Access Protocol
  kerberos     Kerberos
  ldap         Lightweight Directory Access Protocol
  login        Remote login
  lotusnote    Lotus Note
  mgcp         Media Gateway Control Protocol
  ms-sql       Microsoft SQL
  msrpc        Microsoft Remote Procedure Call
  netshow      Microsoft NetShow
  nfs          Network File System
  nntp         Network News Transfer Protocol
  pop2         Post Office Protocol - Version 2
  pop3         Post Office Protocol - Version 3
  realmedia    RealNetwork's Realmedia Protocol
  rtsp         Real Time Streaming Protocol
  sap          SAP
  shell        Remote command
  sip          Session Initiation Protocol
  smtp         Simple Mail Transfer Protocol
  snmp         Simple Network Management Protocol
  sql-net      SQL-NET
  streamworks  StreamWorks Protocol
  sunrpc       SUN Remote Procedure Call
  sybase-sql   Sybase SQL
  tacacs       Login Host Protocol (TACACS)
  telnet       Telnet
  tftp         Trivial File Transfer Protocol
  vdolive      VDOLive Protocol
Lab_B(config)#ip port-map http port 8000
```

Configuring options such as these modifies the default port-mapping of HTTP. You can create multiple ports for the same application, but you'll receive a warning if you try to map an application to the well-known port of another application. You can use the no version of the ip port-map command to remove the configuration, and you can use the show ip port-map command to review the changes and current PAM settings:

```
Lab_B(config)#^Z
Lab_B#show ip port-map
Default mapping: vdolive          port 7000          system defined
Default mapping: sunrpc           port 111           system defined
Default mapping: netshow          port 1755          system defined
Default mapping: cuseeme          port 7648          system defined
Default mapping: tftp             port 69            system defined
Default mapping: rtsp             port 8554          system defined
Default mapping: realmedia        port 7070          system defined
Default mapping: streamworks      port 1558          system defined
Default mapping: ftp              port 21            system defined
Default mapping: telnet           port 23            system defined
Default mapping: rtsp             port 554           system defined
Default mapping: h323             port 1720          system defined
Default mapping: sip              port 5060          system defined
Default mapping: smtp             port 25            system defined
Default mapping: http             port 80            system defined
Default mapping: msrpc            port 135           system defined
Default mapping: exec             port 512           system defined
Default mapping: login            port 513           system defined
Default mapping: sql-net          port 1521          system defined
Default mapping: shell            port 514           system defined
Default mapping: mgcp             port 2427          system defined
Default mapping: http             port 8000          user defined
Lab_B#
```

Did you notice that the HTTP mapping on port 8000 is user-defined, but all the other ports are system-defined? You can also set additional parameters for this command to get more than just one application or port, as follows:

```
Lab_B#show ip port-map http
Default mapping: http             port 80            system defined
Default mapping: http             port 8000          user defined
Lab_B#show ip port-map port 8000
Default mapping: http             port 8000          user defined
Lab_B#
```

Defining Inspection Rules

The *inspection rules* are what you use to define the applications and traffic types that you want to be inspected. Basically, this comes down to a named list that can have multiple lines, similar to an ACL. Most of the time you configure only a single inspection rule on a router, but if you're applying CBAC in two directions, you've got to create two inspection rules. You'll be creating a single inspection rule and applying it in a single direction for our corporate network example.

You should list all the applications that you want CBAC to monitor in the inspection rule. Generic TCP or UDP traffic is also allowed here. I've named the inspection rule IOSFW. Here it is on the Lab_B router:

```
Lab_B#conf t
Lab_B(config)#ip inspect name IOSFW ?
   cuseeme      CUSeeMe Protocol
   fragment     IP fragment inspection
   ftp          File Transfer Protocol
   h323         H.323 Protocol (e.g, MS NetMeeting, Intel Video Phone)
   http         HTTP Protocol
   netshow      Microsoft NetShow Protocol
   rcmd         R commands (r-exec, r-login, r-sh)
   realaudio    Real Audio Protocol
   rpc          Remote Prodedure Call Protocol
   rtsp         Real Time Streaming Protocol
   smtp         Simple Mail Transfer Protocol
   sqlnet       SQL Net Protocol
   streamworks  StreamWorks Protocol
   tcp          Transmission Control Protocol
   tftp         TFTP Protocol
   udp          User Datagram Protocol
   vdolive      VDOLive Protocol
Lab_B(config)#ip inspect name IOSFW ftp
Lab_B(config)#ip inspect name IOSFW h323
Lab_B(config)#ip inspect name IOSFW http
Lab_B(config)#ip inspect name IOSFW tcp
Lab_B(config)#ip inspect name IOSFW udp
Lab_B(config)#^Z
Lab_B#
```

You can see here that this inspection rule is configured to inspect three protocols—FTP, H323, and HTTP—plus all generic TCP and UCP traffic. If you want, you can include parameters for each protocol that control alerts, audit trails, and timeouts, as in the following example.

```
Lab_B#conf t
Lab_B(config)#ip inspect name IOSFW http ?
  alert       Turn on/off alert
  audit-trail Turn on/off audit trail
  java-list   Specify a standard access-list to apply the Java blocking.
              If specified, MUST appear directly after option "http"
  timeout     Specify the inactivity timeout time
  <cr>
Lab_B(config)#ip inspect name IOSFW http alert ?
  off  Turn off alert
  on   Turn on alert
Lab_B(config)#ip inspect name IOSFW http alert on ?
  audit-trail  Turn on/off audit trail
  timeout      Specify the inactivity timeout time
  <cr>
Lab_B(config)#ip inspect name IOSFW http alert on audit-trail ?
  off  Turn off audit trail
  on   Turn on audit trail
Lab_B(config)#ip inspect name IOSFW http alert on audit-trail on
Lab_B(config)#^Z
Lab_B#
```

The ability to define inspection rules is important because there are several types of applications that have special inspection features. For example, when configuring Java applet filtering, you can use ACLs to specify trusted applet sources such as these:

```
Lab_B#conf t
Lab_B(config)#ip inspect name IOSFW http java-list 10 alert on
Lab_B(config)#access-list 10 permit 172.16.2.0 0.0.0.255
Lab_B(config)#access-list 10 permit deny any
Lab_B(config)#^Z
Lab_B#
```

If the applet comes from a trusted site, as specified by the ACL, CBAC allows it through. If not, the applet is stripped. There are also specific inspection rules for IP packet fragmentation, RPC, and SMTP that you can apply to prevent certain types of attacks.

You're almost there! With the inspection rules defined, you're ready for the second-to-last step: applying the inspection rules and ACLs to interfaces.

Applying Inspection Rules and ACLs to Router Interfaces

Let's review what you set out to accomplish in the corporate network example and check your progress. You have a perimeter router (Lab_B) that you've been placing CBAC on, and you've configured alerts and audit trails, global timeouts, PAM, and an inspection rule. Check! But you still need to allow access from the external network to the web server and the DNS server on appropriate ports. In addition, you need to allow your internal users to access the protocols you configured into your inspection rule, as well as give them general TCP and UDP services.

CBAC must be used in conjunction with ACLs. Remember, your inspection rule was to permit your internal clients dynamic access to specified protocols and to generic TCP and UDP services on the external network, while protecting them from any unwanted attacks. Cisco recommends the following guidelines for applying rules and ACLs to interfaces:

- On the interface where traffic initiates (in the corporate network example, the dirty DMZ):
    - Apply an ACL inward that permits only wanted traffic.
    - Apply the CBAC inspection rule in the inward direction that inspects wanted traffic.
- On all other interfaces:
    - Apply an ACL in the inward direction that denies all other traffic except for traffic types not inspected by CBAC such as ICMP.

Let's go ahead and do this on the Lab_B router using the following commands:

```
Lab_B#conf t
Lab_B(config)#access-list 150 permit ip 172.16.1.0 0.0.0.255 any
Lab_B(config)#access-list 150 deny ip any any
Lab_B(config)#int f0/0
Lab_B(config-if)#ip inspect IOSFW in
Lab_B(config-if)#ip access-group 150 in
Lab_B(config-if)#^Z
Lab_B#
```

So far, so good. You've defined an access list for the interface where traffic initiates that permits wanted traffic (the internal 172.16.1.0 network addresses—you're assuming that the firewall is NATing other internal traffic). You've applied this ACL inbound on the internal interface and applied the CBAC inspection rule inbound on this same interface. So now let's protect that external interface using the following commands:

```
Lab_B#conf t
Lab_B(config)#access-list 151 permit tcp any host 172.16.1.2 eq www
Lab_B(config)#access-list 151 permit udp any host 172.16.1.3 eq domain
Lab_B(config)#access-list 151 deny ip any any
Lab_B(config)#int s1/0
Lab_B(config-if)#ip access-group 151 in
Lab_B(config-if)#^Z
Lab_B#
```

If you aren't familiar with CBAC, you might not like the looks of this—didn't you just block everything coming in from the Internet except requests to the web server and the DNS server? The access-list 151 certainly makes it look as if you did! But remember that CBAC is listening to all incoming traffic on F0/0. So when user requests to the Internet arrive there, CBAC, knowing those requests require responses, temporarily changes the ACL (151) to permit conversation between the local hosts and the Internet host. Once the conversation is over (or times out), CBAC removes the changes.

Suppose that a host on the Internet tries to access a local machine other than the web server or the DNS server. The request arrives at interface S1/0, but CBAC has no record of an open session between an internal host and that particular Internet host, and so it hasn't changed the ACL. That packet is denied because the only exceptions to the ACL that will be allowed are those entered by CBAC. Any bad guys who try to make it seem as though they have an established TCP connection when they don't will simply have their packets dropped!

The only items allowed in from the Internet are those allowed by ACL 151, which by default, allows access to the web server and the DNS server. CBAC adds entries so that servers contacted by your internal users can respond to user requests. But when your internal users aren't accessing Internet services, CBAC leaves your network locked up tight!

Did I mention that it's possible to configure both internal and external CBAC on the same router? Cool, huh?

Configuring IP ACLs at the Interface

For CBAC to work properly, you've got to have an ACL in place. Because CBAC dynamically makes changes to the ACL to permit the specific conversations it sees—you can see them too with the `show ip access list` command—the ACL needs to be an extended ACL. In the preceding example, you used `access-list 151`. You may need to have additional permit entries to allow traffic types that CBAC can't predict, such as ICMP, for example.

Testing and Verifying CBAC

As with most IOS commands, there is a set of `show` and `debug` commands that allow you to test and verify the operation of CBAC. You can use the following commands to display CBAC operation:

The `show ip inspect config` command displays information about the entire global timeouts and thresholds configuration for CBAC as well as the inspection rule configuration, excluding interface information.

```
Lab_B#show ip inspect config
Session audit trail is enabled
Session alert is enabled
one-minute (sampling period) thresholds are [400:500] connections
max-incomplete sessions thresholds are [400:500]
max-incomplete tcp connections per host is 50. Block-time 0 minute.
tcp synwait-time is 30 sec -- tcp finwait-time is 5 sec
tcp idle-time is 3600 sec -- udp idle-time is 30 sec
dns-timeout is 5 sec
Inspection Rule Configuration
```

```
Inspection name IOSFW
    ftp alert is on audit-trail is on timeout 3600
    h323 alert is on audit-trail is on timeout 3600
    http java-list 10 alert is on audit-trail is on timeout 3600
    tcp alert is on audit-trail is on timeout 3600
    udp alert is on audit-trail is on timeout 30
```

The show ip inspect interfaces command displays information about the interface configuration.

```
Lab_B#show ip inspect interfaces
Interface Configuration
 Interface FastEthernet0/0
  Inbound inspection rule is IOSFW
    ftp alert is on audit-trail is on timeout 3600
    h323 alert is on audit-trail is on timeout 3600
    http java-list 10 alert is on audit-trail is on timeout 3600
    tcp alert is on audit-trail is on timeout 3600
    udp alert is on audit-trail is on timeout 30
  Outgoing inspection rule is not set
  Inbound access list is 150
  Outgoing access list is not set
```

The show ip inspect name command displays information about the inspection rule configuration.

```
Lab_B#show ip inspect name IOSFW
Inspection name IOSFW
    ftp alert is on audit-trail is on timeout 3600
    h323 alert is on audit-trail is on timeout 3600
    http java-list 10 alert is on audit-trail is on timeout 3600
    tcp alert is on audit-trail is on timeout 3600
    udp alert is on audit-trail is on timeout 30
Lab_B#
```

And you can remove any and all CBAC by doing the following:

```
Lab_B#conf t
Lab_B(config)#no ip inspect
Lab_B(config)#^Z
Lab_B#show ip inspect interfaces
Lab_B#
```

If you do this, you'll wipe out all dynamic ACLs, reset all global timeouts, and delete all existing sessions—so be careful!

Summary

By now, I'm sure you can see that CBAC offers you way tighter security than you can hope to get through the use of ACLs. It can operate like a stateful firewall, keeping track of sessions and dynamically changing access lists to allow the passage of appropriate traffic.

The six steps that Cisco has defined to help you configure CBAC are:

1. Set audit trails and alerts.
2. Set global timeouts and thresholds.
3. Define Port-to-Application Mapping (PAM).
4. Define inspection rules.
5. Apply inspection rules and ACLs to interfaces.
6. Test and verify CBAC.

By using these steps as outlined in this chapter, you can create and maintain a secure and cost-effective internetwork.

Because CBAC is so versatile, it can also be used to prevent certain types of DoS attacks, and it offers you many fine-tuning options, as well as lots of settings for values and timeouts to use to determine appropriate thresholds for your networks. Typically, you'd have to buy more hardware to provide these services, but not with CBAC.

Another example of CBAC's versatility is Port-to-Application Mapping (PAM), which allows you to modify the default values of well-known ports and teach CBAC how to recognize these applications.

And if you need it to, CBAC can generate real-time alerts and audit trails through the use of a Syslog server. This allows you to monitor all enterprise alerts and audit trails at a single, centralized location.

To test and verify the operation of CBAC, use the command `show ip inspect config` to enable the session audit trail and the command `show ip inspect interfaces` to see the CBAC interface configuration.

Exam Essentials

Make sure you know the six steps for configuring CBAC.   Cisco has outlined six steps for CBAC configuration:

1. Set audit trails and alerts.
2. Set global timeouts and thresholds.
3. Define Port-to-Application Mapping (PAM).
4. Define inspection rules.
5. Apply inspection rules and ACLs to interfaces.
6. Test and verify CBAC.

Be sure to know the global timeouts and thresholds and the commands for changing them. You need to know the commands for changing the global timeouts and thresholds, as well as the default values. Refer to Table 5.1 for a listing of all global timeouts and thresholds and how to change them.

Make sure to know the rules for applying ACLs in conjunction with CBAC. Know that CBAC needs an extended ACL to modify for return traffic. Here is what else you must know:

- On the interface where traffic initiates (in the corporate network example, the dirty DMZ), apply an ACL inward that permits only wanted traffic and apply the CBAC inspection rule in the inward direction that inspects wanted traffic.

- On all other interfaces, apply an ACL in the inward direction that denies all other traffic except for traffic types not inspected by CBAC such as ICMP.

Be sure to review the commands to test CBAC, and know the command to disable it. There are three `show ip inspect` commands:

- The `show ip inspect config` command displays information about the entire global timeouts and thresholds configuration for CBAC as well as the inspection rule configuration, excluding interface information.

- The `show ip inspect interfaces` command displays information about the interface configuration.

- The `show ip inspect name` command displays information about the inspection rule configuration.

The `no ip inspect` command in global configuration mode disables all CBAC.

Key Terms

Before you take the exam, be certain you are familiar with the following terms:

access control lists (ACLs)	Intrusion Detection System (IDS)
Cisco IOS Firewall	Port-to-Application Mapping (PAM)
Context-Based Access Control (CBAC)	signatures

Commands Used in This Chapter

Here is the list of commands used in this chapter:

Command	Meaning
(config)#**logging on**	Enables logging.
(config)#**logging** *ip_address*	Logs to the listed IP address.
(config)#**ip inspect audit-trail**	Enables the audit trail.
(config)#**no ip inspect alert-off**	Enables the alerts.
(config)#**ip inspect tcp synwait-time** *time*	Sets how long CBAC will wait for a TCP session to be established before dropping the session. The default is 30 seconds.
(config)#**ip port-map http port** *port_number*	Modifies the default port-mapping of HTTP.
#**show ip port-map**	Displays the current PAM settings.
(config)#**ip inspect** *name*	Creates an inspection rule. The inspection rule defines the applications and traffic types to be inspected.
#**show ip inspect config**	Displays the inspection rule configuration.
#**show ip inspect interfaces**	Displays the inspection rule interface configuration.
#**show ip inspect name** *name*	Provides audit-trail timers for the specified name.

Written Lab

This section asks you 10 write-in-the-answer questions to help you understand the technology that you need to know in order to pass the SECUR exam.

1. When CBAC starts deleting half-open connections, how many must there be per minute before it stops?

2. Which command disables all auditing?

3. Which commands are valid monitoring commands for CBAC?

4. Which command do you use to disable all CBAC functions on the router?

5. Which types of ACLs can CBAC dynamically modify?

6. Which command would you use if you needed to check and see which port(s) CBAC thinks HTTP is running on?

7. True or False: When configuring inspection rules, you can inspect application protocols, generic TCP, and generic UDP all together.

8. _____ provides stateful inspection, can effectively respond to DoS attacks, and adapts to user requests and network conditions. It is neither free with IOS, nor is it static.

9. What type of server do you need to have if you want to enable alerts and audit trails?

10. What are the six steps recommended by Cisco to configure CBAC (in order)?

Review Questions

1. Which of the following commands would you use to change the maximum number of half-open TCP connections per host to 100?

    A. `ip inspect tcp synwait-time 100`

    B. `ip inspect tcp idle-time 100`

    C. `ip inspect max-incomplete high 100`

    D. `ip inspect one-minute high 100`

    E. `ip inspect tcp max-incomplete host 100`

2. Which of the following best describes a half-open connection?

    A. The TCP three-way handshake was completed.

    B. The connection was denied.

    C. The connection failed to reach an established state.

    D. The connection timed out.

3. Which of the following commands would you use to change the maximum total number of half-open TCP connections to 1000?

    A. `ip inspect tcp synwait-time 1000`

    B. `ip inspect tcp idle-time 1000`

    C. `ip inspect max-incomplete high 1000`

    D. `ip inspect one-minute high 1000`

    E. `ip inspect tcp max-incomplete host 1000`

4. Which of the following commands disables all CBAC on the IOS Firewall?

    A. `Router(config)#`**`no ip inspect`**

    B. `Router(config-if)#`**`no ip inspect`**

    C. `Router(config)#`**`no ip cbac`**

    D. `Router(config-if)#`**`no ip cbac`**

5. What is the default time CBAC will wait before closing idle TCP connections?

    A. 10 seconds

    B. 30 seconds

    C. 60 seconds

    D. 600 seconds

    E. 3600 seconds

6. Which of the following commands would you use to change the length of time CBAC will wait for half-open TCP connections to complete before dropping them to 60 seconds?

   A. `ip inspect tcp synwait-time 60`

   B. `ip inspect tcp idle-time 60`

   C. `ip inspect max-incomplete high 60`

   D. `ip inspect one-minute high 60`

   E. `ip inspect tcp max-incomplete host 60`

7. What is the default number of half-open connections that causes CBAC to start deleting them?

   A. 100

   B. 400

   C. 500

   D. 600

   E. 3600

8. Once CBAC starts deleting half-open connections, how many must there be before it stops?

   A. 100

   B. 400

   C. 500

   D. 600

   E. 3600

9. What is the default number of half-open connections per minute that causes CBAC to start deleting them?

   A. 100

   B. 400

   C. 500

   D. 600

   E. 3600

10. Once CBAC starts deleting half-open connections, how many must there be per minute before it stops?

   A. 100

   B. 400

   C. 500

   D. 600

   E. 3600

11. Which of the following commands disables all auditing?

    A. `ip inspect audit-trail`

    B. `no ip inspect audit-trail`

    C. `ip inspect alert off`

    D. `no ip inspect alert off`

12. Which of the following are components of the IOS Firewall? (Choose all that apply.)

    A. Context-Based Access Control (CBAC)

    B. Contextless Access Control (CAC)

    C. Authentication Proxy

    D. Intrusion Detection System (IDS)

    E. Stateful firewall

13. Which of the following commands are valid monitoring commands for CBAC? (Choose all that apply.)

    A. `ip inspect show`

    B. `show ip inspect interfaces`

    C. `show ip inspect config`

    D. `display ip inspect config`

    E. `inspect ip global-parameters`

14. Suppose that you need to disable all CBAC functions on the router. Which of the following commands would you choose?

    A. `Router(config)#`**`ip inspect none`**

    B. `Router(config-if)#`**`no ip inspect`**

    C. `Router(config)#`**`no ip inspect`**

    D. `Router(config-if)#`**`no ip cbac`**

15. Which types of ACL can CBAC dynamically modify?

    A. IP standard

    B. IP extended

    C. Any IP access list

    D. Any access list

16. You need to check and see which port(s) CBAC thinks HTTP is running on. Which of the following commands gives you this information? (Choose all that apply.)

    A. `show ip port-map`

    B. `show ip port 80 port-map`

    C. `show ip http port-map`

    D. `show ip port-map port 80`

    E. `show ip port-map http`

17. When configuring inspection rules, which of the following best describes how protocols can be configured?

    A. You can inspect TCP or UDP, but not both.

    B. You can inspect TCP and UDP, but nothing else.

    C. You can inspect application protocols or TCP.

    D. You can inspect application protocols, generic TCP, and generic UDP all together.

    E. None of the above.

18. Which of the following are properties of CBAC? (Choose all that apply.)

    A. Stateful inspection

    B. Static

    C. Can be used to effectively respond to DoS attacks

    D. Adapts to user requests and network conditions

    E. Free with standard IOS

19. You need to enable alerts and audit trails. Which of the following must you have in order to do this?

    A. CiscoSecure ACS

    B. Windows 2000

    C. Syslog server

    D. TACACS server

    E. RADIUS server

20. What are the six steps recommended by Cisco to configure CBAC (in order)?

   1. Define inspection rules.

   2. Test and verify CBAC.

   3. Set global timeouts and thresholds.

   4. Apply inspection rules and ACLs to interfaces.

   5. Set audit trails and alerts.

   6. Define Port-to-Application Mapping (PAM).

   A. 1, 2, 3, 4, 5, 6

   B. 3, 6, 5, 2, 1, 4

   C. 5, 3, 6, 1, 4, 2

   D. 2, 4, 3, 5, 6, 1

   E. 4, 6, 2, 3, 1, 5

Hands-On Labs

The labs in this chapter will have you configure CBAC on a Cisco router. You will perform the following tasks:

- Lab 5.1: Configure Logging and Audit Trails
- Lab 5.2: Define and Apply Inspection Rules and ACLs
- Lab 5.3: Test and Verify CBAC

The labs in this chapter are based on the corporate network example you've used for configuring the NAS and perimeter router throughout this book. (See the graphic in the "Introduction to CBAC Configuration" section.)

Lab 5.1: Configure Logging and Audit Trails

To configure logging and audit trails, complete the following steps:

1. Log in to your router and enter global configuration mode.

2. On your router, enable logging to the console and the Syslog server:

   ```
   Lab_B(config)#logging on
   Lab_B(config)#logging 192.168.254.251
   ```

3. Enable the audit trail on your router:

   ```
   Lab_B(config)#ip inspect audit-trail
   ```

4. Save your configuration:

   ```
   Lab_B(config)#^Z (Ctrl+Z)
   Lab_B#copy run start
   ```

Lab 5.2: Define and Apply Inspection Rules and ACLs

To define and apply inspection rules and ACLs, complete the following steps:

1. Log in to your router and enter global configuration mode.

2. On your router, define a CBAC rule to inspect all TCP and FTP traffic:

   ```
   Lab_B(config)#ip inspect name MYRULE tcp timeout 300
   Lab_B(config)#ip inspect name MYRULE ftp timeout 300
   ```

3. Define the ACLs to allow outbound ICMP traffic and CBAC traffic (FTP and WWW). Block all other inside-initiated traffic:

   ```
   Lab_B(config)#access-list 101 permit icmp any any
   Lab_B(config)#access-list 101 permit tcp 172.16.1.0 0.0.0.255 any eq ftp
   Lab_B(config)#access-list 101 permit tcp 172.16.1.0 0.0.0.255 any eq www
   Lab_B(config)#access-list 101 deny ip any any
   ```

4. Define ACLs to allow inbound ICMP traffic and CBAC traffic (FTP and WWW) to the inside web server or FTP server. Block all other outside-initiated traffic:

   Lab_B(config)#**access-list 102 permit eigrp any any**

   Lab_B(config)#**access-list 102 permit icmp any any**

   Lab_B(config)#**access-list 102 permit tcp any host 172.16.1.2 eq ftp**

   Lab_B(config)#**access-list 102 permit tcp any host 172.16.1.3 eq www**

   Lab_B(config)#**access-list 102 deny ip any any**

5. Apply the inspection rule and ACL to the inside interface:

   Lab_B(config)#**interface FastEthernet0/0**

   Lab_B(config-if)#**ip inspect MYRULE in**

   Lab_B(config-if)#**ip access-group 101 in**

6. Apply the ACL to the outside interface:

   Lab_B(config-if)#**interface serial0**

   Lab_B(config-if)#**ip access-group 102 in**

7. Save your configuration:

   Lab_B(config-if)#**^Z**

   Lab_B#**copy running-config startup-config**

Lab 5.3: Test and Verify CBAC

To test and verify CBAC on your router, take the following steps:

1. Log in to your router and enter privileged mode.

2. Check the ACLs configured on your router:

   Lab_B#**show access-lists**

3. On your router, use the following show commands to verify CBAC operation:

   Lab_B#**show ip inspect name MYRULE**

   Lab_B#**show ip inspect config**

   Lab_B#**show ip inspect interfaces**

   Lab_B#**show ip inspect sessions**

   Lab_B#**show ip inspect sessions detail**

   Lab_B#**show ip inspect all**

Answers to Written Lab

1. When CBAC starts deleting half-open connections, there must be 400 per minute before CBAC stops.

2. The command `no ip inspect audit-trail` disables all auditing.

3. The valid monitoring commands for CBAC are `show ip inspect interfaces` and `show ip inspect config`.

4. To disable all CBAC functions on the router, use the command `no ip inspect`.

5. CBAC can dynamically modify the IP extended type of ACLs.

6. You can use either `show ip port-map` or `show ip port-map http` to check which port(s) CBAC thinks HTTP is running on.

7. True. You can inspect application protocols, generic TCP, and generic UDP all together when configuring inspection rules.

8. CBAC provides stateful inspection, can effectively respond to DoS attacks, and adapts to user requests and network conditions. It is neither free with IOS, nor is it static.

9. You need to have a Syslog server if you want to enable alerts and audit trails.

10. The six steps recommended by Cisco to configure CBAC are, in order: set audit trails and alerts, set global timeouts and thresholds, define Port-to-Application Mapping (PAM), define inspection rules, apply inspection rules and ACLs to interfaces, and test and verify CBAC.

Answers to Review Questions

1. E. The `ip inspect tcp max-incomplete host 100` command sets the maximum number of half-open TCP connections to a single host to 100.

2. C. CBAC defines a half-open connection as any connection that fails to reach an established state.

3. C. The `ip inspect max-incomplete high 1000` command sets the maximum number of total (regardless of the destination host) half-open TCP connections to a single host to 1000.

4. A. The `no ip inspect` command in global configuration mode disables all CBAC.

5. E. CBAC will wait 1 hour, or 3600 seconds, before deleting idle TCP connections.

6. A. The `ip inspect tcp synwait-time 60` command sets the time CBAC will wait on half-open TCP connections to 60 seconds.

7. C. CBAC, by default, starts deleting half-open connections once there are 500. This is configured using the `ip inspect max-incomplete high` parameter.

8. B. Once CBAC starts deleting half-open connections, by default, it will not stop until there are 400 (or fewer). This is configured using the `ip inspect-max-incomplete low` parameter.

9. C. CBAC, by default, starts deleting half-open connections once there are 500 per minute. This is configured using the `ip inspect one-minute high` parameter.

10. B. Once CBAC starts deleting half-open connections, by default, it will not stop until there are 400 per minute (or fewer). This is configured using the `ip inspect one-minute low` parameter.

11. B. The `no ip inspect audit-trail` command disables the auditing.

12. A, C, D. The three components of the IOS Firewall are CBAC, Authentication Proxy, and IDS.

13. B, C. Both the `show ip inspect interfaces` and `config` commands display information about CBAC configuration. The other commands are all invalid.

14. C. The `no ip inspect` command in global configuration mode disables all CBAC.

15. B. CBAC can only modify IP extended access lists to allow responses back through the firewall.

16. A, E. The `show ip port-map` and `show ip port-map http` commands display the ports configured or mapped to HTTP. The `show ip port-map port 80` command displays only port 80 information.

17. D. You can inspect independent protocols, generic TCP, and UDP traffic.

18. A, C, D.   CBAC provides stateful inspection, can effectively respond to DoS attacks, and adapts to user requests and network conditions. It is neither free with IOS, nor is it static.

19. C.   When you enable audit trails and alerts, you must have a Syslog server configured to receive the alerts and audit logs.

20. C.   The six steps recommended by Cisco to configure CBAC are, in order: set audit trails and alerts, set global timeouts and thresholds, define Port-to-Application Mapping (PAM), define inspection rules, apply inspection rules and ACLs to interfaces, and test and verify CBAC.

Cisco IOS Firewall Authentication and Intrusion Detection

THE FOLLOWING SECUR EXAM TOPICS ARE COVERED IN THIS CHAPTER:

✓ Understanding the Cisco IOS Firewall Authentication Proxy

✓ Configuring the AAA server

✓ Configuring AAA

✓ Configuring the Authentication Proxy

✓ Verifying the Cisco IOS Firewall

✓ Understanding IOS Firewall IDS

✓ Initializing Cisco IOS Firewall IDS

✓ Configuring, disabling, and excluding signatures

✓ Creating and applying audit rules

Picture this…You're the networking/security guru working for a company located in the trendiest part of town—you know, where all the old, industrial brick buildings have been converted to cool lofts and chic, pricey offices with gourmet shops, martini bars, and art galleries at street level? Nice! Congrats—only, there's a catch. Though snappy and stylish, that edgy design house aesthetic spawned an office environment without cubes, doors, or privacy, where all the desks are out in one big open, collaborative, synergetic "space." Said another way, every PC is physically accessible to every user who simply waits for the office to empty out at lunch or after work to do whatever they please on someone else's computer.

And of course you have many different levels of employees in this office, and each one requires specific kinds of access to external networks, including the Internet. Assuming that you can't just give everyone full access to all external resources, how do you deal with this nightmare and configure (implement) access controls?

Well, you could sit down, figure out who sits where, and scribble out some access control lists (ACLs). And it'll take what, a half-nanosecond, for your users to realize: "@#%&! I can't get to the Web from my PC. But if I wait for someone whose machine can get to the Internet to leave, voila! I've got web access!"

So what's your next move? Password-protect the machines? Implement policies about locking screensavers? Those strategies might help a bit, but do you think you'll really be able to get Mr. Know-It-All-VP, who doesn't know diddly about computers, to buy in? And what about shared machines—especially when users sharing the same machine have different security policies? Can you solve that one with an ACL?

All of this highlights a critical issue that you didn't have a very effective solution for in the past. Tying ACLs to devices (IP addresses) was pretty much it, except doing that didn't help a whole lot because what you really need to control are organic life forms, plus other Darwinian wonders known as users. How would you like to be able to attach an ACL to the user rather than to the resource? Well, now you can—that's the objective of the IOS Firewall Authentication Proxy, and it's what we'll be covering in the first part of this chapter.

But the Authentication Proxy is only a partial solution, because once you've got your users squared away, you've still got to keep out spam e-mail, viruses, worms, hackers, and the deranged former employee seeking to sabotage the company's business processes! While it's pretty idealistic to think that you can protect yourself from everyone or everything bent on seriously messing with your system, there is a truly powerful tool that can really help. The IOS Firewall Intrusion Detection System (IDS) gives you more bang for your buck by allowing your IOS router to act as a Cisco

Secure IDS sensor would; it can spot and react to potentially inappropriate or malicious packets. It can even be added into the CSIDS Director for inclusion in a centralized IDS monitoring system. I'm not going to get into the whole "should-you-or-should-you-not-profile" debate. Just know that in network security, you profile suspicious elements. It makes sense not to pat down a Mother Teresa packet while the shoe-bomber packet gets to breeze right through unquestioned!

How does this work? Well, the IOS Firewall IDS bases its profiling capabilities on IDS signatures that delineate the types of traffic that may be nasty. You, as the administrator, get to choose which signatures to deploy and how you want to react when patterns of network traffic match the signature. These IDS protections can be used against internal or external attacks and can be executed in conjunction with the other IOS Firewall features we've been discussing.

I'm going to show you how to configure the IOS Firewall IDS, but first, I'm going to start things off by giving you a brief operational overview and pointing out a few other IDS considerations. Then, I'll take you through the process of enabling the IOS Firewall IDS and manipulating the various available signatures. Finally, I'll show you how to create audit rules and verify your configuration.

Introduction to the Cisco IOS Firewall Authentication Proxy

Back in Chapter 1, "Introduction to Network Security," I stressed how seriously important it is that you create a solid security policy to protect your network (and your job!). This is because the *IOS Firewall Authentication Proxy* allows you to create and apply access control policies to *individuals* instead of to *addresses*. When your users move around, their access policies follow them, regardless of which IP address they happen to be using at any given moment. This technology helps you permit Sales Exec A to use the same username and password to log on to the docked laptop at her desk or to dial up from home or anywhere else. And unless Sales Exec A gives away her username and password, no one else gets to log in and pretend to be her or access her individual rights.

With the IOS Firewall Authentication Proxy in place, users are forced to authenticate before access through the IOS Firewall is granted. When the user attempts to initiate communications through the IOS Firewall, they'll be queried for a username and password, which are then sent to an external AAA server running either TACACS+ or RADIUS. The server responds to the firewall's request with a user profile that defines the specific rights and limitations for that individual user's access and is adopted by the firewall for the duration of the communication.

In order to authenticate to the firewall, users must initiate an HTTP session through it. When they do that, an HTTP window appears that's used for authentication, such as the one you see in Figure 6.1.

FIGURE 6.1   User authentication screen

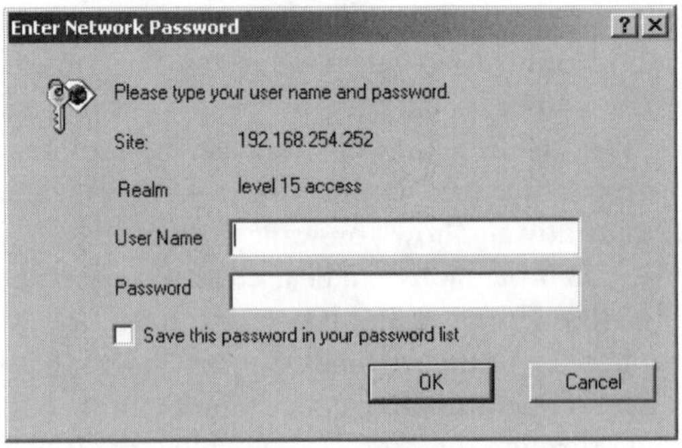

Users must initiate HTTP and successfully authenticate before other traffic types will be allowed—no HTTP first, no Telnet. After authentication, the user's profile dynamically modifies ACLs on the router to allow the user the specified access. If the user exceeds the idle timer (60 minutes by default), they have to re-authenticate and establish a new HTTP session before they can continue. Remember Sales Exec A? Let's say she took her work home, logged onto the Internet, and left the room before the idle time default elapsed. Now suppose she has a daughter who wanders into the room, sits down at her mom's computer, and accesses some chat room that way as well. This could be a problem, right? The good news is that you can change that default setting. I'll show you how later in this chapter.

There are four easy steps to setting up the IOS Firewall Authentication Proxy:

1. Configure the AAA server (CSACS, etc.).

2. Configure AAA on the router.

3. Configure the IOS Firewall Authentication Proxy on the router.

4. Test and verify functionality.

As you can see, the first two steps merely get AAA up and running on the router and server. Once you do that, you add the IOS Firewall Authentication Proxy configuration to the router, then test and verify its functionality. Like I said, it's easy.

Okay, let's walk through these four steps, once again using the same setup for the corporate network that you've been using throughout this book, which is illustrated in the following graphic:

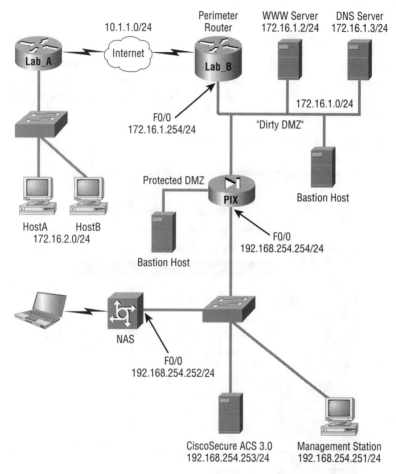

In order to understand this chapter's material, you're going to configure the CSACS server at 192.168.254.253, and configure the Lab_B perimeter router.

Configuring the AAA Server

As I said, the AAA server can be either a TACACS+ or a RADIUS server—you have lots of options here. The IOS Firewall Authentication Proxy supports the following TACACS+ servers:

- CSACS for Windows 2000
- CSACS for Unix
- TACACS+ freeware

The IOS Firewall Authentication Proxy also supports the following RADIUS servers:

- CSACS for Windows 2000
- CSACS for Unix
- Lucent
- Other standard RADIUS servers

The first step in setting up the IOS Firewall Authentication Proxy is to configure the AAA server to support it. You'll use the CSACS for Windows server from the corporate network example for that, and you'll start by selecting Interface Configuration from the navigation bar to configure TACACS+, as illustrated in Figure 6.2.

FIGURE 6.2 Interface configuration for TACACS+

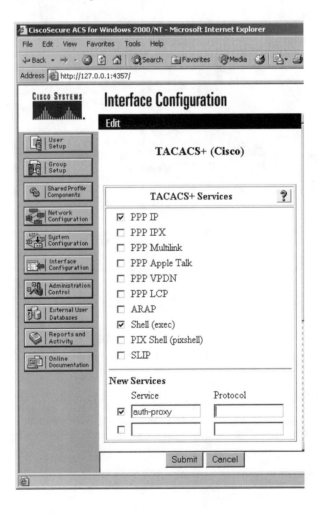

Next, select Group Setup from the navigation bar and edit the settings for your group. Select the Auth-Proxy and Custom Attributes check boxes, then add your ACL using the appropriate syntax (I'll cover that in a minute), as shown in Figure 6.3.

FIGURE 6.3   Group setup for TACACS+

When configuring the ACLs in the AAA server, you use syntax that's similar but not identical to what you use in a router. The similarities make it almost intuitive, but it's also easy to make a mistake if you're not careful. For instance, the following output shows an example of an ACL that allows all traffic after authentication:

```
proxyacl#1=permit ip any any
priv-lvl=15
```

Here's an even more specific example:

```
proxyacl#1=permit tcp any any eq www
proxyacl#2=permit tcp any any eq ftp
proxyacl#3=permit tcp any host 192.168.55.3 eq smtp
priv-lvl=15
```

Combining both of these examples with your past experience with ACLs in the Cisco IOS should help you get the syntax down. Here are a few general rules to keep in mind:

- Only use permit statements, no deny statements.
- The source address must be set to any. These addresses will be dynamically replaced with actual source addresses in operation.
- End each list by setting the privilege level to 15.

At this point, the configuration of the AAA server is complete, but you still have to configure AAA on the router and then configure the Authentication Proxy before you can validate your work here.

Configuring AAA

Now that the CSACS server is configured, let's move on to configuring the router that will act as the IOS Firewall Authentication Proxy. First, you enable AAA on the router in preparation for configuring the IOS Firewall Authentication Proxy by following these six steps:

1. Enable AAA.
2. Configure the authentication protocol.
3. Configure the authorization protocol.
4. Specify the TACACS+ server and key.
5. Create an ACL to allow AAA traffic to the router.
6. Enable the router's HTTP server to use AAA.

I'll go over each of these steps separately while you configure the Lab_B router.

Enabling AAA

First, enable AAA by using the aaa new-model command in global configuration mode:

```
Lab_B#conf t
Lab_B(config)#aaa new-model
Lab_B(config)#^Z
Lab_B#
```

The router is now prepared for further AAA configuration. (Remember, if you want to remove AAA from the router, you can use the no aaa new-model command in global configuration mode.)

Configuring the Authentication Protocol

Next, enable AAA authentication. You can do this several different ways, and you can also specify multiple methods if you want. Here's the configuration on the Lab_B router:

```
Lab_B#conf t
Lab_B(config)#aaa authentication ?
  arap            Set authentication lists for arap.
  attempts        Set the maximum number of authentication attempts
  banner          Message to use when starting login/authentication.
  enable          Set authentication list for enable.
  fail-message    Message to use for failed login/authentication.
  login           Set authentication lists for logins.
  nasi            Set authentication lists for NASI.
  password-prompt Text to use when prompting for a password
  ppp             Set authentication lists for ppp.
  username-prompt Text to use when prompting for a username

Lab_B(config)#aaa authentication login ?
  WORD    Named authentication list.
  default The default authentication list.

Lab_B(config)#aaa authentication login default ?
  enable     Use enable password for authentication.
  group      Use Server-group
  line       Use line password for authentication.
  local      Use local username authentication.
  local-case Use case-sensitive local username authentication.
  none       NO authentication.

Lab_B(config)#aaa authentication login default group ?
  WORD    Server-group name
  radius  Use list of all Radius hosts.
  tacacs+ Use list of all Tacacs+ hosts.

Lab_B(config)#aaa authentication login default group tacacs+
Lab_B(config)#^Z
Lab_B#
```

In this example, you specified the server-group authentication using a TACACS+ server. If necessary, you could have specified an additional authentication method besides TACACS+.

Configuring the Authorization Protocol

As with the authentication protocol, there are a number of choices available for specifying the authorization protocol for AAA. In this case, specify the authorization for the IOS Firewall Authentication Proxy service, which is reflected in the command syntax. Here's how the Lab_B router configuration looks now:

```
Lab_B#conf t
Lab_B(config)#aaa authorization ?
  auth-proxy      For Authentication Proxy Services
  cache           For AAA cache configuration
  commands        For exec (shell) commands.
  config-commands For configuration mode commands.
  configuration   For downloading configurations from AAA server
  exec            For starting an exec (shell).
  network         For network services. (PPP, SLIP, ARAP)
  reverse-access  For reverse access connections

Lab_B(config)#aaa authorization auth-proxy ?
  default  The default authorization list.

Lab_B(config)#aaa authorization auth-proxy default ?
  group  Use server-group.

Lab_B(config)#aaa authorization auth-proxy default group ?
  WORD     Server-group name
  radius   Use list of all Radius hosts.
  tacacs+  Use list of all Tacacs+ hosts.

Lab_B(config)#aaa authorization auth-proxy default group tacacs+
Lab_B(config)#^Z
Lab_B#
```

As with the authentication protocol, you're using TACACS+, but you could have specified multiple authorization protocols had it been necessary.

Specifying the TACACS+ Server and Key

The router certainly needs a TACACS+ server and server key configured, and you can even configure multiple TACACS+ servers. The IOS Firewall Authentication Proxy will query them in the order you enter them. The no tacacs-server host command removes individual servers from the list. Remember, you've designated the CSACS server at 192.168.254.253 in the corporate network example. Here's the Lab_B router configuration:

```
Lab_B#conf t
```

```
Lab_B(config)#tacacs-server host 192.168.254.253
Lab_B(config)#tacacs-server key todd
Lab_B(config)#^Z
Lab_B#
```

Creating an ACL to Allow AAA Traffic to the Router

Now you're going to create an access list that will allow incoming TACACS+ traffic from the CSACS box to the router. You're also going to permit all ICMP traffic, but deny everything else. Here's how Lab_B's output looks now:

```
Lab_B#conf t
Lab_B(config)#access-list 155 permit tcp host 192.168.254.253 eq tacacs host
   ↳ 172.16.1.254
Lab_B(config)#access-list 155 permit icmp any any
Lab_B(config)#access-list 155 deny ip any any
Lab_B(config)#int fast0/0
Lab_B(config-if)#ip access-group 155 in
Lab_B(config)#^Z
Lab_B#
```

Does it seem as if what you just did totally screwed things up? No worries. Remember, just as with CBAC, this ACL isn't going to be what it looks like right off the bat. In a second, when you apply the IOS Firewall Authentication Proxy to this interface, all appropriate network traffic will flow, and all will be well. But even so, there are a few important things to keep in mind when creating this ACL. First, the source address in the first line is the CSACS server, so you've got to be sure to allow traffic types that are consistent with the authentication and authorization methods specified earlier (TACACS+ and/or RADIUS). Secondly, the destination will be the IP address of the interface closest to the CSACS server. And finally, don't forget to explicitly deny all other IP traffic!

Enabling the Router's HTTP Server to Use AAA

You've enabled the HTTP server on the router and told it to use AAA for authentication—check out the configuration on Lab_B now:

```
Lab_B#conf t
Lab_B(config)#ip http server
Lab_B(config)#ip http ?
  access-class     Restrict access by access-class
  authentication   Set http authentication method
  path             Set base path for HTML
  port             HTTP port
  server           Enable HTTP server
```

```
Lab_B(config)#ip http authentication ?
  aaa     Use AAA access control methods
  enable  Use enable passwords
  local   Use local username and passwords
  path    Set base path for HTML
  tacacs  Use tacacs to authorize user

Lab_B(config)#ip http authentication aaa
Lab_B(config)#^Z
Lab_B#
```

Sweet! Now that Lab B's AAA configuration is complete, the foundation is in place for the IOS Firewall Authentication Proxy configuration. If you need a bit of a break, now's a great time to take one.

Configuring the Authentication Proxy

Okay, back to work! With the AAA configuration in place, the Authentication Proxy configuration is a breeze. The first thing to do is to specify the Authentication Proxy idle timeout value. This is the amount of time in minutes that idle connections will be maintained by the Authentication Proxy. The default value is 60 minutes, which may or may not work for you. Remember that example of the Sales Exec and her daughter? Yikes! Okay, let's cut that default time in half. Here's a look at Lab_B router's output:

```
Lab_B#conf t
Lab_B(config)#ip auth-proxy auth-cache-time 30
Lab_B(config-if)#^Z
Lab_B#
```

You can reset this to the default by using the no ip auth-proxy auth-cache-time command in global configuration mode.

Next, you'll create an Authentication Proxy rule and name it **toddlock**:

```
Lab_B#conf t
Lab_B(config)#ip auth-proxy name toddlock ?
  http  HTTP Protocol
  <cr>

Lab_B(config)#ip auth-proxy name toddlock http
Lab_B(config)#^Z
Lab_B#
```

Great—now you'll apply the Authentication Proxy rule to an interface—Fast Ethernet 0/0 on Lab_B:

```
Lab_B#conf t
Lab_B(config)#int fast0/0
Lab_B(config-if)#ip auth-proxy ?
  WORD  Name of authenticaion proxy rule

Lab_B(config-if)#ip auth-proxy name toddlock
Lab_B(config-if)#^Z
Lab_B#
```

You could have used an ACL to control which devices could use the IOS Firewall Authentication Proxy with the command `ip auth-proxy name toddlock http list 50` to create an Authentication Proxy rule. The additional `list 50` parameter refers to the standard IP access list 50 to determine which source addresses could be authenticated. You didn't add that in, so in the preceding configuration, all hosts are prompted for authentication. If you want to limit hosts that have the ability to authenticate out, you can do that using this ACL parameter.

Now that you're through, it's time to see if everything's working. After that, you'll learn about some testing and verification commands.

Testing and Verifying Your Configuration

There are several commands for troubleshooting and validating the operation of the IOS Firewall Authentication Proxy. The syntax of these commands is pretty typical, so if you've made it this far in the book, you could probably guess most, if not all, of the commands! But just in case, I'll briefly explain in this section the show commands, the **debug** commands, and the commands for clearing the cache.

show Commands

There are three primary show commands that you need to know for checking the contents of the IOS Firewall Authorization Proxy cache, the global configuration parameters, and statistics. Here are some examples demonstrated on the Lab_B router:

```
Lab_B#show ip auth-proxy cache
Authentication Proxy Cache
 Client IP 172.16.1.100 Port 2326, timeout 30, state HTTP_INIT

Lab_B#show ip auth-proxy configuration
Authentication global cache time is 30 minutes
Authentication Proxy Rule Configuration
```

```
Auth-proxy name toddlock
    http list not specified auth-cache-time 30 minutes

Lab_B#show ip auth-proxy statistics
Authentication Proxy Statistics
    proxied client number 1
Lab_B#
```

debug Commands

The number of debug commands available varies a bit as you change IOS versions. The following is a demonstration of the debug ip auth-proxy function-trace command from the previous example that hit Cisco's website (represented here by 1.1.1.1):

```
Lab_B#debug ip auth-proxy ?
  function-trace    Auth-Proxy function trace
  object-creation   Authentication Proxy object creations
  object-deletion   Authentication Proxy object deletions
  timers            Authentication Proxy timer related events

Lab_B#debug ip auth-proxy function-trace
AUTH-PROXY Function Trace debugging is on
Lab_B#
00:55:43: AUTH-PROXY FUNC: auth_proxy_fast_path
00:55:43: AUTH-PROXY auth_proxy_find_conn_info :
    find srcaddr - 172.16.1.100, dstaddr - 1.1.1.1
      ip-srcaddr 172.16.1.100
      pak-srcaddr 0.0.0.0

00:55:43: AUTH-PROXY FUNC: auth_proxy_process_path
00:55:43:  SYN SEQ 537346255 LEN 0
00:55:43: dst_addr 3473868035 src_addr 2886730084 dst_port 80 src_port 2328
00:55:43: AUTH-PROXY auth_proxy_find_conn_info :
    find srcaddr - 172.16.1.100, dstaddr - 1.1.1.1
      ip-srcaddr 172.16.1.100
      pak-srcaddr 0.0.0.0

00:55:43: clientport 2327 state 0
00:55:43: AUTH-PROXY FUNC: auth_proxy_fast_path
00:55:43: AUTH-PROXY auth_proxy_find_conn_info :
    find srcaddr - 172.16.1.100, dstaddr - 1.1.1.1
```

```
        ip-srcaddr 172.16.1.100
        pak-srcaddr 0.0.0.0

00:55:43: AUTH-PROXY FUNC: auth_proxy_fast_path
00:55:43: AUTH-PROXY auth_proxy_find_conn_info :
     find srcaddr - 172.16.1.100, dstaddr - 1.1.1.1
        ip-srcaddr 172.16.1.100
        pak-srcaddr 0.0.0.0
Lab_B#
```

Clearing the Cache

And finally, you need to know the commands for maintaining and clearing the cache. Earlier, you set a timeout parameter for inactive sessions, so yes, these sessions will time out on their own eventually, but there may be times when you'll want to clear some or all of the connections and force users to re-authenticate. The following output includes the command-line help and an example of clearing all connections:

```
Lab_B#clear ip auth-proxy ?
  cache  Delete auth-proxy cache entries

Lab_B#clear ip auth-proxy cache ?
  *        Delete all auth-proxy cache
  A.B.C.D  Address to delete

Lab_B#clear ip auth-proxy cache *
Lab_B#
```

Okay, your users are now happily typing in usernames and passwords to access external resources, and you've risen above the challenge described at the beginning of this chapter—nice. Now all you have left to do is check each monitor and look under all the keyboards for those little stickies with usernames and passwords scribbled on them, and you're good to go!

Introduction to the Cisco IOS Firewall IDS

Let me make sure you've got the terminology specific to the *IOS Firewall IDS* straight. I mentioned that the *Intrusion Detection System (IDS)* functions on *signatures*. Well, each signature profiles a specific type of attack or potential problem.

For specific information on signatures and their descriptions, see www.cisco.com or your CSIDS Director documentation.

Let's begin with the main two types of signatures:

- Atomic
- Compound

Atomic signatures trigger based on a single packet, and *compound signatures* trigger based on multiple packets. Atomic signatures are much easier to support for the router because they can evaluate each packet independently. Compound signatures work by buffering previous packets for comparison against current packets to see if traffic trends match their signature, which means that they cost more memory.

Signature types are further defined as

- Info
- Attack

Info signatures are informational—they notice when an information-gathering activity such as a port scan is underway. *Attack signatures* represent malicious activities such as DoS attacks or inappropriate Application-layer calls.

So, you really end up with four types of signatures:

- Info atomic
- Info compound
- Attack atomic
- Attack compound

While you definitely want to defend your network against attacks, you don't need a nuclear device to kill a mouse in your house either; nothing's free, and every precaution you take costs you something. So the key issues to consider when deploying the IOS Firewall IDS are

- Memory usage
- Performance impact
- Signature coverage

I'm bringing this up because the IOS Firewall IDS can have a seriously significant impact on router memory and performance. Some signatures have the capability to monitor not just Layer 3 or Layer 4 functions, but application-level functioning as well. Realize that with such signatures enabled, each packet traversing the router must be inspected—potentially up to the Application layer—and decoding all those headers tends to guzzle resources. The more signatures that are enabled, the worse your mileage will be, and with signatures for 59 common attacks currently included with the IOS Firewall IDS—well, you can imagine the potential impact. And that's nothing. The CSIDS Sensor includes 300 signatures!

The IOS Firewall IDS is an in-line IDS and has a number of options available as reactions to signature matches, so it offers a good bit of flexibility for you in deciding what you want it to do when it sees a problem. Basically, you get three self-explanatory choices of action, which can also be used in combination with one another:

- Alarm
- Reset
- Drop

Alarm means to (surprise) generate an alarm to either a CSIDS Director or a Syslog server, reset sends a TCP reset to both session participants if the packet used TCP, and drop means to immediately drop the packet. Reset does not imply drop—it'll still forward the packet. For this reason, reset and drop are often used together.

With these preliminaries out of the way, let's add the IOS Firewall IDS configuration to your trusty Lab_B router.

Initializing Cisco IOS Firewall IDS

The first thing you'll do is configure the IOS Firewall IDS to notify the Syslog server at 172.16.1.200. Remember that you have the choice of notifying either a Syslog server or a CSIDS Director, and you can see that choice in the following output. Configure it to notify the Syslog server:

```
Lab_B#conf t
Lab_B(config)#ip audit notify ?
  log          Send events as syslog messages
  nr-director  Send events to the nr-director

Lab_B(config)#ip audit notify log
Lab_B(config)#logging 172.16.1.200
Lab_B(config)#^Z
Lab_B#
```

And yes—the no form of the `ip audit notify` command removes event notifications from the router.

Configuring, Disabling, and Excluding Signatures

Only the acutely disturbed like getting spam e-mail. The rest of us resolutely tolerate the pain and hope/pray/chant/scream for the day when every router in the world runs an IOS Firewall IDS with spam protection enabled!

That's right—wanna put that spam back in the can? Here's how! In the following example, you can see how to limit the number of SMTP destination addresses using the IOS Firewall IDS:

```
Lab_B#conf t
Lab_B(config)#ip audit ?
  attack    Specify default action for attack signatures
```

```
info      Specify default action for informational signatures
name      Specify an IDS audit rule
notify    Specify the notification mechanisms (nr-director or log) for the
          ⮑ alarms
po        Specify nr-director's PostOffice information (for sending events
          ⮑ to the nr-directors)
protected Specify addresses that are on a protected network
signature Add a policy to a signature
smtp      Specify SMTP Mail spam threshold

Lab_B(config)#ip audit smtp ?
 spam  Specify the threshold for spam signature
 <cr>

Lab_B(config)#ip audit smtp spam ?
 <1-65535>  Threshold of correspondents to trigger alarm

Lab_B(config)#ip audit smtp spam 100
Lab_B(config)#^Z
Lab_B#
```

By following the context-sensitive help, you can see the parameter definitions in the final ip audit smtp spam 100 command. The default maximum number of recipients is 250; here, you changed it to 100. If only everyone on the Internet would do this, we could realize the dream of a Spamless Internet Utopia! Way cool.

Disabling Signatures

As I said, running signatures noshes resources, so you probably don't want to run every signature available. It's likely you won't need them all anyway, so let's disable signature 3102 on the Lab_B router.

Signature 3102 is an attack compound signature. It's a Sendmail Invalid Sender signature that triggers when the From: field is a pipe (|) symbol.

Here's the command syntax for removing this signature:

```
Lab_B#conf t
Lab_B(config)#ip audit signature ?
 <1-65535>  Signature to be configured
```

```
Lab_B(config)#ip audit signature 3102 ?
  disable  Disable the specified signature
  list     Specify a standard access list to match
  <cr>
```

```
Lab_B(config)#ip audit signature 3102 disable
Lab_B(config)#^Z
Lab_B#
```

But what if you decide that you need the signature back? You use the no form of the command to restore it:

```
Lab_B#conf t
Lab_B(config)#no ip audit signature 3102 disable
Lab_B(config)#^Z
Lab_B#
```

Excluding Signatures by Host or Network

That was easy, but suppose you want to get really surgical and apply a signature *selectively* instead of completely disabling it? You can do that by using an ACL to pick and choose specific hosts and/ or networks that you don't want a given signature to apply to. Here's an example of how:

```
Lab_B#conf t
Lab_B(config)#ip audit signature 3102 ?
  disable  Disable the specified signature
  list     Specify a standard access list to match
  <cr>
```

```
Lab_B(config)#ip audit signature 3102 list 75
Lab_B(config)#access-list 75 deny host 172.16.1.50
Lab_B(config)#access-list 75 deny 192.160.1.0 0.0.0.255
Lab_B(config)#access-list 75 permit any
Lab_B(config)#^Z
Lab_B#
```

This kind of ACL will include deny statements for hosts or networks to exclude them from the signature. And it's got to end with a permit any command to indicate that all other networks and hosts should still be subjected to it.

Creating and Applying Audit Rules

Let's begin tackling this section by defining default actions for both info and attack signature types and then creating an *audit rule*. Then you'll apply the audit rule to an interface and specify a direction.

Setting Default Actions

Recall the three possible actions the IOS Firewall IDS can take when a signature is matched: alarm, reset, or drop. You can use any one or any combination of these actions, but the default is to alarm:

```
Lab_B#conf t
Lab_B(config)#ip audit ?
  attack     Specify default action for attack signatures
  info       Specify default action for informational signatures
  name       Specify an IDS audit rule
  notify     Specify the notification mechanisms (nr-director or log) for the
             ↳ alarms
  po         Specify nr-director's PostOffice information (for sending events to
             ↳ the nr-directors
  protected  Specify addresses that are on a protected network
  signature  Add a policy to a signature
  smtp       Specify SMTP Mail spam threshold

Lab_B(config)#ip audit info ?
  action  Specify the actions

Lab_B(config)#ip audit info action ?
  alarm  Generate events for matching signatures
  drop   Drop packets matching signatures
  reset  Reset the connection (if applicable)
Lab_B(config)#ip audit info action alarm
```

This takes care of the info signatures, leaving them set to the default action of alarm. To change the action for attack signatures to both drop and reset in addition to alarm, check out the following example:

```
Lab_B(config)#ip audit attack ?
  action  Specify the actions
```

```
Lab_B(config)#ip audit attack action ?
  alarm  Generate events for matching signatures
  drop   Drop packets matching signatures
  reset  Reset the connection (if applicable)

Lab_B(config)#ip audit attack action alarm ?
  drop   Drop packets matching signatures
  reset  Reset the connection (if applicable)
  <cr>

Lab_B(config)#ip audit attack action alarm drop ?
  reset  Reset the connection (if applicable)
  <cr>

Lab_B(config)#ip audit attack action alarm drop reset ?
  <cr>

Lab_B(config)#ip audit attack action alarm drop reset
Lab_B(config)#^Z
Lab_B#
```

Look at the context-sensitive help offered in the preceding example and note that after setting the alarm action, you still have the option to drop and/or reset. Also, the option <cr> becomes available only after you add all three actions.

Creating an Audit Rule

Okay, with the default settings out of the way, you're now ready to create an audit rule and give it a name. A little later, you'll apply it to an interface. As with the default actions you just ran through, you can specify a list of actions for the audit rule based on both info and action signatures. Replicating what you did with these two signatures previously and naming your audit rule **toddaudit**, this configuration on the Lab_B router will look like the following:

```
Lab_B#conf t
Lab_B(config)#ip audit name ?
  WORD  Name of audit specfication

Lab_B(config)#ip audit name toddaudit ?
  attack  All attack signatures
  info    All informational signatures
```

```
Lab_B(config)#ip audit name toddaudit info ?
  action  Specify action(s) for matching signatures
  list    Specify a standard access list
  <cr>

Lab_B(config)#ip audit name toddaudit info action ?
  alarm  Generate events for matching signatures
  drop   Drop packets matching signatures
  reset  Reset the connection (if applicable)

Lab_B(config)#ip audit name toddaudit info action alarm
Lab_B(config)#ip audit name toddaudit ?
  attack  All attack signatures
  info    All informational signatures

Lab_B(config)#ip audit name toddaudit attack ?
  action  Specify action(s) for matching signatures
  list    Specify a standard access list
  <cr>

Lab_B(config)#ip audit name toddaudit attack action ?
  alarm  Generate events for matching signatures
  drop   Drop packets matching signatures
  reset  Reset the connection (if applicable)

Lab_B(config)#ip audit name toddaudit attack action alarm ?
  drop   Drop packets matching signatures
  reset  Reset the connection (if applicable)
  <cr>

Lab_B(config)#ip audit name toddaudit attack action alarm drop ?
  reset  Reset the connection (if applicable)
  <cr>

Lab_B(config)#ip audit name toddaudit attack action alarm drop reset ?
  <cr>

Lab_B(config)#ip audit name toddaudit attack action alarm drop reset
Lab_B(config)#^Z
Lab_B#
```

Here again, the context-sensitive help demonstrates the ways you can further define the available parameters.

Applying the Audit Rule

Now that you've created the audit rule, it's time to apply it to an interface. The following example applies the toddaudit audit rule to the fast0/1 interface on the Lab_B router:

```
Lab_B#conf t
Lab_B(config)#int fast0/1
Lab_B(config-if)#ip audit ?
  WORD  Name of audit defined

Lab_B(config-if)#ip audit toddaudit ?
  in   Inbound audit
  out  Outbound audit

Lab_B(config-if)#ip audit toddaudit in ?
  <cr>

Lab_B(config-if)#ip audit toddaudit in
Lab_B(config-if)#^Z
Lab_B#
```

The direction in which you apply the audit rule makes a huge difference in the function of the IOS Firewall IDS. If you choose inbound on an interface, packets will be audited before any ACLs are applied. But if you opt for outbound, packets might be discarded by inbound ACLs on other interfaces before the IOS Firewall IDS has a chance to evaluate them. This could be bad—it means that precious alerts and resets could be totally missed because the IDS is never even given a chance to see these packets! Personally, I like the option of evaluating all packets that try to attack because it helps me refine my security policy and plug any holes. That's why you see the IOS Firewall IDS applied inbound on the Lab_B router in the preceding example.

With everything in place so far, it's now time to define which network is to be protected by the router. Here's the ip audit command on the Lab_B router:

```
Lab_B#conf t
Lab_B(config)#ip audit po protected 172.16.1.1 to 172.16.1.254
Lab_B(config-if)#^Z
Lab_B#
```

Realize that once the audit rule is in place, several—even many—signatures may be scrutinizing packets. The different modules are evaluated in the following order:

1. IP

2. ICMP (if applicable)

3. TCP or UDP

4. Application-level protocol

If a signature match is made, the appropriate action will be taken.

Verifying the Configuration

Okay, it's not a perfect world, and not everything runs smoothly the first time, right? So as you might expect, there are several show commands available to you for verifying and troubleshooting the IOS Firewall IDS. Here's the output from the most useful show command:

```
Lab_B#show ip audit ?
  all            IDS all available information
  configuration  IDS configuration
  interfaces     IDS interfaces
  name           IDS name
  sessions       IDS sessions
  statistics     IDS statistics


Lab_B#show ip audit statistics
Interfaces configured for audit 1
Session creations since subsystem startup or last reset 0
Current session counts (estab/half-open/terminating) [0:0:0]
Maxever session counts (estab/half-open/terminating) [0:0:0]
Last session created never
Last statistic reset never

Post Office is not enabled - No connections are active


Lab_B#show ip audit configuration
Event notification through syslog is enabled
Event notification through Net Director is disabled
Default action(s) for info signatures is alarm
Default action(s) for attack signatures is alarm drop reset
Default threshold of recipients for spam signature is 100
Signature 3102 list 75
PostOffice:HostID:0 OrgID:0 Msg dropped:0
     :Curr Event Buf Size:0  Configured:100
Post Office is not enabled - No connections are active
Audit Rule Configuration
```

```
Audit name toddaudit
    info actions alarm
    attack actions alarm drop reset

Lab_B#show ip audit interface
Interface Configuration
 Interface FastEthernet0/1
  Inbound IDS audit rule is toddaudit
    info actions alarm
    attack actions alarm drop reset
  Outgoing IDS audit rule is not set
Lab_B#
```

You're right! The preceding statistics indicate a largely idle network, but the configuration and interface output points to the work you've done so far and checks out. There are also several **debug** command options available:

```
Lab_B#debug ip audit ?
    detailed         Audit Detailed debug records
    ftp-cmd          Audit FTP commands and responses
    ftp-token        Audit FTP tokens
    function-trace   Audit function trace
    icmp             Audit ICMP packets
    ip               Audit IP packets
    object-creation  Audit Object Creations
    object-deletion  Audit Object Deletions
    rpc              Audit RPC
    smtp             Audit SMTP
    tcp              Audit TCP
    tftp             Audit TFTP
    timers           Audit Timer related events
    udp              Audit UDP

Lab_B#
```

Stopping the IOS Firewall IDS

Sometimes you just gotta pull the plug, and in order to pull it, you have to know where it is. If you really need to kill the IOS Firewall IDS lights, there are several steps to take. First, let's start with the show ip audit configuration screen again to verify that the configuration is still in place:

```
Lab_B#show ip audit configuration
Event notification through syslog is enabled
Event notification through Net Director is disabled
Default action(s) for info signatures is alarm
Default action(s) for attack signatures is alarm drop reset
Default threshold of recipients for spam signature is 100
Signature 3102 list 75
PostOffice:HostID:0 OrgID:0 Msg dropped:0
     :Curr Event Buf Size:0  Configured:100
Post Office is not enabled - No connections are active
Audit Rule Configuration
 Audit name toddaudit
    info actions alarm
    attack actions alarm drop reset
```

Yup—it's there.

Next, use the clear ip audit configuration command to disable IDS, remove all IDS configuration, and release all dynamic resources:

```
Lab_B#clear ip audit configuration
```

And finally (as always), you've got to verify that it did what it was supposed to do, so look at the output from the show ip audit configuration command:

```
Lab_B#show ip audit configuration
Event notification through syslog is enabled
Event notification through Net Director is disabled
Default action(s) for info signatures is alarm
Default action(s) for attack signatures is alarm
Default threshold of recipients for spam signature is 250
PostOffice:HostID:0 OrgID:0 Msg dropped:0
     :Curr Event Buf Size:0  Configured:100
Post Office is not enabled - No connections are active
Lab_B#
```

It's good to go—all values have been reset to the defaults!

Summary

The IOS Firewall was introduced in Chapter 5, "Context-Based Access Control Configuration," which explained CBAC, but this chapter covered two of its critically important additional capabilities:

- Authentication Proxy
- Intrusion Detection System (IDS)

The wonderful new IOS Firewall Authentication Proxy bestows upon the networking world the ability to control user access based on *users* rather than on IP addresses or other device information! In the glowing IOS Firewall world, users are forced to authenticate before accessing external resources. Their now-personalized access policies are being retrieved from centralized AAA servers and following them wherever they roam on the network.

Add to the Authentication Proxy the IOS Firewall IDS—a capable guard with the ability to alert, reset, and drop when security signatures are matched—and you can select which signatures to deactivate, or you can selectively apply signatures using ACLs.

Exam Essentials

Remember the two types of AAA servers you can use for the IOS Authentication Proxy. TACACS+ and RADIUS are the two types of AAA servers you can use for Authentication Proxy.

Know the default idle time for the IOS Firewall Authentication Proxy. The default idle time for the Authentication Proxy is 60 minutes.

Know the different types of signatures for the IOS Firewall IDS. The four types of signatures are info atomic, info compound, attack atomic, and attack compound.

Be familiar with the *show* and *debug* commands for both the IOS Firewall Authentication Proxy and the IOS Firewall IDS. For the IOS Firewall Authentication Proxy, the commands are show ip auth-proxy and debug ip auth-proxy. For the IOS Firewall IDS, the commands are show ip audit and debug ip audit.

Remember the three actions that the IOS Firewall IDS can take when a signature is matched. The three actions the IOS Firewall IDS can take when a signature is matched are alert, reset, and drop.

Key Terms

Before you take the exam, be certain you are familiar with the following terms:

atomic signatures

attack signatures

audit rule

compound signatures

info signatures

Intrusion Detection System (IDS)

IOS Firewall Authentication Proxy

IOS Firewall IDS

signatures

Commands Used in This Chapter

Here is the list of commands used in this chapter:

Command	Meaning
(config)#`aaa new-model`	Prepares the router for AAA configuration.
(config)#`aaa authentication login default group tacacs+`	Enables AAA authentication using TACACS+.
(config)#`aaa authorization auth-proxy default group tacacs+`	Enables AAA authorization using TACACS+.
(config)#`tacacs-server host` *ip-address*	Specifies the TACACS+ server at the designated IP address.
(config)#`tacacs-server key` *key-name*	Specifies the TACACS+ server key.
(config)#`ip http server`	Enables the router's HTTP server.
(config)#`ip http server authentication aaa`	Enables AAA authentication for HTTP.
(config)#`ip auth-proxy auth-cache-time` *time*	Sets the default idle timeout to the specified interval (in minutes).
(config)#`ip auth-proxy name` *name* `http`	Creates an Authentication Proxy rule with the specified name.
(config)#`clear ip auth-proxy cache *`	Clears all Authentication Proxy cache entries.

Command	Meaning
`(config)#ip audit notify log`	Configures the IOS Firewall IDS to log to the Syslog server.
`(config)#logging ip-address`	Specifies the Syslog server at the designated IP address.
`(config)#ip audit signature signature disable`	Disables the specified IDS signature; there's no form to enable.
`(config)#ip audit signature signature list list`	Excludes hosts and networks in the specified list from the designated signature.
`(config)#ip audit info action alarm`	Sets the default action for info to alarm.
`(config)#ip audit attack action alarm drop reset`	Sets the default action for attack to alarm, drop, and reset.
`(config)#ip audit name name info action alarm`	Sets the action for the specified audit rule type info to alarm.
`(config)#ip audit name name attack action alarm drop reset`	Sets the action for the specified audit rule type attack to alarm, drop, and reset.
`(config)#ip audit po protected ip-address to ip-address`	Defines the protected network using the specified IP addresses.

Written Lab

This section asks you 10 write-in-the-answer questions to help you understand the technology that you need to know in order to pass the SECUR exam.

1. List three TACACS+ servers supported by the IOS Firewall Authentication Proxy.

2. What are the three issues to consider when implementing the IOS Firewall IDS?

3. What is the command that clears the cache of all entries when running the IOS Firewall Authorization Proxy?

4. What is the order in which modules are evaluated when a packet is evaluated by the IOS Firewall IDS?

5. What is the command that enables AAA on the router?

6. What is the command to change the default idle time for the IOS Firewall Authentication Proxy to 30 minutes?

7. What actions can the IOS Firewall IDS take when a signature is matched?

8. List four RADIUS servers supported by the IOS Firewall Authentication Proxy.

9. List the four signature-type combinations in the IOS Firewall IDS.

10. What is the correct command to specify a TACACS+ server on a router?

Review Questions

1. Which of the following are issues to consider when implementing the IOS Firewall IDS? (Choose all that apply.)

   A. Memory usage

   B. Signature coverage

   C. User address space

   D. TACACS+ server type

2. In the IOS Firewall IDS, what type of signature triggers on a single packet?

   A. Atomic

   B. Compound

   C. Info

   D. Attack

3. What is the default action for attack signatures in the IOS Firewall IDS?

   A. Alert

   B. Reset

   C. Drop

   D. Reset and drop

   E. Alert, reset, and drop

4. In the IOS Firewall IDS, which types of signatures are informative in nature?

   A. Atomic

   B. Compound

   C. Info

   D. Attack

5. What is the default idle timeout period on the IOS Firewall Authentication proxy?

   A. 60 seconds

   B. 60 minutes

   C. 30 seconds

   D. 30 minutes

   E. 90 seconds

   F. 90 minutes

6. When packets enter an IOS Firewall IDS, which module is evaluated first?

    A. ICMP

    B. IP

    C. TCP/UDP

    D. Application-level protocol

7. When packets enter an IOS Firewall IDS, which module is evaluated last?

    A. ICMP

    B. IP

    C. TCP/UDP

    D. Application-level protocol

8. What types of RADIUS servers are supported by the IOS Firewall Authentication Proxy? (Choose all that apply.)

    A. Active Directory

    B. CiscoSecure ACS for Unix

    C. NDS

    D. Freeware TACACS+

    E. Lucent

    F. CiscoSecure ACS for Windows NT/2000

9. Which of the following best describes the function of the IOS Firewall Authentication Proxy?

    A. Provides dynamic per-user authentication and authorization via TACACS+ and/or RADIUS

    B. Provides dynamic per-user authentication and authorization via CiscoSecure ACS

    C. Provides dynamic per-user authentication via TACACS+ and/or RADIUS

    D. Provides dynamic per-user authorization via TACACS+ and/or RADIUS

    E. Provides dynamic per-user authentication via CiscoSecure ACS

10. Which command tells a router that a Syslog server is available at 10.1.1.2?

    A. `syslog-server 10.1.1.2`

    B. `logging 10.1.1.2`

    C. `ip logging 10.1.1.2`

    D. `ip syslog 10.1.1.2`

11. In the IOS Firewall IDS, which types of signatures indicate a potentially malicious problem?

   A. Atomic

   B. Compound

   C. Info

   D. Attack

12. When configuring the AAA server for the IOS Firewall Authentication Proxy, what privilege level must you set at the end of each list?

   A. 1

   B. 3

   C. 10

   D. 15

   E. *

13. Which TACACS+ servers are supported by the IOS Firewall Authentication Proxy? (Choose all that apply.)

   A. Active Directory

   B. CiscoSecure ACS for Unix

   C. NDS

   D. Freeware TACACS+

   E. Lucent

   F. CiscoSecure ACS for Windows NT/2000

14. Which command would remove all AAA processing from the router?

   A. `clear aaa *`

   B. `aaa new-model`

   C. `clear ip auth-proxy cache *`

   D. `no aaa new-model`

   E. `no clear ip auth-proxy cache *`

15. When a signature in the IOS Firewall IDS matches a packet or packets, which of the following are valid actions? (Choose all that apply.)

   A. Log

   B. Alarm

   C. Activate CBAC

   D. Reset

   E. Drop

16. Which of the following commands will clear all entries of the cache on the IOS Firewall Authentication Proxy?

   A. `clear ip auth-proxy cache all`

   B. `clear ip auth proxy cache`

   C. `clear ip auth-proxy cache *`

   D. `clear ip cache`

   E. `clear auth-proxy cache *`

17. What is the default action for info signatures in the IOS Firewall IDS?

   A. Alert

   B. Reset

   C. Drop

   D. Reset and drop

   E. Alert, reset, and drop

18. In the IOS Firewall IDS, which type of signature matches based on multiple packets?

   A. Atomic

   B. Compound

   C. Info

   D. Attack

19. Which of the following commands successfully changes the default idle timeout of the IOS Firewall Authentication Proxy?

   A. `ip auth-proxy 30`

   B. `ip auth-proxy auth-cache-time 60`

   C. `ip auth-proxy idle-timeout 30`

   D. `ip auth-proxy auth-cache-time 30`

   E. `ip auth-proxy idle-timeout 60`

20. Which command halts all IOS Firewall IDS functions?

   A. `no aaa new-model`

   B. `clear ip audit-configuration`

   C. `no ip audit configuration`

   D. `clear ip audit configuration`

Hands-On Labs

This section will have you configure a Cisco 2600 router with IOS Firewall Authentication Proxy and IDS. If you don't have a Cisco router, please check www.routersim.com for a SECUR router simulator.

The labs covered in this chapter include

- Lab 6.1: Enabling the IOS Firewall Authentication Proxy
- Lab 6.2: Enabling the IOS Firewall IDS

Lab 6.1: Enabling the IOS Firewall Authentication Proxy

This lab will review the basic commands to set up the IOS Firewall Authentication Proxy. Please note that this lab assumes that you have the Secure ACS configured at 10.1.1.2 as outlined in the text.

1. Connect to your router and press Enter.
2. Type the command **enable**.
3. Type the following to enable the IOS firewall authentication proxy:

```
Lab_B#conf t
Lab_B(config)#aaa new-model
Lab_B(config)#aaa authentication login default group tacacs+
Lab_B(config)#aaa authorization auth-proxy default group tacacs+
Lab_B(config)#tacacs-server host 10.1.1.2
Lab_B(config)#tacacs-server key test
Lab_B(config)#access-list 155 permit tcp host 10.1.1.2 eq tacacs host
    ↳ 10.1.1.1
Lab_B(config)#access-list 155 deny ip any any
Lab_B(config)#ip http server
Lab_B(config)#ip http authentication aaa
Lab_B(config)#ip auth-proxy name aptest http
Lab_B(config)#int fast0/0
Lab_B(config-if)#ip access-group 155 in
Lab_B(config-if)#ip auth-proxy aptest
Lab_B(config-if)#^Z
Lab_B#
```

Lab 6.2: Enabling the IOS Firewall IDS

This lab will have you configure the IOS Firewall IDS. This lab assumes you have a Syslog server configured at 10.1.1.3.

1. Connect to your router and press Enter.

2. Type the command **enable**.

3. Type the following to enable the IOS firewall IDS:

```
Lab_B#conf t
Lab_B(config)#ip audit notify log
Lab_B(config)#logging 10.1.1.3
Lab_B(config)#ip audit info action alarm
Lab_B(config)#ip audit attack action alarm drop reset
Lab_B(config)#ip audit name idstest info action alarm
Lab_B(config)#ip audit name idstest attack action alarm drop reset
Lab_B(config)#ip audit po protected 10.1.1.1 to 10.255.255.255
Lab_B(config)#int fast0/1
Lab_B(config-if)#ip audit idstest in
Lab_B(config-if)#^Z
Lab_B#
```

Answers to Written Lab

1. The three TACACS+ servers supported by the IOS Firewall Authentication Proxy are CSACS for Windows NT/2000, CSACS for UNIX, and freeware TACACS+.

2. Memory usage, performance impact, and signature coverage are issues you should consider when implementing the IOS Firewall IDS.

3. The command `clear ip auth-proxy cache` * clears the cache of all entries when running the IOS Firewall Authorization Proxy.

4. The order in which modules are evaluated when a packet is evaluated by the IOS Firewall IDS is IP, ICMP, TCP/UDP, and application-level protocol.

5. The command `aaa new-model` enables AAA on the router.

6. To change the default idle time for the IOS Firewall Authentication Proxy to 30 minutes, use the command `ip auth-proxy auth-cache-time 30`.

7. Alarm, reset, and drop are the actions that the IOS Firewall IDS can take when a signature is matched.

8. The four RADIUS servers supported by the IOS Firewall Authentication Proxy are CSACS for Windows NT/2000, CSACS for UNIX, Lucent, and other standard RADIUS servers.

9. Info atomic, info compound, attack atomic, and attack compound are the four signature-type combinations in the IOS Firewall IOS.

10. To specify a TACACS+ server on a router, use the `tacacs-server host` *ip-address* command.

Answers to Review Questions

1. A, B.   Both memory usage and signature coverage are issues to consider when planning an IOS Firewall IDS implementation. Performance impact was the third item mentioned in the text.

2. A.   Atomic signatures trigger based on a single packet.

3. A.   The default action for attack signatures is to alert.

4. C.   Info signatures are informative in nature.

5. B.   The default idle timeout period for the IOS Authentication Proxy is 60 minutes.

6. B.   IP is evaluated first when packets enter an IOS Firewall IDS.

7. D.   The application-level protocol is evaluated last when packets enter an IOS Firewall IDS.

8. B, E, F.   There are three supported RADIUS servers: CSACS for NT/200, CSACS for Unix, and the Lucent server.

9. A.   The IOS Firewall Authentication Proxy provides dynamic per-user authentication and authorization via TACACS+ and/or RADIUS. While CiscoSecure ACS is a valid server, it is not the only server.

10. B.   The correct command to tell a router that a Syslog server is available is `logging 10.1.1.2`.

11. D.   Attack signatures indicate malicious patterns of traffic.

12. D.   The list must end by setting the privilege level to 15.

13. B, D, F.   The three supported TACACS+ servers are CSACS for NT/2000, CSACS for Unix, and freeware TACACS+ servers.

14. D.   The `no aaa new-model` command is the correct choice to remove all AAA processing from the router.

15. B, D, E.   The three actions that IOS Firewall IDS can take are to alarm, drop, and reset.

16. C.   The `clear ip auth-proxy cache` * command is the correct choice.

17. A.   The default action for info signatures is to alert.

18. B.   Compound signatures evaluate multiple packets.

19. D.   The command `ip auth-proxy auth-cache-time` 30 is the correct syntax to change the default idle timer. While the syntax of answer B is also correct, 60 minutes is the default, and thus answer B will not change the default timeout value.

20. D.   The `clear ip audit configuration` command is entered in global configuration mode.

Chapter 7

Understanding Cisco IOS IPSec Support

THE FOLLOWING SECUR EXAM TOPICS ARE COVERED IN THIS CHAPTER:

- ✓ Understanding Cisco IOS IPSec technologies
- ✓ Using key exchange mechanisms
- ✓ Understanding the Cisco IOS Cryptosystem
- ✓ Establishing IPSec support in Cisco systems products
- ✓ Using tunneling protocols
- ✓ Using virtual private networks

Technology changes things—the way you live, work, communicate—your very needs. The standard 9-to-5 job, with everyone at one location, needed a type of network that is now for the most part obsolete because of current trends such as telecommuting and video conferencing. These business requirements have exponentially increased the demand for users to access secure communications over public networks. Companies now need communications technology such as distributed and virtual private networks to stay competitive—if they want to stay in business now and in the future, that is!

This chapter introduces you to the concept of virtual private networks and describes the solutions you need to meet your company's off-site network access needs. You'll get an in-depth look at how these networks utilize IP Security (IPSec) to provide secure communications over a public network such as the Internet. The chapter concludes with a discussion of the devices that Cisco provides to implement these solutions and an introduction to the Cisco IOS Cryptosystem.

Okay, grab a double latte. This chapter is *very* theory intensive. If you feel lost after reading a section, take a moment to go back and review the material. Don't rush or skim over sections you don't really understand. You need a thorough knowledge of this content to provide the best service to your employer or clients.

Chapter 8, "Cisco IOS IPSec Pre-Shared Keys and Certificate Authority Support," will demonstrate how to implement the solutions discussed in this chapter. So, let's begin the introduction to virtual private networks.

What is a Virtual Private Network?

I'd be pretty willing to bet you've heard the term VPN more than once before. Maybe you even know what one is, but just in case you don't, a *virtual private network (VPN)* allows for the creation of private networks across the Internet, enabling privacy and tunneling of non–TCP/IP protocols. VPNs are used daily to give remote users and disjointed networks connectivity over a public medium such as the Internet instead of using more expensive permanent means.

The types of VPNs are named based on the role they play in a business environment. There are three different categories of VPNs:

Remote access VPNs   *Remote access VPNs* allow remote users like telecommuters to securely access the corporate network whenever and from wherever they need to.

Site-to-site VPNs   A *site-to-site VPN*, also called an *intranet VPN*, allows a company to connect its remote sites to the corporate backbone securely over a public medium such as the Internet instead of requiring more expensive WAN connections like Frame Relay.

Extranet VPNs   *Extranet VPNs* allow an organization's suppliers, partners, and customers to be connected to the corporate network in a limited way for business-to-business (B2B) communications.

Now you're interested, huh? And because VPNs are inexpensive and secure, I'm guessing you're really jonesing to find out how VPNs are created, right? Well, there's more than one way to bring a VPN into being. The first approach uses IPSec to create authentication and encryption services between endpoints on an IP network. The second way is accomplished via tunneling protocols, allowing you to establish a tunnel between endpoints on a network. The tunnel itself is a means for data or protocols to be encapsulated inside another protocol—clean!

I'm going to go over the first way to create a VPN (using IPSec) shortly, but first, I really want to describe four of the most common tunneling protocols in use:

Layer 2 Forwarding (L2F)   *Layer 2 Forwarding (L2F)* is a Cisco Proprietary tunneling protocol. It was Cisco's initial tunneling protocol, and it was created for virtual private dial-up networks (VPDNs). VPDNs allow a device to use a dial-up connection to create a secure connection to a corporate network. L2F was later replaced by Layer 2 Tunneling Protocol (L2TP), which is backward compatible with L2F.

Point-to-Point Tunneling Protocol (PPTP)   *Point-to-Point Tunneling Protocol (PPTP)* was created by Microsoft to allow the secure transfer of data from remote networks to the corporate network.

Layer 2 Tunneling Protocol (L2TP)   *Layer 2 Tunneling Protocol (L2TP)* was created by Cisco and Microsoft to replace L2F and PPTP. L2TP merged the capabilities of both L2F and PPTP into one tunneling protocol.

Generic routing encapsulation (GRE)   *Generic routing encapsulation (GRE)* is another Cisco Proprietary tunneling protocol. It forms virtual point-to-point links, allowing for a variety of protocols to be encapsulated in IP tunnels.

Now that you're clear on exactly what a VPN is and the various types of VPNs available, it's time to dive into IPSec.

Introduction to Cisco IOS IPSec

Here's the $64 question: What is *IP Security (IPSec)*? No, it doesn't have anything to do with an airport screener. Simply put, IPSec is an industry-wide standard suite of protocols and algorithms that allows for secure data transmission over an IP-based network, and it functions at Layer 3 (the Network layer) of the OSI model.

Did you notice I said, "IP-based networks?" That's really important, because by itself, IPSec can't be used to encrypt non–IP traffic. This means that if you run into a situation where you have to encrypt non–IP traffic, you'll need to create a GRE tunnel for it and then use IPSec to encrypt that tunnel.

IPSec runs by utilizing transforms such as protocols and algorithms that give IPSec its direction. There are five steps to IPSec operation. This section will discuss the IPSec transforms and how IPSec works.

 Real World Scenario

IPSec Support in Cisco Systems Products

Numerous Cisco devices can be utilized in the creation of IPSec VPNs. Cisco routers can be used to create router-to-router VPN solutions and client VPN solutions. When attempting to configure IPSec VPNs on routers, you should really be sure you have the correct feature set. The CiscoSecure VPN Concentrator series can be used for remote-user VPN access to your network. The PIX Firewall, discussed in the Appendix, "Introduction to the PIX Firewall," can be used as an endpoint for VPN connections and provide you with the protection of a firewall.

IPSec Transforms

An *IPSec transform* specifies a single security protocol with its corresponding security algorithm, and without these transforms, IPSec wouldn't be able to give you its glorious encryption technologies. It's important to be familiar with these technologies, so let me take a second to define the security protocols and briefly introduce the supporting encryption and hashing algorithms that IPSec relies on.

Security Protocols

The two primary security protocols used by IPSec are *Authentication Header (AH)* and *Encapsulating Security Payload (ESP)*.

Authentication Header (AH)

The AH protocol provides authentication for the data and IP header of a packet using a one-way hash for packet authentication. It works like this: The sender generates a one-way hash, and then the receiver generates the same one-way hash. If the packet has changed in any way, it won't be authenticated, and so, it is dropped. Basically, IPSec relies on AH to guarantee authenticity. AH checks the entire packet, but it doesn't offer any encryption services.

Encapsulating Security Payload (ESP)

No, ESP won't tell you when the NASDAQ's gonna bounce back in spades. But ESP does provide confidentiality, data origin authentication, connectionless integrity, anti-replay service, and limited traffic-flow confidentiality by defeating traffic-flow analysis. Which is almost as good!

There are four components of ESP:

Confidentiality   Confidentiality is provided through the use of symmetric encryption algorithms such as DES or 3DES. Confidentiality can be selected separately from all other services, but the confidentiality selected must be the same on all endpoints of your VPN.

Data origin authentication and connectionless integrity Data origin authentication and connectionless integrity are joint services offered as an option in conjunction with the likewise optional confidentiality.

Anti-replay service You can only use the anti-replay service if data origin authentication is selected. Anti-replay election is based on the receiver, meaning that the service is effective only if the receiver checks the sequence number. In case you were wondering, a replay attack occurs when an attacker snags a copy of an authenticated packet and later transmits it to the intended destination. When the duplicate, authenticated IP packet gets to the destination, it can disrupt services or cause other ugly consequences. The Sequence Number field is designed to foil this type of attack.

Traffic flow For traffic flow confidentiality to work, you have to have tunnel mode selected. Tunnel mode is most effective if it's implemented at a security gateway where tons of traffic amass—a condition that can mask the true source-destination patterns of bad guys trying to breach your network's security.

 Although both confidentiality and authentication are optional, at least one of them must be selected.

Encryption and Hashing Algorithms

Encryption algorithms are used to encrypt and decrypt data, and there's a large number of both encryption and hashing algorithms available for IPSec. A *hashing algorithm* is used to create a (surprise) *hash*—a one-way encryption algorithm that takes an input message of random length and creates a fixed-length output message.

Cisco actually uses a hash variant known as *Hash-Based Message Authentication Code (HMAC)*, which provides an extra level of hashing. This section will discuss Data Encryption Standard (DES), Triple DES, and some variations on the HMAC algorithms.

Data Encryption Standard (DES)

Data Encryption Standard (DES) is known as a symmetric key algorithm, meaning that a single key is used to encrypt and decrypt data. DES utilizes cipher block chaining (CBC) to connect a series of cipher blocks for encrypting data. It uses a 64-bit fixed-length cipher block and a 56-bit key, stored as a 64-bit (eight-octet) quantity with the least significant bit of each octet used as a parity bit. The key used by DES is the same on both sides of the connection. DES functions as follows:

1. The data to be encrypted arrives at the device.
2. DES uses its 56-bit key to encrypt the data.
3. The encrypted data is transmitted to its destination.
4. The encrypted data is received by the decrypting device.
5. The decrypting device uses its 56-bit DES key to decrypt the data.

Triple DES (3DES)

Do you need more security muscle? For a bigger bouncer, try *Triple DES (3DES)*. It's a much beefier version of DES; the main difference is in how traffic encryption takes place. Instead of encrypting data only once before sending it, 3DES does the following:

1. 3DES encrypts the traffic using one 56-bit key.
2. 3DES then decrypts the traffic using another 56-bit key.
3. 3DES then encrypts the traffic once more with another 56-bit key and finally sends the traffic to its destination.

So basically, it's the number of times that 3DES encrypts and decrypts traffic before sending it that makes it such a force, and so much stronger than DES.

Hash-Based Message Authentication Code-Message Digest 5 (HMAC-MD5)

Hash-Based Message Authentication Code-Message Digest 5 (HMAC-MD5), also known as HMAC-MD5-96, is a hashing algorithm that creates a 128-bit secret key. It works by producing a 128-bit authentication value that is truncated using the first 96 bits—hence the name HMAC-MD5-96. This truncated value is then inserted into the authenticator field of AH or ESP and sent to the peer. The peer then computes its own 128-bit authentication value and compares the first 96 bits of it to the truncated value stored in the authenticator field of the packet it just received. If the values match, the device is authenticated.

Hash-Based Message Authentication Code-Secure Hash Algorithm-1 (HMAC-SHA-1)

Hash-Based Message Authentication Code-Secure Hash Algorithm-1 (HMAC-SHA-1), also known as HMAC-SHA-1-96, is HMAC-MD5's big brother. It's a stronger hashing algorithm that creates a 160-bit authenticator value, which is truncated at 96 bits. It works similarly to HMAC-MD5 in that the truncated value is then stored in the AH or ESP authenticator field of the packet and sent to the peer. The peer then computes its own 160-bit authenticator value and compares the first 96 bits of it to the truncated value stored in the authenticator field of the packet it has just received. If the values match, the device is authenticated.

IPSec Operation

I'll be going into greater detail on all the components of IPSec in a bit, but for now, understand that the operation of IPSec can be broken down into five steps:

1. IPSec process initiation
2. IKE phase 1
3. IKE phase 2
4. Data transfer
5. IPSec tunnel termination

IPSec Process Initiation

IPSec process initiation does pretty much what the name implies—it initiates the operation of IPSec. It works a lot like making a phone call. First, you decide *who* you're going to call, and then you look up that person's *phone number*. With IPSec, *who* is the traffic that needs to be encrypted, and the *phone number* is where that traffic encryption needs to take place. Once those decisions have been made, a policy specifying the traffic to encrypt needs to be manually created and then applied to the devices that will form the VPN and encrypt the traffic. These devices are known as *IPSec peers*. So what happens after the policy has been implemented? The answer is simple—when traffic that needs to be encrypted is detected on one of the IPSec peers, IKE phase 1 negotiation begins.

IKE Phase 1

Right now, all you need to know about IKE (Internet Key Exchange) is that it's used to form the IPSec encrypted tunnel. I'll discuss IKE in much more detail later in this chapter. *IKE phase 1* is the term used to describe the process of determining your IKE policy. During this second step of IPSec operation, the goal is to authenticate IPSec peers and to form the IKE tunnel.

What's actually happening in IKE phase 1? Well, first, IKE *security associations (SAs)* are negotiated on the IPSec peers. The IKE SAs are used to specify the type of peer authentication and which Diffie-Hellman (DH) group to use.

Next, an authenticated Diffie-Hellman Key Agreement (discussed later in this chapter) of matching keys is used to authenticate and protect the identities of IPSec peers. And finally, the IKE tunnel is formed for IKE phase 2 negotiation.

It's also worth mentioning that IKE can use either *main mode* or *aggressive mode* for phase 1 negotiation:

Main mode   In main mode, IKE uses three two-way handshakes for phase 1 negotiation:

1. During the first exchange, the security algorithms IKE will use are decided on for the IKE SAs. The security algorithms are specified in the IKE policy that has been configured on the IPSec peers. (Chapter 8 discusses the configuration of IKE policies.)

2. During the second exchange, the Diffie-Hellman Key Agreement is used to generate the shared keying information, which is then used to generate the shared secret keys. Finally, the shared secret keys are used to validate the IPSec peers' identities.

3. During the third exchange, the peer device's identity is verified.

Aggressive mode   Aggressive mode is faster than main mode because it uses only the following two exchanges:

1. During the first exchange, aggressive mode performs both steps 1 and 2 of main mode.

2. During the second exchange, the receiving peer sends back information that is needed to complete the exchange. Finally, the initiator sends back a confirmation.

As you can see, IPSec peer authentication is a priority of IKE phase 1. The completion of IKE phase 1 signals the beginning of the next step, IKE phase 2.

IKE Phase 2

The third step in the IPSec operation is called *IKE phase 2*, which is the process of creating the IPSec policy. The final outcome of IKE phase 2 is the negotiation of IPSec SAs. An IPSec SA is a unidirectional connection established between IPSec peers and is used to determine the IPSec services that will be offered. To say this another way, the IPSec SA specifies the type of encryption and IPSec services that are offered in one direction. Because an IPSec SA is unidirectional, two SAs must be set up: one from the sender to the receiver and one from the receiver to the sender. The IPSec SAs operate over the secure IKE tunnel that was set up in IKE phase 1.

Figure 7.1 illustrates two devices setting up SAs with one another.

FIGURE 7.1 Two devices setting up security associations

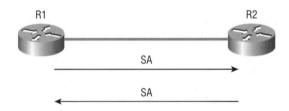

Let me explain the process illustrated in Figure 7.1:

1. R1 sends an SA to R2.

2. R2 accepts the SA.

3. R2 sends the SA back to R1.

4. Two unidirectional SAs are set up.

It's important to remember that a device has an SA for every IPSec device it peers with. These SAs are stored in the devices' security association database (SAD) and are indexed by their *Security Parameter Index (SPI)*.

The SPI is a unique identification mechanism for each SA on a device. When an IPSec packet arrives, the device checks the SPI contained in the packet and compares the SPI in the packet to the SPIs in the device's SAD to determine which IPSec policy is in effect.

Also, make note of the fact that each SA has a unique triple identity consisting of an SPI, an IP destination address, and a security protocol (AH or ESP) identifier. The completion of this step is marked by the formation of an IPSec tunnel. The IPSec tunnel is then used to transport the encrypted traffic.

Data Transfer

Finally, we've reached the step in which traffic will begin to flow. Once the IPSec SAs have been negotiated and the IPSec tunnel has been formed, traffic can begin passing over the IPSec tunnel. The traffic that's allowed to enter the IPSec tunnel is encrypted and decrypted based on the information contained within the IPSec SA.

IPSec Tunnel Termination

IPSec tunnel termination can occur for one of two reasons: it is deleted or the IPSec SA lifetime expires. When an IPSec SA lifetime expires, IKE phase 2 negotiation begins again and, if needed, so does IKE phase 1 negotiation.

Well, it's about time you started learning about the different IPSec components, but before moving on, you might want to go back and review anything that's still unclear. It would be pretty sweet if I could show you how to create a tunnel between this book and your brain so that all this data could just flow into it without studying, huh? Maybe someday, but for now you'll have to deal with the grind. So take a break if you need to, and then let's get into IPSec components.

The Components of IPSec

All rested up? Good—let's get back to it then! You've just learned about how IPSec operates and about IKE. With that foundation in place, you're ready to take a detailed look at the encapsulations that make IPSec possible and at the IKE components. So without further ado, let's get down to the skinny on both IPSec encapsulation and IKE!

IPSec Encapsulation

IPSec handles packet encapsulation through the use of ESP and/or AH. ESP encrypts the payload of a packet, whereas AH provides protection to the entire datagram by embedding the header in the data and verifying the integrity of the IP datagram.

IPSec can encapsulate data by one of two methods: transport mode or tunnel mode.

Transport Mode Encapsulation

Transport mode encapsulation uses the original IP header and inserts the header for ESP and/or AH. In transport mode, the original IP header must contain a routable IP address.

Figure 7.2 illustrates the format of a packet using ESP in transport mode.

FIGURE 7.2   Packet format using ESP in transport mode

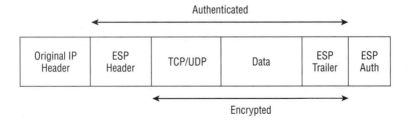

Figure 7.3 illustrates the format of a packet using AH in transport mode.

FIGURE 7.3 Packet format using AH in transport mode

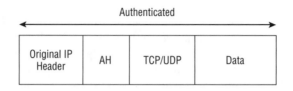

Figure 7.4 illustrates the format of a packet using ESP and AH in transport mode.

FIGURE 7.4 Packet format using ESP and AH in transport mode

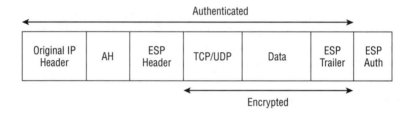

Great! With transport mode down, let's look at tunnel mode.

Tunnel Mode Encapsulation

When you use *tunnel mode* encapsulation, the original IP header doesn't transport the packet. Instead, a new IP header is created using the IP addresses of the IPSec peers as the source and destination of the packet. This mode works great when you're creating a VPN across the Internet because the addresses of the originating devices can be private, so they're less vulnerable to unwanted access. As with transport mode, tunnel mode uses ESP and/or AH.

Figure 7.5 illustrates the format of a packet using ESP in tunnel mode.

FIGURE 7.5 Packet format using ESP in tunnel mode

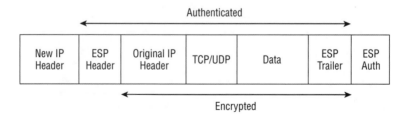

Figure 7.6 illustrates the format of a packet using AH in tunnel mode.

FIGURE 7.6   Packet format using AH in tunnel mode

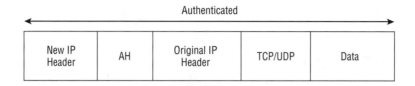

Figure 7.7 illustrates the format of a packet using ESP and AH in tunnel mode.

FIGURE 7.7   Packet format using ESP and AH in tunnel mode

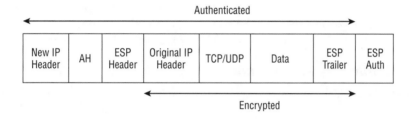

Internet Key Exchange (IKE)

IPSec can be configured with or without Internet Key Exchange (IKE), but it's really a better idea to use IKE. IKE enhances IPSec by providing additional features, flexibility, and ease of configuration for the IPSec standard. It's a hybrid protocol that implements the OAKLEY key exchange and SKEME key exchange inside the Internet Security Association and Key Management Protocol (ISAKMP) framework.

Now's a good time to define some of the terms I just threw at you:

ISAKMP   *Internet Security Association and Key Management Protocol (ISAKMP)* is a protocol framework that defines the payload format, the mechanics of implementing a key exchange protocol, and the negotiation of an SA.

OAKLEY   Having nothing to do with high-tech, seriously cool sunglasses, *OAKLEY* is a key exchange protocol that defines how to derive authenticated keying material.

SKEME   SKEME is a key exchange protocol that defines how to derive authenticated keying material with rapid key refreshment.

Now that you're clear on the terminology, let's get back into the discussion. IKE gives us the goods in the following six ways:

- IKE eliminates the need to manually specify all the IPSec security parameters in the crypto maps at both peers.

- IKE allows you to specify a lifetime for the IPSec security SA.

- IKE allows encryption keys to change during IPSec sessions.

- IKE allows IPSec to provide anti-replay services.

- IKE permits certification authority (CA) support for a manageable, scalable IPSec implementation.

- IKE allows dynamic authentication of peers.

So, how is IKE able to provide these goodies? That's what you're about to find out.

IKE consists of the two phases mentioned earlier in this chapter: IKE phase 1 and IKE phase 2. During phase 1, IKE negotiates the IKE SAs and authenticates the IPSec peers. During phase 2, IKE negotiates the IPSec SAs and creates the IPSec tunnel.

IKE relies heavily on Diffie-Hellman during phase 1, so let's take a closer look at that feature.

Diffie-Hellman Key Agreement

The *Diffie-Hellman (DH) Agreement* is a means for two parties to agree on a shared secret number that is then used to encrypt secret keys for other algorithms such as DES and MD5. DH occurs in phase 1 of IKE negotiation.

 The process of DH occurs over unsecured lines.

Before diving right into how DH works, here's a list of keys you need to understand:

P   P is a randomly generated prime integer.

G   G is a primitive root of P.

Xa   Xa is a private key generated by the formula (G mod P).

Xb   Xb is a private key generated by the formula (G mod P).

Ya   Ya is a public key generated by the formula ((G to the power of Xa) mod P).

Yb   Yb is a public key generated by the formula ((G to the power of Xb) mod P).

ZZ   ZZ is a shared secret key generated by the formula ((Yb to the power of Xa) mod P) on one device and the formula ((Ya to the power of Xb) mod P) on the other device.

Mod stands for a modulus or division.

Now, with the terminology and formulas out of the way, you're ready to get into the six-step process DH goes through in the creation of ZZ. Use the network in Figure 7.8 for reference in this discussion of DH.

FIGURE 7.8   A Diffie-Hellman network

1. The first step of DH uses the generated P value on each device to create the G value. The following steps are what the devices in Figure 7.8 actually go through:

    A. Both R1 and R2 generate a P value.

    B. R1 transmits its P value to R2, and R2 transmits its P value to R1.

    C. Both R1 and R2 use the two P values to create G.

2. The second step of DH uses G and P on each device to generate Xa on one device and Xb on the other device. The routers in Figure 7.8 go through the following process:

    A. R1 uses the formula (G mod P) to create its private key Xa.

    B. R2 uses the formula (G mod P) to create its private key Xb.

3. Now it's time to generate each device's public key. To generate the public keys for R1 and R2, the devices in Figure 7.8 go through the following process:

    A. Using the formula ((G to the power of Xa) mod P), R1 creates its public key Ya.

    B. Using the formula ((G to the power of Xb) mod P), R2 creates its public key Yb.

4. The devices now exchange their public keys. R1 sends its public key, Ya, to R2, and R2 sends its public key, Yb, to R1.

5. R1 and R2 generate the secret shared key ZZ. R1 uses the formula ((Yb to the power of Xa) mod P) to create ZZ, and R2 uses the formula ((Ya to the power of Xb) mod P) to create ZZ.

6. On each device, ZZ encrypts the key that will be used by DES or MD5 for the purpose of encrypting data.

Once this last step has been completed, DH is finished with its initial function. But DH can be used later in IKE phase 2 to generate new keying material for IPSec SAs.

All right, now you understand how DH is used with IKE—great! So let's look at some of the authentication mechanisms available to IKE during phase 1 that it can use to authenticate a peer's identity.

Authentication

I've mentioned authentication several times in this chapter, but I've never gone into any detail. That's exactly what I'm going to do here. Any of the following three authentication types can be used for IKE:

- Pre-shared keys
- RSA-encrypted nonces
- RSA signatures and digital certificates

Pre-Shared Keys

Pre-shared keys must be configured on each IPSec peer, and any keys used have got to be the same on each peer. This is because IKE peers authenticate each other by creating and sending a keyed hash that includes the pre-shared key. Once the receiving peer receives the hash, it attempts to create the same hash by using its configured pre-shared key. Needless to say, the peer is authenticated only if the hashes match.

RSA-Encrypted Nonces

RSA-encrypted nonces are a type of public/private key cryptography that truly is very secure, but it's not very scalable. A nonce is a pseudo-random number. RSA-encrypted nonces can be used to authenticate the IKE exchange and the Diffie-Hellman Key Agreement.

So let's take a look at how RSA-encrypted nonces work. This section could get a little confusing, so I'll use an example.

Suppose you have two devices you want to peer using RSA-encrypted nonces: R1 and R2. You've got to manually generate a public key on both R1 and R2, and then manually enter the public key generated by R1 into R2 and vice versa.

Next, R1 generates a *nonce* that it then encrypts along with its IKE identity using RSA encryption and the public key that was manually entered. R1 transmits the cipher text to R2. While R1 is doing all of this, R2 is doing the same using the public key that you manually entered into it.

Once R1 receives the encrypted packet from R2, it decrypts the packet using its own private RSA key. After the packet has been decrypted, R1 removes both the nonce and R2's IKE identity. R1 then hashes R2's nonce and IKE identity and sends the hash back to R2. R2 is performing all these same functions simultaneously.

After both R1 and R2 receive their respective hash, each device then hashes its own nonce and IKE identity. With that done, each device compares the hash it received with the hash it just generated to determine if they match. If they do, authentication has occurred.

RSA-encrypted nonces are not very scalable because of the fact that you've got to both manually generate and then exchange public keys. Even so, RSA signatures do scale the best.

RSA Signatures and Digital Certificates

RSA signatures rely on digital signatures—something I'll get to in a second. It's actually through the use of digital signatures that RSA signatures overcome the scalability limitations of RSA-encrypted nonces.

You still need to manually generate the public/private key pair on each device when you use RSA signatures. And once you've done that, you've got to register each peer with a *certificate authority (CA)*. When you register a device with the CA, it also registers the public key you've just generated. The CA then issues a signed digital certificate to you, validating that you really are who you say you are. Each peer absolutely must have a signed digital certificate before RSA can be used.

Once each device has a signed digital certificate, they send them, along with their IKE identities, to the other device. The IKE exchange is authenticated by the signed digital certificate.

Why is this good? Well, because using digital certificates eliminates that nasty need to manually enter a device's generated public key in each and every device that it needs to peer with, that's why! It's a significant advantage because it allows for greater scalability.

Now it's time to talk in depth about digital certificates. They contain device-specific information such as the device's name and IP address, as well as its generated public key. This is why a digital certificate can be used in place of manually entering public keys for IKE authentication.

But how does this all work? Well, first of all, the CA that you're using needs to be trusted by the devices that you want to be able to peer with. This occurs when the device first begins talking to the CA. The following are the steps required for a device to receive a signed digital signature from a CA:

1. You must manually generate the public/private key pair on the device.

2. The device requests the specified CA's public key.

3. The CA sends its public key to the device.

4. The device requests a signed digital certificate from the CA. In that request, the device includes device-specific information and its public key.

5. The CA generates the digital signature, incorporating both the device's public key and the CA's private key.

6. The CA sends the signed digital signature back to the device.

So after a device receives its signed digital signature, it offers it to all the devices it wants to peer with. A peer device trusts the device's public key once it verifies the device's signature using the public key from the CA. This entire process is a type of *Digital Signature Standard (DSS)* encryption.

 NOTE   DSS encryption is a mechanism that uses digital signatures to protect data.

Cisco fully supports the use of digital certificates by IKE and implements the following standards:

X.509v3   The standard certificate format. X.509v3 specifies how to form a certificate.

CRLv2   The certificate revocation list, version 2. CRLv2 is a list of revoked certificates, that is, certificates that should no longer be trusted.

Certificate Enrollment Protocol (CEP)   A certificate management protocol jointly developed by Cisco Systems and VeriSign, Inc. CEP is an early implementation of Certificate Request Syntax (CRS), a standard proposed to the Internet Engineering Task Force (IETF). CEP specifies how a device communicates with a CA, including how to retrieve the CA's public key, how to enroll a device with the CA, and how to retrieve a certificate revocation list (CRL). CEP uses RSA's PKCS (Public-Key Cryptography Standards) 7 and 10 as key component technologies. The IETF's Public Key Infrastructure (PKI) Working Group is moving forward to standardize a protocol for these functions, either CRS or an equivalent. When an IETF standard is stable, Cisco will add support for it.

IKE Mode Configuration

IKE mode configuration allows IKE to scale an IPSec policy out to remote users. This is accomplished by permitting a gateway to download an IP address and other network-level configuration through Dynamic Host Configuration Protocol (DHCP) to a client during IKE negotiation. Afterward, this address is used as the inner IP address to be encapsulated under IPSec and can then be matched against an IPSec policy.

The last IKE feature I need to describe is IKE's extended authentication capabilities.

IKE Extended Authentication (XAuth)

Until the advent of IKE extended authentication (XAuth), IKE was only able to support authentication of the device, but not of the user. XAuth introduced a way for IKE to use AAA to authenticate the user after it has authenticated the device, adding an extra level of security to the network.

That's really all there is to understanding IPSec. The following sidebar explores Cisco's IOS Cryptosystem and goes further into the encryption and hash algorithms described earlier.

Cisco IOS Cryptosystem

To put it simply, a *cryptosystem* is a combination of encryption technologies, working in harmony, that are used to encrypt data so that only the intended receiver can decrypt it. Cisco uses the following four technologies to create its IOS Cryptosystem:

- Digital Encryption Standard (DES)

- Message Digest 5 (MD5)

- Digital Signature Standard (DSS)

- Diffie-Hellman Key Agreement

These four technologies perform the following tasks in Cisco's cryptosystem:

- DES encrypts data.

- MD5 creates a message hash.

- DSS verifies peers by exchanging public keys.

- Diffie-Hellman establishes private and public keys that encrypt the keys used by DES and MD5.

When all of these items work together as a team, they create a very secure environment for transmitting data.

Summary

Congratulations—you made it! This chapter introduced you to many new concepts. VPNs are growing in demand, and if you want to remain relevant in today's competitive marketplace, you positively must understand their terms and processes.

Cisco utilizes IPSec VPNs to provide a secure connection over a public network—connections that can be designed based on the business needs of your company. You can use remote-access solutions for telecommuters, site-to-site solutions for remote offices that need access to the corporate network, and extranet solutions to provide your customers and partners with the limited information they need.

Cisco provides a number of products to meet your IPSec needs. Cisco routers, CiscoSecure VPN Concentrators, and PIX Firewalls can all be used to create VPN solutions for your specific situation.

You really must have a thorough understanding of the concepts discussed in this chapter before proceeding to Chapter 8, so if you feel at all shaky on anything covered here, take the time you need to go back and review.

Exam Essentials

Explain virtual private networks.   You must be able to explain how VPNs are used in the creation of secure networks. You need to understand the three different types of VPNs: site-to-site, extranet, and remote access.

List and explain the different tunneling technologies.   The tunneling protocols currently available are GRE, L2F, L2TP, and PPTP. You must be able to explain how each of these protocols is used.

Explain IPSec operation.   You need a solid understanding of the five steps of IPSec operation: how an IPSec process initiates, IKE phase 1, IKE phase 2, data transfer, and IPSec tunnel termination.

Explain the different key exchange methods.   You must be able to list the different key exchange methods: pre-shared keys, RSA-encrypted nonces, and RSA signatures. You need to explain how each one operates and when each should be used.

Explain the Cisco IOS Cryptosystem.   You must be able to explain that a cryptosystem is a combination of encryption technologies, working in harmony, that are used to encrypt data so that only the intended receiver can decrypt it. The Cisco IOS Cryptosystem uses DES, MD5, DSS, and DH.

List the Cisco equipment available for IPSec.   Cisco uses their routers, VPN Concentrators, and the PIX Firewalls for IPSec VPN solutions.

Key Terms

Before you take the exam, be certain you are familiar with the following terms:

aggressive mode

Authentication Header (AH)

certificate authority (CA)

cryptosystem

Data Encryption Standard (DES)

Diffie-Hellman (DH) Agreement

Digital Signature Standard (DSS)

Encapsulating Security Payload (ESP)

encryption algorithms

extranet VPNs

generic routing encapsulation (GRE)

hash

Hash-Based Message Authentication
Code-Message Digest 5 (HMAC-MD5)

hashing algorithm

IKE phase 1

IKE phase 2

Internet Security Association and Key
Management Protocol (ISAKMP)

IP Security (IPSec)

IPSec transform

Layer 2 Forwarding (L2F)

Layer 2 Tunneling Protocol (L2TP)

main mode

nonce

OAKLEY

Point-to-Point Tunneling Protocol (PPTP)

pre-shared keys

remote access VPNs

RSA signatures

RSA-encrypted nonces

security association (SA)

Security Parameter Index (SPI)

site-to-site VPNs

transport mode

Triple DES (3DES)

tunnel mode

virtual private network (VPN)

Written Lab

This section asks you 10 write-in-the-answer questions to help you understand the technology that you need to know in order to pass the SECUR exam.

1. List the two phases of IKE.

2. List the Cisco devices available for IPSec.

3. What are the two symmetric encryption algorithms that provide confidentiality for ESP?

4. How many IPSec SAs are required for a peering session?

5. List the three categories of VPNs.

6. What makes up the Cisco IOS Cryptosystem?

7. What is XAuth's function?

8. What tunneling protocols did L2TP replace?

9. What is an IPSec transform?

10. What is a nonce?

Review Questions

1. Which of the following participate in the Cisco IOS Cryptosystem? (Choose all that apply.)

   A. DH

   B. MD5

   C. ESP

   D. DES

2. When does DH calculate the Xa?

   A. IKE phase 1

   B. IKE phase 2

   C. IKE phase 3

   D. None of the above

3. Which of the following types of authentication requires a user to manually generate keys and then manually exchange the public keys?

   A. Pre-shared keys

   B. RSA-encrypted nonces

   C. RSA signatures

   D. None of the above

4. Which of the following is an encryption algorithm that uses one key to encrypt data, another key to decrypt, and yet another key to encrypt it again before the data is ever sent to the peer?

   A. DES

   B. MD5

   C. 3DES

   D. SHA-1

5. Which IPSec mode generates a new IP header?

   A. Aggressive

   B. Transport

   C. Main

   D. Tunnel

6. What is used by Cisco IOS Cryptosystem to exchange public keys for IPSec?

   A. DES

   B. ESP

   C. MD5

   D. DSS

7. Which of the following authentication methods utilizes a CA server?

   A. Pre-shared keys

   B. RSA-encrypted nonces

   C. RSA signatures

   D. None of the above

8. Which of the following Cisco devices is best used for remote access VPN solutions?

   A. CiscoSecure VPN Concentrator

   B. Cisco Router

   C. PIX Firewall

   D. None of the above

9. Which of the following algorithms produces a 128-bit authentication value that is truncated using the first 96 bits?

   A. HMAC-MD5

   B. HMAC-SHA-1

   C. ESP

   D. 3DES

10. At which of the following OSI layers does IPSec operate?

   A. Network

   B. Data Link

   C. Physical

   D. Transport

11. Which of the following are forms of VPN? (Choose all that apply.)

   A. Site-to-site

   B. Externet

   C. Intranet

   D. Remote access

12. Which VPN solution allows a site in another city to be securely connected to the corporate network over the Internet?

   A. Site-to-site

   B. Extranet

   C. Internet

   D. None of the above

13. Which of the following assigns an "inner" IP address to a remote user that is wrapped inside of the IPSec packet?

   A. IKE aggressive mode

   B. IKE main mode

   C. IKE quick mode

   D. IKE mode configuration

14. When is an IPSec SA negotiated?

   A. IKE phase 1

   B. Tunnel setup

   C. IKE phase 2

   D. IPSec initialization

15. Which of the following tunneling protocols is L2TP backward compatible with?

   A. GRE

   B. L2F

   C. IPSec

   D. PPP

16. Which of the following are used together to uniquely identify an IPSec SA? (Choose all that apply.)

   A. SAD

   B. SPI

   C. IP source address

   D. Security protocol identifier

17. Which type of VPN is best suited for telecommuters?

   A. Extranet

   B. Intranet

   C. Remote access

   D. None of the above

18. Which of the following protocols is used by the Cisco IOS Cryptosystem to encrypt data?

   A. ESP

   B. DES

   C. DSS

   D. DH

19. Which of the following tunneling protocols did Cisco and Microsoft jointly develop?

   A. L2F

   B. L2TP

   C. GRE

   D. PPTP

20. Which of the following statements are true about AH? (Choose all that apply.)

   A. AH encrypts data.

   B. AH provides data integrity.

   C. AH provides anti-replay.

   D. AH performs an integrity check of the whole packet.

Answers to Written Lab

1. IKE phase 1 and IKE phase 2 are the two phases of IKE.

2. The Cisco devices available for IPSec are Cisco routers, CiscoSecure VPN Concentrators, and PIX Firewalls.

3. DES and 3DES are the two symmetric encryption algorithms that provide confidentiality for ESP.

4. Two IPSec SAs are required for a peering session.

5. Remote access, site-to-site, and extranet are the three categories of VPNs.

6. The Cisco IOS Cryptosystem is made up of DES, MD5, DSS, and DH.

7. XAuth provides a method in which IKE can use AAA to authenticate the user after IKE has authenticated the device.

8. L2TP replaced L2F and PPTP.

9. An IPSec transform is a single security protocol with the corresponding security algorithm.

10. A nonce is a pseudo-random number.

Answers to Review Questions

1. A, B, D. The Cisco IOS Cryptosystem consists of DES, MD5, DSS, and DH.

2. A. During IKE phase 1, DH is used to create the private keys, Xa and Xb, and the public keys, Ya and Yb. DH then uses these keys to create the shared secret key ZZ, which is used to encrypt the DES and MD5 keys.

3. B. The first step in using RSA-encrypted nonces requires the user to manually generate the keys. The user must then manually enter the public key created on each device into the device they wish to peer with.

4. C. 3DES is a stronger version of DES that uses three different keys for encrypting data before it is sent to the peer.

5. D. When tunnel mode encapsulation is used, the original IP header is not used to transport the packet. Instead, a new IP header is created using the IP addresses of the IPSec peers as the source and destination of the packet. This mode is great when you are creating a VPN across the Internet because the addresses of the originating devices can be private.

6. D. In Cisco's Cryptosystem, DES is used to encrypt data, MD5 is used to create a message hash, DSS is used to verify peers by exchanging public keys, and Diffie-Hellman is used to establish private and public keys that will be used to encrypt the keys used by DES and MD5.

7. C. RSA signatures utilize a CA server to issue a device a signed digital certificate. This digital certificate is then exchanged with devices they wish to peer with.

8. A. The CiscoSecure VPN Concentrator allows for remote access users, such as telecommuters, to be securely connected into a corporate network.

9. A. HMAC-MD5 is a hashing algorithm that creates a 128-bit secret key. HMAC-MD5 produces a 128-bit authentication value that is truncated using the first 96 bits. This truncated value is then inserted into the authenticator field of AH or ESP and sent to the peer.

10. A. IPSec functions at Layer 3, the Network layer, of the OSI model.

11. A, C, D. There are three types of VPNs: remote access, site-to-site (a.k.a. intranet), and extranet. Answer B is wrong because there isn't an externet VPN type.

12. A. Site-to-site VPN solutions allow a company to connect its remote sites to the corporate backbone securely over a public medium such as the Internet, instead of having to use more expensive WAN connections such as Frame Relay.

13. D. IKE mode configuration allows IKE to scale an IPSec policy out to remote users. This is accomplished by allowing a gateway to download an IP address and other network-level configuration to a client during IKE negotiation. This address is then used as the inner IP address to be encapsulated under IPSec.

14. C. During IKE phase 2, IPSec SAs are negotiated, resulting in the formation of an IPSec tunnel.

15. B.   L2TP was created by Cisco and Microsoft to replace L2F and PPTP. L2TP merged the functionality of L2F and PPTP into one tunneling protocol. L2TP is backward compatible with L2F.

16. B, D.   Each SA has a unique triple identity consisting of a Security Parameter Index (SPI), an IP destination address, and a security protocol (AH or ESP) identifier. So the only correct answers are B and D.

17. C.   Remote access VPNs allow remote users, such as telecommuters, to securely access the corporate network whenever and from wherever the need may arise.

18. B.   The Cisco IOS Cryptosystem uses DES for the encryption of data.

19. B.   L2TP was created by Cisco and Microsoft to replace L2F and PPTP. L2TP merged the functionality of L2F and PPTP into one tunneling protocol.

20. B, C, D.   AH provides an integrity check on the whole packet, and anti-replay AH doesn't offer any encryption services. So answers B, C, and D are correct.

Chapter

8

Cisco IOS IPSec Pre-Shared Keys and Certificate Authority Support

THE FOLLOWING SECUR EXAM TOPICS ARE COVERED IN THIS CHAPTER:

- ✓ Configuring IPSec encryption tasks
- ✓ Preparing for IKE and IPSec
- ✓ Configuring IKE
- ✓ Configuring IPSec
- ✓ Configuring transform set suites
- ✓ Configuring global IPSec Security Association (SA) lifetimes
- ✓ Creating crypto ACLs
- ✓ Creating crypto maps
- ✓ Applying crypto maps to interfaces
- ✓ Testing and verifying IPSec
- ✓ Configuring IPSec manually
- ✓ Configuring IPSec for RSA-encrypted nonces
- ✓ Configuring CA support tasks
- ✓ Understanding CA support
- ✓ Configuring CA support

In another life, I was a professional musician and played guitar in a band. I didn't study a lot of music theory, but I did know a lot about making music and performing it live. In the last chapter, I went over all the theory behind IKE and IPSec with you. Now, I'm going to build upon that material by showing you what to do with it. In this chapter, you're going to learn how to configure IKE and IPSec, because while understanding theory is good, you had better know how to implement it when showtime comes!

Everybody has different strengths and weaknesses. Some people struggle with the theory part of this material but fly through the application, while others experience the opposite. Some of you are just loving every minute of it, handling both the concepts and their implementation with ease. But no matter which category you fall into, the fact remains that you simply have to know this stuff—both in theory and in practice—if you want to pass the test and be capable of actually working with the technologies competently.

And that's exactly the goal of this chapter—to pull together theory and execution and integrate them into one tight package. I've got to be honest with you though; achieving this goal is going to take awhile. This chapter is one of the longest in this book!

Configuring Cisco IOS IPSec for Pre-Shared Keys Site-to-Site

IPSec for pre-shared keys is the easiest of all of the IPSec implementations. Implementing IPSec requires that you configure an IKE policy, pre-shared keys, and IPSec, but it's not very scalable because you've got to manually configure the pre-shared keys on the devices, plus manage them. This can become fairly tangled and messy in large networks. Hear that big sucking sound? Those are the man-hours being consumed if you use IPSec for pre-shared keys on a large network! It's not exactly cost-effective—go for another option in a larger environment. In the next section, you're going to learn the configuration tasks for IPSec and how to plan your approach to implementing IPSec so you can configure it correctly the first time.

Configuring IPSec for pre-shared keys requires you to do these four tasks:

- Prepare for IKE and IPSec.
- Configure IKE.
- Configure IPSec.
- Test and verify IPSec.

By the time you're done with this section, you'll be able to implement site-to-site IPSec for pre-shared keys, so let's get going!

Preparing for IKE and IPSec

Before you get into configuring IPSec utilizing pre-shared keys, you need to plan out your approach. Think of it as a football game—you don't just show up at the field and play. You show up with a decided strategy to win the game, complete with a book of plays you plan to use depending on the circumstances and your opponent. You've also done your research, so you're packing detailed notes on all their codes and signs. It's pretty much the same thing for IPSec. You don't just start configuring IPSec without first coming up with a solid plan of attack.

Here are five questions you need to answer that will help you develop a plan:

- Can the devices you want to peer already ping each other? If not, you need to verify network connectivity. If yes, move on to the next question.

- Does existing packet filtering currently allow IPSec traffic? If not, update the access lists to allow IPSec traffic. If yes, move on to the next question.

- What's the current configuration of the device? Knowing this will allow you to establish two things—the crypto map name already in use and interfaces that currently have crypto maps applied to them. Time to move on to the next question.

- What IKE policy do you want to enforce between the devices that you're going to peer? Asking yourself this question will make you think about the message-encryption and hash algorithms, the authentication method, and the key exchange parameters. These decisions should directly correspond with what you've outlined in your corporate security policy. That done, you're ready for the next question.

- What type of IPSec policy do you want to enforce between the devices with which you wish to peer? To answer this one, you'll have to think about two factors: the IPSec mode you're going to use and which IPSec transforms to use.

Okay, great—now that you've answered these questions (and documented your answers, of course), you're ready to rock! The first step in configuring IPSec utilizing pre-shared keys is to configure IKE on each device.

Configuring IKE

Once your IKE policy has been identified, configuring IKE is relatively simple. Configuring IKE with pre-shared keys is a four-step process:

1. Enable IKE.

2. Create the IKE policy.

3. Configure the IKE identity and pre-shared keys.

4. Verify IKE operation.

Enabling IKE

To configure IKE, it's got to be enabled first. You enable IKE by entering the following command in global configuration mode:

`crypto isakmp enable`

Once the preceding command has been entered, IKE will be enabled on the device. If you ever need to disable it, enter the following command, also in global configuration mode:

`no crypto isakmp enable`

Don't use the no `crypto isakmp enable` command lightly—disabling all IKE operation on a device can have serious ramifications.

Creating the IKE Policy

With IKE enabled, you now need to create the IKE policy. Doing this requires you to have already answered the following questions:

- What priority will you give the policy? Lower numbers indicate a higher priority in the policy and vice versa. This is critical when a device has multiple IKE policies configured.

- What type of message encryption will you use? The default is DES, but you can change it to 3DES if you have the right feature set.

- What message hash will you use? The default is sha, but you can change it to MD5.

- What authentication method do you want to use? The default is rsa-sig, but it can be changed to pre-shared or rsa-encr. The example in this book will use pre-shared keys.

- What Diffie-Hellman group do you want to use? The default is 1, but it can be changed to 2. Group 1 is 768-bit Diffie-Hellman; group 2 is 1024-bit Diffie-Hellman.

- What lifetime would you like to set for the IKE Security Association (SA)? The default is 86,400, but that can be changed.

Don't forget that the policy you have set on one device must be the same as the policy you set on the devices you wish to peer with. The exceptions are: first, the priority given to the policy, which is locally significant; and second, the lifetime that's negotiated during IKE phase 1.

To create the IKE policy, enter the following command in global configuration mode, where *priority* is a value between 1 and 10,000.

`crypto isakmp policy priority`

Once you enter this command, the IKE policy is created with all the default values, and the router is placed in IKE policy configuration mode. All of the configuration in this section is accomplished while in this mode.

Next, you need to specify which message-encryption algorithm to use by entering the following command:

`encryption {des | 3des}`

After configuring the message-encryption algorithm, you configure the message hash by entering the following command:

`hash {sha | md5}`

Now you configure the authentication method by entering the following command:

`authentication {rsa-sig | rsa-encr | pre-share}`

Because this section discusses only pre-shared keys, you need to use the `pre-share` keyword.

Next, you configure the Diffie-Hellman group by entering the following command:

`group {1 | 2}`

All right, hang in there. You're in the home stretch! To finish this off, you configure the IKE SA lifetime by entering the following command, where *seconds* is a value between 60 and 86,400:

`lifetime seconds`

Entering the commands discussed in this section is all you need to do if you want to change the default value or change a value that's already been configured. If you want to create a new IKE policy or enter IKE policy configuration mode, you've got to enter the `crypto isakmp policy priority` command.

Configuring the IKE Identity and Pre-Shared Keys

Okay, your IKE policy has been created and configured on all of the devices—nice! Now it's time to set the IKE identity and configure the pre-shared key that is used during IKE negotiations to authenticate peers.

Because you're reading this book, you probably know that a device can use either the router's IP address or the router's hostname for its identity. By default, devices use their IP address as their IKE identity. This is important because unless you want to set the device to use its hostname instead, or the device is already using the hostname and you want to change it back to use the device's IP address, you don't need to configure a thing. To accomplish one of these tasks, just enter the following command in global configuration mode:

`crypto isakmp identity {address | hostname}`

 WARNING
If you choose to use a device's hostname for IKE identity, make sure a DNS server is available for name resolution. Your other option is to manually enter the hostname of the device in the hostname table of all devices you wish to peer with.

Once you've nailed the IKE identity, it's time to configure the pre-shared key. But first, you need to determine which pre-shared key to use on all the devices you wish to peer. When you've made your decision, enter the following command in global configuration mode on each device, where *keystring* is the pre-shared key you want to use, *peer-address* is the IP address of the remote device, and *peer-hostname* is the hostname of the remote device:

`crypto isakmp key keystring {address peer-address | hostname peer-hostname}`

This command needs to be entered on a device for each device it wishes to peer with.

 NOTE
Use the address keyword if the remote peer is using an IKE identity of the address. Use the hostname keyword if the remote peer is using an IKE identity of the hostname.

I know, I know! That was a ton of input, so let's take a second to put it all together visually. The following graphic illustrates a potential network for setting up a VPN. Remember our corporate network example? You'll be using it again for Exercise 8.1.

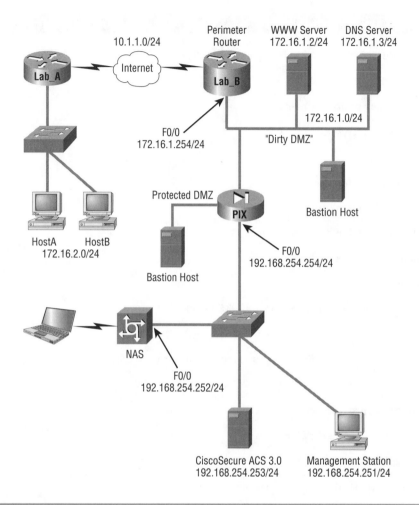

 Word of advice: If you are taking the SECUR exam, which is probably a sure bet because you're reading this book, it would be wise to set up some routers and configure the next lab!

EXERCISE 8.1

Setting Up a VPN Using IKE

In this exercise, I'm going to guide you through configuring IKE using a VPN between the Lab_A device and the Lab_B device with the following parameters:

- Lab_A interface Serial 0/0 with IP address 10.1.1.1 /24

- Lab_B interface Serial 1/0 with IP address 10.1.1.2 /24

- Lab_A IKE policy priority equals 2

- Lab_B IKE policy priority equals 2

- 3DES message encryption

- MD5 message hash

- Authentication method is pre-share

- Default Diffie-Hellman group for both devices

- Default IKE SA lifetime for both devices

- IKE Identity is address for both devices

- Pre-shared key is cisco

Enter the following commands to create your IKE policies:

Lab_A#**conf t**

Enter configuration commands, one per line. End with CNTL/Z.

Lab_A(config)#**crypto isakmp enable**

Lab_A(config)#**crypto isakmp policy 2**

Lab_A(config-isakmp)#**encryption 3des**

Lab_A(config-isakmp)#**hash md5**

Lab_A(config-isakmp)#**authentication pre-share**

Lab_A(config-isakmp)#**exit**

Lab_A(config)#**crypto isakmp key cisco address 10.1.1.2**

Lab_A(config)#**^Z**

Lab_A#

Lab_B#**conf t**

Enter configuration commands, one per line. End with CNTL/Z.

Lab_B(config)#**crypto isakmp enable**

```
Lab_B(config)#crypto isakmp policy 2

Lab_B(config-isakmp)#encryption 3des

Lab_B(config-isakmp)#hash md5

Lab_B(config-isakmp)#authentication pre-share

Lab_B(config-isakmp)#exit

Lab_B(config)#crypto isakmp key cisco address 10.1.1.1

Lab_B(config)#^Z

Lab_B#
```

Did you notice that the Diffie-Hellman group command and the lifetime command weren't entered? That's because the default settings were used, so you didn't need to use those commands.

Once the configuration is complete, you must always be able to verify what you have configured. The next section will explain how to do this.

Verifying the IKE Policy

Now that the IKE policies have been configured, you need to verify that the device accepted them. You do this via the show crypto isakmp policy command, which displays the IKE policies currently configured on a device. With this in mind, let's verify the IKE policies on the Lab_A and Lab_B devices:

```
Lab_A#show crypto isakmp policy
Protection suite of priority 2
    encryption algorithm:     3DES--Triple Data Encryption Standard (168 bit
      ↳keys)
    hash algorithm:           Message Digest 5
    authentication method:    Pre-Shared Key
    Diffie-Hellman group:     #1 (768 bit)
    lifetime:                 86400 seconds, no volume limit
Default protection suite
    encryption algorithm:     DES--Data Encryption Standard
    hash algorithm:           Secure Hash Standard
    authentication method:    Rivest-Shamir-Adleman Signature (56 bit keys)
    Diffie-Hellman group:     #1 (768 bit)
```

```
    lifetime:                   86400 seconds, no volume limit
Lab_A#


Lab_B#show crypto isakmp policy
Protection suite of priority 2
    encryption algorithm:       3DES--Triple Data Encryption Standard
    hash algorithm:             Message Digest 5
    authentication method:      Pre-Shared Key
    Diffie-Hellman group:       #1 (768 bit)
    lifetime:                   86400 seconds, no volume limit
Default protection suite
    encryption algorithm:       DES--Data Encryption Standard
    hash algorithm:             Secure Hash Standard
    authentication method:      Rivest-Shamir-Adleman Signature
    Diffie-Hellman group:       #1 (768 bit)
    lifetime:                   86400 seconds, no volume limit
Lab_B#
```

Sweet—everything looks great! Now that you've verified that your IKE policies are actually configured on each device, you're ready to move on and configure IPSec.

Configuring IPSec

Just like pre-shared keys, there are important steps that you should keep in mind when configuring IPSec on your routers. Configuring IPSec on each device is a five-step process:

1. Create the transform set.

2. Set the IPSec SA lifetime.

3. Create the access list that specifies the traffic to encrypt.

4. Create the crypto map.

5. Apply the crypto map to an interface.

Creating the Transform Set

A transform set is your tool for protecting the data flow. It's made up of payload authentication, payload encryption, and an IPSec mode. For devices to peer, the transform set must match on each device, except (obviously) for their names. Also, in order for a transform set to be valid, it must have a unique name on the device and at least one transform. To configure a transform set, enter the following command in global configuration mode:

crypto ipsec transform-set *transform-set-name* {[*transform1*] [*transform2*]
      ↳ [*transform3*]}

The variables for the preceding command are as follows:

- *transform-set-name*: This should be a unique name for the transform set.
- *transform1*: This can be ah-md5-hmac or ah-sha-hmac.
- *transform2*: This can be esp-des, esp-3des, or esp-null.
- *transform3*: This can be esp-md5-hmac or esp-sha-hmac.

After you've issued the preceding command, the device enters transform set configuration mode, in which the IPSec mode for the transform set can be configured. The default IPSec mode is tunnel. To change the IPSec mode, enter the following command:

mode {**tunnel** | **transport**}

When you're configuring transform sets, it's really important to make sure that both the transforms and the IPSec mode are the same on the device you want to peer.

Setting the IPSec SA Lifetime

To make sure you're clear on this, an *IPSec SA lifetime* is what you use to determine how long IPSec SAs remain valid until they need to be renegotiated. There are two ways in which you can configure the IPSec SA. The first is globally, and the second is per crypto map sequence. When you go with the configured-globally option, the IPSec SA lifetime is applied to each and every crypto map that exists on the device. And it's important to know that a global IPSec SA lifetime can be overridden by configuring a crypto map–specific IPSec SA lifetime. For now, I'm going to stick with global IPSec SA lifetimes. You'll learn about the crypto map–specific IPSec SA lifetimes later in this chapter.

There are two types of global IPSec SA lifetimes that exist on a device: seconds and kilobytes. The seconds global IPSec SA lifetime specifies the number of seconds that an IPSec SA remains active before it expires. The kilobytes global IPSec SA lifetime specifies the amount of traffic that can be transmitted between peers for a given IPSec SA before the SA expires.

To change the seconds global IPSec SA from its default of 3600 seconds, enter the following command in global configuration mode, where *seconds* is a value between 120 and 86,400:

```
crypto ipsec security-association lifetime seconds seconds
```

To change the kilobytes global IPSec SA from its default of 4,608,000 kilobytes, enter the following command, where *kilobytes* represents a value between 2560 and 4,608,000:

```
crypto ipsec security-association lifetime kilobytes kilobytes
```

Remember that both the kilobytes and seconds global IPSec SA lifetimes exist on a device at the same time.

Creating the Access List

So far you've created the transform set and set the global IPSec lifetimes. But what good is IPSec if you haven't specified any traffic to protect? That's where access lists come into play.

IPSec uses extended access lists to perform the following tasks:

- Choose the outbound traffic to protect.
- Process inbound traffic for selecting IPSec traffic.
- Process inbound traffic for filtering out traffic that should have been protected.
- When processing IKE negotiations, they determine whether to accept requests for IPSec SAs.

I'm not going to explain how to create extended access lists here. If you need more information on extended access lists, they're covered in detail in the *CCNA Study Guide* (Sybex, 2002).

 Cisco recommends using symmetrical access lists for IPSec because doing so causes both outbound and inbound traffic to be compared against the same access list.

Creating the Crypto Map

IPSec SAs are established through the use of a crypto map, which is basically a combination of one or more sequences where each sequence represents an IPSec SA.

Each crypto map sequence specifies the following:

- What traffic to protect
- The remote peer the protected traffic should be sent to
- The transforms to use to protect the traffic
- Whether the IPSec SA will be established via IKE or manually
- Other parameters such as a description and a crypto map IPSec SA lifetime

All sequences of a crypto map are tied together by the name of the respective crypto map. Each sequence can be one of the following types:

Cisco   This sequence specifies that Cisco Encryption Technology will be used to protect traffic instead of IPSec.

IPSec-manual   The IPSec-manual sequence specifies that IKE will not be used to establish IPSec SA. This type of sequence is discussed in more detail later in this chapter.

IPSec-isakmp   This sequence specifies that IKE will be used to establish IPSec SAs.

Dynamic   The dynamic sequence specifies that this sequence references a pre-existing crypto map. This book does not cover dynamic crypto maps because they are beyond the scope of the SECUR exam.

To create a crypto map sequence that utilizes IKE, enter the following command in global configuration mode, where *map-name* is the name of the crypto map and *seq-num* is the sequence number of the crypto map sequence, which is a value between 1 and 65,535:

```
crypto map map-name seq-num ipsec-isakmp
```

Logically, the sequence number is what you use to specify the order that traffic is compared to the crypto map; the lowest sequence number is compared first. So it's a very good idea to give the sequences that will be matched most often a lower sequence number—they'll process through more quickly that way.

 Real World Scenario

When Would You Need More Than One Sequence?

Because an interface can have only one crypto map applied to it, you can run into a bit of trouble when you need more than one IPSec tunnel to form over an interface. The following graphic illustrates a network that would need two IPSec tunnels over the same interface:

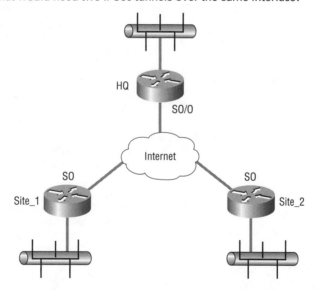

Company XYZ is made up of three sites: HQ, Site_1, and Site_2. All of the sites are connected to the Internet for WAN connectivity. The HQ site needs to have one IPSec tunnel connection to Site_1 and one IPSec tunnel connection to Site_2. How do you do this when you already know that an interface can have only one crypto map applied to it? All you need to do is create a crypto map with two sequences—one for the connection to Site_1 and the other for the connection to Site_2.

Once you've created the sequence with the `crypto map` command, the device enters crypto map configuration mode. This is where you get to configure the specific parameters of the sequence. Table 8.1 lists the commands you can enter in crypto map configuration mode for a sequence using IKE.

TABLE 8.1 Crypto Map Configuration Mode Commands

Command	Purpose
`match address {access-list-number	name}`	A mandatory command that specifies the extended access list to use for defining the traffic to protect
`set peer {peer-address	peer-hostname}`	A mandatory command that specifies the IPSec peer
`set transform-set transform-set-name [transform-set-name2...transform-set-name6]`	A mandatory command that specifies a list of transform sets, in order of priority, to use for protecting traffic.
`description text`	An optional command that can be used to provide a description for a crypto map sequence
`set security-association lifetime seconds seconds`	An optional command that can be used to override the seconds global IPSec SA life-time for the sequence
`set security-association lifetime kilobytes kilobytes`	An optional command that can be used to override the kilobytes global IPSec SA life-time for the sequence
`set pfs {group1	group2}`	An optional command that can be used to specify the Diffie-Hellman group to use when requesting new security associations for this sequence
`set security-association level per-host`	An optional command that can be used to specify that separate IPSec SAs should be requested for each source/destination host pair

You can configure multiple peers for each sequence—very cool when you want to set a backup path for the IPSec tunnel in case the primary path goes down. When multiple peers are set for a sequence, the device begins with the first one entered and proceeds down the list until an IPSec SA is set up.

Once you've created your crypto map, you need to apply it to an interface.

Applying the Crypto Map

When you create IPSec tunnels without using GRE tunnels, the crypto map has to be applied to the outgoing interface. If you use GRE tunnels instead, you need to apply the crypto map to both the tunnel interface and the egress interfaces. The egress interfaces are any that may be used to form the GRE tunnel. You can have more than one GRE interface.

To apply a crypto map to an interface, enter the following command in interface configuration mode, where *map-name* is the name of the crypto map being applied to the interface:

```
crypto map map-name
```

For redundancy, you could apply the same *crypto map set* to more than one interface. The default behavior is as follows:

- Each interface will have its own piece of the security association database.
- The IP address of the local interface will be used as the local address for IPSec traffic originating from or destined to that interface.

If you decide to apply the same crypto map set to multiple interfaces, you need to specify an identifying interface. Doing this causes the following:

- The per-interface portion of the IPSec security association database (SAD) will be established one time and shared for traffic through all the interfaces that share the same crypto map.
- The IP address of the identifying interface will be used as the local address for IPSec traffic originating from or destined to those interfaces sharing the same crypto map set.

To designate the identifying interface, enter the following command in global configuration mode, where *map-name* is the name of the crypto map and *local-id* is the IP address of the identifying interface:

```
crypto map map-name local-address local-id
```

You must use this `crypto map` command if you are applying a crypto map to a GRE tunnel because the crypto map will be applied to both the tunnel interface and the egress interface.

When you specify an identifying interface, you must use the IP address of that interface whenever you configure the peer statements on the remote peers.

Before you move on to the final step in the process of configuring IPSec for pre-shared keys—testing and verifying IPSec—let's run through a sample IPSec configuration.

In Exercise 8.2, you'll build upon the configuration you began in the IKE section of this chapter. For a refresher, the following graphic illustrates the network you began configuring:

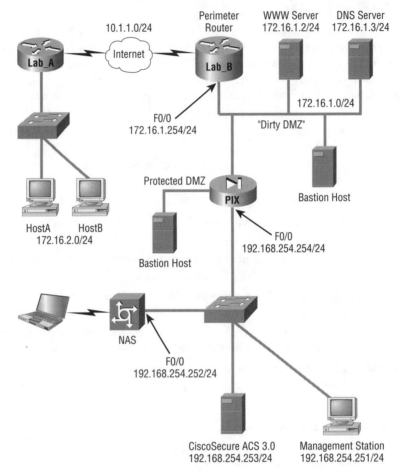

But before you jump into configuring IPSec, let's take another look at how the devices have been configured so far:

```
Lab_A#conf t
Enter configuration commands, one per line.  End with CNTL/Z.
Lab_A(config)#crypto isakmp enable
Lab_A(config)#crypto isakmp policy 2
Lab_A(config-isakmp)#encryption 3des
Lab_A(config-isakmp)#hash md5
Lab_A(config-isakmp)#authentication pre-share
Lab_A(config-isakmp)#exit
Lab_A(config)#crypto isakmp key cisco address 10.1.1.2
```

```
Lab_A(config)#^Z
Lab_A#

Lab_B#conf t
Enter configuration commands, one per line.  End with CNTL/Z.
Lab_B(config)#crypto isakmp enable
Lab_B(config)#crypto isakmp policy 2
Lab_B(config-isakmp)#encryption 3des
Lab_B(config-isakmp)#hash md5
Lab_B(config-isakmp)#authentication pre-share
Lab_B(config-isakmp)#exit
Lab_B(config)#crypto isakmp key cisco address 10.1.1.1
Lab_B(config)#^Z
Lab_B#
```

EXERCISE 8.2

Configuring IPSec on Our Sample Corporate Network

Now you're ready to configure IPSec. You need to add IPSec to your currently configured network with IKE using the following steps:

1. Create a transform set on each device named **test** using esp-des and tunnel mode.

2. Leave the global IPSec SA lifetimes set to their defaults.

3. Create a symmetrical extended access list on each device that will permit traffic from networks 172.16.2.0 /24 and 172.16.1.0 /24.

4. Create a crypto map on each device using the name **test1** and sequence number **100**. Each sequence should use the transform set test and the extended access list just created, and set the peer to the IP address of the outgoing interface of the remote device.

5. Apply the crypto map to each device's outgoing interface.

6. Use the following commands to configure the Lab_A router:

```
Lab_A#conf t

Enter configuration commands, one per line.  End with CNTL/Z.

Lab_A(config)#crypto ipsec tramsform-set test esp-des

Lab_A(cfg-crypto-trans)#exit

Lab_A(config)#access-list 100 permit ip 172.16.2.0 0.0.0.255 172.16.1.0 0.0.0.255
```

EXERCISE 8.2 *(continued)*

```
Lab_A(config)#access-list 100 permit ip 172.16.1.0 0.0.0.255 172.16.2.0 0.0.0.255

Lab_A(config)#cryto map test1 100 ipsec-isakmp

Lab_A(config-crypto-map)#match address 100

Lab_A(config-crypto-map)#set transform-set test

Lab_A(config-crypto-map)#set peer 10.1.1.2

Lab_A(config-crypto-map)#exit

Lab_A(config)#interface s0/0

Lab_A(config-if)#crypto map test1

Lab_A(config-if)#^Z

Lab_A#


Lab_B#conf t

Enter configuration commands, one per line.  End with CNTL/Z.

Lab_B(config)#crypto ipsec tramsform-set test esp-des

Lab_B(cfg-crypto-trans)#exit

Lab_B(config)#access-list 100 permit ip 172.16.2.0 0.0.0.255 172.16.1.0 0.0.0.255

Lab_B(config)#access-list 100 permit ip 172.16.1.0 0.0.0.255 172.16.2.0 0.0.0.255

Lab_B(config)#cryto map test1 100 ipsec-isakmp

Lab_B(config-crypto-map)#match address 100

Lab_B(config-crypto-map)#set transform-set test

Lab_B(config-crypto-map)#set peer 10.1.1.1

Lab_B(config-crypto-map)#exit

Lab_B(config)#interface s1/0

Lab_B(config-if)#crypto map test1

Lab_B(config-if)#^Z

Lab_B#
```

As always, you have to be able to verify your configurations. The next section will guide you through this process.

Testing and Verifying IPSec

It's test-and-verify time again. With network operations, you just can't skip these steps. So now you're going to take some time to review the commands you need to use to verify IPSec operation.

The show crypto isakmp sa command is one of the most widely used commands for verifying IKE operation after IPSec has been configured. It gives you information about all of the active IKE SAs on the device. Here's a sample of the output you'll get when you use this command:

```
Lab_A#show crypto isakmp sa
   dst       src       state     conn-id  slot
10.1.1.2  10.1.1.1  QM_IDLE      82        0
```

Have a problem? For troubleshooting, it may be important to reset IKE SAs using the clear crypto isakmp *conn-id* command. With it, you can clear a single IKE SA. Alternatively, you can use the clear crypto isakmp * command to clear all active IKE SAs.

If you need more information, use the debug crypto isakmp command to display messages about IKE events. In addition, you can use the debug crypto ipsec command to learn even more.

If you want to get a look at the configuration of all IPSec transform sets on a certain device, use the show crypto ipsec transform-set command. Here's a sample of its output:

```
Lab_A#show crypto ipsec transform-set
Transform set test: { esp-des }
   will negotiate = { Tunnel,  },
```

The aptly named show crypto map command is what you use to display the configuration of all crypto maps currently configured on a device—a great way to find out if someone blew their crypto map configuration.

To verify that an IPSec SA is working okay, use the show crypto ipsec sa command. Below is a sample of its output:

```
Lab_A#show crypto ipsec sa
interface: Serial0/0
   Crypto map tag: test1, local addr. 10.1.1.1
   local  ident (addr/mask/prot/port):
   (10.1.1.1/255.255.255.255/0/0)
   remote ident (addr/mask/prot/port):
   (10.1.1.2/255.255.255.255/0/0)
   current_peer: 10.1.1.2
     PERMIT, flags={origin_is_acl,}
   #pkts encaps: 10, #pkts encrypt: 10, #pkts digest 10
```

```
#pkts decaps: 10, #pkts decrypt: 10, #pkts verify 10
#send errors 10, #recv errors 0

 local crypto endpt.: 10.1.1.1, remote crypto endpt.: 10.1.1.2
 path mtu 1500, media mtu 1500
 current outbound spi: 20890A6F

 inbound esp sas:
  spi: 0x257A1039(628756537)
    transform: esp-des ,
    in use settings ={Tunnel, }
    slot: 0, conn id: 26, crypto map: test1
    sa timing: remaining key lifetime (k/sec): (4607999/90)
    IV size: 8 bytes
    replay detection support: Y

 inbound ah sas:

 outbound esp sas:
  spi: 0x20890A6F(545852015)
    transform: esp-des ,
    in use settings ={Tunnel, }
    slot: 0, conn id: 27, crypto map: test1
    sa timing: remaining key lifetime (k/sec): (4607999/90)
    IV size: 8 bytes
    replay detection support: Y

 outbound ah sas:
```

And there are also several commands that you can use to reset an IPSec SA. Table 8.2 lists these commands and describes what they do.

TABLE 8.2 IPSec SA *clear* Commands

Command	Purpose
clear crypto sa	Resets all IPSec SAs on a device
clear crypto sa peer {*ip-address* | *peer-name*}	Resets the IPSec SA for the specified peer

TABLE 8.2 IPSec SA *clear* Commands *(continued)*

Command	Purpose
clear crypto sa map *map-name*	Resets the IPSec SA for the specified crypto map
clear crypto sa entry *destination-address protocol spi*	Resets the IPSec SA for the specified address, protocol, and SPI
clear crypto sa counters	Resets the IPSec traffic counters for all IPSec SAs on the device

Okay, everyone, it's reward time—you've made it, now celebrate! Seriously! That's all there is to configuring IPSec utilizing pre-shared keys. You're not completely done yet though, because next I'm going to show you how to configure IPSec without using IKE. If you're on a roll, great—keep going! But at least get some more coffee or get up and stretch or something, because truthfully, you're really only about halfway through this chapter!

Configuring IPSec Manually

If you configure IPSec manually, you don't have to use IKE. But doing this means you'll have to specify the inbound and outbound keys to use on each device for establishing the IPSec SA manually. And no doubt you remember me telling you that wasn't such a great idea back in Chapter 7, "Understanding Cisco IOS IPSec Support," for two reasons—it's not as secure as using IKE, and it's harder to scale.

It follows then that you don't need to bother creating an IKE policy if you manually configure IPSec, right? Right, but you don't get to skip any of the other steps that were laid out for configuring IPSec utilizing pre-shared keys, so don't get too excited.

Anyway, other than having to give the inbound and outbound keys your personal attention, the main difference in configuring IPSec manually is how you create the crypto map. Let's look at that now. While in global configuration mode, you're going to create a manual crypto map sequence by entering the following command, where *map-name* is the name of the crypto map and *seq-num* is the sequence number of the crypto map sequence, a value between 1 and 65,535:

crypto map *map-name* *seq-num* ipsec-manual

All of the commands defined previously in Table 8.1 still apply to manual crypto map sequences, but there are four more mandatory commands that must be entered in crypto map configuration mode that are listed in Table 8.3.

TABLE 8.3   Additional Commands for Manual Crypto Map Sequences

Command	Purpose
set session-key inbound ah *spi hex-key-string*	A mandatory command that specifies the inbound key to use for Authentication Header (AH)
set session-key outbound ah *spi hex-key-string*	A mandatory command that specifies the outbound key to use for AH
set session-key inbound esp *spi* cipher *hex-key-string* [authenticator *hex-key-string*]	A mandatory command that specifies the inbound key to use for ESP
set session-key outbound esp *spi* cipher *hex-key-string* [authenticator *hex-key-string*]	A mandatory command that specifies the outbound key to use for ESP

WARNING   The outbound key of one device must be the same as the inbound key of the remote peer.

Configuring IPSec for RSA-Encrypted Nonces

RSA-encrypted nonces require you to perform two tasks: manually generate the public/private keys and then manually enter the public key of a device on the remote peer. Configuring IPSec for RSA-encrypted nonces is a five-step process:

1. Prepare for IPSec using RSA-encrypted nonces. This includes planning how to distribute the public keys.
2. Generate the RSA public/private keys manually.
3. Configure IKE using RSA-encrypted nonces.
4. Configure IPSec.
5. Test and verify IPSec.

You'll work through each of these steps in this section, beginning with the first step.

Preparing for IPSec Using RSA-Encrypted Nonces

Sorry—you still need to answer all those questions outlined in the "Preparing for IKE and IPSec" section at the very beginning of this chapter, plus one more: What's your plan for distributing the public keys to potential peers? (This has to be accomplished out of band.)

Generating the RSA Public/Private Keys Manually for RSA-Encrypted Nonces

This step is actually the biggest change from configuring IPSec utilizing pre-shared keys. It's also the most involved step. When generating the RSA public/private keys manually, you've got five steps to follow:

1. Plan for configuring RSA.

2. Configure the device's hostname and domain name.

3. Generate the RSA public/private keys.

4. Manually enter the RSA public key on remote devices.

5. Manage the RSA keys.

Planning for Configuring RSA

There are a few more questions to answer before you jump in and configure RSA so that the number of errors that can occur during configuration are kept to a minimum:

- What peers will use RSA encryption? Make a list of these devices.

- What type of RSA keys will you use? You have two choices: general-usage or special-usage keys.

- What size of key modulus—a value between 360 and 2048 bits—do you want to use? The higher the bit value, the stronger the encryption.

Configuring the Device's Hostname and Domain Name for RSA-Encrypted Nonces

Armed with the answers to the preceding questions, you're ready to begin configuring these three items:

- Hostname

- Domain name

- Static hostname-to-address mapping for each peer

Because RSA encryption uses these three items for IKE identity, they must be properly configured in order for RSA to function. To configure the hostname of a device, enter the following command in global configuration mode, where *hostname* is the name of the device:

```
hostname hostname
```

The domain name is used in conjunction with the hostname to produce the fully qualified domain name for the device. You configure this by entering the following command in global configuration mode, where *domain-name* is the name of the domain:

```
ip domain-name domain-name
```

If a DNS server isn't available, you only need to configure a static hostname-to-address mapping for each peer by entering the following command in global configuration mode:

ip host *name* [*tcp-port-number*] *address1* [*address2...address8*]

The parameters for the preceding command are as follows:

- *name*: The name of the remote device.

- *tcp-port-number*: The CP port number to connect to when using the defined hostname in conjunction with an EXEC connect or Telnet command.

- *address1*: The IP address you want bound to the hostname.

- *address2...address8*: You can bind seven more addresses to the hostname.

Generating the RSA Public/Private Keys

Now you're ready to generate the RSA public/private keys on each device, but before issuing the command to generate the keys, you need to decide if you want to create special-usage keys or *general-usage keys*. Special-usage keys generate two public/private key pairs per device—a good choice when you're using RSA signatures and RSA-encrypted nonces on the same device and you don't want them using the same keys. General-usage keys create one public/private key pair that will be used by both RSA signatures and RSA-encrypted nonces.

With the key-type decision out of the way, it's time to start configuring. Enter the following command in global configuration mode:

crypto key generate rsa [**usage-keys**]

Be sure to use the usage-keys keyword when you want to generate special-usage keys.

Once you've entered the command to generate the keys, the device prompts you to enter the modulus length. This value tells the device the level of encryption strength to use—the higher the number, the stronger the encryption. Keep in mind that entering a higher value also means that it'll take longer to generate those keys.

All right, let's take a second and see what this process really looks like on a device. Oh, and keep in mind that this device already has its hostname and domain name configured. Here it is:

```
Lab_A#conf t
Enter configuration commands, one per line.  End with CNTL/Z.
Lab_A(config)#crypto key generate rsa
The name for the keys will be: Lab_A.mycorp.com
Choose the size of the key modulus in the range of 360 to 2048 for your
    ⮡Signature Keys.
Choosing a key modulus greater than 512 may take a few minutes.
How many bits in the modulus [512]: 512
Generating RSA keys…
[OK]
% Key pair was generated at 10:22:30 UTC Dec 23 2002
Lab_A(config)#
```

Once your RSA keys have been generated, you need a way to view them so you can take the public key from one device and input it into another one. To check out the RSA public key, just enter the following command in privileged-exec mode:

`show crypto key mypubkey rsa`

Here's a sample of what Lab_A would then show you:

```
Lab_A#show crypto key mypubkey rsa
Key name: Lab_A.mycorp.com
 Usage: General Purpose Key
 Key Data:
  005C300D 06092A86 4886F70D 01010105 00034B00 30480241 00C5E23B 55D6AB22
     ⮡04AEF1BA A54028A6 9ACC01C5 129D99E4 64CAB820 847EDAD9 DF0B4E4C 73A05DD2
     ⮡BD62A8A9 FA603DD2 E2A8A6F8 98F76E28 D58AD221 B583D7A4 71020301 0001
```

The information below the words "Key Data" is the public key. Since you need to input this key into any device you want to peer with, it's a brilliant idea to copy it down so you can transmit it out of band to remote devices.

Entering the RSA Public Key on Remote Devices Manually

Before you can enter the public key on any remote devices, you need to get into public key chain configuration mode. Do this by entering this command while in global configuration mode:

`crypto key pubkey-chain rsa`

You must specify whether the key is an addressed key or a named key. How the IKE identity has been configured on the device that generated the key decides this. If the IKE identity is address, you use the addressed key; if it's hostname, use the named key. You can also specify whether the key is an encryption key or a signature key with the following rules:

- Encryption specifies that the key will be an encryption special-usage key. Use this when you have generated special-usage keys and you are inputting the encryption key.

- Signature specifies that the key will be a signature special-usage key. Use this when you have generated special-usage keys and you are inputting the signature key.

- Not specifying the type of key makes it a general-purpose key. Use this when you generate general-usage keys.

While in public key chain configuration mode, enter one of the following commands:

`addressed-key` *key-address* {`encryption` | `signature`}

`named-key` *key-name* {`encryption` | `signature`}

In the `addressed-key` command, *key-address* is the IP address of the device that generated the key. In the `named-key` command, *key-name* is the fully qualified domain name of the device that generated the key.

Once you've specified the type of key and entered public key configuration mode, it's time to issue the key-string command. After that, you input the public key. Once you've done that, use the quit command to return to public key configuration mode. Here's the output caused by entering the key generated by Lab_A on Lab_B:

```
Lab_B#conf t
Enter configuration commands, one per line.  End with CNTL/Z.
Lab_B(config)#crypto key pubkey-chain rsa
Lab_B(config-pubkey-chain)#addressed-key 10.1.1.1
Lab_B(config-pubkey-key)#key-string
Lab_B(config-pubkey)#005C300D 06092A86 4886F70D 01010105 00034B00 30480241
   ↳00C5E23B 55D6AB22 04AEF1BA A54028A6 9ACC01C5 129D99E4 64CAB820 847EDAD9
   ↳DF0B4E4C 73A05DD2 BD62A8A9 FA603DD2 E2A8A6F8 98F76E28 D58AD221 B583D7A4
    ↳71020301 0001
Lab_B(config-pubkey)#quit
Lab_B(config-pubkey-key)#^Z
Lab_B#
```

Verify that the key has been accepted by entering the command show crypto key pubkey-chain rsa in privileged-exec mode:

```
Lab_B#show crypto key pubkey-chain rsa
Codes: M -  Manually configured, C - Extracted from Certificate


Code  Usage    IP-Address    Name
M     General  10.1.1.1
```

To check out the actual key that you or someone else entered, use the show crypto key pubkey-chain rsa {address *address* | name *name*} command in privileged-exec mode:

```
Lab_B#show crypto key pubkey-chain rsa address 10.1.1.1
Key name:
Key address: 10.1.1.1
 Usage: General Purpose Key
 Source: Manual
 Data:
 005C300D 06092A86 4886F70D 01010105 00034B00 30480241 00C5E23B 55D6AB22
   ↳04AEF1BA A54028A6 9ACC01C5 129D99E4 64CAB820 847EDAD9 DF0B4E4C 73A05DD2
   ↳BD62A8A9 FA603DD2 E2A8A6F8 98F76E28 D58AD221 B583D7A4 71020301 0001
```

Managing the RSA Keys

To keep your system clean, it's crucial to remove keys that are no longer valid. To spruce things up, get into public key chain configuration mode and issue the no form of either the addressed-key command or the named-key command.

It's nice that those last three steps in this process are pretty much identical to those for configuring pre-shared keys, huh?

Configuring IKE Using RSA-Encrypted Nonces

You're going to configure IKE almost exactly the same way as you did for pre-shared keys. The one exception is the authentication method. Instead of entering the authentication pre-shared command, you enter the authentication rsa-encr command. Verify that the IKE policy works the same way using the same commands you used earlier.

Configuring IPSec for RSA-Encrypted Nonces

IPSec for RSA-encrypted nonces is configured in the same exact way as IPSec utilizing pre-shared keys—no exceptions. For a refresher on configuring IPSec, refer back to the section titled "Configure IPSec" earlier in this chapter.

Testing and Verifying IPSec for RSA-Encrypted Nonces

And lastly, to verify IPSec for RSA-encrypted nonces, you use the same commands you used in the "Testing and Verifying IPSec" section earlier in this chapter, along with the show commands described in this section.

Configuring Cisco IOS IPSec Certificate Authority Support Site-to-Site

IPSec for CA is the most scalable of all IPSec implementations because it allows a device to receive a digital certificate from a CA server that it uses to identify itself for IPSec peering.

This section describes all the steps you'll need to learn how to configure IPSec for CA.

Configuring CA Support Tasks

To configuring IPSec for CA, you must complete these five tasks:

- Prepare for IKE and IPSec.
- Configure CA support.
- Configure IKE.
- Configure IPSec.
- Test and verify IPSec.

When you find yourself at the end of this section, you'll be able to implement site-to-site IPSec for CA. Did you notice that some of these tasks overlap with the ones described previously in IPSec for pre-shared keys? Well, sometimes the ball really does bounce your way—I'm only going to touch on the overlapping ones briefly.

Preparing for IKE and IPSec

Once again, you need to answer those questions back in the "Preparing for IKE and IPSec" section of this chapter, but this time, you get two additional questions to ponder:

- Which CA server are you going to use? You need to determine that in order to assign your certificate.

- Do you need to use trusted root CA servers? You need to configure them if you intend to peer with devices that aren't using the same CA server as you are.

Configuring CA Support

Remember back a bit when I suggested taking that break? Did you take it? If so, you're good to go. If not—ummmm…well, live and learn. This step is actually the greatest departure from the method used in configuring IPSec utilizing pre-shared keys; there's lots of new stuff to learn in this section. If you want to configure CA support, you've got to successfully complete each of the following nine steps:

1. Manage NVRAM memory usage.
2. Configure the device's hostname and domain name.
3. Generate the RSA public/private keys.
4. Declare a CA.
5. Configure a root CA (trusted root).
6. Authenticate the CA.
7. Request the device's certificate.
8. Verify CA interoperability.
9. Save your configurations.

Managing NVRAM Memory Usage

Certificates are stored locally on a device—something that usually won't give you any memory-related grief. But it can, so if you think your situation warrants it or if you just don't want to take any chances, enter the following command in global configuration mode:

```
crypto ca certificate query
```

Doing this ensures that the device retrieves certificates from the CA server only when needed.

> Some ugly issues can arise when retrieving certificates if the CA server is down, so be sure the certificate server is up and running before performing your query.

Configuring the Device's Hostname and Domain Name for CA

I'm not going to go over this step again because you do it the exact same way as you did for RSA-encrypted nonces. If you need a review, refer to the section "Configuring the Device's Hostname and Domain Name for RSA-Encrypted Nonces" earlier in this chapter.

Generating the RSA Public/Private Keys Manually for CA

This step is also accomplished the same way as it was for RSA-encrypted nonces, so refer back to the "Generating the RSA Public/Private Keys Manually for RSA-Encrypted Nonces" section earlier in this chapter if you need a review.

Declaring a CA

Okay, let's move on. In order for CA to operate, you must first designate a CA server that you'll request your certificates from. Let's define a few terms before diving into configuration:

Simple Certificate Enrollment Protocol (SCEP) *Simple Certificate Enrollment Protocol (SCEP)* is a CA interoperability protocol that permits compliant IPSec peers and CAs to communicate so that the IPSec peer can obtain and use digital certificates from the CA.

Certificate revocation lists (CRL) *Certificate revocation lists (CRL)* are lists of certificates that have been revoked and are no longer valid. IPSec peers can obtain the CRL from the CA server and should check the CRL every time an IPSec peer attempts to establish a new IKE SA.

Registration authority (RA) A *registration authority (RA)* is a server that acts as a proxy for the CA so that CA functions can continue when the CA is offline.

Now that you're clear on these terms, you ready to start configuring.

All people name their kids, most people name their dogs, and some people even name their cars. You will name your CA. This first step for declaring your CA is done by entering the following command in global configuration mode, where *name* is the name you will use to refer to the CA:

```
crypto ca identity name
```

Entering this command places the device in ca-identity configuration mode where you can spell out the CA-specific information such as the enrollment URL.

Which is what you're going to do next: enter the URL of your CA. This is the address to which the router will send certificate requests. To configure the enrollment URL, enter the following command in ca-identity configuration mode, where *url* is the URL to which the certificate requests will be sent:

`enrollment url` *url*

If the CA server you are communicating with provides an RA, you need to enable enrollment RA support by entering the following command in ca-identity configuration mode:

`enrollment mode ra`

Each of the next four commands will also be entered in this mode.

If your CA server provides an RA and supports Lightweight Directory Access Protocol (LDAP), and your CA server supports both RA and LDAP, you'll need to specify a URL to query. To specify a URL to query, enter the following command, where *url* is the LDAP URL to query for retrieving certificates:

`query url` *url*

By default, a device requires that an IPSec peer's certificate be checked against the appropriate CRL before accepting the certificate. Sometimes a device won't be able to obtain the CRL, and when that happens, it responds by rejecting the IPSec peer. To avoid this snag, use the following command:

`crl optional`

By default, devices send the CA server certificate requests every minute until they receive a valid certificate in return. You can change this default behavior with the following command, where *minutes* is a value between 1 and 60:

`enrollment retry period` *minutes*

Devices also send CA server certificate requests until they receive a valid certificate back—something you'd probably love some control over. Good news: You can limit the number of times a device will request the certificate via this command, where *number* is a value between 1 and 100:

`enrollment retry count` *number*

That's all, folks—you've now successfully declared your CA server. But before moving on, let's take a look at how this works.

In the following example, device Lab_A is configured to declare a CA that is creatively dubbed test_ca. The enrollment URL is `http://ca_server`. The CA doesn't support RA or LDAP, and the device is configured to ignore the CRL if one can't be found:

```
Lab_A#conf t
Enter configuration commands, one per line.  End with CNTL/Z.
```

```
Lab_A(config)#crypto ca identity test_ca
Lab_A(ca-identity)#enrollment url http://ca_server
Lab_A(ca-identity)#crl optional
Lab_A(ca-identity)#^Z
Lab_A#
```

Configuring a Root CA (Trusted Root)

A trusted root CA is the aptly named CA server that devices will trust certificates from even if those devices aren't enrolled with that CA. This is important to point out because you need to know that an IPSec peer may be enrolled with a different CA server than your device.

Like I said, the first thing you need to do is come up with a name you'll use to refer to your trusted root CA. Do this by entering the following command in global configuration mode, where *name* is the name you'll use for the trusted root CA:

```
crypto ca trusted-root name
```

When you enter the preceding command, you put the device into trusted root configuration mode—the place from which you'll specify the trusted root–specific information such as the URL that trusted root certificates will be received from.

Once your trusted root has its name squared away, you need to decide if the device will use the SCEP protocol or the TFTP protocol to query the trusted root CA. If the SCEP protocol is your winner, enter this command in trusted root configuration mode, where *url* is the URL of the trusted root CA:

```
root CEP url
```

The next three commands are all issued from within the trusted root configuration mode.

If you want to use the TFTP protocol, use the following command instead, where *url* is the URL of the trusted root CA:

```
root TFTP url
```

If the trusted root CA is utilizing an HTTP proxy server, you need to define the URL of the proxy server with the following command, where *url* is the URL of the trusted root CA proxy server:

```
root PROXY url
```

You also get an option to indicate the URL to query using LDAP for CRLs from the trusted root server. To make this your reality, use the following command, where *ldap-url* is the LDAP URL to use for querying:

```
crl query ldap-url
```

With your CA server declared and everything, including your trusted root servers configured so nicely, it's time to move on to authentication.

Authenticating the CA

You have finally arrived—Easy Street, baby! Yes, it's true that you still have to authenticate those declared and trusted root CA servers, but doing that is a day at the beach! You need only one command to authenticate a CA server. From within global configuration mode, enter the following command, where *name* is the name you used for the CA server:

crypto ca authenticate *name*

Once your CA server is authenticated, it receives the public key of the CA server. After you've entered the preceding command, the device asks if you accept the certificate, to which you reply either yes or no. Here's an example of authenticating the CA server declared on device Lab_A:

```
Lab_A#conf t
Enter configuration commands, one per line.  End with CNTL/Z.
Lab_A(config)#crypto ca authenticate test_ca
Certificate has the following attributes:
Fingerprint: 0123 4567 89AB CDEF 0123
Do you accept this certificate? [yes/no]#y
Lab_A(config)#
```

Requesting the Device's Certificate

After authenticating the CA, a device needs to request its own certificate from the CA server. To request a certificate, enter the following command in global configuration mode, where *name* is the name you used for the CA server:

crypto ca enroll *name*

Entering the preceding command starts the inquisition—you're then asked a number of questions, as you can see in the following output:

```
Lab_A#conf t
Enter configuration commands, one per line.  End with CNTL/Z.
Lab_A(config)#crypto ca enroll test_ca
%
% Start certificate enrollment ..
% Create a challenge password. You will need to verbally provide this password
       ↳to the CA Administrator in order to revoke your certificate. For security
       ↳reasons your password will not be saved in the configuration. Please make
       ↳ a note of it.
Password: cisco
Re-enter password: cisco
```

```
% The subject name in the certificate will be: Lab_A.mycorp.com
% Include the router serial number in the subject name? [yes/no]: no
% Include an IP address in the subject name [yes/no]? yes
Interface: serial0/0
Request certificate from CA [yes/no]? yes
% Certificate request sent to Certificate Authority
% The certificate request fingerprint will be displayed.
% The 'show crypto ca certificate' command will also show the fingerprint.
Lab_A(config)#
```

Verifying and Saving Your Configurations

Now once again, it's verification time. Verifying CA interoperability introduces two new show commands to the group you met earlier in the "Entering the RSA Public Key on Remote Devices Manually" section earlier in this chapter. Your new friends are

- The show crypto ca certificates command that can be entered in privileged-exec mode to display information about a device's certificate, the CA server certificate, and any RA certificates

- The show crypto ca roots command that can also be entered in privileged-exec mode to display information about the CA roots configured on the device

You should always save your configuration after you make changes. After all this work, it would be a shame to lose it all now!

Use the copy system:running-config nvram:startup-config command to save your configuration. This saves the RSA keys as well. Saving to a TFTP server or using the Remote Copy Protocol (RCP) to save your configuration will not save the RSA keys.

Configuring IKE Using CA

IKE is configured the same way it was for pre-shared keys and RSA-encrypted nonces with one exception: the authentication method used. You need to enter the command authentication rsa-sig in IKE policy configuration mode. You verify the IKE policy using the same commands I showed you earlier.

Configuring IPSec for CA

IPSec for CA is configured in the same exact way as IPSec utilizing pre-shared keys and IPSec for RSA-encrypted nonces with no exceptions. If you're less than clear on this, refer back to the section titled "Configuring IPSec" earlier in this chapter.

Sweet—you're almost there—stay with me! Before moving on to testing and verifying IPSec for CA, let's look at how all these steps come together.

To help you see the whole picture, you're going to configure IPSec for CA between devices Lab_A and Lab_B in Exercise 8.3. Recall once again the corporate network shown in the following graphic:

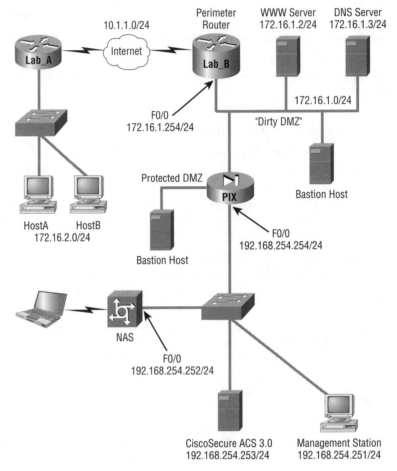

Let's get started by dividing the process of configuring IPSec for CA into four steps:

1. Generate RSA public/private keys.
2. Configure CA support.
3. Configure IKE.
4. Configure IPSec.

Both hostnames and domain names have already been configured on the devices.

EXERCISE 8.3

Configuring IPSec for the CA Network

This exercise will have you configure IPSec using CA on the corporate network example.

1. First, you need to generate the public/private keys on each device using the following commands:

Lab_A#**conf t**

Enter configuration commands, one per line.   End with CNTL/Z.

Lab_A(config)#**crypto key generate rsa**

The name for the keys will be: Lab_A.mycorp.com

Choose the size of the key modulus in the range of 360 to 2048 for your

    ↳Signature Keys.

Choosing a key modulus greater than 512 may take a few minutes.

How many bits in the modulus [512]: **512**

Generating RSA keys…

[OK]

% Key pair was generated at 10:22:30 UTC Dec 23 2002

Lab_A(config)#

Lab_B#**conf t**

Enter configuration commands, one per line.   End with CNTL/Z.

Lab_B(config)#**crypto key generate rsa**

The name for the keys will be: Lab_B.mycorp.com

Choose the size of the key modulus in the range of 360 to 2048 for your

    ↳Signature Keys.

Choosing a key modulus greater than 512 may take a few minutes.

How many bits in the modulus [512]: **512**

Generating RSA keys…

[OK]

EXERCISE 8.3 *(continued)*

% Key pair was generated at 10:22:30 UTC Dec 23 2002

Lab_B(config)#

2. Next, you need to configure CA support on each device using the following parameters:

    CA name: test_ca.

    Enrollment URL: http://ca_server.

    The devices need to ignore the CRL if one cannot be found.

    The CA server doesn't support LDAP.

    Use the following commands to configure CA support:

Lab_A(config)#**crypto ca identity test_ca**

Lab_A(ca-identity)#**enrollment url http://ca_server**

Lab_A(ca-identity)#**crl optional**

Lab_A(ca-identity)#**exit**

Lab_A(config)#**crypto ca authenticate test_ca**

Certificate has the following attributes: Fingerprint: 0123 4567 89AB CDEF 0123

Do you accept this certificate? [yes/no]#**y**

Lab_A(config)#**crypto ca enroll test_ca**

%

% Start certificate enrollment.

% Create a challenge password. You will need to verbally provide this password
    ↳to the CA Administrator in order to revoke your certificate. For security
    ↳reasons your password will not be saved in the configuration. Please make
    ↳a note of it.

Password: **cisco**

Re-enter password: **cisco**

% The subject name in the certificate will be: Lab_A.mycorp.com

% Include the router serial number in the subject name? [yes/no]: **no**

EXERCISE 8.3 *(continued)*

% Include an IP address in the subject name [yes/no]? **yes**

Interface: **serial0/0**

Request certificate from CA [yes/no]? **yes**

% Certificate request sent to Certificate Authority

% The certificate request fingerprint will be displayed.

% The 'show crypto ca certificate' command will also show the fingerprint.

Lab_A(config)#

Lab_B(config)#**crypto ca identity test_ca**

Lab_B(ca-identity)#**enrollment url http://ca_server**

Lab_B(ca-identity)#**crl optional**

Lab_B(ca-identity)#**exit**

Lab_B(config)#**crypto ca authenticate test_ca**

Certificate has the following attributes: Fingerprint: 0123 4567 89AB CDEF 0123

Do you accept this certificate? [yes/no]#**y**

Lab_B(config)#**crypto ca enroll test_ca**

%

% Start certificate enrollment.

% Create a challenge password. You will need to verbally provide this password

    ↳to the CA Administrator in order to revoke your certificate. For security

    ↳reasons your password will not be saved in the configuration. Please make

    ↳a note of it.

Password: **cisco**

Re-enter password: **cisco**

% The subject name in the certificate will be: Lab_A.mycorp.com

% Include the router serial number in the subject name? [yes/no]: **no**

EXERCISE 8.3 *(continued)*

% Include an IP address in the subject name [yes/no]? **yes**

Interface: **serial1/0**

Request certificate from CA [yes/no]? **yes**

% Certificate request sent to Certificate Authority

% The certificate request fingerprint will be displayed.

% The 'show crypto ca certificate' command will also show the fingerprint.

Lab_B(config)#

3. Configure IKE between the Lab_A device and the Lab_B device with the following parameters:

    Lab_A interface Serial 0/0 with IP address 10.1.1.1 /24

    Lab_B interface Serial 1/0 with IP address 10.1.1.2 /24

    Lab_A IKE policy priority equals 2

    Lab_B IKE policy priority equals 2

    3DES message encryption

    MD5 message hash

    Authentication method: rsa-sig

    Default Diffie-Hellman group for both devices

    Default IKE SA lifetime for both devices

    IKE identity as the address for both devices

    Use the following commands to configure IKE:

    Lab_A(config)#**crypto isakmp enable**

    Lab_A(config)#**crypto isakmp policy 2**

    Lab_A(config-isakmp)#**encryption 3des**

    Lab_A(config-isakmp)#**hash md5**

    Lab_A(config-isakmp)#**authentication rsa-sig**

    Lab_A(config-isakmp)#**exit**

    Lab_A(config)#

Lab_B(config)#**crypto isakmp enable**

Lab_B(config)#**crypto isakmp policy 2**

Lab_B(config-isakmp)#**encryption 3des**

Lab_B(config-isakmp)#**hash md5**

Lab_B(config-isakmp)#**authentication rsa-sig**

Lab_B(config-isakmp)#**exit**

Lab_B(config)#

4. Finally, it's time to configure IPSec, moving through the following list from beginning to end:

    Create a transform set on each device named **test** using esp-des and tunnel mode.

    Leave the global IPSec SA lifetimes set to their defaults.

    Create a symmetrical extended access list on each device that will permit traffic from networks 172.16.2.0 /24 and 172.16.1.0 /24.

    Create a crypto map on each device using the name **test1** and sequence number **100**.

    Each sequence should use the transform set test and the extended access list just created, and set the peer to the IP address of the outgoing interface of the remote device.

    Apply the crypto map to each device's outgoing interface.

    Use the following commands to configure IPSec:

Lab_A(config)#**crypto ipsec tramsform-set test esp-des**

Lab_A(cfg-crypto-trans)#**exit**

Lab_A(config)#**access-list 100 permit ip 172.16.2.0 0.0.0.255 172.16.1.0 0.0.0.255**

Lab_A(config)#**access-list 100 permit ip 172.16.1.0 0.0.0.255 172.16.2.0 0.0.0.255**

Lab_A(config)#**cryto map test1 100 ipsec-isakmp**

Lab_A(config-crypto-map)#**match address 100**

Lab_A(config-crypto-map)#**set transform-set test**

Lab_A(config-crypto-map)#**set peer 10.1.1.2**

Lab_A(config-crypto-map)#**exit**

```
Lab_A(config)#interface s0/0

Lab_A(config-if)#crypto map test1

Lab_A(config-if)#^Z

Lab_A#


Lab_B(config)#crypto ipsec tramsform-set test esp-des

Lab_B(cfg-crypto-trans)#exit

Lab_B(config)#access-list 100 permit ip 172.16.2.0 0.0.0.255 172.16.1.0 0.0.0.255

Lab_B(config)#access-list 100 permit ip 172.16.1.0 0.0.0.255 172.16.2.0 0.0.0.255

Lab_B(config)#cryto map test1 100 ipsec-isakmp

Lab_B(config-crypto-map)#match address 100

Lab_B(config-crypto-map)#set transform-set test

Lab_B(config-crypto-map)#set peer 10.1.1.1

Lab_B(config-crypto-map)#exit

Lab_B(config)#interface s1/0

Lab_B(config-if)#crypto map test1

Lab_B(config-if)#^Z

Lab_B#
```

Yes, you did it! You've configured IPSec for CA support all the way through! Start planning the festivities, call all your friends, order the food, and practice your acceptance speech—oh, wait. Oops, sorry. There's one more thing...

Testing and Verifying IPSec for CA

Verification. You've got to verify stuff, and IPSec for CA is no exception. You complete this one last gasp of a task using the same commands you learned earlier in the "Testing and Verifying IPSec" section in this chapter, along with the show commands I introduced you to in this section.

Summary

Do you feel as though you've run a marathon? Has your sanity been compromised by this gauntlet? Do you now have weird little twitches or find yourself staring at absolutely nothing for untold periods of time? No worries; it'll pass, I promise—really! Yup, this chapter was a long puppy, packed with tons of stuff to remember.

It is imperative that you can configure IPSec, starting with how to configure IPSec utilizing pre-shared keys. In addition, you need to know how to create IKE policies and configure pre-shared keys. Configuring IPSec without IKE is created using the IPSec-manual crypto map. Manually configuring IPSec requires you to specify the inbound and outbound keys used for establishing IPSec peers.

In addition to IPSec with IKE, you can use RSA-encrypted nonces with IPSec. These require you to manually generate RSA keys and then manually input the public key into all the devices you intend to peer with. However, don't try this with large networks!

Configuring IPSec can also be accomplished using CA—the most scalable of all the implementation types. CAs allow a device to request a certificate from a CA server and use that certificate in all of its peering attempts.

Yes, indeed. You certainly covered a tremendous amount of material in this chapter, so don't feel bad if you didn't get it all on your first read through. Go ahead—take however much time you need to go back and review any areas you feel a bit shaky about. But not yet—you've accomplished a ton—it's reward time. Take a break, have that party, and go to Vegas—whatever—you truly deserve it! Congratulations! Chapter 9, "Cisco IOS Remote Access Using Cisco Easy VPN," will be ready and waiting when you can think and form coherent sentences again. The best news about Chapter 9 is that it is short and sweet and it covers Easy VPN. Sounds nice, doesn't it? Oh, and did I mention it's the last chapter in this book? Sweet.

Exam Essentials

Understand the tasks required for IPSec utilizing pre-shared keys.   Configuring IPSec with pre-shared keys requires the following four tasks, in this order:

1. Prepare for IKE and IPSec.
2. Configure IKE.
3. Configure IPSec.
4. Test and verify IPSec.

You must be able to perform each of these four tasks.

Implement an IKE policy.   Given the need for IKE, you must be able to create an IKE policy. Once the IKE policy is created, you must be able to implement it on the devices you wish to peer.

Implement IPSec with IKE.   You must be able to implement IPSec once you have configured IKE. This requires you to configure global IPSec SA lifetimes, transform sets, extended access lists, crypto maps, and then apply the crypto map to an interface.

Implement IPSec without IKE.   You must be able to implement IPSec without the use of IKE. This requires you to manually configure the appropriate inbound and outbound session keys.

Implement RSA-encrypted nonces.   Given a scenario that requires the use of RSA-encrypted nonces, you must be able to implement it. This requires generating RSA public/private keys, manually entering the public key on devices you wish to peer with, configuring IKE using RSA-encrypted nonces, and configuring IPSec.

Understand the tasks required for IPSec with CA.   Configuring IPSec with CA requires the following five tasks:

1.   Prepare for IKE and IPSec.
2.   Configure CA support.
3.   Configure IKE.
4.   Configure IPSec.
5.   Test and verify IPSec.

You must be able to perform each of these five tasks.

Implement IPSec with CA.   Given a scenario that requires the use of CA servers, you must be able to implement it. This requires you to generate RSA public/private keys, declare a CA server, configure trusted root servers, authenticate the CA servers, request a certificate, configure IKE using RSA signatures, and configure IPSec.

Key Terms

Before you take the exam, be certain you are familiar with the following terms:

certificate revocation lists (CRL)	IPSec SA lifetime
crypto map set	registration authority (RA)
general-usage keys	Simple Certificate Enrollment Protocol (SCEP)

Commands Used in This Chapter

Here is the list of commands used in this chapter:

Command	Purpose
(config-pubkey-chain)#**addressed-key** *key-address* {**encryption** | **signature**}	Specifies that the entered RSA public key is an addressed key.
(config-isakmp)#**authentication** {**rsa-sig** | **rsa-encr** | **pre-share**}	Configures the authentication method for an IKE policy.
#**clear crypto isakmp** *conn-id*	Used to reset an IKE SA.
#**clear crypto isakmp** *	Used to reset all IKE SAs on a device.
#**clear crypto sa**	Resets all IPSec SAs on a device.
#**clear crypto sa peer** {*ip-address* | *peer-name*}	Resets the IPSec SA for the specified peer.
#**clear crypto sa map** *map-name*	Resets the IPSec SA for the specified crypto map.
#**clear crypto sa entry** *destination-address protocol spi*	Resets the IPSec SA for the specified address, protocol, and SPI.
#**clear crypto sa counters**	Resets the IPSec traffic counters for all IPSec SAs on the device.
(ca-identity)#**crl optional**	Allows a device to accept IPSec peering without the use of a CRL.
(ca-identity)#**crl query** *ldap-url*	Specifies that a device use LDAP when querying for CRLs.
<config>#**crypto ca authenticate** *name*	Used to authenticate a CA server.
<config>#**crypto ca certificate query**	Disables the local storing of certificates on a device.
<config>#**crypto ca enroll** *name*	Used to request a certificate from the CA server.
<config>#**crypto ca identity** *name*	Specifies a name for referring to a CA server.
<config>#**crypto ca trusted-root** *name*	Specifies a name for referring to a trusted root CA server.
<config>#**crypto key pubkey-chain rsa**	Places a device in public key chain configuration mode.

Command	Purpose
<config>#**crypto ipsec security-association lifetime seconds** *seconds*	A global lifetime command that specifies the number of seconds an IPSec SA will remain active before it expires.
<config>#**crypto ipsec security-association lifetime kilobytes** *kilobytes*	A global lifetime command that specifies the number of kilobytes an IPSec SA can transmit before it expires.
<config>#**crypto ipsec transform-set** *transform-set-name* {[*transform1*] [*transform2*] [*transform3*]}	Configures a transform set on a device.
<config>#**crypto isakmp enable**	Enables IKE.
<config>#**crypto isakmp identity** {**address**	**hostname**}	Specifies whether IKE will use an IP address or the device's hostname as its IKE identity.
<config>#**crypto isakmp key keystring** {**address** *peer-address*	**hostname** *peer-hostname*}	Creates a pre-shared key on a device.
<config-if>#**crypto map** *map-name*	Applies a crypto map to an interface.
<config>#**crypto map** *map-name* **local-address** *local-id*	Used to specify the identifying interface for a crypto map.
<config>#**crypto map** *map-name* *seq-num* **ipsec-isakmp**	Creates a crypto map sequence that utilizes IKE.
<config>#**crypto map** *map-name* *seq-num* **ipsec-manual**	Creates a crypto map sequence that doesn't use IKE.
<config>#**crypto isakmp policy** *priority*	Creates an IKE policy.
#**debug crypto ipsec**	Provides detailed information about the current operation of IPSec.
#**debug crypto isakmp**	Provides detailed information about the current operation of IKE.
(config-crypto-map)#**description** *text*	An optional command for configuring manual IPSec and IPSec with IKE that can be used to provide a description for a crypto map sequence.
(config-isakmp)#**encryption** {**des**	**3des**}	Configures the message-encryption algorithm for an IKE policy.
(ca-identity)#**enrollment mode ra**	Enables a device for RA support.

Command	Purpose
`(ca-identity)#enrollment retry count number`	Specifies the maximum number of times a device will attempt to request a certificate.
`(ca-identity)#enrollment retry period minutes`	Specifies the amount of a time a device will wait in between sending certificate requests.
`(ca-identity)#enrollment url url`	Specifies the URL for a device to send certificate queries to.
`<config>#crypto key generate rsa [usage-keys]`	Generates the RSA public/private key pairs.
`(config-isakmp)#group {1	2}`	Configures the Diffie-Hellman group for an IKE policy.
`(config-isakmp)#hash {sha	md5}`	Configures the message hash for an IKE policy.
`<config>#hostname hostname`	Specifies the hostname of a device.
`<config>#ip domain-name domain-name`	Specifies the domain name of a device.
`<config>#ip host name [tcp-port-number] address1 [address2...address8]`	Creates a static IP address-to-hostname mapping.
`(config-pubkey-key)#key-string`	Allows you to enter the public key of a remote device into your local device.
`(config-isakmp)#lifetime seconds`	Configures the IKE SA lifetime for an IKE policy.
`(config-crypto-map)#match address {access-list-number	name}`	A mandatory command for configuring manual IPSec and IPSec with IKE that specifies the extended access list to use for defining the traffic to protect.
`(cfg-crypto-trans)#mode {tunnel	transport}`	Configures the IPSec mode to be used.
`(config-pubkey-chain)#named-key key-name {encryption	signature}`	Specifies that the entered RSA public key is a named key.
`#no crypto isakmp enable`	Disables IKE.
`(ca-identity)#query url url`	Specifies an LDAP URL to query for certificates.
`(ca-identity)#root CEP url`	Specifies that SCEP will be used for querying a trusted root CA server.
`(ca-identity)#root TFTP url`	Specifies that TFTP will be used for querying a trusted root CA server.

Command	Purpose
`(ca-identity)#root PROXY url`	Specifies the URL of the HTTP proxy server the trusted root is using.
`(config-crypto-map)#set peer {peer-address	peer-hostname}`	A mandatory command for configuring manual IPSec and IPSec with IKE that specifies the IPSec peer.
`(config-crypto-map)#set transform-set transform-set-name [transform-set-name2...transform-set-name6]`	A mandatory command for configuring manual IPSec and IPSec with IKE that specifies a list of transform sets, in order of priority, to use for protecting traffic.
`(config-crypto-map)#set security-association lifetime seconds seconds`	An optional command for configuring manual IPSec and IPSec with IKE that can be used to override the seconds global IPSec SA lifetime for the sequence.
`(config-crypto-map)#set security-association lifetime kilobytes kilobytes`	An optional command for configuring manual IPSec and IPSec with IKE that can be used to override the kilobytes global IPSec SA lifetime for the sequence.
`(config-crypto-map)#set pfs {group1	group2}`	An optional command for configuring manual IPSec and IPSec with IKE that can be used to specify the Diffie-Hellman group to use when requesting new SAs for this sequence.
`(config-crypto-map)#set security-association level per-host`	An optional command for configuring manual IPSec and IPSec with IKE that can be used to specify that separate IPSec SAs should be requested for each source/destination host pair.
`(config-crypto-map)#set session-key inbound ah spi hex-key-string`	A mandatory command for configuring manual IPSec that specifies the inbound key to use for AH.
`(config-crypto-map)#set session-key outbound ah spi hex-key-string`	A mandatory command for configuring manual IPSec that specifies the outbound key to use for AH.
`(config-crypto-map)#set session-key inbound esp spi cipher hex-key-string [authenticator hex-key-string]`	A mandatory command for configuring manual IPSec that specifies the inbound key to use for ESP.
`(config-crypto-map)#set session-key outbound esp spi cipher hex-key-string [authenticator hex-key-string]`	A mandatory command for configuring manual IPSec that specifies the outbound key to use for ESP.

Command	Purpose
`#show crypto ca certificates`	Displays information about a device's certificate, the CA server certificate, and any RA certificates.
`#show crypto ca roots`	Displays information about the CA roots configured on the device.
`#show crypto key mypubkey rsa`	Displays the public key generated on a device.
`#show crypto key pubkey-chain rsa`	Displays the public keys manually entered on a device.
`#show crypto key pubkey-chain rsa {address address | name name}`	Displays a specific public key that was manually entered on a device.
`#show crypto ipsec sa`	Displays information about all currently active IPSec SAs on a device.
`#show crypto ipsec transform-set`	Displays the configuration of all transform sets currently configured on a device.
`#show crypto isakmp policy`	Used to display the IKE policies currently configured on a device.
`#show crypto isakmp sa`	Used to display information about all current IKE SAs on a device.
`#show crypto map`	Displays the configuration of all crypto maps currently configured on a device.

Written Lab

This section asks you 10 write-in-the-answer questions to help you understand the technology that you need to know in order to pass the SECUR exam.

1. What are the four tasks required for IPSec using pre-shared keys?
2. What are the five tasks required for IPSec using CA?
3. What IKE authentication method would you use for RSA-encrypted nonces?
4. What command must you type before you can manually enter the public key of a remote device into your local device?
5. What is the first configuration step required when configuring IPSec with CA?
6. What command is used to configure a pre-shared key on a device?

7. What command can be used to show the configuration of all crypto maps currently configured on a device?

8. What is the default message-encryption algorithm used by IKE?

9. What command would be used to create a crypto map sequence that didn't use IKE?

10. What IKE authentication method would you use for CA?

Review Questions

1. Which of the following statements are true about the `crypto ipsec security-association lifetime` command? (Choose all that apply.)

    A. It configures global IPSec SA lifetime values used when negotiating IPSec SAs.

    B. It can configure the global IPSec SA lifetime values based on kilobytes.

    C. It defines the outbound traffic to be protected by IPSec.

    D. The values can be overridden for a crypto map.

2. Which of the following commands can be used to specify Diffie-Hellman group 1 or group 2 for a crypto map?

    A. `set peer`

    B. `group`

    C. `set pfs`

    D. None of the above

3. Which of the following commands would you use to reset all IKE SAs configured on a device?

    A. `clear crypto sa counters`

    B. `clear crypto isakmp`

    C. `clear crypto isakmp *`

    D. `clear crypto isakmp` *conn-id*

4. Which of the following would be a more secure approach for configuring pre-shared keys between peers?

    A. Use the same key on all peers.

    B. Use different keys on every device.

    C. Use different keys for every pair of peers.

    D. Use the same key for every pair of peers.

5. Which of the following commands can be used to provide error messages that occur for IKE events?

    A. `show crypto isakmp log`

    B. `debug crypto ipsec`

    C. `show crypto ipsec sa`

    D. `debug crypto isakmp`

6. When creating more than one crypto map sequence, what does a low sequence number represent?

   A. Low priority

   B. High priority

   C. The total number of interfaces the sequence can be applied to

   D. It has no relevance.

7. Why do you need to pay attention when entering peer RSA public keys?

   A. Once a key is entered, there is no way to change it.

   B. Improperly entered keys can cause IPSec peers to never form.

   C. They are long.

   D. You don't enter RSA public keys.

8. Which of the following IKE authentication methods require you to manually generate keys? (Choose all that apply.)

   A. pre-shared

   B. rsa-sig

   C. rsa-encr

   D. rsa-ca

9. Which of the following are required to configure RSA keys? (Choose all that apply.)

   A. Configure the device's hostname.

   B. Configure the device's domain name.

   C. Configure an encryption method.

   D. Manage the keys.

10. Which of the following commands verifies the configuration of IKE policies?

    A. show crypto isakmp sa

    B. show crypto map

    C. show crypto ike policy

    D. None of the above

11. Which of the following commands would you use when verifying network connectivity during the preparing for IPSec phase?

    A. telnet

    B. ping

    C. show running-configuration

    D. show startup-configuration

12. What command is used to enable IKE?

    A. `show crypto isakmp policy`

    B. `crypto isakmp key`

    C. `crypto isakmp policy`

    D. `crypto isakmp enable`

13. Which of the following commands will display information about all of the certificates on a device?

    A. `show crypto ca certificates`

    B. `show ca certificate`

    C. `show crypto ca all`

    D. `show crypto ca roots`

14. Which of the following steps must be completed in order to support IPSec with CA? (Choose all that apply.)

    A. Configure a CA server.

    B. Configure CA support.

    C. Configure IKE.

    D. Configure IPSec.

15. Which of the following commands configures an IP address-to-hostname mapping?

    A. `ip host`

    B. `hostname`

    C. `ip domain-name`

    D. `ip map host`

16. For which of the following must you define a domain name? (Choose all that apply.)

    A. IPSec with pre-shared keys

    B. IPSec-manual

    C. IPSec with RSA-encrypted nonces

    D. IPSec with CA

17. When setting the IKE identity of a peer to a hostname, when would you need to specify the IP address of the peer?

    A. Always

    B. When DNS is working for name resolution

    C. When DNS is not working for name resolution

    D. Never

18. How many transforms can be associated with a transform set?

    A. 1

    B. 2

    C. 3

    D. 4

19. Which of the following are steps needed to configure IPSec? (Choose all that apply.)

    A. Create an access list.

    B. Create a transform set.

    C. Create an IKE policy.

    D. Apply a crypto map to an interface.

20. Which of the following types of access lists can be used for IPSec? (Choose all that apply).

    A. Extended IP access lists

    B. Standard IP access lists

    C. Extended named IP access lists

    D. Standard named IP access lists

Hands-On Labs

This section will test your ability to configure IPSec with pre-shared keys. Use the following graphic as your guide.

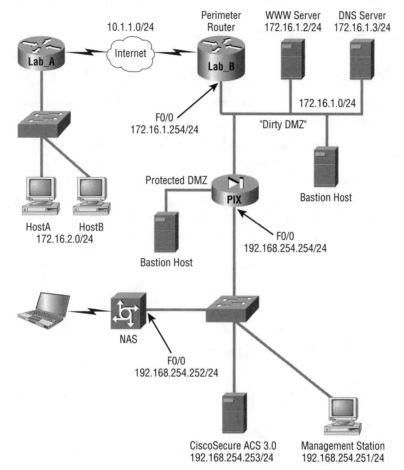

The following interfaces will be used:

- Lab_A interface Serial 0/0 with IP address 10.1.1.1 /24
- Lab_B interface Serial 1/0 with IP address 10.1.1.2 /24

This section includes the following labs:

- Lab 8.1: Configure IKE on Lab_A and Lab_B
- Lab 8.2: Configure IPSec on Lab_A and Lab_B

Lab 8.1: Configure IKE on Lab_A and Lab_B

This lab will have you configure IKE on routers Lab_A and Lab_B from the previous graphic.

1. Create an IKE policy on Lab_A and Lab_B with priority 2.

2. Use 3DES encryption, MD5 message hash, and pre-shared authentication on Lab_A and Lab_B.

3. Use the pre-shared key **cisco** on Lab_A and Lab_B.

Lab 8.2: Configure IPSec on Lab_A and Lab_B

This lab will have you configure IPSec on routers Lab_A and Lab_B from the previous graphic.

1. Create a transform set named **test** using esp-des and tunnel mode on Lab_A and Lab_B.

2. Create a symmetrical extended access list that will permit traffic from networks 172.16.2.0 /24 and 172.16.1.0 /24 on Lab_A and Lab_B.

3. Create a crypto map using the name **test1** and sequence number **100** on Lab_A and Lab_B.

4. The crypto maps created should use the transform set test and the extended access list just created, and set the peer to the IP address of the outgoing interface of the remote device.

5. Apply the crypto map to Lab_A's and Lab_B's outgoing interfaces.

Answers to Written Lab

1. The four tasks required for IPSec using pre-shared keys are prepare for IKE and IPSec, configure IKE, configure IPSec, and test and verify IPSec.

2. The five tasks required for IPSec using CA are prepare for IKE and IPSec, configure CA support, configure IKE, configure IPSec, and test and verify IPSec.

3. Use the IKE authentication method rsa-encr for RSA-encrypted nonces.

4. You type the command `key-string` before manually entering the public key of a remote device into your local device.

5. You must first configure a hostname and a domain name when configuring IPSec with CA.

6. Use the command `crypto isakmp key` *keystring* {`address` *peer-address* | `hostname` *peer-hostname*} to configure a pre-shared key on a device.

7. To show the configuration of all crypto maps currently configured on a device, use the command `show crypto map`.

8. DES is the default message-encryption algorithm used by IKE.

9. Use the command `crypto map` *map-name seq-num* `ipsec-manual` to create a crypto map sequence that doesn't use IKE.

10. The IKE authentication method rsa-sig is used for CA.

Answers to Review Questions

1. A, B, D. The crypto ipsec security-association lifetime command defines the global IPSec SA lifetime based on kilobytes and seconds. This is the amount of time and the number of kilobytes that will pass before an SA needs to be renegotiated. These values can be overridden at the crypto map level.

2. C. To set the Diffie-Hellman group to use for a crypto map, enter the command set pfs {1 | 2} in crypto map configuration mode.

3. C. To reset all active IKE SAs on a device, use the * keyword with the clear crypto isakmp command. If you just want to reset a particular IKE SA, use the clear crypto isakmp conn-id command.

4. C. When configuring pre-shared keys, each pair of peers must have the same key configured. However, for security you should assign a different key for each pair of peers.

5. D. When you need to know the errors that occur for IKE events, use the debug crypto isakmp command. When you need to view this information for IPSec events, use the debug crypto ipsec command.

6. B. The sequence number of a crypto map sequence represents the priority of the sequence: the lower the sequence number, the higher the priority.

7. B. When manually entering peer RSA public keys, you must pay attention. If a key is entered improperly, it can cause IPSec peers to never form.

8. B, C. When using the RSA-encrypted nonces or the RSA signatures authentication method for IKE, you must manually generate the RSA public/private key pair.

9. A, B, D. When configuring RSA keys, you must plan for RSA, configure the device's hostname and domain name, generate the keys, manually enter the public keys, and manage the keys.

10. D. When you need to verify the configuration of IKE policies on a device, use the show crypto isakmp policy command. So the only correct answer is D.

11. B. When you need to verify basic network connectivity, use the ping command.

12. D. To enable IKE, which is the first step in creating and configuring IKE policies, use the crypto isakmp enable command.

13. A. To display information about a device's certificate, the CA server certificate, and any registration authority certificates, use the show crypto ca certificates command.

14. B, C, D. To support IPSec with CA, you must prepare for IKE and IPSec, configure CA support, configure IKE, configure IPSec, and test and verify IPSec.

15. A. To configure a static IP address-to-hostname mapping, use the ip host command.

16. A, C, D.   You must configure a hostname and a domain name whenever you configure IPSec using RSA-encrypted nonces or CA. The reason for this is that RSA uses the hostname and the domain name in the identification of a device.

17. C.   When the IKE identity of a peer is set to a hostname, you do not need to specify the IP address unless DNS is working for name resolution. You would then need to create a hostname-to-IP address mapping on the device for the remote peer.

18. C.   A transform set must have at least one transform associated with it, but can have up to three.

19. A, B, D.   When configuring IPSec, you must create the transform set, set the IPSec SA lifetime, create the access list that will specify the traffic to encrypt, create the crypto map, and apply the crypto map to an interface.

20. A, C.   IPSec uses extended named or numbered IP access lists for defining the traffic to encrypt.

Answers to Hands-On Labs

Here are the answers to the hands-on labs.

Answer to Lab 8.1

```
Lab_A#conf t
Enter configuration commands, one per line.  End with CNTL/Z.
Lab_A(config)#crypto isakmp enable
Lab_A(config)#crypto isakmp policy 2
Lab_A(config-isakmp)#encryption 3des
Lab_A(config-isakmp)#hash md5
Lab_A(config-isakmp)#authentication pre-share
Lab_A(config-isakmp)#exit
Lab_A(config)#crypto isakmp key cisco address 10.1.1.2
Lab_A(config)#^Z
Lab_A#


Lab_B#conf t
Enter configuration commands, one per line.  End with CNTL/Z.
Lab_B(config)#crypto isakmp enable
Lab_B(config)#crypto isakmp policy 2
Lab_B(config-isakmp)#encryption 3des
Lab_B(config-isakmp)#hash md5
Lab_B(config-isakmp)#authentication pre-share
Lab_B(config-isakmp)#exit
Lab_B(config)#crypto isakmp key cisco address 10.1.1.1
Lab_B(config)#^Z
Lab_B#
```

Answer to Lab 8.2

```
Lab_A#conf t
Enter configuration commands, one per line.  End with CNTL/Z.
Lab_A(config)#crypto ipsec tramsform-set test esp-des
Lab_A(cfg-crypto-trans)#exit
Lab_A(config)#access-list 100 permit ip 172.16.2.0 0.0.0.255 172.16.1.0
    ↪0.0.0.255
```

```
Lab_A(config)#access-list 100 permit ip 172.16.1.0 0.0.0.255 172.16.2.0
    ↳0.0.0.255
Lab_A(config)#cryto map test1 100 ipsec-isakmp
Lab_A(config-crypto-map)#match address 100
Lab_A(config-crypto-map)#set transform-set test
Lab_A(config-crypto-map)#set peer 10.1.1.2
Lab_A(config-crypto-map)#exit
Lab_A(config)#interface s0/0
Lab_A(config-if)#crypto map test1
Lab_A(config-if)#^Z
Lab_A#

Lab_B#conf t
Enter configuration commands, one per line.  End with CNTL/Z.
Lab_B(config)#crypto ipsec tramsform-set test esp-des
Lab_B(cfg-crypto-trans)#exit
Lab_B(config)#access-list 100 permit ip 172.16.2.0 0.0.0.255 172.16.1.0
    ↳0.0.0.255
Lab_B(config)#access-list 100 permit ip 172.16.1.0 0.0.0.255 172.16.2.0
    ↳0.0.0.255
Lab_B(config)#cryto map test1 100 ipsec-isakmp
Lab_B(config-crypto-map)#match address 100
Lab_B(config-crypto-map)#set transform-set test
Lab_B(config-crypto-map)#set peer 10.1.1.1
Lab_B(config-crypto-map)#exit
Lab_B(config)#interface s1/0
Lab_B(config-if)#crypto map test1
Lab_B(config-if)#^Z
Lab_B#
```

Chapter

9

Cisco IOS Remote Access Using Cisco Easy VPN

THE FOLLOWING SECUR EXAM TOPICS ARE COVERED IN THIS CHAPTER:

- ✓ Understanding Cisco Easy VPN
- ✓ Understanding the Easy VPN Server
- ✓ Understanding the Cisco VPN 3.5 Client
- ✓ Setting up the Easy VPN Server
- ✓ Setting up the Cisco VPN 3.5 Client

This short (yes, I really did say short) chapter introduces a very cool development in VPN technology: Cisco Easy VPN. While it really can cut down considerably on labor, Cisco's Easy VPN won't work for you in every situation. I'll list which VPN features are supported and which are not, and I'll include an overview of Cisco VPN 3.5 Client Software.

I'm also going to present a sweet configuration example that will focus on how you can make the Easy VPN Server into an IOS router (a relatively new feature) and make the Easy VPN Remote into the VPN 3.5 Client.

In addition, I'll explain some great tools you can use to eliminate unnecessary user interference when installing the VPN 3.5 Client Software. This chapter wraps up with a hands-on lab where you'll get to install the Cisco VPN 3.5 Client on a Windows machine. Nice, huh? Let's get going!

Configuring IOS Remote Access Using Cisco Easy VPN

"Easy is as easy does," so the saying goes. Are you ready for something that's really as easy as its name implies? After eight pretty intense chapters—especially that last one—you're probably thinking, "Uh huh, yeah, sure. He said, 'Easy.' Ha ha ha!" Well, I tell you no lie. Look no further, because Cisco has become your genie—ready and waiting to grant your wish by bringing you the aptly named Cisco Easy VPN!

Now, you're right. Virtual private networks (VPNs) have been around for some time, and you know there are many ways to configure them because we also covered some VPN configurations in Chapter 7, "Understanding Cisco IOS IPSec Support." VPNs can be as simple as two fixed IOS routers establishing a VPN between them, or they can be more complex, with multiple, mobile PC users and VPN Concentrators. Management in the first scenario is typically a snap, but in the second scenario, it's a lot more complicated—more like handling a snapping turtle!

This section focuses on a new feature in IOS that allows any capable IOS router to act as a VPN server, permitting your remote clients to establish VPN connections to the IOS router acting as a VPN server. So kick back, relax, and let me guide you through this cool technology.

Introduction to Cisco Easy VPN

Cisco Easy VPN consists of two primary components: the *Easy VPN Server* and the *Easy VPN Remote*. The Easy VPN Server can be any of the following devices:

- IOS router
- PIX Firewall
- VPN Concentrator device

The Easy VPN Server acts as a head-end device for either site-to-site or remote access VPN clients. It has the ability to push security policies to Easy VPN Remote clients before connections are actually established, ensuring that those clients always have current policies in place. Remember, anything that helps you to manage multiple remote devices is a very good thing. Easy VPN Server definitely goes a long way toward helping Cisco Easy VPN earn the moniker "easy."

The Easy VPN Remote can be either a site-to-site device or the remote access VPN Client. In fact, it can be anything on the following list of devices:

- IOS router (800, 900, and 1700 series)
- PIX Firewall
- VPN 3002 Hardware Client device
- VPN 3.5 Client Software

As I said, the Easy VPN Remote can receive security policies from the Easy VPN Server, which minimizes the amount of configuration and maintenance required on remote devices and cuts your aggravation dramatically—especially if you have an ever-growing number of them.

You can see that there are quite a few possible combinations of Easy VPN Server and Easy VPN Remote options. The remainder of this chapter focuses specifically on how the Easy VPN Server becomes an IOS router, as well as how the Easy VPN Client becomes the VPN 3.5 Client Software.

The option of using the IOS router as the Easy VPN Server is a fairly recent development. The ability to use an IOS router instead of a PIX Firewall or VPN Concentrator as the head-end to Easy VPN Clients offers a world of possibilities when establishing VPN connections throughout your existing, installed infrastructure. This flexibility is great, and adding VPN server capabilities to IOS can really deliver the goods for you.

So, limiting our talk to this combination of server and remote, let's take a deeper look into the Easy VPN Server and VPN 3.5 Client.

The Easy VPN Server

As of IOS release 12.2(8)T, the Cisco Easy VPN Server is available on an IOS router to support either the hardware Easy VPN Remote devices or the VPN 3.*x* Client.

End users have the capability to establish IPSec communications with these IOS routers, and the IOS routers acting as Easy VPN Servers have the ability to push security policies to these remote devices. The 12.2(8)T Easy VPN Server release of IOS adds support for the following VPN functions:

- Mode configuration version 6 support

- Xauth version 6 support

- IKE Dead Peer Detection (DPD)

- Split Tunneling control

- Initial contact

- Group-based policy control

The IKE DPD is a form of keepalive for VPN connections. There are a number of problems that could cause a VPN remote device to "disappear" or lose connectivity without being able to inform the VPN server. Ever had a dial-in line die? That's only one example. *IKE Dead Peer Detection (DPD)* from the VPN server will send "R-U-THERE?" messages to idle VPN remote devices. If the idle devices fail to respond, the VPN server assumes the connection has been broken and responds by recovering the resources dedicated to maintaining that particular connection.

Split Tunneling control gives the VPN remote the ability to maintain intranet and Internet access at the same time. Without Split Tunneling enabled, the remote will send all traffic—intranet and Internet—across the tunnel. If the VPN remote device is already Internet connected, it may not be necessary to have Internet traffic filled through the tunnel.

Initial contact solves this particular problem. Imagine that a VPN remote device is attached to a VPN server, and the connection is broken for some reason. The VPN remote device attempts to re-establish the VPN connection, only to find that its connection attempts are denied because it supposedly already has an established connection! "But," you sputter, "I'm not there anymore, I'm here! What's up with this?" In the formerly unforgiving world of VPN, those tortured cries would simply have been ignored—or they would have flooded Help Desks—until now, that is! Initial contact is supported by all Cisco VPN devices, meaning that whenever a new VPN connection is to be established, any previous connection information is reset.

But the Easy VPN Server does not support all possible IPSec options. Table 9.1 illustrates the options that are and are not supported.

TABLE 9.1   Easy VPN Supported and Unsupported Options

Options	Supported	Unsupported
Authentication algorithm	HMAC-MD5 HMAC-SHA1	
Authentication types	Pre-shared keys RSA digital signatures	Digital Signature Standard (DSS)

TABLE 9.1   Easy VPN Supported and Unsupported Options *(continued)*

Options	Supported	Unsupported
Diffie-Hellman (DH) groups	2 5	1
IKE encryption algorithms	DES 3DES	
IPSec encryption algorithms	DES 3DES NULL	
IPSec protocol identifiers	ESP IPCOMP-LZS	Authentication Header (AH)
IPSEC protocol mode	Tunnel	Transport

And I have to note a couple more options that aren't supported: manual keys and perfect forward security (PFS).

Let's move on to the Cisco VPN 3.5 Client and how it is installed and configured.

Introduction to the Cisco VPN 3.5 Client

The *Cisco VPN 3.5 Client* can be used to establish VPN connections to any of the Easy VPN Server devices listed earlier in this chapter, including an IOS router. Cisco VPN 3.5 Client is also available via Cisco Connection Online (CCO) to customers with SMARTnet support.

The Cisco VPN 3.5 Client is available for the following operating systems:

- Windows 95, 98, Me, NT 4.0, 2000, and XP
- Linux (Intel)
- Solaris (Ultra-Sparc 32-bit)
- Mac OS X 10.1

Once installed, the VPN Client allows you to configure and select a number of possible VPN servers. When you launch the VPN Client, the window shown in Figure 9.1 appears.

FIGURE 9.1   Launching VPN Client

Since no connections are configured, you need to add one by clicking the New button. When you do this, the New Connection Entry Wizard appears, illustrated in Figure 9.2. This window prompts you to give the connection a name and gives you the option of adding a description for the new connection entry.

FIGURE 9.2   Creating a new connection entry

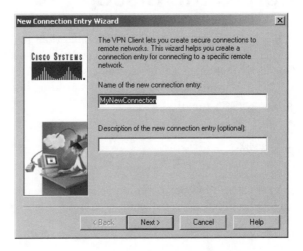

After naming the connection, you click the Next button and enter the IP address of the VPN server you're connecting to in the window illustrated in Figure 9.3.

FIGURE 9.3   Identifying the VPN server to be connected to

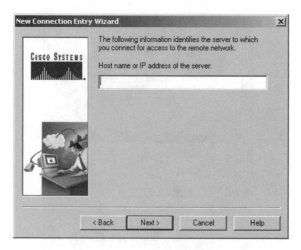

Next, you're queried for group access or certificate information. This is the only remotely challenging part of the Easy VPN concept, and it isn't even that bad. But if you're not doing this yourself, you'll need to provide users with the correct information so they can fill out the screen shown in Figure 9.4.

FIGURE 9.4   Entering group access information

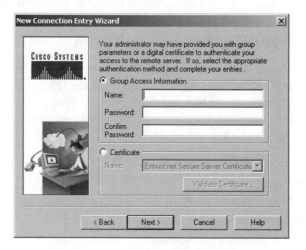

You'll get one last chance to make any changes when you're asked if you want to save the connection information. Once this is done, click Connect from the initial screen, as you can see in Figure 9.5.

FIGURE 9.5   Connecting your VPN server

You can add as many connections as you want and then select one to use from the pull-down menu before connecting.

The VPN 3.5 Client supports many VPN features. In fact, it's so supportive, it doesn't have some of the limitations that the IOS Easy VPN Server does. This requires a little thought when configuring connections to avoid incompatibilities. Here's an example—VPN Client supports Diffie-Hellman groups 1, 2, and 5, but as you know, the Easy VPN Server doesn't support DH1.

Easy VPN Server Configuration Tasks

Easy VPN Server configuration uses skills and commands I've already covered in previous chapters. Basically, you need to configure AAA and then configure IPSec. There are some optional features you can configure such as DPD, but they're not required.

Cisco has defined the following seven steps to configuring the Easy VPN Server:

1. Enable policy lookup via AAA.

2. Define group policy for mode configuration push.

3. Apply mode configuration and Xauth to crypto maps.

4. Enable Reverse Route Injection (RRI) for the VPN Client (optional).

5. Enable IKE Dead Peer Detection (optional).

6. Configure RADIUS server support (optional).

7. Verify the Easy VPN Server.

Each step itself consists of multiple steps. Step 1 involves enabling AAA. Steps 2 and 3 involve configuring IPSec. Steps 4 through 6 are specific to Easy VPN Server configuration, but as mentioned previously, they're optional. Finally, in step 7, the `show crypto map` *interface* command can be used to verify Easy VPN Server operation.

Pre-Configuring the Cisco VPN 3.5 Client

I know that this book isn't a how-to on customer relations, but I've often observed a direct correlation between users having software-related decisions to make and an increase in annoying telephone conversations between users and engineers. Therefore, it's usually in everyone's best interest to just remove that tempting ability from the keyboards of your expert users altogether. This is especially helpful because you're ultimately concerned about the security of the entire network—your control is utterly essential to getting the job done right. Cisco seems to understand the ruinous potential of this little conflict and has provided a way to streamline the installation of the VPN 3.5 Client on Windows.

As the administrator of a Cisco VPN 3.5 Client installation, you have the ability to pre-configure the connection configuration covered in the section "Introduction to the Cisco VPN 3.5 Client" earlier in this chapter. And there's more. You can even protect the user from making messy, uninformed decisions during the installation of the VPN Client, such as, "Which directory should I install the software into?" You do this by creating three text files, which you then place in the same directory as the `setup.exe` file you used to install the VPN Client software:

The *oem.ini* file   The *oem.ini* file installs the VPN Client without user intervention. You get to perform tasks such as force the machine to reload after installation, select the directory to install the software into, and even my personal favorite, turn off all user prompts during installation—yes! In the end, the only thing the user is left to do is double-click the `setup.exe` icon, and the file takes care of every standard query that follows during installation.

The *vpnclient.ini* file   The `vpnclient.ini` file is used to configure the global parameters of the VPN Client, which are not normally queried as part of the installation wizard and are therefore not covered in the `oem.ini` file. You can customize these global parameters to whatever settings are appropriate for your environment.

The *.pcf* files   *.pcf* files add connection entries. You need to create one file for each connection you want to add, and you can use as many entries as you wish. Just put them in the same directory as the `setup.exe` file, and they'll be added to the VPN Client.

 Refer to the documentation that came with your particular VPN Client software for the exact syntax of these files.

So there you have it. By using these three files, you can completely pre-configure the Cisco VPN 3.5 Client and reclaim the network that is rightfully yours! The only thing left to do is send out a memo and somehow get users to run the `setup.exe` program on the VPN Client machine.

Summary

You have to admit—this chapter really was easy and truly short. The Cisco Easy VPN solution that Cisco provides can be deployed in various ways, and the new Cisco features allow you to employ the Easy VPN Server to act as an IOS router and employ the Easy VPN Remote as the VPN 3.5 Client.

It is important to understand which features are supported and which features are not supported in the VPN 3.5 Client. For example, the Easy VPN Client supports 3DES, which is important, but it does not support DSS, Diffie-Hellman group 1 (DH1), and Authentication Header (AH).

It is important to understand the process of adding a connection to the VPN 3.5 Client, which was covered in detail in this chapter. If you have to, review the "Introduction to the Cisco VPN 3.5 Client" section until you really understand the process.

By truly understanding the process of adding a connection to the VPN 3.5 Client, you can then streamline the installation of the VPN Client, while ensuring that the ultimate control of your network remains where it should—in your trusty, capable hands!

Exam Essentials

Make sure to know the supported and unsupported IPSec features of the Easy VPN Server (see Table 9.1). DSS, DH group 1, and AH are not supported features.

Know which files are used for which functions when pre-configuring the VPN 3.5 Client. The oem.ini file is used to install without user prompts, the vpnclient.ini file is used to pre-configure global parameters, and the .pcf files are used to configure connections (one .pcf file per connection).

Know which devices can act as Easy VPN Servers and which devices can act as Easy VPN Remotes. The Easy VPN Server can be an IOS router, PIX Firewall, or VPN Concentrator. The Easy VPN Remote can be an IOS router, PIX Firewall, VPN 3002 Hardware Client, or VPN 3.5 Client Software.

Know the seven tasks for Easy VPN Server configuration. The seven Easy VPN Server configuration tasks are

1. Enable policy lookup via AAA.
2. Define group policy for mode configuration push.
3. Apply mode configuration and Xauth to crypto maps.
4. Enable Reverse Route Injection (RRI) for the VPN Client (optional).
5. Enable IKE Dead Peer Detection (optional).
6. Configure RADIUS server support (optional).
7. Verify the Easy VPN Server.

Key Terms

Before you take the exam, be certain you are familiar with the following terms:

Cisco VPN 3.5 Client

Easy VPN Remote

Easy VPN Server

IKE Dead Peer Detection (DPD)

initial contact

`oem.ini`

`.pcf`

Written Lab

This section asks you 10 write-in-the-answer questions to help you understand the technology that you need to know in order to pass the SECUR exam.

1. List the two Diffie-Hellman groups supported by the Cisco Easy VPN.
2. Which file do you modify to remove user prompts when installing the Cisco VPN 3.5 Client?
3. List the encryption algorithms supported by the Cisco Easy VPN Server.
4. List the devices that can be an Easy VPN Server.
5. Which IPSec protocol mode is supported by the Cisco Easy VPN Server?
6. Which files do you modify to pre-configure connections when installing the Cisco VPN 3.5 Client?
7. List the IPSec protocol identifiers supported by the Cisco Easy VPN Server.
8. Which IPSec protocol mode is not supported by the Cisco Easy VPN Server?
9. Which operating systems are supported by the Cisco VPN 3.5 Client Software?
10. List the IPSec protocol identifiers not supported by the Cisco Easy VPN Server.

Review Questions

1. Which IPSec authentication types are supported by the Cisco Easy VPN Server? (Choose all that apply.)

   A. Pre-shared keys

   B. RSA digital signatures

   C. DSS

   D. DES

   E. 3DES

2. Which IOS is the minimum required in order to run the IOS Easy VPN Server?

   A. 11.3(18)T

   B. 12.1(8)T

   C. 12.2(8)T

   D. 12.2(12)T

3. Which of the following are supported by the Cisco Easy VPN server? (Choose all that apply.)

   A. Authentication using DSS

   B. DH1

   C. DH2

   D. Manual keys

   E. Perfect forward secrecy (PFS)

   F. DH5

4. Which of the following can be used as a Cisco Easy VPN Server? (Choose all that apply.)

   A. VPN 3.5 Client Software

   B. IOS router

   C. PIX Firewall

   D. Cisco VPN Concentrator

   E. All of the above

5. Which types of IPSec encryption algorithms are supported by the Cisco Easy VPN? (Choose all that apply.)

   A. NULL

   B. ESP

   C. DES

   D. 3DES

   E. HMAC-MD5

6. You want your remote users to send their Internet requests directly to the Internet and not through the VPN tunnel. Which of the following features enables this?

   A. Xauth version 6

   B. DPD

   C. Split Tunneling

   D. Initial contact

7. Suppose that you are going to pre-configure the Cisco VPN 3.5 Client, and you want to remove all user prompts and force the PC to reboot when the installation is finished. Which of the following files would you modify?

   A. `setup.exe`

   B. `oem.ini`

   C. `vpnclient.ini`

   D. `*.pcf`

8. Which of the following is the first task you need to perform when configuring the Easy VPN Server?

   A. Verify Easy VPN Server.

   B. Configure RADIUS server support (optional).

   C. Apply mode configuration and Xauth to crypto maps.

   D. Enable Reverse Route Injection for the VPN Client (optional).

   E. Enable policy lookup via AAA.

   F. Define group policy for mode configuration push.

   G. Enable IKE Dead Peer Detection (optional).

9. Which of the following DH groups are supported by the Cisco Easy VPN Server? (Choose all that apply.)

   A. DH1

   B. DH2

   C. DH3

   D. DH4

   E. DH5

   F. DH6

10. Suppose that you are going to pre-configure the Cisco VPN 3.5 Client, and you want to add pre-configured connections to the pull-down menu. Which of the following files would you modify?

    A. `setup.exe`

    B. `oem.ini`

    C. `vpnclient.ini`

    D. `*.pcf`

11. Which IPSec protocol modes are supported by the Cisco Easy VPN Server?

    A. Tunnel mode

    B. Transport mode

    C. Both A and B

    D. Neither A nor B

12. When users get disconnected and then attempt to reconnect, they are denied because they have existing connections. Which of the following solves this problem?

    A. Xauth version 6

    B. DPD

    C. Split Tunneling

    D. Initial contact

13. Suppose that you are going to pre-configure the Cisco VPN 3.5 Client, and you want to pre-configure global profiles. Which of the following files would you modify?

    A. `setup.exe`

    B. `oem.ini`

    C. `vpnclient.ini`

    D. `*.pcf`

14. Which of the following DH groups is *not* supported by the Cisco Easy VPN Server?

    A. DH1

    B. DH2

    C. DH3

    D. DH4

    E. DH5

    F. DH6

15. Which of the following can be used as a Cisco Easy VPN Remote?

   A. VPN 3.5 Client Software

   B. IOS router

   C. PIX Firewall

   D. Cisco VPN 3002 Hardware Client

   E. All of the above

16. Which operating systems are supported by the Cisco VPN 3.5 Client Software? (Choose all that apply.)

   A. HP-UX

   B. OS2

   C. Linux (Intel)

   D. Mac OS X

   E. Palm OS

   F. Windows

   G. Solaris (Ultra-Sparc 32-bit)

17. Suppose that you are going to pre-configure the Cisco VPN 3.5 Client, and you have already configured the files you want to use for the pre-configuration. Which directory do you place them in for the install?

   A. /etc

   B. /windows/system

   C. The same directory as the `setup.exe` for the VPN 3.5 Client

   D. /windows/bin

18. Which of the following DH groups are supported by the Cisco VPN 3.5 Client? (Choose all that apply.)

   A. DH1

   B. DH2

   C. DH3

   D. DH4

   E. DH5

   F. DH6

19. You have devices that lose connection, but their connections never seem to get cleaned up. Which of the following will help solve this problem?

    A. Xauth version 6

    B. DPD

    C. Split Tunneling

    D. Initial contact

20. Which IPSec protocol identifiers are supported by the Cisco Easy VPN Server? (Choose all that apply.)

    A. DH2

    B. DES

    C. ESP

    D. IPCOMP-LZS

    E. IPSEC AH

Hands-On Lab

This lab will have you install the Cisco VPN 3.5 Client Software on a Windows machine.

Lab 9.1: Installing the Cisco VPN 3.5 Client Software on Windows

You need to download the VPN 3.5 Client Software from CCO or use the software provided with a VPN Concentrator. To access CCO, you need a SMARTnet contract.

1. Extract the software from the zip file and run the **setup.exe** file.

2. You may be prompted to disable the Windows IPSec policy agent. If you are, click Yes.

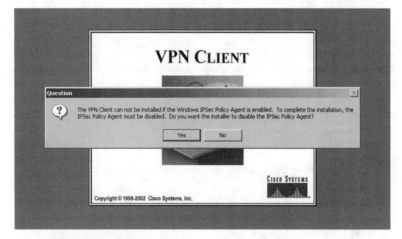

3. When the screen introducing the Installshield Wizard comes up, click Next.

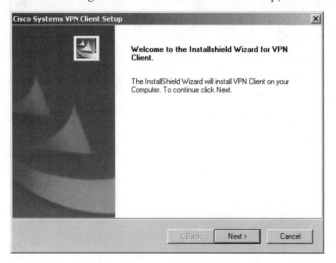

4. When the software license agreement appears, make sure to read it thoroughly. Once you understand it and agree to all of the terms, click Yes.

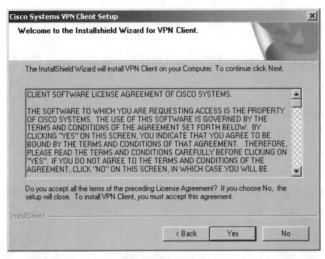

5. Verify the directory to install the software into and click Next.

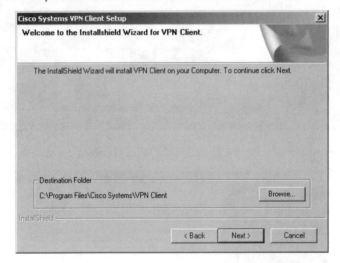

6. When prompted to restart your machine, make your selection and then click Finish.

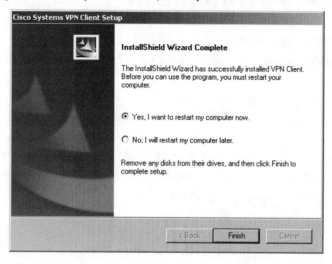

Answers to Written Lab

1. Cisco Easy VPN supports DH groups 2 and 5.

2. To remove user prompts when installing the Cisco VPN 3.5 Client, you modify the `oem.ini` file.

3. The Cisco Easy VPN Server supports the DES and 3DES encryption algorithms.

4. A Cisco IOS router, a Cisco PIX Firewall, or a Cisco VPN Concentrator can be an Easy VPN Server.

5. Tunnel mode is the IPSec protocol supported by the Cisco Easy VPN Server.

6. You modify the `*.pcf` files, one per connection, when installing the Cisco VPN 3.5 Client.

7. The IPSec protocol identifiers supported by the Cisco Easy VPN Server are ESP and IPCOMP-LZS.

8. Transport mode is the IPSec protocol mode not supported by the Cisco Easy VPN Server.

9. The operating systems supported by the Cisco VPN 3.5 Client Software are Solaris (Ultra-Sparc 32-bit), Mac OS X, Windows, and Linux (Intel).

10. IPSec AH is not supported by the Cisco Easy VPN Server.

Answers to Review Questions

1. A, B.   Pre-shared keys and RSA digital signatures are supported authentication types. DSS is not supported. DES and 3DES are encryption algorithms, not authentication types.

2. C.   You must have at least 12.2(8)T to run the IOS Easy VPN Server.

3. C, F.   DH groups 2 and 5 are supported. DSS, DH1, PFS, and manual keys are not supported.

4. B, C, D.   An IOS router, PIX Firewall, or VPN Concentrator can act as a Cisco Easy VPN Server. The VPN 3.5 Client Software cannot.

5. A, C, D.   DES, 3DES, and NULL are the three types of IPSec encryption supported by the Cisco Easy VPN.

6. C.   Split Tunneling enables remote user traffic destined for the Internet to go directly to the Internet and not across the VPN tunnel.

7. B.   The `oem.ini` file is used to remove all user prompts and force the PC to reboot when the installation is finished.

8. E.   Enabling policy lookup via AAA is the first configuration task for the Easy VPN Server.

9. B, E.   DH groups 2 and 5 are supported by the Cisco Easy VPN Server.

10. D.   You would configure and add one `.pcf` file for each connection you wish to add to the VPN 3.5 Client.

11. A.   Tunnel mode is supported by the Cisco Easy VPN Server; transport mode is not.

12. D.   Initial contact allows Cisco VPN devices to clear existing connections when devices attempt to establish new connections.

13. C.   You would modify the `vpnclient.ini` file to pre-configure global profiles.

14. A.   DH group 1 (DH1) is not supported by the Cisco Easy VPN Server.

15. E.   Any of these can be used as Cisco Easy VPN Remotes.

16. C, D, F, G.   The Cisco VPN 3.5 Client Software is available for Linux (Intel), Mac OS X, Windows, and Solaris (Ultra-Sparc 32-bit).

17. C.   The `oem.ini`, `vpnclient.ini`, and `.pcf` files are placed in the same directory as the `setup.exe` file.

18. A, B, E.   The VPN 3.5 Client supports DH groups 1, 2, and 5.

19. B.   DPD (Dead Peer Detection) allows Cisco VPN devices to identify connections where the communications peer has "died" and to recover the allocated resources.

20. C, D.   ESP and IPCOMP-LZS are the IPSec protocol identifiers supported by the Cisco Easy VPN Server. IPSec AH is not supported. DH2 and DES are not IPSec protocol identifiers.

Appendix A

Introduction to the PIX Firewall

This appendix is by no means meant to be a comprehensive guide to the installation and configuration of PIX Firewalls. Instead, it gives you an introduction to the information covered in the CCSP PIX exam, including the features and basic configuration of PIX Firewalls. (Please go to www .sybex.com for information about Sybex's Study Guides on the CCSP exams.)

Here are some of the topics covered in this appendix:

- The advantages of using a PIX Firewall to protect your network

- How a firewall passes traffic from one interface to another and the rules that traffic must follow

- The basics of configuring a PIX Firewall: how to navigate the different modes, how to configure interfaces, and how to save configurations

- How you can influence the traffic between interfaces, that is, how you can control exactly which traffic crosses the firewall

- How to enable AAA on PIX Firewalls

- Some of the advanced features available on the PIX Firewall

Be prepared—there are a lot of configuration details, and many new commands and syntax will be introduced.

The Cisco Packet Internet eXchange (PIX) Firewall

The PIX Firewall is a tool used to prevent unauthorized access between any two (or more) networks. The PIX Firewall uses a secure, real-time, embedded operating system.

Many other competing firewalls run on top of another operating system such as Unix or Windows NT. The problem with this is that Unix and Windows NT (or even Cisco's IOS) have well-known security issues. This means that potential intruders can attack the operating system of the box your firewall is running using commonly available information! So much for the firewall....

Since the PIX Firewall uses a proprietary operating system (called Finesse), it is much more difficult to attack. There is no source code floating around that a potential hacker might use to break into your PIX Firewall.

PIX Firewall interfaces must be purchased from Cisco or Cisco resellers. No other interfaces are supported, because vendors would not be able to provide drivers to work with the closed operating system used by the PIX Firewall. Currently, the following interface types are available:

- Single-port 10/100BaseT Ethernet
- Four-port 10/100BaseT Ethernet
- Token Ring
- FDDI

Network Separation

Consider the following PIX Firewall separating three distinct networks:

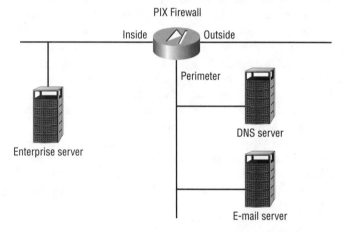

Because all traffic between these three networks must physically pass through the PIX Firewall, it is in the ultimate position to control and potentially limit all access between these networks. These networks are labeled *inside*, *perimeter*, and *outside*. They each have a separate function:

Inside network   The inside network is your internal network where you keep your protected resources such as enterprise servers or other internal-access devices, along with your internal users.

Outside network   The outside network is the open, untrusted Internet.

Perimeter network   Also called a *DMZ* (for *de-militarized zone*), the perimeter network is where you host services such as DNS (Domain Name System) servers, e-mail servers, web and FTP servers, and so on. These services are generally made available to users from the outside network.

Some of you may recognize this terminology from the classic three-part firewall.

The administrator has the ability to control what the PIX Firewall lets through. There are many functions that the PIX Firewall can accomplish, but once it is installed, there are only three ways to get traffic through a PIX Firewall. You will learn about these next.

Three Ways through a PIX Firewall

The PIX Firewall has ultimate control over what traffic goes between the networks it separates, and it gives a great deal of control to the administrator in configuring which traffic is to be permitted and which traffic is not allowed. The PIX Firewall can permit traffic between networks using three methods:

- Cut-through proxy user authentication
- Static route
- Adaptive Security Algorithm (ASA)

Cut-Through Proxy User Authentication

The cut-through proxy user authentication method performs user authentication at the Application layer. When a user requests a resource through the PIX Firewall, the firewall intercepts that request and forces the user to provide a username and password. The firewall then authenticates this user against a security server using either the TACACS+ or the RADIUS security protocol (as discussed in Chapter 3, "Configuring CiscoSecure ACS and TACACS+"). Assuming that the security policy allows this particular user to access this resource, the user's request is forwarded through the firewall. This method can be used for either inbound or outbound requests.

One common problem with proxy servers is that they must evaluate the contents of each and every packet passing through them. This is a processor-expensive operation and can introduce a potential bottleneck into the network. The PIX Firewall gets around this requirement by using a cut-through proxy technique. Once the user's request has been approved, the PIX Firewall establishes a data flow between the two communicating partners. All traffic between that user and the resource then flows directly through the PIX Firewall, without needing to have each individual packet "proxied."

Static Route

You can enter static routes on a PIX Firewall. The syntax is similar to that used on a Cisco router, but it is not the same. You must specify an interface name in the command, as in the following examples:

```
route outside 0.0.0.0 0.0.0.0 172.19.20.1 1
route inside 10.0.0.0 255.0.0.0 10.1.1.1
```

This syntax should look familiar to those of you with router experience. The only difference is the addition of the `inside` and `outside` parameters, which are the interface names. The "Configuring Interfaces" section later in this appendix discusses the naming of interfaces.

The routing protocol that the PIX Firewall supports is RIP (Routing Information Protocol). Earlier PIX Firewall versions support only RIP version 1 (RIPv1). RIP version 2 (RIPv2) is supported as of PIX Firewall version 5.1(1).

Adaptive Security Algorithm

The Adaptive Security Algorithm (ASA) uses a "stateful" approach to connection security. ASA checks each inbound packet against connection state information stored in memory.

The ASA follows a set of rules:

- No packets can cross the firewall without a connection and state, and the connection and state must be recorded in the ASA table.

- Outbound connections (connections from a higher security to a lower security interface) are allowed, except those specifically denied using outbound lists.

- Inbound connections (connections from a lower security to a higher security interface) are denied, except those specifically allowed using conduits.

- Any packet attempting to bypass the previous rules is dropped and logged to Syslog.

- All ICMP packets are denied unless specifically permitted using the `conduit permit icmp` command.

PIX Firewall Configuration Basics

Anyone familiar with configuring Cisco routers using Cisco's IOS will be at home when configuring a PIX Firewall. The command-line interface (CLI) is similar for the two products, but as mentioned earlier, it is not exactly the same. There are a number of differences, such as the ability to enter any command while in configuration mode on the PIX Firewall. Here, you'll start your configuration by first changing from user to enable mode, then to configuration mode:

```
toddfw>enable
toddfw#config t
toddfw(config)#^Z
toddfw#disable
toddfw>
```

First, you enter privileged mode using the `enable` command, and then you enter configuration mode using the `config t` command. Notice how the prompt changes, just as during router configuration. Then you enter ^Z (Ctrl-Z) to go back to privileged mode, after which you enter the `disable` command to go back to user mode (called unprivileged mode). Now, you need to set an enable password:

```
toddfw>enable
toddfw#config t
toddfw(config)#enable password todd
toddfw(config)#^Z
toddfw#show password
```

Notice that you set the password from privileged mode. Also, when you enter the `show passwd` command, the password is shown encrypted.

Configuring Interfaces

Now, let's configure some interfaces! You need to assign duplex settings, interface names, and IP addresses. Take a look at a simple firewall:

PIX Firewall

| Inside | | Outside |
| 172.16.10.1 | | 192.168.30.1 |

This PIX Firewall has two interfaces: one internal and one external. The internal interface is meant to have IP address 172.16.10.1, and the external interface is to have the IP address 192.168.30.1. Here is how you configure these interfaces:

```
toddfw#config t
toddfw(config)#nameif ethernet0 inside sec100
toddfw(config)#nameif ethernet1 outside sec0
toddfw(config)#interface ethernet0 auto
toddfw(config)#interface ethernet1 auto
toddfw(config)#ip address inside 172.16.10.1 255.255.255.0
toddfw(config)#ip address outside 192.168.30.1 255.255.255.0
toddfw(config)#^Z
toddfw#
```

In this example, you use three commands to configure these interfaces: the nameif command, the interface command, and the ip address command. Let's take a closer look at the arguments for each of these commands and how these arguments are used.

The *nameif* Command

The nameif command is used to give the interface a name and specify its security level. It has the following syntax:

```
nameif hardware_id if_name security_level
```

The interface name is then used throughout the configuration whenever referencing that interface.

The *security_level* parameter specifies the security level of the interface on a scale of 0 to 100. You use 0 for the outside network and 100 for the inside network. DMZ or perimeter networks have some number between 1 and 99. You'll learn more about security levels in the "Configuring Access through the PIX Firewall" section later in this appendix.

The *interface* Command

The interface command is used to specify the speed on the interface and can be used to enable or disable the interface. It has the following syntax:

```
interface hardware_id hardware_speed
```

In the previous example, you set each Ethernet interface to auto. You can set the interface to 10-megabit half duplex using the following command:

toddfw(config)#**interface ethernet0 10baset**

Or you can set the interface to 100-megabit full duplex using this command:

toddfw(config)#**interface ethernet0 100full**

The *ip address* Command

The ip address command, as you might expect, is used to assign an IP address to the interface. Here is its syntax:

ip address *if_name ip_address* [*netmask*]

Unlike with a router, where you use an interface-configuration mode to set the IP address on an interface, for the PIX Firewall, you specify the name you gave that interface using the name-if command. Other than this difference, the command is similar to the router command and is straightforward.

Default Gateway Assignment

One last thing you need to do is to assign a default gateway using the route command (mentioned in the "Static Route" section earlier in this appendix). Here is how you set the default gateway:

toddfw(config)#**route outside 0.0.0.0 0.0.0.0 192.168.30.2**
toddfw(config)#**^Z**
toddfw#

Testing the Configuration with Ping and ARP

Now that you have the IP addresses configured, you can do a bit of testing. Let's start with a ping:

toddfw#**ping inside 172.16.10.45**
172.16.10.45 response received -- 0ms
172.16.10.45 response received -- 0ms
172.16.10.45 response received -- 0ms
toddfw#

Note that you specify the name of the interface closest to the ping target. The ping command makes three attempts to reach the specified IP address.

If you want to ping *through* a PIX Firewall, you must create an ICMP conduit, covered in the "Configuring Inbound Access" section later in this appendix.

Finally, let's check the contents of the ARP cache to make sure that the MAC address for the host you pinged in the preceding example is present:

```
toddfw#show arp
inside 172.16.10.45 00d0.b78f.3553
toddfw#
```

Saving Your Configuration

Those of you who remember the old router commands for saving and displaying the configuration files will find this refreshing. To save the current firewall configuration to flash memory, do the following:

```
toddfw#write memory
Building configuration…

[OK]
toddfw#
```

You can also save the configuration to a floppy disk or to a TFTP (Trivial File Transfer Protocol) server on the network.

To erase the configuration stored in flash memory, you can use this command:

```
toddfw#write erase
Erase PIX configuration in Flash Memory? [confirm] y

toddfw#
```

And finally, to show the current running configuration, use this command:

```
toddfw#write terminal
Building configuration…

…
```

If you remember these commands from the old IOS days, great! You are so old that you probably drive 10 miles per hour under the speed limit in the left lane, with your turn signal on! If you know the new router commands such as show running-config and copy running-config startup-config, well, once upon a time, this is how we used to do it.

Configuring Access through the PIX Firewall

Now that you've mastered the basics of firewall configuration, named and addressed the interfaces, and saved your configuration, the next task at hand is to configure access through the PIX

Firewall. As mentioned earlier, when interfaces are defined, they are given a security level number between 0 and 100. 0 is used for the outside interface, and 100 is used for the inside interface. Perimeter or DMZ interfaces are assigned numbers between 1 and 99.

As traffic goes between interfaces, it is placed into one of two categories: outbound or inbound. Which category it falls into depends on the security levels of the interfaces it is traversing:

- Outbound connections are for higher security to lower security interfaces.

- Inbound connections are for lower security to higher security interfaces.

The PIX Firewall uses different methods for passing traffic in each of these categories. Let's look at each category and talk about how to allow traffic in that direction.

Configuring Outbound Access

You may recall from the introduction of the ASA earlier in this appendix that outbound connections are allowed unless specifically prohibited. However, you need to do a bit of configuration to start traffic flowing in outbound situations. In most instances, you use the nat and global commands to accomplish this.

The PIX Firewall anticipates that you are using Network Address Translation (NAT). Although it is possible to run the firewall without using NAT, Cisco strongly recommends against it. Use NAT on the firewall if at all possible.

To configure outbound access using the nat and global commands, you must first start with a diagram of your PIX Firewall, showing all interfaces and their associated names and security levels. Consider the diagram shown here:

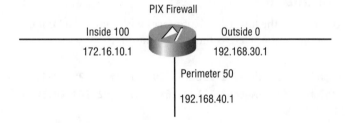

Here is a summary of the configuration of this PIX Firewall:

Interface	Security Level	IP Address
Inside	100	172.16.10.1
Outside	0	192.168.30.1
Perimeter	50	192.168.40.1

Now you must decide where you will have outbound access. Remember that outbound access is where traffic originates on an interface with a higher security level destined for an interface with a lower security level. This occurs in only the following situations:

- Inside to outside

- Inside to perimeter
- Perimeter to outside

There will never be outbound traffic originating on the outside interface because its security level is 0. Traffic from the outbound interface can never go to another interface with a lower security level!

The *nat* Command

You use the nat command to specify each *higher* security level interface you want to be able to access *lower* security level interfaces. Here is your configuration:

```
toddfw#config t
toddfw(config)#nat (inside) 1 0 0
toddfw(config)#nat (perimeter) 1 0 0
toddfw(config)#^Z
toddfw#
```

Notice that, once again, you did not specify the outside interface, because outbound connections cannot originate there. Each nat command allows users of the specified interface (in parentheses) to access lower security interfaces. So, in this example, the first nat command allows users on the inside interface to access both the perimeter and outside interfaces. The second nat command allows users on the perimeter interface to access the outside interface (the only other interface with a lower security level).

The *global* Command

Now you need to configure the lower-level interfaces with the global command to finalize the outbound traffic configuration. Here is the configuration:

```
toddfw#config t
toddfw(config)#global (outside) 1 192.168.30.2 netmask 255.255.255.0
toddfw(config)#global (perimeter) 1 192.168.40.10-192.168.40.100
   ↳netmask 255.255.255.0
toddfw(config)#^Z
toddfw#
```

In this configuration, you've done two different things. First, you're assuming that the outbound interface IP address is a registered Internet address and that you do not have an unlimited number of registered Internet addresses to use for NAT. Therefore, in the preceding configuration of the external or outbound interface, you're using Port Address Translation (PAT). With PAT, each outbound client connection can use a separate port on the single translated address, allowing you to service more than 64,000 connections from a single IP address!

On the perimeter interface (where you're translating and have essentially unlimited address space), you have specified a range of addresses to be used in translation when this interface is accessed from other interfaces (in this outbound case, from the inside interface). The "Outbound Access Control" section later in this appendix discusses limiting outbound user access using access control lists (ACLs).

Configuring Inbound Access

Great! With the outbound connections configured, you're halfway done. Recall that inbound connections are denied unless specifically allowed. This is the opposite of outbound behavior. You need to do a bit of configuration to allow any inbound connections. You use the static and conduit commands to accomplish this.

As with outbound access, let's begin with a diagram. Consider the network shown here:

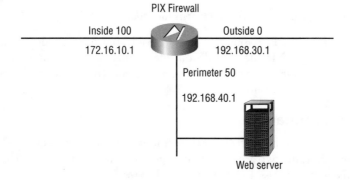

PIX Firewall

Inside 100   Outside 0

172.16.10.1   192.168.30.1

Perimeter 50

192.168.40.1

Web server

With many configuration tasks, using a network diagram can help prevent con-figuration errors. It's always easier to start with a diagram of the PIX Firewall showing all the interfaces, their names, and their security levels. Put this infor-mation in a table and then decide where inbound and outbound access must be configured.

This example uses the same configuration as the diagram for outbound access, with the addi-tion of a web server in the DMZ at IP address 192.168.40.2. You want to allow external users to access this server through the outbound interface. Here is the configuration you must add:

```
toddfw#config t
toddfw(config)#static (perimeter, outside) 192.168.30.5 192.168.40.2 netmask
    ↳255.255.255.255
toddfw(config)#conduit permit host 192.168.30.5 eq www any
toddfw(config)#^Z
toddfw#
```

You may need to do a clear xlate before configuring inbound access—to ensure that the translation entry isn't already taken dynamically—so that you can do the static translation.

Let's take a closer look at the static and conduit commands, as well as another command you can add for protocol control: fixup protocol.

The *static* Command

In the preceding example, the `static` command statically translates the outside address 192 .168.30.5 to the perimeter address 192.168.40.2. You then register the address 192.168.30.5 in your external DNS server as the IP address of your web server to be accessed from the Internet (not the actual server at 192.168.40.2).

The `static` command specifies the involved interfaces and addresses using the following formula:

```
static (inside, outside) outside_addr inside_addr
```

Remember this formula! Everyone all together: inside, outside, outside, inside. Inside, outside, outside, inside. Again? Inside, outside, outside, inside. Good! If you follow this formula, you can't go wrong with the `static` commands on the exam. (But be aware that this static functionality changes with NAT disabled!)

The *conduit* Command

The `conduit` command in the preceding example looks similar to the `access-list` syntax from the IOS; however, the two are not interchangeable. This `conduit` command permits any host to access the static address 192.168.30.5 on the www port.

The `conduit` commands can become more complex as you add interfaces. Additionally, some services require multiple `conduit` statements, including the following services:

- discard
- dns
- echo
- ident
- pptp
- rpc
- syslog
- tacacs-ds
- talk
- time

The *fixup protocol* Command

Do you know every potential security hole on every service you must allow through the firewall? I certainly don't! The PIX Firewall allows you to use the `fixup protocol` command to further control Application-layer protocols.

For example, suppose that you want to add a mail server to your network diagram at 192.168.40.6, but you also want to use the PIX Mail Guard feature with this server. The Mail Guard feature allows only certain SMTP commands to be sent to the mail server. Here is the configuration:

```
toddfw#config t
```

```
toddfw(config)#static (perimeter, outside) 192.168.30.6 192.168.40.6
       ↳netmask 255.255.255.0
toddfw(config)#conduit permit host 192.168.30.5 eq smtp any
toddfw(config)#fixup protocol smtp 25
toddfw(config)#^Z
toddfw#
```

Configuring Multiple Interfaces and AAA on the PIX Firewall

Congratulations! You have now covered the basics of configuring the PIX Firewall and learned how to allow both inbound and outbound traffic. These functions are the "meat and potatoes" of the configuration; everything else is merely details. Unfortunately, mere details have caused many a pager to go off at 2:00 A.M.! In this section, you need to look at some of these details. This section discusses two issues: configuring multiple interfaces and how to integrate PIX into the AAA environment.

Configuring Multiple Interfaces

The first section of this appendix discussed the interfaces available on the PIX Firewall and how they must be purchased through either Cisco or a Cisco reseller. There are many ways to include the PIX Firewall in your network. Let's take a look at two methods.

The following illustration depicts a typical three-part firewall, where there is an external router, an internal router (the PIX box), and a DMZ:

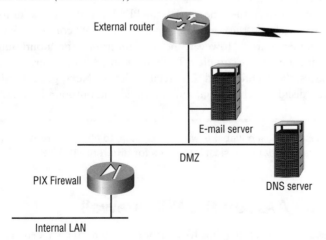

Notice that the PIX box is in an ideal position to protect the internal network from outside threats. However, what is protecting any assets placed in the DMZ? Of course, you can use ACLs on the router to offer some protection, but you may not be fully using the capabilities of your PIX Firewall.

Next, consider this network diagram:

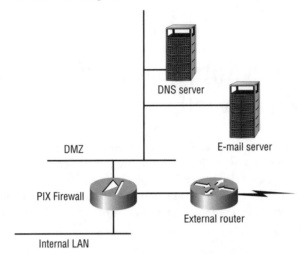

Now the PIX Firewall has been moved to act as a router between the internal network, the external network, and both DMZ networks. The PIX Firewall still has the ability to protect internal assets as in the typical three-part firewall scenario, but it now sits between the external, untrusted Internet and one DMZ. This gives the PIX Firewall the ability to offer protection to DMZ-located servers as well as internal servers. In situations such as hosting mail gateways (as discussed earlier), this setup allows the PIX Firewall to use its Mail Guard feature to protect assets otherwise left open in a DMZ.

Of course, to work between these networks, the PIX Firewall needs additional interfaces. With the addition of interfaces, the configuration becomes more complex. Basic configuration commands extend rather simply. However, the configuration of both outbound and inbound traffic becomes significantly more complex. To figure it out, draw a diagram of the PIX Firewall showing all interfaces, their names, and their security levels. Next, put this information in a table. Then you can decide where to configure inbound and outbound access.

Visit the Cisco website (www.cisco.com) to check current limitations and the availability of physical interfaces for different PIX Firewalls.

Implementing AAA on the PIX Firewall

Now that the firewall is in place, it's time to incorporate it into the AAA environment. The first step is to do the initial AAA configuration, where you specify the location of the security servers and the protocols used to communicate with them. You'll then learn how to enable each *A* in AAA separately.

AAA can be used to authenticate in a number of different situations on the PIX Firewall:

- FTP, HTTP, and Telnet traffic, either inbound or outbound
- Enable mode access to the PIX Firewall
- Serial console access on the PIX Firewall

Initial AAA Configuration

The first thing to do is to specify a security server to be used for authentication and the protocol to be used for this communication. Earlier in this book, we discussed in some detail the operation of CSNT as a security server, as well as the TACACS+ and RADIUS protocols. Here, you'll begin configuring your PIX Firewall to use a security server. Suppose that you have the network configuration shown here:

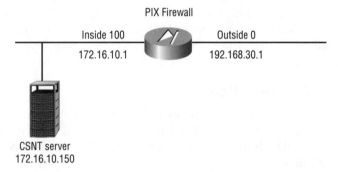

You want the PIX Firewall to use the security server at 172.16.10.150 to authenticate users. Here's the configuration to define the protocol and the location of the security server:

```
toddfw#config t
toddfw(config)#aaa-server AUTH1 protocol tacacs+
toddfw(config)#aaa-server AUTH1 host 172.16.10.150 keykey timeout 5
toddfw(config)#^Z
toddfw#
```

In this example, you used the `aaa-server` command twice. The first `aaa-server` command specifies the group tag AUTH1 and the communications protocol TACACS+. You can configure up to 16 separate group tags. (You may use different groups of security servers for different types of authentication.)

The second `aaa-server` command is used to define a security server in the AUTH1 group. It specifies the group tag (AUTH1), the security server (`host 172.16.10.150`), the encryption key (`keykey`), and the timeout in seconds to be used with this security server (`timeout 5`). Up to 16 security servers can be configured per group tag.

Implementing Authentication

Authentication can be forced on either inbound or outbound connections. The PIX Firewall can use either TACACS+ or RADIUS to communicate with the security server when using authentication. Let's go ahead and add authentication:

```
toddfw#config t
toddfw(config)#aaa authentication any inbound 0 0 AUTH1
toddfw(config)#aaa authentication any outbound 0 0 AUTH1
toddfw(config)#^Z
toddfw#
```

This configuration requires authentication for any access, either inbound or outbound. In the aaa authentication command, the any keyword refers to the authentication service. It could be HTTP, FTP, or Telnet; the any keyword enables authentication for all TCP services.

The next parameter refers to either inbound or outbound connections. You've used two separate statements to require authentication for both inbound and outbound connections. The 0 0 parameter is used to specify local and foreign addresses. In this example, you use 0 to indicate any address. Finally, you specify the group tag you want that particular traffic authenticated against.

Implementing Authorization

As with authentication, authorization can be used for either inbound or outbound connections. However, authorization requires that the PIX Firewall use TACACS+ when communicating with the security server. RADIUS communication between the firewall and security server will not support authorization.

Here is the configuration to add authorization to your PIX Firewall:

```
toddfw#config t
toddfw(config)#aaa authorization any inbound 0 0
toddfw(config)#aaa authorization ftp outbound 0 0
toddfw(config)#^Z
toddfw#
```

In this example, you require authorization for any inbound traffic, but you only require authorization for outbound FTP traffic.

Implementing Accounting

Finally, let's enable accounting to keep track of what your users are doing. Suppose that you wish to have the PIX Firewall report to the security server everything that your inbound users are doing. Here is the configuration:

```
toddfw#config t
toddfw(config)#aaa accounting any inbound 0 0 AUTH1
toddfw(config)#^Z
toddfw#
```

The PIX Firewall now sends attribute-value pairs to the security server on all inbound traffic. This information can then be used as an audit trail for billing information, security information, or network management information.

Configuring Advanced PIX Firewall Features

There are many additional features included in the PIX Firewall, and new ones are being added all the time. This section looks at some of the possibilities and presents a quick look at the configuration for a few of them.

The PIX Firewall is obviously intended to be a central component in your network topology. Any such device deserves a bit of additional attention with respect to fault tolerance and manageability. Fortunately, the PIX Firewall supports both of these needs with its *failover*, or *hot standby*, capability and the Cisco Security Manager utility. Other features covered in this section include outbound access, logging, SNMP support, Java applet blocking, URL filtering, and password recovery.

Failover

You can provide fault tolerance to your system by adding a standby PIX Firewall. Consider this network (it's the same one used as an example earlier in the appendix):

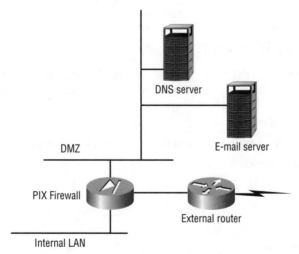

In this situation, should the PIX Firewall fail, all access between the internal network and the DMZ (and the outside world, for that matter) would fail. Such an outage would certainly not be desirable and may provide you with extensive blocks of free time (in other words, unemployment).

Now, consider the network diagram shown here:

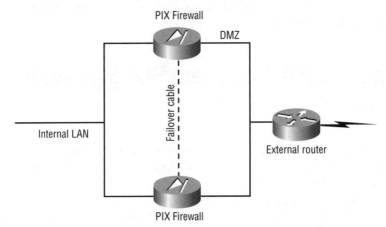

In this network, there are two PIX Firewalls, connected by a failover cable. This cable must be present for this configuration to work! When running properly, the configurations between the two firewalls are synchronized, and the second, or standby, PIX Firewall will not take over until the first one has failed.

When you use the PIX Firewall's failover feature, the active (primary) firewall must have an Unrestricted license. The backup (secondary) firewall can have a Failover license.

Cisco Security Manager

The Cisco Security Manager (CSM) utility allows for the centralized management of up to 100 PIX Firewalls. A Windows application, CSM requires Microsoft Windows NT Server 4.0 to run.

CSM provides the following:

- Real-time event notification using e-mail, paging gateways, or scripts
- Filtered event notifications
- Policy-consistency checking
- Backup
- Distribution
- Web-based reporting

Outbound Access Control

Outbound access is the equivalent of an ACL. However, the syntax for ACLs here is different from the router syntax with which you may already be familiar. PIX Firewall uses two commands—outbound and apply—to enforce ACLs. Let's jump back to a sample network used earlier in this appendix, which looks like this:

PIX Firewall

Inside   Outside

172.16.10.1   192.168.30.1

Now, suppose that you want to deny your inside users access to the external web pages. Here is how you could implement this policy:

```
toddfw#config t
toddfw(config)#outbound 12 deny 172.16.10.1 255.255.255.0 80 tcp
toddfw(config)#apply (inside) 12 outgoing_src
toddfw(config)#^Z
toddfw#
```

The outbound command has a number of parameters. The 12 specifies a list ID, same as with an ACL. The deny keyword—well, denies the specified traffic. The IP addresses are not source or destination addresses yet; that is determined by the apply command. Finally, TCP port 80 is specified.

The apply command must first specify which interface the policy will be applied to. In the preceding example, you used the outgoing_src parameter to indicate that addresses in the outbound command are source addresses. Had you used the outgoing_dest parameter instead, the IP addresses specified in the outbound command would have been interpreted as destination addresses. Using these commands, you can limit many types of outbound traffic, much as you would control access by using ACLs on a router.

Logging

PIX Firewalls support a number of logging options. From the previous example, here is a sample configuration of how to add logging to the PIX Firewall:

```
toddfw#config t
toddfw(config)#logging on
toddfw(config)#logging facility 20
toddfw(config)#logging host 172.16.10.50
toddfw(config)#^Z
toddfw#
```

Using these commands, you have enabled logging, specified the logging facility on the Syslog server, and specified the IP address of the security server where Syslog messages are to be sent.

SNMP Support

The PIX Firewall can be configured to support SNMP messages, as in the following example:

```
toddfw#config t
toddfw(config)#snmp-server community todd1
toddfw(config)#snmp-server contact Todd Lammle
toddfw(config)#snmp-server enable traps
toddfw(config)#^Z
toddfw#
```

In this example, you have entered the community string, specified a contact for problems, and told the PIX Firewall to enable the sending of traps (traps are sent via Syslog).

Java Applet Blocking

Java may present a problem to your network security. When you allow your internal users to download port 80 (HTTP) objects, these objects might contain hidden Java code that could be harmful to your internal data. The PIX Firewall allows you to block these hidden Java programs. This is achieved using the outbound and apply commands. Here is the configuration:

```
toddfw#config t
toddfw(config)#outbound 13 deny 172.16.10.1 255.255.255.0 java
toddfw(config)#apply (inside) 13 outgoing_src
toddfw(config)#^Z
toddfw#
```

As you can see, this is simply an ACL in the format introduced in the "Outbound Access" section earlier in this appendix, but in this example, the type of access is specified as java.

URL Filtering

URL filtering is a new command in the PIX Firewall release 4.2. It gives you the ability to use a third-party URL filter list (from WebSENSE) to control the content your users may be accessing. Here is the configuration:

```
toddfw#config t
toddfw(config)#url-server (inside) 172.16.10.55
toddfw(config)#filter url http 0 0 0 0
toddfw(config)#^Z
toddfw#
```

This assumes that the device at IP address 172.16.10.55 is configured as a WebSENSE URL server. On the URL server, you can configure which categories of content are deemed appropriate or inappropriate for your network.

Password Recovery

So what happens if you lose the enable password for your PIX Firewall? Well, you need to do password recovery. This is not like the password recovery on an IOS router! You need the following:

- A working PC

- A terminal-emulation program

- The PIX Password Lockout utility

The password-recovery procedure requires approximately 10 minutes of outage for the PIX Firewall, so plan accordingly. For detailed instructions, including files that may be required and specific steps for password recovery with or without a floppy disk, see the Cisco online help.

Glossary

10BaseT   Part of the original IEEE 802.3 standard, 10BaseT is the Ethernet specification of 10Mbps baseband that uses two pairs of twisted-pair, Category 3, 4, or 5 cabling—one pair to send data and the other to receive. 10BaseT has a distance limit of about 100 meters per segment. See also: *Ethernet* and *IEEE 802.3*.

100BaseT   Based on the IEEE 802.3u standard, 100BaseT is the Fast Ethernet specification of 100Mbps baseband that uses UTP wiring. 100BaseT sends link pulses (containing more information than those used in 10BaseT) over the network when no traffic is present. See also: *10BaseT, Fast Ethernet,* and *IEEE 802.3*.

100BaseTX   Based on the IEEE 802.3u standard, 100BaseTX is the 100Mbps baseband Fast Ethernet specification that uses two pairs of UTP or STP wiring. The first pair of wires receives data; the second pair sends data. To ensure correct signal timing, a 100BaseTX segment cannot be longer than 100 meters.

A

A&B bit signaling   Used in T1 transmission facilities and sometimes called *24th channel signaling*. Each of the 24 T1 subchannels in this procedure uses one bit of every sixth frame to send supervisory signaling information.

AAA   Authentication, Authorization, and Accounting: A system developed by Cisco to provide network security. See also: *authentication, authorization,* and *accounting*.

AAL   ATM adaptation layer: A service-dependent sublayer of the Data Link layer that accepts data from other applications and brings it to the ATM layer in 48-byte ATM payload segments. CS and SAR are the two sublayers that form AALs. Currently, the four types of AAL recommended by the ITU-T are AAL1, AAL2, AAL3/4, and AAL5. AALs are differentiated by the source-destination timing they use, whether they are CBR or VBR, and whether they are used for connection-oriented or connectionless mode data transmission. See also: *AAL1, AAL2, AAL3/4, AAL5, ATM,* and *ATM layer*.

AAL1   ATM adaptation layer 1: One of four AALs recommended by the ITU-T, it is used for connection-oriented, time-sensitive services that need constant bit rates, such as isochronous traffic and uncompressed video. See also: *AAL*.

AAL2   ATM adaptation layer 2: One of four AALs recommended by the ITU-T, it is used for connection-oriented services that support a variable bit rate, such as voice traffic. See also: *AAL*.

AAL3/4   ATM adaptation layer 3/4: One of four AALs (a product of two initially distinct layers) recommended by the ITU-T, supporting both connectionless and connection-oriented links. Its primary use is in sending SMDS packets over ATM networks. See also: *AAL*.

AAL5   ATM adaptation layer 5: One of four AALs recommended by the ITU-T, it is used to support connection-oriented VBR services primarily to transfer classical IP over ATM and LANE traffic. This least complex of the AAL recommendations uses simple and efficient AAL (SEAL), offering lower bandwidth costs and simpler processing requirements but also providing reduced bandwidth and error-recovery capacities. See also: *AAL*.

AARP   AppleTalk Address Resolution Protocol: The protocol in an AppleTalk stack that maps Data Link–layer addresses to Network-layer addresses.

AARP probe packets   Packets sent by the AARP to determine whether a given node ID is being used by another node in a nonextended AppleTalk network. If the node ID is not in use, the sending node appropriates that node's ID. If the node ID is in use, the sending node selects a different ID and then sends out more AARP probe packets. See also: *AARP*.

ABM   Asynchronous Balanced Mode: When two stations can initiate a transmission, ABM is an HDLC (or one of its derived protocols) communication technology that supports peer-oriented, point-to-point communications between both stations.

ABR   Area border router: An OSPF router that is located on the border of one or more OSPF areas. ABRs are used to connect OSPF areas to the OSPF backbone area.

access control list (ACL)   Sometimes called the *poor man's firewall*, a record kept by routers that uses specific test conditions to determine "interesting" traffic to and from the router for certain network services.

access control server (ACS)   A process that connects asynchronous devices to a WAN or LAN using terminal emulation software. Sometimes referred to as a *network access server*, it provides synchronous or asynchronous routing of supported protocols. See also: *network access server*.

access layer   One of the layers in Cisco's three-layer hierarchical model. The access layer provides users with access to the internetwork.

access link   A link used with switches that is part of only one virtual LAN (VLAN). Trunk links carry information from multiple VLANs.

access list   A set of test conditions kept by routers that determines "interesting" traffic to and from the router for various services on the network.

access method   The manner in which network devices approach gaining access to the network itself.

access rate   Defines the bandwidth rate of the circuit. For example, the access rate of a T1 circuit is 1.544Mbps. In Frame Relay and other technologies, there may be a fractional T1 connection—256Kbps, for example. However, the access rate and clock rate is still 1.544Mbps.

access server   See: *access control server (ACS)*.

accounting   The third part of AAA that collects and sends security server information for billing, auditing, and reporting information.

acknowledgment   Verification sent from one network device to another signifying that an event has occurred. May be abbreviated as ACK. Contrast with: *NAK*.

ACR   Allowed cell rate: A designation defined by the ATM Forum for managing ATM traffic. Dynamically controlled using congestion control measures, the ACR varies between the minimum cell rate (MCR) and the peak cell rate (PCR). See also: *MCR* and *PCR*.

active monitor   The mechanism used to manage a Token Ring. The network node with the highest MAC address on the ring becomes the active monitor and is responsible for management tasks such as preventing loops and ensuring that tokens are not lost.

Adaptive Security Algorithm (ASA)   Provides stateful security for all TCP/IP sessions. ASA protects sensitive and private resources.

address learning   Used with transparent bridges to learn the hardware addresses of all devices on an internetwork. The switch then filters the network with the known hardware (MAC) addresses.

address mapping   By translating network addresses from one format to another, this methodology permits different protocols to operate interchangeably.

address mask   A bit combination descriptor identifying which portion of an address refers to the network or subnet and which part refers to the host. Sometimes simply called the *mask*. See also: *subnet mask*.

address resolution   The process used for resolving differences between computer addressing schemes. Address resolution typically defines a method for tracing Network-layer (Layer 3) addresses to Data Link–layer (Layer 2) addresses. See also: *address mapping*.

adjacency   The relationship made between defined neighboring routers and end nodes—using a common media segment—to exchange routing information.

administrative distance   A number between 0 and 255 that expresses the value of trustworthiness of a routing information source. The lower the number, the higher the integrity rating.

administrative weight (AW)   A value designated by a network administrator to rate the preference given to a network link. It is one of four link metrics exchanged by PNNI topology state packets (PTSPs) to test ATM network resource availability.

ADSU   ATM data service unit: The terminal adapter used to connect to an ATM network through an HSSI-compatible mechanism. See also: *DSU*.

advertising   The process whereby routing or service updates are transmitted at given intervals, allowing other routers on the network to maintain a record of viable routes.

AEP   AppleTalk Echo Protocol: A test for connectivity between two AppleTalk nodes where one node sends a packet to another and receives an echo, or copy, in response.

AES   Advanced Encryption Standard: The National Institute of Standards and Technology (NIST) created AES as a new Federal Information Processing Standard (FIPS) publication and as privacy transforms for IPSec and Internet Key Exchange (IKE). AES has a variable key length—the algorithm can specify a 128-bit key (the default), a 192-bit key, or a 256-bit key.

AFI   Authority and format identifier: The part of an NSAP ATM address that delineates the type and format of the IDI section of an ATM address.

AFP   AppleTalk Filing Protocol: A Presentation-layer protocol supporting AppleShare and MacOS File Sharing that permits users to share files and applications on a server.

aggressive mode   An IKE initiate feature, aggressive mode allows you to configure IKE pre-shared keys as RADIUS tunnel attributes for IPSec peers, giving you the ability to scale your IKE pre-shared keys in a hub-and-spoke topology.

AIP   ATM Interface Processor: Supporting AAL3/4 and AAL5, this interface for Cisco 7000 series routers minimizes performance bottlenecks at the UNI. See also: *AAL3/4 and AAL5*.

algorithm   A set of rules or a process used to solve a problem. In networking, algorithms are typically used for finding the best route for traffic from a source to its destination.

alignment error   An error occurring in Ethernet networks in which a received frame has extra bits, that is, a number not divisible by eight. Alignment errors are generally the result of frame damage caused by collisions.

all-routes explorer packet   An explorer packet that can move across an entire SRB network, tracing all possible paths to a given destination. Also known as an *all-rings explorer packet*. See also: *explorer packet*, *local explorer packet*, and *spanning explorer packet*.

AM   Amplitude modulation: A modulation method that represents information by varying the amplitude of the carrier signal. See also: *modulation*.

AMI   Alternate mark inversion: A line-code type on T1 and E1 circuits that shows zeros as "01" during each bit cell, and ones as "11" or "00," alternately, during each bit cell. The sending device must maintain ones density in AMI but not independently of the data stream. Also known as *binary coded alternate mark inversion*. Contrast with: *B8ZS*. See also: *ones density*.

amplitude   An analog or digital waveform's highest value.

analog transmission   Signal messaging whereby information is represented by various combinations of signal amplitude, frequency, and phase.

ANSI   American National Standards Institute: The organization of corporate, government, and other volunteer members that coordinates standards-related activities, approves U.S. national standards, and develops U.S. positions in international standards organizations. ANSI assists in the creation of international and U.S. standards in disciplines such as communications, networking, and a variety of technical fields. It publishes over 13,000 standards for engineered products and technologies ranging from screw threads to networking protocols. ANSI is a member of the IEC and ISO.

anti-replay   Replay attacks occur when a hacker records a session from a user, then replays that session to fool the receiving device into thinking that it is the original user. Anti-replay provides security by enabling the receiving device to reject these replays either by using a sequence number within an IPSec session or with the help of a data authentication service.

anycast   An ATM address that can be shared by more than one end system, allowing requests to be routed to a node that provides a particular service.

AppleTalk   Currently in two versions, the group of communication protocols designed by Apple Computer for use in Macintosh environments. The earlier Phase 1 protocols support one physical network with only one network number that resides in one zone. The later Phase 2 protocols support more than one logical network on a single physical network, allowing networks to exist in more than one zone. See also: *zone*.

Application layer   Layer 7 of the OSI reference network model, supplying services to application procedures (such as electronic mail or file transfer) that are outside the OSI model. This layer chooses and determines the availability of communicating partners and the resources necessary to make the connection, coordinates partnering applications, and forms a consensus on procedures for controlling data integrity and error recovery. See also: *Data Link layer*, *Network layer*, *Physical layer*, *Presentation layer*, *Session layer*, and *Transport layer*.

Application-layer attack   Involves an application with well-known weaknesses that can be easily exploited.

ARA   AppleTalk Remote Access: A protocol for Macintosh users establishing their access to resources and data from a remote AppleTalk location.

area   A logical, rather than physical, set of segments (based on CLNS, DECnet, or OSPF), along with their attached devices. Areas are commonly connected to other areas using routers to create a single autonomous system. See also: *autonomous system*.

ARM   Asynchronous response mode: An HDLC communication mode using one primary station and at least one additional station in which transmission can be initiated from either the primary station or from one of the secondary stations.

ARP   Address Resolution Protocol: Defined in RFC 826, the protocol that traces IP addresses to MAC addresses. See also: *RARP*.

AS path prepending   The use of route maps to lengthen the autonomous system path by adding false ASNs.

ASBR   Autonomous system boundary router: An area border router placed between an OSPF autonomous system and a non-OSPF network that operates both OSPF and an additional routing protocol, such as RIP. ASBRs must be located in a non-stub OSPF area. See also: *ABR*, *non-stub area*, and *OSPF*.

ASCII   American Standard Code for Information Interchange: An eight-bit code for representing characters, consisting of seven data bits plus one parity bit.

ASICs   Application-specific integrated circuits: Used in Layer 2 switches to make filtering decisions. The ASIC looks in the filter table of MAC addresses and determines which port the destination hardware address of a received hardware address is destined for. The frame will be allowed to traverse only that one segment. If the hardware address is unknown, the frame is forwarded out all ports.

ASN.1   Abstract Syntax Notation One: An OSI language used to describe types of data that is independent of computer structures and depicting methods. Described by ISO International Standard 8824.

ASP   AppleTalk Session Protocol: A protocol employing ATP to establish, maintain, and tear down sessions and sequence requests. See also: *ATP*.

AST   Automatic spanning tree: A function that supplies one path for spanning explorer frames traveling from one node in the network to another, supporting the automatic resolution of spanning trees in SRB networks. AST is based on the IEEE 802.1 standard. See also: *IEEE 802.1* and *SRB*.

asynchronous transmission   Digital signals sent without precise timing, usually with different frequencies and phase relationships. Asynchronous transmissions generally enclose individual characters in control bits (called *start* and *stop bits*) that show the beginning and end of each character. Contrast with: *isochronous transmission* and *synchronous transmission*.

ATCP   AppleTalk Control Program: The protocol for establishing and configuring AppleTalk over PPP, defined in RFC 1378. See also: *PPP*.

ATDM   Asynchronous time-division multiplexing: A technique for sending information, it differs from normal TDM in that the time slots are assigned when necessary rather than preassigned to certain transmitters. Contrast with: *FDM, statistical multiplexing,* and *TDM*.

ATG   Address translation gateway: The mechanism within Cisco DECnet routing software that enables routers to route multiple, independent DECnet networks and to establish a user-designated address translation for chosen nodes between networks.

ATM   Asynchronous Transfer Mode: The international standard, identified by fixed-length 53-byte cells, for transmitting cells in multiple service systems, such as voice, video, or data. Transit delays are reduced because the fixed-length cells permit processing to occur in the hardware. ATM is designed to maximize the benefits of high-speed transmission media, such as SONET, E3, and T3.

ATM ARP server   A device that supplies logical subnets running classical IP over ATM with address-resolution services.

ATM endpoint   The initiating or terminating connection in an ATM network. ATM endpoints include servers, workstations, ATM-to-LAN switches, and ATM routers.

ATM Forum The international organization founded jointly by Northern Telecom, Sprint, Cisco Systems, and NET/ADAPTIVE in 1991 to develop and promote standards-based implementation agreements for ATM technology. The ATM Forum broadens official standards developed by ANSI and ITU-T and creates implementation agreements before official standards are published.

ATM layer A sublayer of the Data Link layer in an ATM network that is service-independent. To create standard 53-byte ATM cells, the ATM layer receives 48-byte segments from the AAL and attaches a 5-byte header to each. These cells are then sent to the physical layer for transmission across the physical medium. See also: *AAL*.

ATMM ATM Management: A procedure that runs on ATM switches, managing rate enforcement and VCI translation. See also: *ATM*.

ATM user-user connection A connection made by the ATM layer to supply communication between at least two ATM service users, such as ATMM processes. These communications can be unidirectional or bidirectional, using one or two VCCs, respectively. See also: *ATM layer* and *ATMM*.

atomic signatures Cisco IOS uses signatures to discover patterns of misuse in the network. Atomic signatures trigger based on a single packet; compound signatures trigger on multiple packets. Atomic signatures are easier for the router to support. They evaluate each packet independently, whereas compound signatures must buffer previous packets for comparison against current packets to see if traffic trends match their signature. Operatively, this means that atomic signatures cost less memory than compound signatures. Contrast with: *compound signatures*.

ATP AppleTalk Transaction Protocol: A Transport-level protocol that enables reliable transactions between two sockets, where one client requests the other client to perform a given task and to report the results. ATP fastens the request and response together, assuring a loss-free exchange of request-response pairs.

attack signatures Used within an IDS to detect malicious activity.

attenuation In communication, a weakening or loss of signal energy, typically caused by distance.

audit rule Signatures are used by an administrator to keep track of the network traffic and set up alarms. Audit rules specify which signatures should be applied to packet traffic and the actions to be taken when a match is found. See also *atomic signatures*.

AURP AppleTalk Update-based Routing Protocol: A technique for encapsulating AppleTalk traffic in the header of a foreign protocol that allows the connection of at least two noncontiguous AppleTalk internetworks through a foreign network (such as TCP/IP) to create an AppleTalk WAN. The connection made is called an *AURP tunnel*. By exchanging routing information between exterior routers, the AURP maintains routing tables for the complete AppleTalk WAN. See also: *AURP tunnel*.

AURP tunnel A connection made in an AURP WAN that acts as a single, virtual link between AppleTalk internetworks separated physically by a foreign network such as a TCP/IP network. See also: *AURP*.

authentication The first part of the AAA model that verifies users for access onto the network, typically using a username and password. Authentication also identifies users using login and passwords, challenge and response, and encryption.

Authentication, Authorization, and Accounting (AAA) The model used to provide security on a network using a Cisco network access server (NAS). See also: *authentication, authorization*, and *accounting*.

Authentication Header (AH) A security protocol embedded in data that provides authentication and optional replay-detection services.

authority zone A portion of the domain-name tree associated with DNS for which one name server is the authority. See also: *DNS*.

authorization The second part of the AAA network security model that provides the method for remote access control, including one-time authorization or authorization for each service, per-user account list and profile, user group support, and support of upper-layer protocols.

auto duplex A setting on Layer 1 and Layer 2 devices that sets the duplex of a switch or hub port automatically.

automatic call reconnect A function that enables automatic call rerouting away from a failed trunk line.

autonomous confederation A collection of self-governed systems that depend more on their own network accessibility and routing information than on information received from other systems or groups.

autonomous switching The ability of Cisco routers to process packets more quickly by using the ciscoBus to switch packets independently of the system processor.

autonomous system (AS) A group of networks under mutual administration that share the same routing methodology. Autonomous systems are subdivided by areas and must be assigned an individual 16-bit number by the IANA. See also: *area*.

autoreconfiguration A procedure executed by nodes within the failure domain of a Token Ring, wherein nodes automatically perform diagnostics, trying to reconfigure the network around failed areas.

auxiliary port The console port on the back of Cisco routers that allows you to dial the router and make console configuration settings.

B

B8ZS   Binary 8-zero substitution: A line-code type, interpreted at the remote end of the connection, that uses a special code substitution whenever eight consecutive zeros are transmitted over the link on T1 and E1 circuits. This technique assures ones density independent of the data stream. Also known as *bipolar 8-zero substitution*. Contrast with: *AMI*. See also: *ones density*.

backbone   The basic portion of the network that provides the primary path for traffic sent to and initiated from other networks.

back end   A node or software program supplying services to a front end. See also: *server*.

bandwidth   The gap between the highest and lowest frequencies employed by network signals. More commonly, it refers to the rated throughput capacity of a network protocol or medium.

bandwidth on demand (BoD)   This function allows an additional B channel to be used to increase the amount of bandwidth available for a particular connection.

baseband   A feature of a network technology that uses only one carrier frequency. Ethernet is an example. Also called *narrowband*. Compare to: *broadband*.

baseline   Baseline information includes historical data about the network and routine utilization information. This information can be used to determine whether there were recent changes made to the network that may contribute to the problem at hand.

Basic Management Setup   Used with Cisco routers when in setup mode. Provides only enough management and configuration to get the router working so someone can telnet into the router and configure it.

bastion host   A computer located on the perimeter of your network that plays a crucial part in implementing your network security policy. Bastion hosts may also serve to provide web services and public access systems.

baud   Synonymous with bits per second (bps), if each signal element represents one bit. It is a unit of signaling speed equivalent to the number of separate signal elements transmitted per second.

B channel   Bearer channel: A full-duplex, 64Kbps channel in ISDN that transmits user data. Compare to: *D channel*, *E channel*, and *H channel*.

BDR   Backup designated router: This is used in an OSPF network to back up the designated router in case of failure.

beacon   An FDDI device or Token Ring frame that points to a serious problem with the ring, such as a broken cable. The beacon frame carries the address of the station thought to be down. See also: *failure domain*.

BECN   Backward explicit congestion notification: BECN is the bit set by a Frame Relay network in frames moving away from frames headed into a congested path. A DTE that receives frames with the BECN may ask higher-level protocols to take necessary flow control measures. Compare to: *FECN*.

BGP4   BGP Version 4: Version 4 of the interdomain routing protocol most commonly used on the Internet. BGP4 supports CIDR and uses route-counting mechanisms to decrease the size of routing tables. See also: *CIDR*.

BGP Identifier   This field contains a value that identifies the BGP speaker. This is a random value chosen by the BGP router when sending an OPEN message.

BGP neighbors   Two routers running BGP that begin a communication process to exchange dynamic routing information; they use a TCP port at Layer 4 of the OSI reference model. Specifically, TCP port 179 is used. Also known as *BGP peers*.

BGP peers   See: *BGP neighbors*.

BGP speaker   A router that advertises its prefixes or routes.

bidirectional shared tree   A method of shared tree multicast forwarding. This method allows group members to receive data from the source or the rendezvous point, whichever is closer.

binary   A two-character numbering method that uses ones and zeros. The binary numbering system underlies all digital representation of information.

BIP   Bit interleaved parity: A method used in ATM to monitor errors on a link, sending a check bit or word in the link overhead for the previous block or frame. This allows bit errors in transmissions to be found and delivered as maintenance information.

BISDN   Broadband ISDN: ITU-T standards created to manage high-bandwidth technologies such as video. BISDN currently employs ATM technology along SONET-based transmission circuits, supplying data rates between 155Mbps and 622Mbps and beyond. See also: *BRI*, *ISDN*, and *PRI*.

bit-oriented protocol   Regardless of frame content, the class of Data Link–layer communication protocols that transmits frames. Bit-oriented protocols, as compared with byte-oriented, supply more efficient and trustworthy full-duplex operation. Compare with: *byte-oriented protocol*.

Boot ROM   Used in routers to put the router into bootstrap mode. Bootstrap mode then boots the device with an operating system. The ROM can also hold a small Cisco IOS.

bootstrap protocol   A protocol used to dynamically assign IP addresses and gateways to requesting clients.

border gateway   A router that facilitates communication with routers in different autonomous systems.

border peer The device in charge of a peer group; it exists at the edge of a hierarchical design. When any member of the peer group wants to locate a resource, it sends a single explorer to the border peer. The border peer then forwards this request on behalf of the requesting router, thus eliminating duplicate traffic.

border router Typically defined within Open Shortest Path First (OSPF) as a router that connected an area to the backbone area. However, a border router can be a router that connects a company to the Internet as well. See also: *OSPF.*

BPDU Bridge Protocol Data Unit: A Spanning-Tree Protocol initializing packet that is sent at definable intervals for the purpose of exchanging information among bridges in networks.

BRI Basic Rate Interface: The ISDN interface that facilitates circuit-switched communication between video, data, and voice; it is made up of two B channels (64Kbps each) and one D channel (16Kbps). Compare with: *PRI.* See also: *BISDN.*

bridge A device for connecting two segments of a network and transmitting packets between them. Both segments must use identical protocols to communicate. Bridges function at the Data Link layer, Layer 2 of the OSI reference model. The purpose of a bridge is to filter, send, or flood any incoming frame, based on the MAC address of that particular frame.

bridge group Used in the router configuration of bridging, bridge groups are defined by a unique number. Network traffic is bridged between all interfaces that are a member of the same bridge group.

bridge identifier Used to find and elect the root bridge in a Layer 2 switched internetwork. The bridge ID is a combination of the bridge priority and the base MAC address.

bridge priority Sets the STP priority of the bridge. All bridge priorities are set to 32768 by default.

bridging loop Loops occur in a bridged network if more than one link to a network exists and the STP protocol is not turned on.

broadband A transmission methodology for multiplexing several independent signals onto one cable. In telecommunications, broadband is classified as any channel with bandwidth greater than 4kHz (typical voice grade). In LAN terminology, it is classified as a coaxial cable on which analog signaling is employed. Also known as *wideband.* Contrast with: *baseband.*

broadcast A data frame or packet that is transmitted to every node on the local network segment (as defined by the broadcast domain). Broadcasts are known by their broadcast address, which is a destination network and host address with all the bits turned on. Also called *local broadcast.* Compare with: *directed broadcast.*

broadcast domain A group of devices receiving broadcast frames initiating from any device within the group. Because they do not forward broadcast frames, broadcast domains are generally surrounded by routers.

broadcast storm An undesired event on the network caused by the simultaneous transmission of any number of broadcasts across the network segment. Such an occurrence can overwhelm network bandwidth, resulting in timeouts.

buffer A storage area dedicated to handling data while in transit. Buffers are used to receive/store sporadic deliveries of data bursts, usually received from faster devices, compensating for the variations in processing speed. Incoming information is stored until everything is received prior to sending data on. Also known as an *information buffer*.

bursting Some technologies, including ATM and Frame Relay, are considered burstable. This means that user data can exceed the bandwidth normally reserved for the connection; however, this cannot exceed the port speed. An example of this would be a 128Kbps Frame Relay CIR on a T1; depending on the vendor, it may be possible to send more than 128Kbps for a short time.

bus Any physical path, typically wires or copper, through which a digital signal can be used to send data from one part of a computer to another.

BUS Broadcast and unknown servers: In LAN emulation, the hardware or software responsible for resolving all broadcasts and packets with unknown (unregistered) addresses into the point-to-point virtual circuits required by ATM. See also: *LANE, LEC, LECS,* and *LES*.

bus topology A linear LAN architecture in which transmissions from various stations on the network are reproduced over the length of the medium and are accepted by all other stations. Contrast with: *ring*.

BX.25 AT&T's use of X.25. See also: *X.25*.

bypass mode An FDDI and Token Ring network operation that deletes an interface.

bypass relay A device that enables a particular interface in the Token Ring to be closed down and effectively taken off the ring.

byte-oriented protocol Any type of data-link communication protocol that, in order to mark the boundaries of frames, uses a specific character from the user character set. These protocols have generally been superseded by bit-oriented protocols. Compare to: *bit-oriented protocol*.

C

cable range In an extended AppleTalk network, the range of numbers allotted for use by existing nodes on the network. The value of the cable range can be anywhere from a single to a sequence of several touching network numbers. Node addresses are determined by their cable range value.

CAC Connection admission control: The sequence of actions executed by every ATM switch while connection setup is performed in order to determine if a request for connection is violating the guarantees of QoS for established connections. Also, CAC is used to route a connection request through an ATM network.

call admission control   A device for managing traffic in ATM networks, determining the possibility of a path containing adequate bandwidth for a requested VCC.

call establishment   Used to reference an ISDN call setup scheme when the call is working.

call priority   In circuit-switched systems, the defining priority given to each originating port; it specifies in which order calls will be reconnected. Additionally, call priority identifies which calls are allowed during a bandwidth reservation.

call setup time   The length of time necessary to effect a switched call between DTE devices.

CBR   Constant bit rate: An ATM Forum QoS class created for use in ATM networks. CBR is used for connections that rely on precision clocking to guarantee trustworthy delivery. Compare to: *ABR* and *VBR*.

CD   Carrier Detect: A signal indicating that an interface is active or that a connection generated by a modem has been established.

CDP   Cisco Discovery Protocol: Cisco's proprietary protocol that is used to tell a neighbor Cisco device about the type of hardware, software version, and active interfaces that the Cisco device is using. It uses a SNAP frame between devices and is not routable.

CDVT   Cell delay variation tolerance: A QoS parameter for traffic management in ATM networks specified when a connection is established. The allowable fluctuation levels for data samples taken by the PCR in CBR transmissions are determined by the CDVT. See also: *CBR* and *PCR*.

cell   In ATM networking, the basic unit of data for switching and multiplexing. Cells have a defined length of 53 bytes, including a 5-byte header that identifies the cell's data stream and 48 bytes of payload. See also: *cell relay*.

cell payload scrambling   The method by which an ATM switch maintains framing on some medium-speed edge and trunk interfaces (T3 or E3 circuits). Cell payload scrambling rearranges the data portion of a cell to maintain the line synchronization with certain common bit patterns.

cell relay   A technology that uses small packets of fixed size, known as cells. Their fixed length enables cells to be processed and switched in hardware at high speeds, making this technology the foundation for ATM and other high-speed network protocols. See also: *cell*.

Centrex   A local exchange carrier service, providing local switching that resembles that of an on-site PBX. Centrex has no on-site switching capability. Therefore, all customer connections return to the CO. See also: *CO*.

CER   Cell error ratio: The ratio in ATM of transmitted cells having errors to the total number of cells sent in a transmission within a certain span of time.

certificate authority (CA)   A server responsible for managing and issuing digital certificates—especially X.509 certificates—and vouching for the binding between the data items in a certificate.

certificate management A system for device authentication that enables better network security. Cisco fully supports the X509.V3 certificate system for device authentication and the Simple Certificate Enrollment Protocol (SCEP), a protocol for communicating with certificate authorities. Other vendors, including Verisign, Entrust Technologies, and Microsoft, support Cisco SCEP and are interoperable with Cisco devices.

certificate revocation list (CRL) A list issued by the certificate authority that contains certificates that are no longer valid.

CGMP Cisco Group Management Protocol: A proprietary protocol developed by Cisco. The router uses CGMP to send multicast membership commands to Catalyst switches.

channelized E1 Operating at 2.048Mpbs, an access link that is sectioned into 29 B channels and one D channel, supporting DDR, Frame Relay, and X.25. Compare to: *channelized T1*.

channelized T1 Operating at 1.544Mbps, an access link that is sectioned into 23 B channels and one D channel of 64Kbps each, where individual channels or groups of channels connect to various destinations, supporting DDR, Frame Relay, and X.25. Compare to: *channelized E1*.

CHAP Challenge Handshake Authentication Protocol: Supported on lines using PPP encapsulation, CHAP is a security feature that identifies the remote end, helping keep out unauthorized users. After CHAP is performed, the router or access server determines whether a given user is permitted access. It is a newer, more secure protocol than PAP. Compare to: *PAP*.

character-mode access The most common form of router authentication that uses different passwords to authenticate users depending on the line the user is connecting through. Also known as *line authentication*.

checksum A test for ensuring the integrity of sent data. It is a number calculated from a series of values taken through a sequence of mathematical functions, typically placed at the end of the data from which it is calculated, and then recalculated at the receiving end for verification. Compare to: *CRC*.

choke packet When congestion exists, it is a packet sent to inform a transmitter that it should decrease its sending rate.

CIDR Classless interdomain routing: A method supported by classless routing protocols, such as OSPF and BGP4, based on the concept of ignoring the IP class of address, permitting route aggregation and VLSM that enable routers to combine routes in order to minimize the routing information that needs to be conveyed by the primary routers. It allows a group of IP networks to appear to other networks as a unified, larger entity. In CIDR, IP addresses and their subnet masks are written as four dotted octets, followed by a forward slash and the numbering of masking bits (a form of subnet notation shorthand). See also: *BGP4*.

CIP Channel Interface Processor: A channel attachment interface for use in Cisco 7000 series routers that connects a host mainframe to a control unit. This device eliminates the need for an FBP to attach channels.

CIR Committed information rate: Averaged over a minimum span of time and measured in bps, a Frame Relay network's agreed-upon minimum rate of transferring information.

circuit switching Used with dial-up networks such as PPP and ISDN. Passes data, but needs to set up the connection first—just like making a phone call.

Cisco FRAD Cisco Frame-Relay Access Device: A Cisco product that supports Cisco IPS Frame Relay SNA services, connecting SDLC devices to Frame Relay without requiring an existing LAN. May be upgraded to a fully functioning multiprotocol router. Can activate conversion from SDLC to Ethernet and Token Ring, but does not support attached LANs. See also: *FRAD*.

CiscoFusion Cisco's name for the internetworking architecture under which its Cisco IOS operates. It is designed to "fuse" together the capabilities of its disparate collection of acquired routers and switches.

Cisco IOS Firewall The Cisco IOS Firewall offers top-of-the-line security and policy enforcement for connections within an organization (intranet) and between partner networks (extranets), as well as for securing Internet connectivity for remote and branch offices.

Cisco IOS Firewall Context-Based Access Control (CBAC) See: *Context-Based Access Control (CBAC)*.

Cisco IOS software Cisco Internet Operating System software: The essential core of Cisco's product line of routers and switches that enables common functionality, scalability, and security for all products under its CiscoFusion umbrella. See also: *CiscoFusion*.

CiscoSecure ACS 2.3 for UNIX (CSU) CiscoSecure Access Control Server (ACS) 2.2.2 for UNIX (Solaris) software. The CiscoSecure ACS software uses either the Terminal Access Controller Access Control System (TACACS+) or the Remote Authentication Dial-In User Service (RADIUS) protocols to provide you with network security and tracking.

CiscoSecure ACS 3.0 for Windows NT or Windows 2000 (CS ACS) Network security software that helps you authenticate users by controlling dial-in access to a network access server (NAS) device, Cisco PIX Firewall, or router.

CiscoSecure Integrated Software (CSIS) An inspection feature which provides firewall support for multimedia applications that require delivery of data with real-time properties, such as audio and video conferencing.

CiscoSecure User Database A database maintained by CiscoSecure ACS 3.0 for Windows NT or Windows 2000 to screen network users. When a user-access request arrives at CiscoSecure ACS 3.0 for Windows NT or Windows 2000, it goes to the CiscoSecure User Database first to check for information regarding that user.

CiscoSecure VPN 3.5 Client Enables you to establish secure, end-to-end encrypted tunnels.

Cisco Security Manager (CSM) A scalable, thorough security policy management system for policy enforcement points (PEPs), specifically PIX Firewalls. CSM allows administrators to define, distribute, enforce, and audit multiple distributed firewall security policies from one central location.

CiscoView   GUI-based management software for Cisco networking devices, enabling dynamic status, statistics, and comprehensive configuration information. Displays a physical view of the Cisco device chassis and provides device-monitoring functions and fundamental troubleshooting capabilities. May be integrated with a number of SNMP-based network management platforms.

Class A network   Part of the Internet Protocol hierarchical addressing scheme. Class A networks have only 8 bits for defining networks and 24 bits for defining hosts on each network.

Class B network   Part of the Internet Protocol hierarchical addressing scheme. Class B networks have 16 bits for defining networks and 16 bits for defining hosts on each network.

Class C network   Part of the Internet Protocol hierarchical addressing scheme. Class C networks have 24 bits for defining networks and only 8 bits for defining hosts on each network.

classful routing   Routing protocols that do not send subnet mask information when a route update is sent out.

classical IP over ATM   Defined in RFC 1577, the specification for running IP over ATM that maximizes ATM features. Also known as *CIA*.

classless routing   Routing that sends subnet mask information in the routing updates. Classless routing allows variable-length subnet mask (VLSM) and supernetting. Routing protocols that support classless routing are RIP version 2, EIGRP, and OSPF.

CLI   Command-line interface: Allows you to configure Cisco routers and switches with maximum flexibility.

CLP   Cell loss priority: The area in the ATM cell header that determines the likelihood of a cell being dropped during network congestion. Cells with CLP = 0 are considered insured traffic and are not apt to be dropped. Cells with CLP = 1 are considered best-effort traffic that may be dropped during congested episodes, delivering more resources to handle insured traffic.

CLR   Cell loss ratio: The ratio of discarded cells to successfully delivered cells in ATM. CLR can be designated a QoS parameter when establishing a connection.

CO   Central office: The local telephone company office where all loops in a certain area connect and where circuit switching of subscriber lines occurs.

collapsed backbone   A nondistributed backbone where all network segments are connected to each other through an internetworking device. A collapsed backbone can be a virtual network segment at work in a device such as a router, hub, or switch.

collision   The effect of two nodes sending transmissions simultaneously in Ethernet. When they meet on the physical media, the frames from each node collide and are damaged. See also: *collision domain*.

collision domain   The network area in Ethernet over which frames that have collided will spread. Collisions are propagated by hubs and repeaters, but not by LAN switches, routers, or bridges. See also: *collision*.

composite metric   Used with routing protocols, such as IGRP and EIGRP, that use more than one metric to find the best path to a remote network. Both IGRP and EIGRP use bandwidth and delay of the line by default. However, the maximum transmission unit (MTU), load, and reliability of a link can be used as well.

compound signatures   Cisco IOS uses signatures to discover patterns of misuse in the network. Compound signatures trigger based on multiple packets by buffering previous packets for comparison against current packets to see if traffic trends match their signature. Atomic signatures trigger based on a single packet and can evaluate each packet independently. Atomic signatures are much easier to support for the router. Operatively, this means that compound signatures cost more memory than atomic signatures. Contrast with: *atomic signatures*.

compression   A technique to send more data across a link than would normally be permitted by representing repetitious strings of data with a single marker.

conduit   Most organizations must permit untrusted hosts onto resources in their trusted network, with a common example being an internal web server. By default, the Cisco PIX denies connections from outside hosts to inside hosts. A conduit allows these types of connections onto your trusted network.

configuration register   A 16-bit configurable value stored in hardware or software that determines how Cisco routers function during initialization. In hardware, the bit position is set using a jumper. In software, the bit position is set by specifying specific bit patterns used to set startup options, configured using a hexadecimal value with configuration commands.

configuration weakness   Cisco defines configuration weaknesses as unsecured user accounts, system accounts with easily guessed passwords, misconfigured Internet services, unsecured default settings in products, and misconfigured network equipment, all of which undermine security in your network.

congestion   Traffic that exceeds the network's ability to handle it.

congestion avoidance   To minimize delays, the method an ATM network uses to control traffic entering the system. Lower priority traffic is discarded at the edge of the network when indicators signal it cannot be delivered, thus using resources efficiently.

congestion collapse   The situation that results from the retransmission of packets in ATM networks where little or no traffic successfully arrives at destination points. It usually happens in networks made of switches with ineffective or inadequate buffering capabilities, combined with poor packet discard or ABR congestion feedback mechanisms.

connection ID   Identifications given to each Telnet session into a router. The `show sessions` command displays the connections a local router has to a remote router. The `show users` command displays the connection IDs of users telnetted into your local router.

connectionless   Data transfer that occurs without the creation of a virtual circuit. It has no overhead, best-effort delivery, and is not reliable. Contrast with: *connection-oriented*. See also: *virtual circuit*.

connection-oriented   A data transfer method that sets up a virtual circuit before any data is transferred. Uses acknowledgments and flow control for reliable data transfer. Contrast with: *connectionless*. See also: *virtual circuit*.

console port   Typically an RJ-45 port on a Cisco router and switch that allows CLI capability.

Context-Based Access Control (CBAC)   CBAC intelligently filters TCP and UDP packets based on Application-layer protocol session information. You can configure CBAC to permit specified TCP and UDP traffic through a firewall only when the connection is initiated from within the network you want to protect. CBAC can inspect traffic for sessions that originate from either side of the firewall, and CBAC can be used for intranet, extranet, and Internet perimeters of your network.

control direct VCC   One of three control connections defined by Phase I LAN emulation; a bidirectional virtual control connection (VCC) established in ATM by an LEC to an LES. See also: *control distribute VCC*.

control distribute VCC   One of three control connections defined by Phase 1 LAN emulation; a unidirectional virtual control connection (VCC) set up in ATM from an LES to an LEC. Usually, the VCC is a point-to-multipoint connection. See also: *control direct VCC*.

convergence   The process required for all routers in an internetwork to update their routing tables and create a consistent view of the network using the best possible paths. No user data is passed during a convergence time.

core layer   The top layer in the Cisco three-layer hierarchical model, which helps you design, build, and maintain Cisco hierarchical networks. The core layer passes packets quickly to distribution-layer devices only. No packet filtering should take place at this layer.

cost   An arbitrary value, based on hop count, bandwidth, or other calculation, that is typically assigned by a network administrator and used by the routing protocol to compare different routes through an internetwork. Routing protocols use cost values to select the best path to a certain destination; the lowest cost identifies the best path. Also known as *path cost*. See also: *routing metric*.

count to infinity   A problem occurring in routing algorithms that are slow to converge where routers keep increasing the hop count to particular networks. To avoid this problem, various solutions have been implemented into each of the different routing protocols. Some of those solutions include defining a maximum hop count (defining infinity), route poisoning, poison reverse, and split horizon.

CPCS   Common part convergence sublayer: One of two AAL sublayers that is service-dependent, it is further segmented into the CS and SAR sublayers. The CPCS prepares data for transmission across the ATM network; it creates the 48-byte payload cells that are sent to the ATM layer. See also: *AAL* and *ATM layer*.

CPE   Customer premises equipment: Items such as telephones, modems, and terminals installed at customer locations and connected to the telephone company network.

crankback In ATM, a correction technique that is used when a node somewhere on a chosen path cannot accept a connection setup request, blocking the request. The path is rolled back to an intermediate node, which then uses generic connection admission control (GCAC) to attempt to find an alternate path to the final destination.

CRC Cyclical redundancy check: A methodology that detects errors, whereby the frame recipient makes a calculation by dividing frame contents with a prime binary divisor and compares the remainder to a value stored in the frame by the sending node. Contrast with: *checksum*.

crypto map set IPSec SAs are established through the use of a crypto map, which is basically a combination of one or more sequences where each sequence represents an IPSec SA.

cryptosystem A combination of encryption technologies, working in harmony, that encrypt data so that only the intended receiver can decrypt it.

CSAccupdate service The CSAccupdate service processes the ODBC import tables and updates local and remote CiscoSecure ACS installations.

CSMA/CD Carrier sense multiple access/collision detect: A technology defined by the Ethernet IEEE 802.3 committee. Each device senses the cable for a digital signal before transmitting. Also, CSMA/CD allows all devices on the network to share the same cable, but one at a time. If two devices transmit at the same time, a frame collision will occur and a jamming pattern will be sent; the devices will stop transmitting, wait a predetermined amount of time, and then try to transmit again.

CSU Channel service unit: A digital mechanism that connects end-user equipment to the local digital telephone loop. Frequently referred to along with the data service unit as CSU/DSU. *See also: DSU.*

CTD Cell transfer delay: For a given connection in ATM, the time period between a cell exit event at the source user-network interface (UNI) and the corresponding cell entry event at the destination. The CTD between these points is the sum of the total inter-ATM transmission delay and the total ATM processing delay.

cut-through frame switching A frame-switching technique that flows data through a switch so that the leading edge exits the switch at the output port before the packet finishes entering the input port. Frames will be read, processed, and forwarded by devices that use cut-through switching as soon as the destination address of the frame is confirmed and the outgoing port is identified.

D

data authentication Verifies data using two concepts: data integrity, which makes sure that no data has been changed or manipulated, and data origin authentication, which makes sure that the data actually came from the correct source.

data circuit-terminating equipment (DCE) Used to provide clocking to DTE equipment.

data compression See: *compression.*

data direct VCC A bidirectional point-to-point virtual control connection (VCC) set up between two LECs in ATM and one of three data connections defined by Phase 1 LAN emulation. Because data direct VCCs do not guarantee QoS, they are generally reserved for UBR and ABR connections. Compare to: *control distribute VCC* and *control direct VCC.*

data encapsulation The process in which the information in a protocol is wrapped, or contained, in the data section of another protocol. In the OSI reference model, each layer encapsulates the layer immediately above it as the data flows down the protocol stack.

Data Encryption Standard (DES) In Cisco's cryptosystem, DES encrypts data, MD5 creates a message hash, DSS verifies peers by exchanging public keys, and Diffie-Hellman establishes private and public keys that encrypt the keys used by DES and MD5. When all of these processes work in tandem, they provide a secure environment for transmitting data. See also: *cryptosystem.*

data frame Protocol data unit encapsulation at the Data Link layer of the OSI reference model. Encapsulates packets from the Network layer and prepares the data for transmission on a network medium.

datagram A logical collection of information transmitted as a Network-layer unit over a medium without a previously established virtual circuit. IP datagrams have become the primary information unit of the Internet. At various layers of the OSI reference model, the terms *cell, frame, message, packet,* and *segment* also define these logical information groupings.

Data Link Control layer Layer 2 of the SNA architectural model, it is responsible for the transmission of data over a given physical link and compares somewhat to the Data Link layer of the OSI model.

Data Link layer Layer 2 of the OSI reference model, it ensures the trustworthy transmission of data across a physical link and is primarily concerned with physical addressing, line discipline, network topology, error notification, ordered delivery of frames, and flow control. The IEEE has further segmented this layer into the MAC sublayer and the LLC sublayer. Also known as the *Link layer.* Can be compared somewhat to the Data Link Control layer of the SNA model. See also: *Application layer, LLC, MAC, Network layer, Physical layer, Presentation layer, Session layer,* and *Transport layer.*

data terminal equipment See: *DTE.*

DCC Data Country Code: Developed by the ATM Forum, one of two ATM address formats designed for use by private networks. Compare to: *ICD.*

DCE Data communications equipment (as defined by the EIA) or data circuit-terminating equipment (as defined by the ITU-T): The mechanisms and links of a communications network that make up the network portion of the user-to-network interface, such as modems. The DCE supplies the physical connection to the network, forwards traffic, and provides a clocking signal to synchronize data transmission between DTE and DCE devices. Compare to: *DTE.*

D channel   1) Data channel: A full-duplex, 16Kbps (BRI) or 64Kbps (PRI) ISDN channel. Compare to: *B channel*, *E channel*, and *H channel*. 2) In SNA, anything that provides a connection between the processor and main storage with any peripherals.

DDP   Datagram Delivery Protocol: Used in the AppleTalk suite of protocols as a connectionless protocol that is responsible for sending datagrams through an internetwork.

DDR   Dial-on-demand routing: A technique that allows a router to automatically initiate and end a circuit-switched session per the requirements of the sending station. By mimicking keepalives, the router fools the end station into treating the session as active. DDR permits routing over ISDN or telephone lines via a modem or external ISDN terminal adapter.

DE   Discard eligible: Used in Frame Relay networks to tell a switch that a frame can be discarded if the switch is too busy. The DE is a field in the frame that is turned on by transmitting routers if the committed information rate (CIR) is oversubscribed or set to 0.

dedicated line   Point-to-point connection that does not share any bandwidth.

default route   The static routing table entry used to direct frames whose next hop is not spelled out in the dynamic routing table.

delay   The time elapsed between a sender's initiation of a transaction and the first response they receive. Also, the time needed to move a packet from its source to its destination over a path. See also: *latency*.

demarc   The demarcation point between the customer premises equipment (CPE) and the telco's carrier equipment.

demodulation   A series of steps that return a modulated signal to its original form. When receiving, a modem demodulates an analog signal to its original digital form (and, conversely, modulates the digital data it sends into an analog signal). See also: *modulation*.

demultiplexing   The process of converting a single multiplex signal, comprising more than one input stream, back into separate output streams. See also: *multiplexing*.

denial-of-service (DoS) attacks   The result of an intentional or benign assault on a network that interferes with regular traffic by overwhelming the Internet server. If a server is flooded with too many needless connection requests, the result is that it ignores legitimate requests and denies service to them. The TCP intercept feature implements software to protect TCP servers from TCP SYN-flooding attacks, which are a type of denial-of-service attack.

designated bridge   In the process of forwarding a frame from a segment to the route bridge, the bridge with the lowest path cost.

designated port   Used with the Spanning-Tree Protocol (STP) to designate forwarding ports. If there are multiple links to the same network, STP will shut down a port to stop network loops.

designated router (DR)   An OSPF router that creates LSAs for a multiaccess network and is required to perform other special tasks in OSPF operations. Multiaccess OSPF networks that maintain a minimum of two attached routers identify one router that is chosen by the OSPF Hello protocol, which makes possible a decrease in the number of adjacencies necessary on a multiaccess network. This in turn reduces the quantity of routing protocol traffic and the physical size of the database.

destination address   The address for the network devices that will receive a packet.

DHCP   Dynamic Host Configuration Protocol: DHCP is a superset of the BootP protocol. This means that it uses the same protocol structure as BootP, but it has enhancements added. Both of these protocols use servers that dynamically configure clients when requested. The two major enhancements are address pools and lease times.

dial backup   Dial backup connections are typically used to provide redundancy to Frame Relay connections. The backup link is activated over an analog modem.

Diffie-Hellman (DH) Agreement   A means for two parties to agree upon a shared secret number that will then be used to encrypt secret keys for other algorithms, such as DES and MD5. DH occurs in phase 1 of IKE negotiation.

Digital Signature Standard (DSS)   To provide encryption services, Cisco implements the following standards: Digital Signature Standard (DSS), the Diffie-Hellman (DH) public key algorithm, and Data Encryption Standard (DES). DSS authenticates peer routers based on public key cryptography.

directed broadcast   A data frame or packet that is transmitted to a specific group of nodes on a remote network segment. Directed broadcasts are known by their broadcast address, which is a destination subnet address with all the bits turned on.

dirty DMZ   The part of a network that's using real Internet IP addresses. See also: *DMZ*.

discovery mode   Also known as *dynamic configuration*, this technique is used by an Apple-Talk interface to gain information from a working node about an attached network. This information is subsequently used by the interface for self-configuration.

distance-vector routing algorithm   In order to find the shortest path, this group of routing algorithms repeats on the number of hops in a given route, requiring each router to send its complete routing table with each update, but only to its neighbors. Routing algorithms of this type tend to generate loops, but they are fundamentally simpler than their link-state counterparts. See also: *link-state routing algorithm* and *SPF*.

distribution layer   The middle layer of the Cisco three-layer hierarchical model, which helps you design, install, and maintain Cisco hierarchical networks. The distribution layer is the point where access-layer devices connect. Routing is performed at this layer.

DLCI   Data-link connection identifier: Used to identify virtual circuits in a Frame Relay network.

DLSw   Data-link switching: IBM developed DLSw in 1992 to provide support for SNA (Systems Network Architecture) and NetBIOS protocols in router-based networks. SNA and NetBIOS are nonroutable protocols that do not contain any logical Layer 3 network information. DLSw encapsulates these protocols into TCP/IP messages that can be routed and is an alternative to Remote Source-Route Bridging (RSRB).

DLSw+   Cisco's implementation of DLSw. In addition to support for the RFC standards, Cisco added enhancements intended to increase scalability and to improve performance and availability. See also: *DLSw*.

DMZ   The de-militarized zone (DMZ) is a neutral zone between the public network and the corporate intranet and is protected by firewalls limiting access from the outside network to hosts located on its LAN. An external firewall is used to control access to the DMZ, while an internal firewall is used to prevent access to any internal hosts (corporate site). See also: *dirty DMZ*.

DNS   Domain Name System: Used to resolve host names to IP addresses.

DSAP   Destination service access point: The service access point of a network node, specified in the destination field of a packet. See also: *SSAP* and *SAP*.

DSR   Data set ready: When a DCE is powered up and ready to run, this EIA/TIA-232 interface circuit is also engaged.

DSU   Data service unit: This device is used to adapt the physical interface on a data terminal equipment (DTE) mechanism to a transmission facility such as T1 or E1 and is also responsible for signal timing. It is commonly grouped with the channel service unit and referred to as the CSU/DSU. See also: *CSU*.

DTE   Data terminal equipment: Any device located at the user end of a user-network interface (UNI) serving as a destination, a source, or both. DTE includes devices such as multiplexers, protocol translators, and computers. The connection to a data network is made through data channel equipment (DCE) such as a modem, using the clocking signals generated by that device. See also: *DCE*.

DTR   Data terminal ready: An activated EIA/TIA-232 circuit communicating to the DCE the state of preparedness of the DTE to transmit or receive data.

DUAL   Diffusing Update Algorithm: Used in Enhanced IGRP, this convergence algorithm provides loop-free operation throughout an entire route's computation. DUAL grants routers involved in a topology revision the ability to synchronize simultaneously, while routers unaffected by this change are not involved. See also: *Enhanced IGRP*.

DVMRP   Distance Vector Multicast Routing Protocol: Based primarily on the Routing Information Protocol (RIP), this Internet gateway protocol implements a common, condensed-mode IP multicast scheme, using IGMP to transfer routing datagrams between its neighbors. See also: *IGMP*.

DXI   Data eXchange Interface: Described in RFC 1482, DXI defines the effectiveness of a network device such as a router, bridge, or hub to act as a front-end processor (FEP) to an ATM network by using a special DSU that accomplishes packet encapsulation.

dynamic entries   Used in Layer 2 and Layer 3 devices to dynamically create a table of either hardware addresses or logical addresses dynamically.

dynamic routing   Also known as *adaptive routing*, this technique automatically adapts to traffic or physical network revisions.

dynamic VLAN   An administrator will create an entry in a special server with the hardware addresses of all devices on the internetwork. The server will then dynamically assign used VLANs.

E

E1   Generally used in Europe, a wide-area digital transmission scheme carrying data at 2.048Mbps. E1 transmission lines are available for lease from common carriers for private use.

E.164   1) Evolved from standard telephone numbering system, the standard recommended by ITU-T for international telecommunication numbering, particularly in ISDN, SMDS, and BISDN. 2) Label of a field in an ATM address containing numbers in E.164 format.

Easy VPN Remote   The Easy VPN Remote can be either a site-to-site device or the remote access VPN Client. The Easy VPN Remote can receive security policies from the Easy VPN Server, which minimizes the amount of configuration and maintenance required on remote devices.

Easy VPN Server   Acts as a head-end device for either site-to-site or remote access VPN clients. It can push security policies to Easy VPN Remote clients before connections are actually established, ensuring that those clients always have up-to-date policies in place.

eavesdropping   An attacker who is eavesdropping uses a packet sniffer to glean sensitive information by "listening" to data streams between two sites or to steal username/password combinations, either on a private carrier or on a public network. Even if applications such as Lotus Notes were to encrypt traffic within their own streams, a sniffer could still detect sites using Notes in a form of traffic analysis. The attacker could then concentrate on transmissions involving that application. Also called *passive eavesdropping* and *packet sniffing*.

eBGP   External Border Gateway Protocol: Used to exchange route information between different autonomous systems.

E channel   Echo channel: A 64Kbps ISDN control channel used for circuit switching. A specific description of this channel can be found in the 1984 ITU-T ISDN specification, but was dropped from the 1988 version. See also: *B channel*, *D channel*, and *H channel*.

edge device   A device that enables packets to be forwarded between legacy interfaces (such as Ethernet and Token Ring) and ATM interfaces based on information in the Data Link and Network layers. An edge device does not take part in the running of any Network-layer routing protocol; it merely uses the route description protocol in order to get the forwarding information required.

EEPROM   Electronically erasable programmable read-only memory: Programmed after their manufacture, these nonvolatile memory chips can be erased if necessary using electric power and reprogrammed. See also: *EPROM* and *PROM*.

EFCI   Explicit Forward Congestion Indication: A congestion feedback mode permitted by ABR service in an ATM network. The EFCI may be set by any network element that is in a state of immediate or certain congestion. The destination end system is able to carry out a protocol that adjusts and lowers the cell rate of the connection based on the value of the EFCI. See also: *ABR*.

EIGRP   See: *Enhanced IGRP*.

EIP   Ethernet Interface Processor: A Cisco 7000 series router interface processor card, supplying 10Mbps AUI ports to support Ethernet Version 1 and Ethernet Version 2 or IEEE 802.3 interfaces with a high-speed data path to other interface processors.

ELAN   Emulated LAN: An ATM network configured using a client/server model in order to emulate either an Ethernet or Token Ring LAN. Multiple ELANs can exist at the same time on a single ATM network and are made up of a LAN Emulation Client (LEC), a LAN Emulation Server (LES), a broadcast and unknown server (BUS), and a LAN Emulation Configuration Server (LECS). ELANs are defined by the LANE specification. See also: *LANE, LEC, LECS,* and *LES*.

ELAP   EtherTalk Link Access Protocol: In an EtherTalk network, the link-access protocol constructed above the standard Ethernet Data Link layer.

Encapsulating Security Payload (ESP)   A security protocol that completely encapsulates user data and combines data confidentiality and protection with optional authentication and replay-detection services. ESP can be used either by itself or in conjunction with AH.

encapsulation   The technique used by layered protocols in which a layer adds header information to the protocol data unit (PDU) from the layer above. As an example, in Internet terminology, a packet would contain a header from the Physical layer, followed by a header from the Network layer (IP), followed by a header from the Transport layer (TCP), followed by the application protocol data.

encryption   Applies a certain algorithm to data. Encryption changes the data's appearance to make it unrecognizable to those who are not authorized to see the information. Cisco currently provides a Network-layer encryption solution for ensuring the confidentiality, integrity, and authenticity of data communications across a public network.

endpoints   See: *BGP neighbors*.

end-to-end VLANs   VLANs that span the switch-fabric from end to end; all switches in end-to-end VLANs understand about all configured VLANs. End-to-end VLANs are configured to allow membership based on function, project, department, and so on.

Enhanced IGRP (EIGRP)   Enhanced Interior Gateway Routing Protocol: An advanced routing protocol created by Cisco, combining the advantages of link-state and distance-vector protocols. Enhanced IGRP has superior convergence attributes, including high operating efficiency. See also: *IGP*, *OSPF*, and *RIP*.

enterprise network   A privately owned and operated network that joins most major locations in a large company or organization.

EPROM   Erasable programmable read-only memory: Programmed after their manufacture, these nonvolatile memory chips can be erased, if necessary, using high-power light and reprogrammed. See also: *EEPROM* and *PROM*.

ESF   Extended Superframe: Made up of 24 frames with 192 bits each, with the 193rd bit providing other functions including timing. This is an enhanced version of SF. See also: *SF*.

Ethernet   A baseband LAN specification created by the Xerox Corporation and then improved through joint efforts of Xerox, Digital Equipment Corporation, and Intel. Ethernet is similar to the IEEE 802.3 series standard and, using CSMA/CD, operates over various types of cables at 10Mbps. Also called *DIX (Digital/Intel/Xerox) Ethernet*. See also: *10BaseT*, *Fast Ethernet*, and *IEEE*.

EtherTalk   A data-link product from Apple Computer that permits AppleTalk networks to be connected by Ethernet.

excess burst size   The amount of traffic by which the user may exceed the committed burst size.

excess rate   In ATM networking, traffic exceeding a connection's insured rate. The excess rate is the maximum rate less the insured rate. Depending on the availability of network resources, excess traffic can be discarded during congestion episodes. Compare to: *maximum rate*.

expansion   The procedure of directing compressed data through an algorithm, restoring information to its original size.

expedited delivery   An option that can be specified by one protocol layer, communicating either with other layers or with the identical protocol layer in a different network device, requiring that identified data be processed faster.

explorer frames   Used with source-route bridging to find the route to the remote bridged network before a frame is transmitted.

explorer packet   An SNA packet transmitted by a source Token Ring device to find the path through a source route–bridged network.

extended IP access list   An IP access list that filters the network by logical address, protocol field in the Network-layer header, and even the port field in the Transport-layer header.

extended IPX access list   An IPX access list that filters the network by logical IPX address, protocol field in the Network-layer header, or even socket number in the Transport-layer header.

Extended Setup   Used in setup mode to configure the router with more detail than Basic Setup mode. Allows multiple-protocol support and interface configuration.

extranet VPN   Gives your organization the ability to connect suppliers, partners, and customers to your corporate network in a limited fashion for business-to-business (B2B) communications.

F

failure domain   The region in which a failure has occurred in a Token Ring. When a station gets information that a serious problem, such as a cable break, has occurred with the network, it sends a beacon frame that includes the station reporting the failure, its NAUN, and everything between. This defines the failure domain. Beaconing then initiates the procedure known as autoreconfiguration. See also: *autoreconfiguration* and *beacon*.

fallback   In ATM networks, this mechanism is used for scouting a path if it isn't possible to locate one using customary methods. The device relaxes requirements for certain characteristics, such as delay, in an attempt to find a path that meets a certain set of the most important requirements.

Fast Ethernet   Any Ethernet specification with a speed of 100Mbps. Fast Ethernet is ten times faster than 10BaseT, while retaining qualities such as MAC mechanisms, MTU, and frame format. These similarities make it possible for existing 10BaseT applications and management tools to be used on Fast Ethernet networks. Fast Ethernet is based on an extension of IEEE 802.3 specification (IEEE 802.3u). Compare to: *Ethernet*. See also: *100BaseT*, *100BaseTX*, and *IEEE*.

fast switching   A Cisco feature that uses a route cache to speed packet switching through a router. Contrast with: *process switching*.

fault tolerance   The extent to which a network device or a communication link can fail without communication being interrupted. Fault tolerance can be provided by added secondary routes to a remote network.

FDDI   Fiber Distributed Data Interface: A LAN standard, defined by ANSI X3T9.5 that can run at speeds up to 200Mbps and uses token-passing media access on fiber-optic cable. For redundancy, FDDI can use a dual-ring architecture.

FDM   Frequency-division multiplexing: A technique that permits information from several channels to be assigned bandwidth on one wire based on frequency. See also: *TDM*, *ATDM*, and *statistical multiplexing*.

FECN   Forward explicit congestion notification: A bit set by a Frame Relay network that informs the DTE receptor that congestion was encountered along the path from source to destination. A device receiving frames with the FECN bit set can ask higher priority protocols to take flow-control action as needed. See also: *BECN*.

FEIP   Fast Ethernet Interface Processor: An interface processor employed on Cisco 7000 series routers, supporting up to two 100Mbps 100BaseT ports.

filtering   Used to provide security on the network with access lists.

firewall   A barrier purposefully erected between any connected public networks and a private network. A firewall is made up of a router or access server or several routers or access servers, and it uses access lists and other methods to ensure the security of the private network.

fixed configuration router   A router that cannot be upgraded with any new interfaces.

Flash   Electronically erasable programmable read-only Memory (EEPROM). Used to hold the Cisco IOS in a router by default.

flash memory   Developed by Intel and licensed to other semiconductor manufacturers, it is nonvolatile storage that can be erased electronically and reprogrammed. Flash memory is physically located on an EEPROM chip. It permits software images to be stored, booted, and rewritten as needed. Cisco routers and switches use flash memory to hold the IOS by default. See also: *EPROM* and *EEPROM*.

flat network   A network that is one large collision domain and one large broadcast domain.

floating routes   Used with dynamic routing to provide backup routes in case of failure.

flooding   When traffic is received on an interface, it is then transmitted to every interface connected to that device with the exception of the interface from which the traffic originated. This technique can be used for traffic transfer by bridges and switches throughout the network.

flow control   A methodology used to ensure that receiving units are not overwhelmed with data from sending devices. *Pacing*, as it is called in IBM networks, means that when buffers at a receiving unit are full, a message is transmitted to the sending unit to temporarily halt transmissions until all the data in the receiving buffer has been processed and the buffer is again ready for action.

FQDN   Fully qualified domain names: Used within the DNS domain structure to provide name-to-IP address resolution on the Internet. An example of an FQDN is bob.acme.com.

FRAD   Frame Relay access device: Any device affording a connection between a LAN and a Frame Relay WAN. See also: *Cisco FRAD* and *FRAS*.

fragment   Any portion of a larger packet that has been intentionally segmented into smaller pieces. A packet fragment does not necessarily indicate an error and can be intentional. See also: *fragmentation*.

fragmentation   The process of intentionally segmenting a packet into smaller pieces when sending data over an intermediate network medium that cannot support the larger packet size.

FragmentFree   LAN switch type that reads into the data section of a frame to make sure fragmentation did not occur. Sometimes called *modified cut-through*.

frame   A logical unit of information sent by the Data Link layer over a transmission medium. The term *frame* often refers to the header and trailer, employed for synchronization and error control, that surround the data contained in the unit.

frame identification (frame tagging)   VLANs can span multiple connected switches, which Cisco calls a *switch-fabric*. Switches within this switch-fabric must keep track of frames as they are received on the switch ports, and they must keep track of the VLAN they belong to as the frames traverse this switch-fabric. Frame tagging performs this function. Switches can then direct frames to the appropriate port.

Frame Relay   A more efficient replacement of the X.25 protocol (an unrelated packet relay technology that guarantees data delivery). Frame Relay is an industry-standard, shared-access, best-effort, switched Data Link-layer encapsulation that services multiple virtual circuits and protocols between connected mechanisms.

Frame Relay bridging   Defined in RFC 1490, this bridging method uses the identical spanning-tree algorithm as other bridging operations but permits packets to be encapsulated for transmission across a Frame Relay network.

Frame Relay switching   When a router at a service provider provides packet switching for Frame Relay packets. A process that activates an interface that has been deactivated by the pruning process. It is initiated by an IGMP membership report sent to the router.

frame tagging   See: *frame identification*.

framing   Encapsulation at the Data Link layer of the OSI model. It is called framing because the packet is encapsulated with both a header and a trailer.

FRAS   Frame Relay access support: A feature of Cisco IOS software that enables SDLC, Ethernet, Token Ring, and Frame Relay–attached IBM devices to be linked with other IBM mechanisms on a Frame Relay network. See also: *FRAD*.

frequency   The number of cycles of an alternating current signal per time unit, measured in hertz (cycles per second).

FSIP   Fast Serial Interface Processor: The Cisco 7000 routers' default serial interface processor, it provides four or eight high-speed serial ports.

FTP   File Transfer Protocol: The TCP/IP protocol used for transmitting files between network nodes, it supports a broad range of file types and is defined in RFC 959. See also: *TFTP*.

full duplex   The capacity to transmit information between a sending station and a receiving unit at the same time. See also: *half duplex*.

full mesh   A type of network topology where every node has either a physical or a virtual circuit linking it to every other network node. A full mesh supplies a great deal of redundancy but is typically reserved for network backbones because of its expense. See also: *partial mesh*.

G

general-usage keys   General-usage keys create one public/private key pair that will be used by both RSA signatures and RSA-encrypted nonces.

generic routing encapsulation (GRE)   A Cisco Proprietary tunneling protocol. It forms virtual point-to-point links, allowing for a variety of protocols to be encapsulated in IP tunnels.

GMII   Gigabit MII: Media-independent interface that provides eight bits at a time of data transfer.

GNS   Get Nearest Server: On an IPX network, a request packet sent by a customer for determining the location of the nearest active server of a given type. An IPX network client launches a GNS request to get either a direct answer from a connected server or a response from a router disclosing the location of the service on the internetwork to the GNS. GNS is part of IPX and SAP. See also: *IPX* and *SAP*.

grafting   A process that activates an interface that has been deactivated by the pruning process. It is initiated by an IGMP membership report sent to the router.

GRE   Generic routing encapsulation: A tunneling protocol created by Cisco with the capacity for encapsulating a wide variety of protocol packet types inside IP tunnels, thereby generating a virtual point-to-point connection to Cisco routers across an IP network at remote points. IP tunneling using GRE permits network expansion across a single-protocol backbone environment by linking multiprotocol subnetworks in a single-protocol backbone environment.

guard band   The unused frequency area found between two communications channels, furnishing the space necessary to avoid interference between the two.

H

half duplex   The capacity to transfer data in only one direction at a time between a sending unit and receiving unit. See also: *full duplex*.

handshake   Any series of transmissions exchanged between two or more devices on a network to ensure synchronized operations.

hash   A one-way encryption algorithm that takes an input message of arbitrary length and creates a fixed-length output message. For example, AH—the protocol that provides authentication for the data and IP header of a packet—uses a one-way hash for packet authentication. The sender generates a one-way hash, and then the receiver generates the same one-way hash.

Hash-based Message Authentication Code (HMAC)   There are a variety of encryption and hashing algorithms available for IPSec. Encryption algorithms encrypt and decrypt data. A hashing algorithm is used to create a hash. Cisco uses a hash variant known as HMAC, which provides an extra level of hashing.

hashing algorithm   Used to create a hash.

H channel   High-speed channel: A full-duplex, ISDN primary rate channel operating at a speed of 384Kbps. See also: *B channel*, *D channel*, and *E channel*.

HDLC   High-level data link control: Using frame characters, including checksums, HDLC designates a method for data encapsulation on synchronous serial links and is the default encapsulation for Cisco routers. HDLC is a bit-oriented synchronous Data Link-layer protocol created by ISO and derived from SDLC. However, most HDLC vendor implementations (including Cisco's) are proprietary. See also: *SDLC*.

helper address   The unicast address specified, which instructs the Cisco router to change the client's local broadcast request for a service into a directed unicast to the server.

hierarchical addressing   Any addressing plan employing a logical chain of commands to determine location. IP addresses are made up of a hierarchy of network numbers, subnet numbers, and host numbers to direct packets to the appropriate destination.

HIP   HSSI Interface Processor: An interface processor used on Cisco 7000 series routers, providing one HSSI port that supports connections to ATM, SMDS, Frame Relay, or private lines at speeds up to T3 or E3.

holddown   The state a route is placed in so that routers can neither advertise the route nor accept advertisements about it for a defined time period. Holddown is used to discover bad information about a route from all routers in the network. A route is generally placed in holddown when one of its links fails.

hop   The movement of a packet between any two network nodes. See also: *hop count*.

hop count   A routing metric that calculates the distance between a source and a destination. RIP employs hop count as its sole metric. See also: *hop* and *RIP*.

host address   A logical address configured by an administrator or server on a device that logically identifies this device on an internetwork.

Host-to-Host layer   The layer in the Internet Protocol suite that is equal to the Transport layer of the OSI model.

HSCI   High-Speed Communication Interface: Developed by Cisco, a single-port interface that provides full-duplex synchronous serial communications capability at speeds up to 52Mbps.

HSRP   Hot Standby Router Protocol: A protocol that provides high network availability and provides nearly instantaneous hardware failover without administrator intervention. It generates a Hot Standby router group, including a lead router that lends its services to any packet being transferred to the Hot Standby address. If the lead router fails, it will be replaced by any of the other routers—the standby routers—that monitor it.

HSSI   High-Speed Serial Interface: A network-standard physical connector for high-speed serial linking over a WAN at speeds of up to 52Mbps.

HTML attacks   Such attacks can include Java applets and ActiveX controls. Their modus operandi is to pass destructive programs across the network and load them through a user's browser.

hubs   Physical-layer devices that are really just multiple port repeaters. When an electronic digital signal is received on a port, the signal is reamplified or regenerated and forwarded out all segments except the segment from which the signal was received.

I

ICD   International Code Designator: Adapted from the subnetwork model of addressing, this assigns the mapping of Network-layer addresses to ATM addresses. HSSI is one of two ATM formats for addressing created by the ATM Forum to be utilized with private networks. See also: *DCC*.

ICMP   Internet Control Message Protocol: Documented in RFC 792, it is a Network layer Internet protocol for the purpose of reporting errors and providing information pertinent to IP packet procedures.

IEEE   Institute of Electrical and Electronics Engineers: A professional organization that, among other activities, defines standards in a number of fields within computing and electronics, including networking and communications. IEEE standards are the predominant LAN standards used today throughout the industry. Many protocols are commonly known by the reference number of the corresponding IEEE standard.

IEEE 802.1   The IEEE committee specification that defines the bridging group. The specification for STP (Spanning-Tree Protocol) is IEEE 802.1d. The STP uses SPA (spanning-tree algorithm) to find and prevent network loops in bridged networks. The specification for VLAN trunking is IEEE 802.1q.

IEEE 802.3   The IEEE committee specification that defines the Ethernet group, specifically the original 10Mbps standard. Ethernet is a LAN protocol that specifies Physical layer and MAC sublayer media access. IEEE 802.3 uses CSMA/CD to provide access for many devices on the same network. Fast Ethernet is defined as 802.3u, and Gigabit Ethernet is defined as 802.3q. See also: *CSMA/CD*.

IEEE 802.5   IEEE committee that defines Token Ring media access.

IGMP   Internet Group Management Protocol: Employed by IP hosts, the protocol that reports their multicast group memberships to an adjacent multicast router.

IGP   Interior Gateway Protocol: Any protocol used by the Internet to exchange routing data within an independent system. Examples include RIP, IGRP, and OSPF.

IGRP   Interior Gateway Routing Protocol: Cisco Proprietary distance-vector routing algorithm. Upgrade from the RIP protocol.

IKE Dead Peer Detection (DPD)   A form of keepalive for VPN connections.

IKE phase 1   In IKE phase 1, the main concern is to authenticate IPSec peers. This is done by negotiating matching IKE security associations (SAs), performing an authenticated Diffie-Hellman agreement of matching keys (which authenticates and protects the identities of IPSec peers), and setting up a tunnel for IKE phase 2 negotiation. See also: *Diffie-Hellman Agreement*, *security association (SA)*, and *IPSec*.

IKE phase 2   During IKE phase 2, a unidirectional connection is established between IPSec peers that is used to determine the IPSec services to be offered. The final outcome of IKE phase 2 is the negotiation of IPSec security associations (SAs).

ILMI   Integrated (or Interim) Local Management Interface: A specification created by the ATM Forum, designated for the incorporation of network-management capability into the ATM UNI. Integrated Local Management Interface cells provide for automatic configuration between ATM systems. In LAN emulation, ILMI can provide sufficient information for the ATM end station to find an LECS. In addition, ILMI provides the ATM NSAP (network service access point) prefix information to the end station.

in-band management   The management of a network device "through" the network. Examples include using Simple Network Management Protocol (SNMP) or Telnet directly via the local LAN. Compare to: *out-of-band management*.

in-band signaling   Configuration of a router from within the network. Examples are Telnet, Simple Network Management Protocol (SNMP), or a network management station (NMS).

info signatures   There are two types of signatures: info and attack. Info signatures are informational, that is, they notice when an information-gathering activity is underway, such as a port scan. Attack signatures represent malicious activities, such as a DoS attack or inappropriate Application-layer calls. See also: *attack signatures*.

initial contact   Initial contact is supported by all Cisco VPN devices, meaning that whenever a new VPN connection is to be established, any previous connection information is reset.

insured burst   In an ATM network, it is the largest, temporarily permitted data burst exceeding the insured rate on a PVC and not tagged by the traffic-policing function for being dropped if network congestion occurs. This insured burst is designated in bytes or cells.

interarea routing   Routing between two or more logical areas. Contrast with: *intra-area routing*. See also: *area*.

interface   Connection to the trusted, untrusted, or DMZ ports on a Cisco PIX Firewall.

interface processor   Any of several processor modules used with Cisco 7000 series routers. See also: *AIP, CIP, EIP, FEIP, HIP, MIP,* and *TRIP*.

Internet   The global "network of networks" whose popularity has exploded in the last few years. Originally a tool for collaborative academic research, it has become a medium for exchanging and distributing information of all kinds. The Internet's need to link disparate computer platforms and technologies has led to the development of uniform protocols and standards that have also found widespread use within corporate LANs. See also: *TCP/IP* and *MBONE*.

internet Before the rise of the Internet, this lowercase form was shorthand for "internetwork" in the generic sense. Now rarely used. See also: *internetwork*.

Internet Key Exchange (IKE) A hybrid protocol that uses part OAKLEY and part of another protocol suite called SKEME inside the Internet Security Association and Key Management Protocol (ISAKMP) framework. You can use IKE to establish a shared security policy and authenticated keys for services (such as IPSec) that require keys. IKE authenticates each peer in an IPSec transaction, negotiates security policy, and handles the exchange of session keys.

Internet layer The layer in the Internet Protocol suite of protocols that provide network addressing and routing through an internetwork.

Internet protocol Any protocol belonging to the TCP/IP protocol stack. See also: *TCP/IP*.

Internet Security Association and Key Management Protocol (ISAKMP) A protocol framework that defines the mechanics of implementing a key exchange protocol and negotiation of a security policy.

internetwork Any group of private networks interconnected by routers and other mechanisms, typically operating as a single entity.

internetworking Broadly, anything associated with the general task of linking networks to each other. The term encompasses technologies, procedures, and products. When you connect networks to a router, you are creating an internetwork.

intra-area routing Routing that occurs within a logical area. Contrast with: *interarea routing*.

Intrusion Detection System (IDS) The IDS is particularly valuable at perimeter points within the network or at peering points between networks. The IDS contains the profiles or signatures for 59 common attacks that run the gamut from the breach of security types to information-gathering attacks. When a packet matches one of these signatures, the IDS can react with an alarm (can be sent to the Director or a Syslog server), it can drop the packet, or it can reset the TCP session.

Inverse ARP Inverse Address Resolution Protocol: A technique by which dynamic mappings are constructed in a network, allowing a device such as a router to locate the logical network address and associate it with a permanent virtual circuit (PVC). Commonly used in Frame Relay to determine the far-end node's TCP/IP address by sending the Inverse ARP request to the local DLCI.

IOS Firewall Authentication Proxy Gives you the ability to control user access based on users rather than on IP addresses or other device information. It forces users to authenticate before accessing external resources, so their access policies are retrieved from centralized AAA servers and thus follow the users regardless of where they go on the network. See also: *AAA*.

IOS Firewall IDS The IOS Firewall IDS gives the ability to alert, reset, and drop when security signatures are matched. As the administrator, you have the ability to select which signatures to deactivate, or to even selectively apply signatures using ACLs. See *Intrusion Detection System (IDS)*.

IP   Internet Protocol: Defined in RFC 791, it is a Network-layer protocol that is part of the TCP/IP stack and allows connectionless service. IP furnishes an array of features for addressing, type-of-service specification, fragmentation and reassembly, and security.

IP address   Often called an *Internet address*, this is an address uniquely identifying any device (host) on the Internet (or any TCP/IP network). Each address consists of four octets (32 bits), represented as decimal numbers separated by periods (a format known as *dotted-decimal*). Every address is made up of a network number, an optional subnetwork number, and a host number. The network and subnetwork numbers together are used for routing, while the host number addresses an individual host within the network or subnetwork. The network and subnetwork information is extracted from the IP address using the subnet mask. There are five classes of IP addresses (A–E), which allocate different numbers of bits to the network, subnetwork, and host portions of the address. See also: *CIDR, IP,* and *subnet mask.*

IPCP   IP Control Protocol: The protocol used to establish and configure IP over PPP. See also: *IP* and *PPP.*

IP multicast   A technique for routing that enables IP traffic to be reproduced from one source to several endpoints or from multiple sources to many destinations. Instead of transmitting only one packet to each individual point of destination, one packet is sent to a multicast group specified by only one IP endpoint address for the group.

IPSec   IP Security: A system of open standards for providing security between two systems. IPSec works at the Network layer.

IPSec client   A host that participates in a tunnel created between a security gateway and itself to protect data.

IPSec SA lifetime   The `crypto IPSec security-association lifetime` command defines the global IPSec SA lifetime based on kilobytes and seconds.

IPSec transform   A single security protocol with the corresponding security algorithm.

IPX   Internetwork Packet eXchange: Network-layer protocol (Layer 3) used in Novell NetWare networks for transferring information from servers to workstations. Similar to IP and XNS.

IPXCP   IPX Control Protocol: The protocol used to establish and configure IPX over PPP. See also: *IPX* and *PPP.*

IPXWAN   Protocol used for new WAN links to provide and negotiate line options on the link using IPX. After the link is up and the options have been agreed upon by the two end-to-end links, normal IPX transmission begins.

ISDN   Integrated Services Digital Network: Offered as a service by telephone companies, a communication protocol that allows telephone networks to carry data, voice, and other digital traffic. See also: *BISDN, BRI,* and *PRI.*

IS-IS   Intermediate System-to-Intermediate System: An OSI link-state hierarchical routing protocol.

ISL routing Inter-Switch Link routing: A Cisco Proprietary method of frame tagging in a switched internetwork. Frame tagging is a way to identify the VLAN membership of a frame as it traverses a switched internetwork.

isochronous transmission Asynchronous data transfer over a synchronous data link, requiring a constant bit rate for reliable transport. Compare to: *asynchronous transmission* and *synchronous transmission*.

ITU-T International Telecommunication Union-Telecommunication Standardization Sector: A group of engineers that develops worldwide standards for telecommunications technologies.

K

Kerberos An authentication and encryption method that can be used by Cisco routers to ensure that data cannot be "sniffed" off of the network. Kerberos was developed at MIT and was designed to provide strong security using the Data Encryption Standard (DES) cryptographic algorithm. Kerberos provides an alternative approach whereby a trusted third-party authentication service is used to verify users' identities. See also: *Data Encryption Standard (DES)*.

L

LAN Local area network: Broadly, any network linking two or more computers and related devices within a limited geographical area (up to a few kilometers). LANs are typically high-speed, low-error networks within a company. Cabling and signaling at the Physical and Data Link layers of the OSI are dictated by LAN standards. Ethernet, FDDI, and Token Ring are among the most popular LAN technologies. Compare to: *MAN*.

LANE LAN emulation: The technology that allows an ATM network to operate as a LAN backbone. To do so, the ATM network is required to provide multicast and broadcast support, address mapping (MAC-to-ATM), SVC management, in addition to an operable packet format. Additionally, LANE defines Ethernet and Token Ring ELANs. See also: *ELAN*.

LAN switch A high-speed, multiple-interface transparent bridging mechanism, transmitting packets between segments of data links, usually referred to specifically as an *Ethernet switch*. LAN switches transfer traffic based on MAC addresses. Multilayer switches are a type of high-speed, special purpose, hardware-based router. See also: *multilayer switch* and *store-and-forward packet switching*.

LAPB Link Accessed Procedure, Balanced: A bit-oriented Data Link–layer protocol that is part of the X.25 stack and has its origin in SDLC. See also: *SDLC* and *X.25*.

LAPD Link Access Procedure on the D channel: The ISDN Data Link–layer protocol used specifically for the D channel and defined by ITU-T Recommendations Q.920 and Q.921. LAPD evolved from LAPB and is created to comply with the signaling requirements of ISDN basic access.

latency Broadly, the time it takes a data packet to get from one location to another. In specific networking contexts, it can mean either 1) the time elapsed (delay) between the execution of a request for access to a network by a device and the time the mechanism actually is permitted transmission, or 2) the time elapsed between when a mechanism receives a frame and the time that frame is forwarded out of the destination port.

Layer 2 Forwarding (L2F) A Cisco Proprietary tunneling protocol and their initial tunneling protocol created for virtual private dial-up networks (VPDN).

Layer 2 Tunneling Protocol (L2TP) Created by Cisco and Microsoft to replace L2F and PPTP. L2TP merges the functionality of L2F and PPTP into one tunneling protocol.

Layer 3 switch See: *multilayer switch*.

layered architecture Industry-standard way of creating applications to work on a network. Layered architecture allows the application developer to make changes in only one layer instead of in the whole program.

LCP Link Control Protocol: The protocol designed to establish, configure, and test data-link connections for use by PPP. See also: *PPP*.

leaky bucket An analogy for the generic cell rate algorithm (GCRA) used in ATM networks for checking the conformance of cell flows from a user or network. The bucket's "hole" is understood to be the prolonged rate at which cells can be accommodated, and the "depth" is the tolerance for cell bursts over a certain time period.

learning bridge A bridge that transparently builds a dynamic database of MAC addresses and the interfaces associated with each address. Transparent bridges help to reduce traffic congestion on the network.

LE ARP LAN Emulation Address Resolution Protocol: The protocol providing the ATM address that corresponds to a MAC address.

leased lines Permanent connections between two points leased from the telephone companies.

LEC LAN Emulation Client: Software providing the emulation of the link-layer interface that allows the operation and communication of all higher-level protocols and applications to continue. The LEC runs in all ATM devices, which include hosts, servers, bridges, and routers. See also: *ELAN* and *LES*.

LECS LAN Emulation Configuration Server: An important part of emulated LAN services, providing the configuration data that is furnished upon request from the LES. These services include address registration for Integrated Local Management Interface (ILMI) support, configuration support for the LES addresses and their corresponding emulated LAN identifiers, and an interface to the emulated LAN. See also: *LES* and *ELAN*.

LES LAN Emulation Server: The central LANE component that provides the initial configuration data for each connecting LEC. The LES typically is located on either an ATM-integrated router or a switch. Responsibilities of the LES include configuration and support for the LEC, address registration for the LEC, database storage and response concerning ATM addresses, and interfacing to the emulated LAN. See also: *ELAN*, *LEC*, and *LECS*.

line authentication See: *character-mode access*.

link-state routing algorithm A routing algorithm that allows each router to broadcast or multicast information regarding the cost of reaching all its neighbors to every node in the internetwork. Link-state algorithms provide a consistent view of the network and are therefore not vulnerable to routing loops. However, this is achieved at the cost of somewhat greater difficulty in computation and more widespread traffic (compared with distance-vector routing algorithms). See also: *distance-vector routing algorithm*.

LLAP LocalTalk Link Access Protocol: In a LocalTalk environment, the Data Link–layer protocol that manages node-to-node delivery of data. This protocol provides node addressing and management of bus access, and it also controls data sending and receiving to assure packet length and integrity.

LLC Logical Link Control: Defined by the IEEE, the higher of two Data Link–layer sublayers. LLC is responsible for error detection (but not correction), flow control, framing, and software-sublayer addressing. The predominant LLC protocol, IEEE 802.2, defines both connectionless and connection-oriented operations. See also: *Data Link layer* and *MAC*.

LMI Local Management Interface: An enhancement to the original Frame Relay specification. Among the features it provides are a keepalive mechanism, a multicast mechanism, global addressing, and a status mechanism.

LNNI LAN Emulation Network-to-Network Interface: In the Phase 2 LANE specification, an interface that supports communication between the server components within one ELAN.

load balancing The act of balancing packet load over multiple links to the same remote network.

local explorer packet In a Token Ring SRB network, a packet generated by an end system to find a host linked to the local ring. If no local host can be found, the end system will produce one of two solutions: a spanning explorer packet or an all-routes explorer packet.

local loop Connection from a demarcation point to the closest switching office.

LocalTalk Utilizing CSMA/CD, in addition to supporting data transmission at speeds of 230.4Kbps, LocalTalk is Apple Computer's proprietary baseband protocol, operating at the Data Link and Physical layers of the OSI reference model.

LPD Line Printer Daemon: Used in the Unix world to allow printing to an IP address.

LSA Link-state advertisement: Contained inside link-state packets (LSPs), these advertisements are usually multicast packets, containing information about neighbors and path costs, that are employed by link-state protocols. Receiving routers use LSAs to maintain their link-state databases and, ultimately, routing tables.

LUNI LAN Emulation User-to-Network Interface: Defining the interface between the LAN Emulation Client (LEC) and the LAN Emulation Server (LES), LUNI is the ATM Forum's standard for LAN emulation on ATM networks. See also: *LES* and *LECS*.

M

MAC Media Access Control: The lower sublayer in the Data Link layer, it is responsible for hardware addressing, media access, and error detection of frames. See also: *Data Link layer* and *LLC*.

MAC address A Data Link layer hardware address that every port or device needs in order to connect to a LAN segment. These addresses are used by various devices in the network for accurate location of logical addresses. MAC addresses are defined by the IEEE standard and their length is six characters, typically using the burned-in address (BIA) of the local LAN interface. Variously called *hardware address*, *physical address*, *burned-in address*, or *MAC layer address*.

MacIP In AppleTalk, the Network-layer protocol encapsulating IP packets in Datagram Delivery Protocol (DDP) packets. MacIP also supplies substitute ARP services.

Main mode In this mode, IKE uses three two-way handshakes for phase 1 negotiation. See also: *IKE phase 1*.

MAN Metropolitan area network: Any network that encompasses a metropolitan area, that is, an area typically larger than a LAN but smaller than a WAN. See also: *LAN*.

Manchester encoding A method for digital coding in which a mid-bit–time transition is employed for clocking, and a 1 (one) is denoted by a high-voltage level during the first half of the bit time. This scheme is used by Ethernet and IEEE 802.3.

man-in-the-middle attack An individual between you and the network to which you are connected who gathers everything you send and receive. For a man-in-the middle attack to be possible, the attacker must have access to network packets traveling across the networks.

masquerading Also known as *IP spoofing*, it is fairly easy to stop once you understand how it works. An IP spoofing attack happens when someone outside your network pretends to be a trusted computer by using an IP address that's within the range of your network's IP addresses.

maximum burst Specified in bytes or cells, the largest burst of information exceeding the insured rate that will be permitted on an ATM permanent virtual connection for a short time and will not be dropped even if it goes over the specified maximum rate. Compare to: *insured burst*. See also: *maximum rate*.

maximum rate   The maximum permitted data throughput on a particular virtual circuit, equal to the total of insured and uninsured traffic from the traffic source. Should traffic congestion occur, uninsured information may be deleted from the path. Measured in bits or cells per second, the maximum rate represents the highest throughput of data the virtual circuit is ever able to deliver and cannot exceed the media rate. Compare to: *excess rate*. See also: *maximum burst*.

MBONE   Multicast backbone: The multicast backbone of the Internet, it is a virtual multicast network made up of multicast LANs, including point-to-point tunnels interconnecting them.

MBS   Maximum burst size: In an ATM signaling message, this metric, coded as a number of cells, is used to convey the burst tolerance.

MCDV   Maximum cell delay variation: The maximum two-point CDV objective across a link or node for the identified service category in an ATM network. The MCDV is one of four link metrics that are exchanged using PNNI topology state packets (PTSPs) to verify the available resources of an ATM network. Only one MCDV value is assigned to each traffic class.

MCLR   Maximum cell loss ratio: The maximum ratio of cells in an ATM network that fail to transit a link or node compared with the total number of cells that arrive at the link or node. MCDV is one of four link metrics that are exchanged using PNNI topology state packets (PTSPs) to verify the available resources of an ATM network. The MCLR applies to cells in VBR and CBR traffic classes whose CLP bit is set to zero. See also: *CBR*, *CLP*, and *VBR*.

MCR   Minimum cell rate: A parameter determined by the ATM Forum for traffic management of the ATM networks. MCR is specifically defined for ABR transmissions and specifies the minimum value for the allowed cell rate (ACR). See also: *ACR* and *PCR*.

MCTD   Maximum cell transfer delay: In an ATM network, the total of the maximum cell delay variation and the fixed delay across the link or node. MCTD is one of four link metrics that are exchanged using PNNI topology state packets (PTSPs) to verify the available resources of an ATM network. There is one MCTD value assigned to each traffic class. See also: *MCDV*.

MD5 authentication   MD5 (Message Digest 5) is a hash algorithm. HMAC is a keyed hash variant used to authenticate data.

MIB   Management Information Base: Used with SNMP management software to gather information from remote devices. The management station can poll the remote device for information, or the MIB running on the remote station can be programmed to send information on a regular basis.

MII   Media-independent interface: Used in Fast Ethernet and Gigabit Ethernet to provide faster bit transfer rates of four and eight bits at a time. Contrast to AUI interface that is one bit at a time.

MIP   Multichannel Interface Processor: The resident interface processor on Cisco 7000 series routers, providing up to two channelized T1 or E1 connections by serial cables connected to a CSU. The two controllers are capable of providing 24 T1 or 30 E1 channel groups, with each group being introduced to the system as a serial interface that can be configured individually.

mips   Millions of instructions per second: A measure of processor speed.

MLP   Multilink PPP: A technique used to split, recombine, and sequence datagrams across numerous logical data links.

MMP   Multichassis Multilink PPP: A protocol that supplies MLP support across multiple routers and access servers. MMP enables several routers and access servers to work as a single, large dial-up pool with one network address and ISDN access number. MMP successfully supports packet fragmenting and reassembly when the user connection is split between two physical access devices.

modem   Modulator-demodulator: A device that converts digital signals to analog and vice versa so that digital information can be transmitted over analog communication facilities, such as voice-grade telephone lines. This is achieved by converting digital signals at the source to analog for transmission and reconverting the analog signals back into digital form at the destination. See also: *modulation* and *demodulation*.

modem eliminator   A mechanism that makes possible a connection between two DTE devices without modems by simulating the commands and physical signaling required.

modulation   The process of modifying some characteristic of an electrical signal, such as amplitude (AM) or frequency (FM), in order to represent digital or analog information. See also: *AM*.

MOSPF   Multicast OSPF: An extension of the OSPF unicast protocol that enables IP multicast routing within the domain. See also: *OSPF*.

MPOA   Multiprotocol over ATM: An effort by the ATM Forum to standardize how existing and future Network-layer protocols such as IP, IPv6, AppleTalk, and IPX run over an ATM network with directly attached hosts, routers, and multilayer LAN switches.

MTU   Maximum transmission unit: The largest packet size, measured in bytes, that an interface can handle.

multicast   Broadly, any communication between a single sender and multiple receivers. Unlike broadcast messages, which are sent to all addresses on a network, multicast messages are sent to a defined subset of the network addresses; this subset has a group multicast address, which is specified in the packet's destination address field. See also: *broadcast* and *directed broadcast*.

multicast address   A single address that points to more than one device on the network by specifying a special non-existent MAC address specified in that particular multicast protocol. Identical to *group address*. See also: *multicast*.

multicast send VCC   A two-directional point-to-point virtual control connection (VCC) arranged by an LEC to a BUS, it is one of the three types of informational links specified by phase 1 LANE. See also: *control distribute VCC* and *control direct VCC*.

multilayer switch   A highly specialized, high-speed, hardware-based type of LAN router, a multilayer switch filters and forwards packets based on their Layer 2 MAC addresses and Layer 3 network addresses. It's possible that even Layer 4 addresses can be read. Sometimes called a *Layer 3 switch*. See also: *LAN switch*.

multilink   Used to combine multiple async or ISDN links to provide combined bandwidth.

multiplexing   The process of converting several logical signals into a single physical signal for transmission across one physical channel. Contrast with: *demultiplexing*.

N

NAK   Negative acknowledgment: A response sent from a receiver telling the sender that the information was not received or contained errors. Compare to: *acknowledgment*.

NAT   Network Address Translation: An algorithm instrumental in minimizing the requirement for globally unique IP addresses. NAT permits an organization whose addresses are not all globally unique to connect to the Internet nevertheless, by translating those addresses into globally routable address space.

NBP   Name Binding Protocol: In AppleTalk, the transport-level protocol that interprets a socket client's name, entered as a character string, into the corresponding DDP address. NBP gives AppleTalk protocols the capacity to discern user-defined zones and names of mechanisms by showing and keeping translation tables that map names to their corresponding socket addresses.

neighboring routers   Two routers in OSPF that have interfaces to a common network. On networks with multiaccess, these neighboring routers are dynamically discovered using the Hello protocol of OSPF.

NetBEUI   NetBIOS Extended User Interface: An improved version of the NetBIOS protocol used in a number of network operating systems, including LAN Manager, Windows NT, LAN Server, and Windows for Workgroups, implementing the OSI LLC2 protocol. NetBEUI formalizes the transport frame not standardized in NetBIOS and adds more functions. See also: *OSI*.

NetBIOS   Network Basic Input/Output System: The API employed by applications residing on an IBM LAN to ask for services, such as session termination or information transfer, from lower-level network processes.

NetView   A mainframe network product from IBM used for monitoring SNA (Systems Network Architecture) networks. It runs as a VTAM (virtual telecommunications access method) application.

NetWare   A widely used NOS created by Novell, providing a number of distributed network services and remote file access.

network access layer The bottom layer in the Internet Protocol suite that provides media access to packets.

network access server (NAS) A server that works with CiscoSecure ACS software to authenticate and authorize users. The CiscoSecure ACS sits on a network that dial-in users and other types of outside users access through a network access server (NAS). As users log in through the NAS, the CiscoSecure ACS exchanges data and instructions with the NAS, authenticating and authorizing users on the basis of user and group profiles that are stored in either a local or network database. After CiscoSecure ACS authenticates and authorizes users for the proper level of network access, it tracks individual user access and stores this information in a database from which it can later be retrieved for accounting or analyzing network security and usage.

network address Used with the logical network addresses to identify the network segment in an internetwork. Logical addresses are hierarchical in nature and have at least two parts: network and host. An example of a hierarchical address is 172.16.10.5, where 172.16 is the network and 10.5 is the host address.

network equipment weaknesses Defined as any default setting that allows access to equipment without hindrance.

Network layer In the OSI reference model, the Network layer is Layer 3—the layer in which routing is implemented, enabling connections and path selection between two end systems. See also: *Application layer*, *Data Link layer*, *Physical layer*, *Presentation layer*, *Session layer*, and *Transport layer*.

NFS Network File System: One of the protocols in Sun Microsystems' widely used file system protocol suite, allowing remote file access across a network. The name is loosely used to refer to the entire Sun protocol suite, which also includes RPC, XDR (External Data Representation), and other protocols.

NHRP Next Hop Resolution Protocol: In a nonbroadcast multiaccess (NBMA) network, the protocol employed by routers in order to dynamically locate MAC addresses of various hosts and routers. NHRP enables systems to communicate directly without requiring an intermediate hop, thus facilitating increased performance in ATM, Frame Relay, X.25, and SMDS systems.

NHS Next Hop Server: Defined by the NHRP protocol, this server maintains the next-hop resolution cache tables, listing IP-to-ATM address maps of related nodes and nodes that can be reached through routers served by the NHS.

NIC Network interface card: An electronic circuit board placed in a computer. The NIC provides network communication to a LAN.

NLSP NetWare Link Services Protocol: Novell's link-state routing protocol, based on the IS-IS model.

NMP Network Management Processor: A Catalyst 5000 switch processor module used to control and monitor the switch.

node address   Used to identify a specific device in an internetwork. Can be a hardware address, which is burned into the network interface card, or a logical network address, which an administrator or server assigns to the node.

nonce   A pseudo-random number. RSA-encrypted nonces can be used to authenticate the IKE exchange and the Diffie-Hellman Agreement.

non-stub area   In OSPF, a resource-consuming area carrying a default route, intra-area routes, inter-area routes, static routes, and external routes. Non-stub areas are the only areas that can have virtual links configured across them and exclusively contain an anonymous system boundary router (ASBR). Compare to: *stub area*. See also: *ASBR* and *OSPF*.

NRZ   Nonreturn to zero: One of several encoding schemes for transmitting digital data. NRZ signals sustain constant levels of voltage with no signal shifting (no return to zero-voltage level) during a bit interval. If there is a series of bits with the same value (1 or 0), there will be no state change. The signal is not self-clocking. See also: *NRZI*.

NRZI   Nonreturn to zero inverted: One of several encoding schemes for transmitting digital data. A transition in voltage level (either from high to low or vice versa) at the beginning of a bit interval is interpreted as a value of 1; the absence of a transition is interpreted as a 0. Thus, the voltage assigned to each value is continually inverted. NRZI signals are not self-clocking. See also: *NRZ*.

NT1   Network termination 1: An ISDN designation to devices that understand ISDN standards.

NT2   Network termination 2: An ISDN designation to devices that do not understand ISDN standards. To use an NT2, you must use a terminal adapter (TA).

NVRAM   Nonvolatile RAM: Random-access memory that keeps its contents intact while power is turned off.

O

OAKLEY   A key exchange protocol that defines how to derive authenticated keying material.

OC   Optical carrier: A series of physical protocols, designated as OC-1, OC-2, OC-3, and so on, for SONET optical signal transmissions. OC signal levels place STS frames on a multimode fiber-optic line at various speeds, of which 51.84Mbps is the lowest (OC-1). Each subsequent protocol runs at a speed divisible by 51.84. See also: *SONET*.

octet   Base-8 numbering system used to identify a section of a dotted decimal IP address. Also referred to as a *byte*.

oem.ini   File that can be used to install the VPN Client without user intervention.

ones density   Also known as *pulse density*, this is a method of signal clocking. The CSU/DSU retrieves the clocking information from data that passes through it. For this scheme to work, the data needs to be encoded to contain at least one binary 1 for each eight bits transmitted. See also: *CSU* and *DSU*.

operating system weakness   Any default setting that allows access through the operating system to any network implementation.

OSI   Open System Interconnection: International standardization program designed by ISO and ITU-T for the development of data networking standards that make multivendor equipment interoperability a reality.

OSI reference model   Open System Interconnection reference model: A conceptual model defined by the International Organization for Standardization (ISO) describing how any combination of devices can be connected for the purpose of communication. The OSI model divides the task into seven functional layers, forming a hierarchy with the applications at the top and the physical medium at the bottom, and it defines the functions each layer must provide. See also: *Application layer*, *Data Link layer*, *Network layer*, *Physical layer*, *Presentation layer*, *Session layer*, and *Transport layer*.

OSPF   Open Shortest Path First: A link-state, hierarchical IGP routing algorithm derived from an earlier version of the IS-IS protocol, whose features include multipath routing, load balancing, and least-cost routing. OSPF is the suggested successor to RIP in the Internet environment. See also: *Enhanced IGRP*, *IGP*, and *IP*.

OUI   Organizational Unique Identifier: Assigned by the IEEE to an organization that makes network interface cards. The organization then puts this OUI on each and every card they manufacture. The OUI is 3 bytes (24 bits) long. The manufacturer then adds a 3-byte identifier to uniquely identify the host on an internetwork. The total length of the address is 48 bits (6 bytes) and is called a *hardware address* or *MAC address*.

out-of-band management   Management "outside" of the network's physical channels. For example, using a console connection not directly interfaced through the local LAN or WAN or a dial-in modem. Compare to: *in-band management*.

out-of-band signaling   Within a network, any transmission that uses physical channels or frequencies separate from those ordinarily used for data transfer. For example, the initial configuration of a Cisco Catalyst switch requires an out-of-band connection via a console port.

P

packet   In data communications, the basic logical unit of information transferred. A packet consists of a certain number of data bytes, wrapped or encapsulated in headers, and/or trailers that contain information about where the packet came from, where it's going, and so on. The various protocols involved in sending a transmission add their own layers of header information, which the corresponding protocols in receiving devices then interpret.

packet-mode access   One of three packet-mode methods that are used for router authentication. Async, group-async BRI, and serial (PRI) are all considered packet-mode access methods.

packet switch   A physical device that makes it possible for a communication channel to share several connections, its functions include finding the most efficient transmission path for packets.

packet switching   A networking technology based on the transmission of data in packets. Dividing a continuous stream of data into small units—packets—enables data from multiple devices on a network to share the same communication channel simultaneously but also requires the use of precise routing information.

PAM   Port-to-Application Mapping: Allows you to modify the default values of well-known ports, and thus teach CBAC how to recognize these familiar applications in their new homes.

PAP   Password Authentication Protocol: In Point-to-Point Protocol (PPP) networks, a method of validating connection requests. The requesting (remote) device must send an authentication request, containing a password and ID, to the local router when attempting to connect. Unlike the more secure CHAP (Challenge Handshake Authentication Protocol), PAP sends the password unencrypted and does not attempt to verify whether the user is authorized to access the requested resource; it merely identifies the remote end. See also: *CHAP*.

parity checking   A method of error-checking in data transmissions. An extra bit (the parity bit) is added to each character or data word so that the sum of the bits will be either an odd number (in odd parity) or an even number (even parity).

partial mesh   A type of network topology in which some network nodes form a full mesh (where every node has either a physical or a virtual circuit linking it to every other network node), but others are attached to only one or two nodes in the network. A typical use of partial-mesh topology is in peripheral networks linked to a fully meshed backbone. See also: *full mesh*.

password attacks   An attack to obtain user or password information. If a hacker creates a program that repeatedly attempts to identify a user account and/or password, it's called a *brute-force attack*. And if it's successful, the hacker will gain access to all resources the stolen username and password usually provides to the now ripped-off corporate user.

.pcf   You need to create one connection entry for each connection you want to add, and can use as many entries as you wish in the .pcf file. Just put them in the same directory as the setup.exe, and they'll be added to the client.

PCM   Pulse code modulation: The process by which analog data is converted into digital information.

PCR   Peak cell rate: As defined by the ATM Forum, the parameter specifying, in cells per second, the maximum rate at which a source may transmit.

PDN   Public data network: Generally for a fee, a PDN offers the public access to a computer communication network operated by private concerns or government agencies. Small organizations can take advantage of PDNs, aiding them to create WANs without investing in long-distance equipment and circuitry.

PDU Protocol data unit: The processes at each layer of the OSI model. PDUs at the Transport layer are called *segments*; PDUs at the Network layer are called *packets* or *datagrams*; and PDUs at the Data Link layer are called *frames*. The Physical layer uses bits.

perfect forward secrecy (PFS) PFS is called "perfect" because if one security key is compromised in a session, the session is still secure because multiple keys are used and no key is derived from any other key.

perimeter router Your first line of defense for Internet connections. It also defines the de-militarized zone (DMZ) and is used to protect the bastion hosts residing there. You can also use a perimeter router to prevent the Private Internet eXchange (PIX) from being vulnerable to a direct attack, and it can even provide an alarm system for you if anyone does try and break into it.

PGP Pretty Good Privacy: A popular public-key/private-key encryption application offering protected transfer of files and messages.

phantom router Used in a Hot Standby Routing Protocol (HSRP) network to provide an IP default gateway address to hosts.

Physical layer The lowest layer—Layer 1—in the OSI reference model, it is responsible for converting data packets from the Data Link layer (Layer 2) into electrical signals. Physical-layer protocols and standards define, for example, the type of cable and connectors to be used, including their pin assignments and the encoding scheme for signaling 0 and 1 values. See also: *Application layer, Data Link layer, Network layer, Presentation layer, Session layer,* and *Transport layer.*

PIM Protocol Independent Multicast: A multicast protocol that handles the IGMP requests as well as requests for multicast data forwarding.

PIM DM Protocol Independent Multicast dense mode: PIM DM utilizes the unicast route table and relies on the source root distribution architecture for multicast data forwarding.

PIM SM Protocol Independent Multicast sparse mode: PIM SM utilizes the unicast route table and relies on the shared root distribution architecture for multicast data forwarding.

ping Packet Internet groper: A Unix-based Internet diagnostic tool consisting of a message sent to test the accessibility of a particular device on the IP network. The acronym (from which the "full name" was formed) reflects the underlying metaphor of submarine sonar. Just as the sonar operator sends out a signal and waits to hear it echo ("ping") back from a submerged object, the network user can ping another node on the network and wait to see if it responds.

PKI Public key infrastructure: A system of CAs (and, optionally, RAs and other supporting servers and agents) that perform some set of certificate management, archive management, key management, and token management functions for a community of users in an application of asymmetric cryptography. See also: *certificate authority (CA).*

pleisochronous Nearly synchronous, except that clocking comes from an outside source instead of being embedded within the signal as in synchronous transmissions.

PLP Packet Level Protocol: Occasionally called *X.25 level 3* or *X.25 Protocol*, a Network-layer protocol that is part of the X.25 stack.

PNNI Private Network-Network Interface: An ATM Forum specification for offering topology data used for the calculation of paths through the network among switches and groups of switches. It is based on well-known link-state routing procedures and allows for automatic configuration in networks whose addressing scheme is determined by the topology.

point-to-multipoint connection In ATM, a communication path going only one way, connecting a single system at the starting point, called the *root node*, to systems at multiple points of destination, called *leaves*. See also: *point-to-point connection*.

point-to-point connection In ATM, a channel of communication that can be directed either one way or both ways between two ATM end systems. See also: *point-to-multipoint connection*.

Point-to-Point Tunneling Protocol (PPTP) Created by Microsoft to allow the secure transfer of data from remote networks to the corporate network. See also: *Layer 2 Tunneling Protocol (L2TP)*.

poison reverse updates Transmitted by a router back to the originator (thus ignoring the split-horizon rule) after route poisoning has occurred. Typically used with DV routing protocols in order to overcome large routing loops and offer explicit information when a subnet or network is not accessible (instead of merely suggesting that the network is unreachable by not including it in updates). See also: *route poisoning*.

policy weakness Involves problems with the corporate security policy, such as the lack of a written policy and the lack of a disaster recovery plan. Policy weaknesses leave your systems and networking professionals vulnerable.

polling The procedure of orderly inquiry, used by a primary network mechanism, to determine if secondary devices have data to transmit. A message is sent to each secondary, granting the secondary the right to transmit.

POP 1) Point of presence: The physical location where an interexchange carrier has placed equipment to interconnect with a local exchange carrier. 2) Post Office Protocol (currently at version 3): A protocol used by client e-mail applications for the recovery of mail from a mail server.

port address translation (PAT) Provides the same service as NAT, but PAT can allow thousands of users to use the same IP Internet address. PAT uses the source port number from each user to keep them unique and to allow the use of a few IP addresses. In contrast, NAT uses one-to-one translation, which means that each user must be translated to a real IP address. Also called *NAT Overload*.

port security Used with Layer 2 switches to provide some security. Not typically used in production because it is difficult to manage. Allows only certain frames to traverse administrator-assigned segments.

port numbers Used at the Transport layer with TCP to keep track of host-to-host virtual circuits.

POTS   Plain old telephone service: This refers to the traditional analog phone service that is found in most installations.

PPP   Point-to-Point Protocol: The protocol most commonly used for dial-up Internet access, superseding the earlier SLIP. Its features include address notification, authentication via CHAP or PAP, support for multiple protocols, and link monitoring. PPP has two layers: the Link Control Protocol (LCP) establishes, configures, and tests a link; and then any of the various Network Control Protocols (NCPs) transport traffic for a specific protocol suite, such as IPX. See also: *CHAP*, *PAP*, and *SLIP*.

Presentation layer   Layer 6 of the OSI reference model, it defines how data is formatted, presented, encoded, and converted for use by software at the Application layer. See also: *Application layer*, *Data Link layer*, *Network layer*, *Physical layer*, *Session layer*, and *Transport layer*.

Pre-shared keys   Must be configured on each IPSec peer, and those used must be the same on each peer. The IKE peers authenticate each other by creating and sending a keyed hash that includes the pre-shared key. Once the receiving peer receives the hash, it attempts to create the same hash by using its configured pre-shared key. If the hashes match, the peer is authenticated.

PRI   Primary Rate Interface: A type of ISDN connection between a PBX and a long-distance carrier, which is made up of a single 64Kbps D channel in addition to 23 (T1) or 30 (E1) B channels. See also: *ISDN*.

priority queueing   A routing function in which frames temporarily placed in an interface output queue are assigned priorities based on traits such as packet size or type of interface.

private IP addresses   IP addresses that are reserved and blocked on the Internet so they can be used on private networks. See also: *IP address*.

process/application layer   Upper layer in the Internet Protocol stack. Responsible for network services.

process switching   As a packet arrives on a router to be forwarded, it's copied to the router's process buffer, and the router performs a lookup on the Layer 3 address. Using the route table, an exit interface is associated with the destination address. The processor forwards the packet with the added new information to the exit interface, while the router initializes the fast-switching cache. Subsequent packets bound for the same destination address follow the same path as the first packet.

PROM   Programmable read-only memory: ROM that is programmable only once, using special equipment. Compare to: *EPROM*.

propagation delay   The time it takes data to traverse a network from its source to its destination.

protocol   In networking, the specification of a set of rules for a particular type of communication. The term is also used to refer to the software that implements a protocol.

protocol stack   A collection of related protocols.

pruning   The act of trimming down the shortest path tree. This deactivates interfaces that do not have group participants.

Proxy ARP   Proxy Address Resolution Protocol: Used to allow redundancy in case of a failure with the configured default gateway on a host. Proxy ARP is a variation of the ARP protocol in which an intermediate device, such as a router, sends an ARP response on behalf of an end node to the requesting host.

PSE   Packet switch exchange: The X.25 term for a switch.

PSN   Packet-switched network: Any network that uses packet-switching technology. Also known as *packet-switched data network (PSDN)*. See also: *packet switching*.

PSTN   Public switched telephone network: Colloquially referred to as *plain old telephone service (POTS)*. A term that describes the assortment of telephone networks and services available globally.

PVC   Permanent virtual circuit: In a Frame Relay network, a logical connection, defined in software, that is maintained permanently. Compare to: *SVC*. See also: *virtual circuit*.

PVP   Permanent virtual path: A virtual path made up of PVCs. See also: *PVC*.

PVP tunneling   Permanent virtual path tunneling: A technique that links two private ATM networks across a public network using a virtual path, wherein the public network transparently trunks the complete collection of virtual channels in the virtual path between the two private networks.

Q

QoS   Quality of Service: A set of metrics used to measure the quality of transmission and service availability of any given transmission system.

queue   Broadly, any list of elements arranged in an orderly fashion and ready for processing, such as a line of people waiting to enter a movie theater. In routing, it refers to a backlog of information packets waiting in line to be transmitted over a router interface.

R

R reference point   Used with ISDN networks to identify the connection between an NT1 and an S/T device. The S/T device converts the four-wire network to the two-wire ISDN standard network.

RAM Random access memory: Used by all computers to store information. Cisco routers use RAM to store packet buffers and routing tables, along with the hardware addresses cache.

RARP Reverse Address Resolution Protocol: The protocol within the TCP/IP stack that maps MAC addresses to IP addresses. See also: *ARP.*

rate queue A value, assigned to one or more virtual circuits, that specifies the speed at which an individual virtual circuit transmits data to the remote end. Every rate queue identifies a segment of the total bandwidth available on an ATM link. The sum of all rate queues should not exceed the total available bandwidth.

RCP Remote Copy Protocol: A protocol for copying files to or from a file system that resides on a remote server on a network, using TCP to guarantee reliable data delivery.

redistribution Command used in Cisco routers to inject the paths found from one type of routing protocol into another type of routing protocol. For example, networks found by RIP can be inserted into an IGRP network.

redundancy In internetworking, the duplication of connections, devices, or services that can be used as a backup in the event that the primary connections, devices, or services fail.

registration authority (RA) A server that acts as a proxy for the CA so that CA functions can continue when the CA is offline. See also: *certificate authority (CA).*

reload An event or command that causes Cisco routers to reboot.

remote access VPN Allows remote users, such as telecommuters, to securely access the corporate network whenever and from wherever the need may arise.

Remote Authentication Dial-In User Service (RADIUS) A distributed client/server system that secures networks against unauthorized access.

replaying See *session replay.*

repudiation Prevents a third party from being able to prove that a communication between two other parties ever took place. You do this if you do not want your communications to be traceable.

rerouting attack Occurs when packets from user A are rerouted to user B so that user B can intercept the packets and misuse them. A router's routing updates can then be manipulated to cause traffic to flow to unauthorized destinations.

RIF Routing Information Field: In source-route bridging, a header field that defines the path direction of the frame or token. If the Route Information Indicator (RII) bit is not set, the RIF is read from source to destination (left to right). If the RII bit is set, the RIF is read from the destination back to the source, so the RIF is read right to left. It is defined as part of the Token Ring frame header for source-routed frames, which contains path information.

ring   Two or more stations connected in a logical circular topology. In this topology, which is the basis for Token Ring, FDDI, and CDDI, information is transferred from station to station in sequence.

ring topology   A network logical topology comprising a series of repeaters that form one closed loop by connecting unidirectional transmission links. Individual stations on the network are connected to the network at a repeater. Physically, ring topologies are generally organized in a closed-loop star. Compare to: *bus topology* and *star topology.*

RIP   Routing Information Protocol: The most commonly used interior gateway protocol in the Internet. RIP employs hop count as a routing metric. See also: *Enhanced IGRP, IGP, OSPF,* and *hop count.*

RJ connector   Registered jack connector: Used with twisted-pair wiring to connect the copper wire to network interface cards, switches, and hubs.

robbed-bit signaling   Used in Primary Rate Interface clocking mechanisms.

ROM   Read-only memory: Chip used in computers to help boot the device. Cisco routers use a ROM chip to load the bootstrap, which runs a power-on self test, and then finds and loads the IOS in flash memory by default.

root bridge   Used with the Spanning-Tree Protocol to stop network loops from occurring. The root bridge is elected by having the lowest bridge ID. The bridge ID is determined by the priority (32,768 by default on all bridges and switches) and the main hardware address of the device. The root bridge determines which of the neighboring Layer 2 devices' interfaces become the designated and nondesignated ports.

routed protocol   Routed protocols (such as IP and IPX) are used to transmit user data through an internetwork. By contrast, routing protocols (such as RIP, IGRP, and OSPF) are used to update routing tables between routers.

route flap   A route that is being announced in an up/down fashion.

route poisoning   Used by various DV routing protocols in order to overcome large routing loops and offer explicit information about when a subnet or network is not accessible (instead of merely suggesting that the network is unreachable by not including it in updates). Typically, this is accomplished by setting the hop count to one more than the maximum. See also: *poison reverse updates.*

router   A Network-layer mechanism, either software or hardware, using one or more metrics to decide on the best path to use for transmission of network traffic. Sending packets between networks by routers is based on the information provided on network layers. Historically, this device has sometimes been called a *gateway.*

route summarization   In various routing protocols, such as OSPF, EIGRP, and IS-IS, the consolidation of publicized subnetwork addresses so that a single summary route is advertised to other areas by an area border router.

routing   The process of forwarding logically addressed packets from their local subnetwork toward their ultimate destination. In large networks, the numerous intermediary destinations a packet might travel before reaching its destination can make routing very complex.

routing domain   Any collection of end systems and intermediate systems that operate under an identical set of administrative rules. Every routing domain contains one or several areas, all individually given a certain area address.

routing metric   Any value that is used by routing algorithms to determine whether one route is superior to another. Metrics include such information as bandwidth, delay, hop count, path cost, load, MTU, reliability, and communication cost. Only the best possible routes are stored in the routing table, while all other information may be stored in link-state or topological databases. See also: *cost*.

routing protocol   Any protocol that defines algorithms to be used for updating routing tables between routers. Examples include IGRP, RIP, and OSPF.

routing table   A table kept in a router or other internetworking mechanism that maintains a record of only the best possible routes to certain network destinations and the metrics associated with those routes.

RP   Route Processor: Also known as a supervisory processor, a module on Cisco 7000 series routers that holds the CPU, system software, and most of the memory components used in the router.

RSA-encrypted nonces   A type of public/private key cryptography that is truly very secure, but it's not very scalable. A nonce is a pseudo-random number. RSA-encrypted nonces can be used to authenticate the IKE exchange and the Diffie-Hellman Agreement. See also: *nonce*.

RSA signatures   Used every time an IPSec tunnel is established to authenticate the IKE SA. Diffie-Hellman is used to derive the shared secret encryption key for the protection of data across the IKE SA, including the negotiation of the IPSec policy to be used.

RSP   Route/Switch Processor: A processor module combining the functions of RP and SP used in Cisco 7500 series routers. See also: *RP and SP*.

RTS   Request To Send: An EIA/TIA-232 control signal requesting permission to transmit data on a communication line.

S

S reference point   An ISDN reference point that works with a T reference point to convert a four-wire ISDN network to the two-wire ISDN network needed to communicate with the ISDN switches at the network provider.

sacrificial hosts   A term used for bastion hosts because the odds are so good that they'll be attacked. See also: *bastion host*.

sampling rate   The rate at which samples of a specific waveform amplitude are collected within a specified period of time.

SAP   1) Service access point: A field specified by IEEE 802.2 that is part of an address specification. 2) Service Advertising Protocol: The Novell NetWare protocol that supplies a way to inform network clients of resources and services availability on the network, using routers and servers. See also: *IPX*.

SCR   Sustainable cell rate: An ATM Forum parameter used for traffic management, it is the long-term average cell rate for VBR connections that can be transmitted.

SDH   Synchronous Digital Hierarchy: One of the standards developed for Fiber Optic Transmission Systems (FOTS).

SDLC   Synchronous Data Link Control: A protocol used in SNA Data Link–layer communications. SDLC is a bit-oriented, full-duplex serial protocol that is the basis for several similar protocols, including HDLC and LAPB. See also: *HDLC and LAPB*.

security association (SA)   An instance of security policy and keying material applied to a data flow, uniquely identified by destination address (IPSec endpoint), security protocol (AH or ESP), and security parameter index (SPI). Both IKE and IPSec use SAs, although SAs are independent of one another. IPSec SAs are unidirectional, and they are unique in each security protocol. A set of SAs is needed for a protected data pipe, one per direction per protocol. For example, if you have a pipe that supports ESP between peers, one ESP SA is required for each direction.

security gateway   A network system that provides an interface between two networks.

security level   Definition of the danger implied by a signature. Signatures are given one of four security levels: info, low, medium, and high.

Security Parameter Index (SPI)   The SPI is a unique part of the identification mechanism for each SA on a device. When an IPSec packet arrives, the device checks the SPI contained in the packet and compares it to those in its SAD to determine which policy is in force. Each SA has a unique triple identity consisting of a Security Parameter Index (SPI), an IP Destination Address, and a security protocol (AH or ESP) identifier. The completion of this step is marked by the formation of an IPSec tunnel. See also: *security association (SA)*.

security policy   Policy typically created and enforced by organizations to help achieve and maintain a secure network.

seed router   In an AppleTalk network, the router that is equipped with the network number or cable range in its port descriptor. The seed router specifies the network number or cable range for other routers in that network section and answers to configuration requests from non-seed routers on its connected AppleTalk network, permitting those routers to affirm or modify their configurations accordingly. Every AppleTalk network needs at least one seed router physically connected to each network segment.

server   Hardware and software that provide network services to clients.

session   1) Session layer of OSI model, which is responsible for keeping track of user data and keeping it separate on the network. 2) Reliable sessions can be set up between hosts.

session hijacking   When two hosts communicate, they typically use the TCP protocol at the Transport layer to set up a reliable session. This session can be "hijacked" by making the hosts believe that they are sending packets to a valid host when in fact, they're delivering their packets to a hijacker.

Session layer   Layer 5 of the OSI reference model, responsible for creating, managing, and terminating sessions between applications and overseeing data exchange between presentation layer entities. See also: *Application layer, Data Link layer, Network layer, Physical layer, Presentation layer,* and *Transport layer.*

session replay   Occurs when a sequence of packets or application commands are captured, manipulated, and replayed by hackers with the intent of causing harm.

set-based   Set-based routers and switches use the `set` command to configure devices. Cisco is moving away from set-based commands and is using the command-line interface (CLI) on all new devices.

setup mode   Mode that a router will enter if no configuration is found in nonvolatile RAM when the router boots. Allows the administrator to configure a router step by step. Not as robust or flexible as the command-line interface.

SF   Super Frame: A super frame (also called a D4 frame) consists of 12 frames with 192 bits each; the 193rd bit provides other functions, including error checking. SF is frequently used on T1 circuits. A newer version of the technology is Extended Super Frame (ESF), which uses 24 frames. See also: *ESF.*

shared tree   A method of multicast data forwarding. Shared trees use an architecture in which multiple sources share a common rendezvous point.

signaling packet   An informational packet created by an ATM-connected mechanism that wants to establish connection with another such mechanism. The packet contains the QoS parameters needed for connection and the ATM NSAP address of the endpoint. The endpoint responds with a message of acceptance if it is able to support the desired QoS, and the connection is established. See also: *QoS.*

signatures   The IOS Firewall IDS works based on IDS signatures. These signatures profile different types of traffic that may not be desirable. You, as the administrator of the IDS, have the ability to choose which of these signatures you wish to deploy and how you wish to react to them when patterns of network traffic match the signature.

silicon switching   A type of high-speed switching used in Cisco 7000 series routers, based on the use of a separate processor (the Silicon Switch Processor, or SSP). See also: *SSE.*

simplex   The mode at which data or a digital signal is transmitted. Simplex is a way of transmitting in only one direction. Half duplex transmits in two directions but only in one direction at a time. Full duplex transmits both directions simultaneously.

site-to-site VPN   An alternative WAN infrastructure that is used to connect branch offices, home offices, or business partners' sites to all or portions of a company's network.

sliding window   The method of flow control used by TCP, as well as several Data Link–layer protocols. This method places a buffer between the receiving application and the network data flow. The "window" available for accepting data is the size of the buffer minus the amount of data already there. This window increases in size as the application reads data from it and decreases as new data is sent. The receiver sends the transmitter announcements of the current window size, and it may stop accepting data until the window increases above a certain threshold.

SLIP   Serial Line Internet Protocol: An industry-standard serial encapsulation for point-to-point connections that supports only a single routed protocol, TCP/IP. SLIP is the predecessor to PPP. See also: *PPP*.

SMDS   Switched Multimegabit Data Service: A packet-switched, datagram-based WAN networking technology offered by telephone companies that provides high speed.

SMTP   Simple Mail Transfer Protocol: A protocol used on the Internet to provide electronic mail services.

smurf attack   This attack sends a large amount of ICMP (Internet Control Message Protocol) echo (ping) traffic to IP broadcast addresses from a supposedly valid host that is traceable.

SNA   System Network Architecture: A complex, feature-rich network architecture similar to the OSI reference model but with several variations; created by IBM in the 1970s and essentially composed of seven layers.

SNAP   Subnetwork Access Protocol: SNAP is a frame used in Ethernet, Token Ring, and FDDI LANs. Data transfer, connection management, and QoS selection are three primary functions executed by the SNAP frame.

snapshot routing   Snapshot routing takes a point-in-time capture of a dynamic routing table and maintains it even when the remote connection goes down. This allows the use of a dynamic routing protocol without requiring the link to remain active, which might incur per-minute usage charges.

SNMP   Simple Network Management Protocol: This protocol polls SNMP agents or devices for statistical and environmental data. This data can include device temperature, name, performance statistics, and much more. SNMP works with MIB objects that are present on the SNMP agent. This information is queried and then sent to the SNMP server.

socket   1) A software structure that operates within a network device as a destination point for communications. 2) In AppleTalk networks, an entity at a specific location within a node; AppleTalk sockets are conceptually similar to TCP/IP ports.

soft tokens   See *token cards*.

software weakness   Any default setting that allows access through an application or other type of software to any system.

SOHO   Small office/home office: A contemporary term for remote users.

SONET   Synchronous Optical Network: The ANSI standard for synchronous transmission on fiber-optic media, developed at Bell Labs. It specifies a base signal rate of 51.84Mbps and a set of multiples of that rate, known as optical carrier levels, up to 2.5Gbps.

source tree   A method of multicast data forwarding. Source trees use the architecture of the source of the multicast traffic as the root of the tree.

SP   Switch Processor: Also known as a *ciscoBus controller*, it is a Cisco 7000 series processor module acting as governing agent for all CxBus activities.

span   A full-duplex digital transmission line connecting two facilities.

SPAN   Switched Port Analyzer: A feature of the Catalyst 5000 switch, offering freedom to manipulate within a switched Ethernet environment by extending the monitoring ability of the existing network analyzers into the environment. At one switched segment, the SPAN mirrors traffic onto a predetermined SPAN port, while a network analyzer connected to the SPAN port is able to monitor traffic from any other Catalyst switched port.

spanning explorer packet   Sometimes called *limited-route* or *single-route explorer packet*, it pursues a statically configured spanning tree when searching for paths in a source-route bridging network. See also: *all-routes explorer packet, explorer packet*, and *local explorer packet*.

spanning tree   A subset of a network topology, within which no loops exist. When bridges are interconnected into a loop, the bridge, or switch, cannot identify a frame that has been forwarded previously, so there is no mechanism for removing a frame as it passes the interface numerous times. Without a method for removing these frames, the bridges continuously forward them—consuming bandwidth and adding overhead to the network. Spanning trees prune the network to provide only one path for any packet. See also: *Spanning-Tree Protocol* and *spanning-tree algorithm*.

spanning-tree algorithm (STA)   An algorithm that creates a spanning tree using the Spanning-Tree Protocol (STP). See also: *spanning tree* and *Spanning-Tree Protocol*.

Spanning-Tree Protocol (STP)   The bridge protocol (IEEE 802.1d) that enables a learning bridge to dynamically avoid loops in the network topology by creating a spanning tree using the spanning-tree algorithm. Spanning-tree frames called *bridge protocol data units (BPDUs)* are sent and received by all switches in the network at regular intervals. The switches participating in the spanning tree don't forward the frames; instead, they're processed to determine the spanning-tree topology itself. Cisco Catalyst series switches use STP 802.1d to perform this function. See also: *BPDU, learning bridge, MAC address, spanning tree*, and *spanning-tree algorithm*.

SPF   Shortest path first algorithm: A routing algorithm used to decide on the shortest-path spanning tree. Sometimes called *Dijkstra's algorithm* and frequently used in link-state routing algorithms. See also: *link-state routing algorithm*.

SPID   Service profile identifier: A number assigned by service providers or local telephone companies and assigned by administrators to a BRI port. SPIDs are used to determine subscription services of a device connected via ISDN. ISDN devices use SPID when accessing the telephone company switch that initializes the link to a service provider.

split horizon   Useful for preventing routing loops, a type of distance-vector routing rule where information about routes is prevented from leaving the router interface through which that information was received.

spoofing   1) In dial-on-demand routing (DDR), where a circuit-switched link is taken down to save toll charges when there is no traffic to be sent, spoofing is a scheme used by routers that causes a host to treat an interface as if it were functioning and supporting a session. The router pretends to send "spoof" replies to keepalive messages from the host in an effort to convince the host that the session is up and running. See also: *DDR*. 2) The illegal act of sending a packet labeled with a false address, in order to deceive network security mechanisms such as filters and access lists.

spooler   A management application that processes requests submitted to it for execution in a sequential fashion from a queue. A good example is a print spooler.

SPX   Sequenced Packet Exchange: A Novell NetWare transport protocol that augments the datagram service provided by Network layer (Layer 3) protocols, it was derived from the Switch-to-Switch Protocol of the XNS protocol suite.

SQE   Signal quality error: In an Ethernet network, a message sent from a transceiver to an attached machine that the collision-detection circuitry is working.

SRB   Source-route bridging: Created by IBM, the bridging method used in Token Ring networks. The source determines the entire route to a destination before sending the data and includes that information in route information fields (RIFs) within each packet. Contrast with: *transparent bridging*.

SRT   Source-route transparent bridging: A bridging scheme developed by IBM, merging source-route and transparent bridging. SRT takes advantage of both technologies in one device, fulfilling the needs of all end nodes. Translation between bridging protocols is not necessary. Compare to: *SR/TLB*.

SR/TLB   Source-route translational bridging: A bridging method that allows source-route stations to communicate with transparent bridge stations, aided by an intermediate bridge that translates between the two bridge protocols. Used for bridging between Token Ring and Ethernet. Compare to: *SRT*.

SSAP   Source service access point: The SAP of the network node identified in the Source field of the packet. See also: *DSAP* and *SAP*.

SSE   Silicon Switching Engine: The software component of Cisco's silicon switching technology, hard-coded into the Silicon Switch Processor (SSP). Silicon switching is available only on the Cisco 7000 with an SSP. Silicon-switched packets are compared to the silicon-switching cache on the SSE. The SSP is a dedicated switch processor that offloads the switching process from the route processor, providing a fast-switching solution, but packets must still traverse the backplane of the router to get to the SSP and then back to the exit interface.

standard IP access list   IP access list that uses only the source IP addresses to filter a network.

standard IPX access list   IPX access list that uses only the source and destination IPX addresses to filter a network.

star topology   A LAN physical topology with endpoints on the network converging at a common central switch (known as a *hub*) using point-to-point links. A logical ring topology can be configured as a physical star topology using a unidirectional, closed-loop star rather than point-to-point links; that is, connections within the hub are arranged in an internal ring. See also: *bus topology* and *ring topology*.

startup range   If an AppleTalk node does not have a number saved from the last time it was booted, then the node selects from the range of values from 65280 to 65534.

state transitions   Digital signaling scheme that reads the "state" of the digital signal in the middle of the bit cell. If it is five volts, the cell is read as a 1. If the state of the digital signal is zero volts, the bit cell is read as a 0.

static route   A route whose information is purposefully entered into the routing table and takes priority over those chosen by dynamic routing protocols.

static VLANs   Static VLANs are manually configured port by port. This is the method typically used in production networks.

statistical multiplexing   Multiplexing in general is a technique that allows data from multiple logical channels to be sent across a single physical channel. Statistical multiplexing dynamically assigns bandwidth only to input channels that are active, optimizing available bandwidth so that more devices can be connected than with other multiplexing techniques. Also known as *statistical time-division multiplexing* or *stat mux*.

STM-1   Synchronous Transport Module level 1: In the European SDH standard, one of many formats identifying the frame structure for the 155.52Mbps lines that are used to carry ATM cells.

store-and-forward packet switching   A technique in which the switch first copies each packet into its buffer and performs a cyclical redundancy check (CRC). If the packet is error-free, the switch then looks up the destination address in its filter table, determines the appropriate exit port, and sends the packet.

STP   1) Shielded twisted-pair: A two-pair wiring scheme, used in many network implementations, that has a layer of shielded insulation to reduce EMI. 2) Spanning-Tree Protocol. See also: *Spanning-Tree Protocol*.

stub area   An OSPF area carrying a default route, intra-area routes, and inter-area routes, but no external routes. Configuration of virtual links cannot be achieved across a stub area, and stub areas are not allowed to contain an ASBR. See also: *non-stub area*, *ASBR*, and *OSPF*.

stub network   A network having only one connection to a router.

STUN   Serial tunnel: A technology used to connect an HDLC link to an SDLC link over a serial link.

subarea   A portion of an SNA network made up of a subarea node and its attached links and peripheral nodes.

subarea node   An SNA communications host or controller that handles entire network addresses.

subchannel   A frequency-based subdivision that creates a separate broadband communications channel.

subinterface   One of many virtual interfaces available on a single physical interface.

subnet   See: *subnetwork*.

subnet address   The portion of an IP address that is specifically identified by the subnet mask as the subnetwork. See also: *IP address*, *subnetwork*, and *subnet mask*.

subnet mask   Also simply known as *mask*, a 32-bit address mask used in IP to identify the bits of an IP address that are used for the subnet address. Using a mask, the router does not need to examine all 32 bits, only those selected by the mask. See also: *address mask* and *IP address*.

subnetwork   1) Any network that is part of a larger IP network and is identified by a subnet address. A network administrator segments a network into subnetworks in order to provide a hierarchical, multilevel routing structure, and at the same time protect the subnetwork from the addressing complexity of networks that are attached. Also known as a *subnet*. See also: *IP address*, *subnet mask*, and *subnet address*. 2) In OSI networks, the term specifically refers to a collection of ESs and ISs controlled by only one administrative domain, using a solitary network connection protocol.

summarization   Term used to describe the process of summarizing multiple routing table entries into one entry.

supernetting   See: *summarization*.

SVC   Switched virtual circuit: A dynamically established virtual circuit, created on demand and dissolved as soon as transmission is over and the circuit is no longer needed. In ATM terminology, it is referred to as a *switched virtual connection*. See also: *PVC*.

switch   1) In networking, a device responsible for multiple functions such as filtering, flooding, and sending frames. It works using the destination address of individual frames. Switches operate at the Data Link layer of the OSI model. 2) Broadly, any electronic/mechanical device allowing connections to be established as needed and terminated if no longer necessary.

switch block   The switch block is a combination of Layer 3 switches and Layer 3 routers. The Layer 2 switches connect users in the wiring closet into the Access layer and provide 10 or 100Mbps dedicated connections. 1900/2820 and 2900 Catalyst switches can be used in the switch block.

switch-fabric   Term used to identify a Layer 2 switched internetwork with many switches.

switched LAN   Any LAN implemented using LAN switches. See also: *LAN switch*.

synchronous transmission   Signals transmitted digitally with precision clocking. These signals have identical frequencies and contain individual characters encapsulated in control bits (called *start/stop bits*) that designate the beginning and ending of each character. See also: *asynchronous transmission* and *isochronous transmission*.

SYN flood attack   A very popular hacking technique used to cause a denial of service (DoS) to real users. What happens is that SYN packets are sent from a client with a spoofed IP address at a rate faster than the TCP stack on the host is set to time out. This means that all the resources will be used up and leave nothing for legitimate users.

Syslog   A protocol used to monitor system log messages by a remote device.

T

T reference point   Used with an S reference point to change a four-wire ISDN network to a two-wire ISDN network.

T1   Digital WAN that uses 24 DS0s at 64K each to create a bandwidth of 1.536Mbps, minus clocking overhead, providing 1.544Mbps of usable bandwidth.

T3   Digital WAN that can provide bandwidth of 44.763Mbps.

TACACS+   Terminal Access Controller Access Control System Plus: An enhanced version of TACACS, this protocol is similar to RADIUS. TACACS+ is a Cisco Proprietary security application that provides centralized authentication of users attempting to log in to a router or network access server. See also: *RADIUS*.

tagged traffic   ATM cells with their cell loss priority (CLP) bit set to 1. Also referred to as *discard-eligible (DE) traffic*. Tagged traffic can be eliminated in order to ensure trouble-free delivery of higher-priority traffic, if the network is congested. See also: *CLP*.

tag switching   Based on the concept of label swapping, where packets or cells are designated to defined-length labels that control the manner in which data is to be sent, tag switching is a high-performance technology used for forwarding packets. It incorporates Data Link layer (Layer 2) switching and Network layer (Layer 3) routing and supplies scalable, high-speed switching in the network core.

TCP   Transmission Control Protocol: A connection-oriented protocol that is defined at the Transport layer of the OSI reference model. Provides reliable delivery of data.

TCP connection   Connection defined as a user from an untrusted network connecting with a virtual circuit to a host on a trusted network.

TCP Intercept   Cisco's answer to TCP SYN-flooding attacks (DoS attacks). The TCP Intercept feature implements software to protect TCP servers from this type of attack.

TCP/IP   Transmission Control Protocol/Internet Protocol: The suite of protocols underlying the Internet. TCP and IP are the most widely known protocols in that suite. See also: *IP* and *TCP*.

TCP/IP weakness   There are many problems with the IP stack, especially in Microsoft products. Session replaying is a weakness that is found in TCP. Both SNMP and SMTP are listed by Cisco as inherently insecure protocols in the TCP/IP stack.

TDM   Time-division multiplexing: A technique for assigning bandwidth on a single wire, based on preassigned time slots, to data from several channels. Bandwidth is allotted to each channel regardless of a station's ability to send data. See also: *ATDM*, *FDM*, and *multiplexing*.

TE   Terminal equipment: Any peripheral device that is ISDN-compatible and attached to a network, such as a telephone or computer. TE1s are devices that are ISDN-ready and understand ISDN signaling techniques. TE2s are devices that are not ISDN-ready and do not understand ISDN signaling techniques. A terminal adapter must be used with a TE2.

TE1   A device with a four-wire, twisted-pair digital interface is referred to as terminal equipment type 1. Most modern ISDN devices are of this type.

TE2   Devices known as terminal equipment type 2 do not understand ISDN signaling techniques, and a terminal adapter must be used to convert the signaling.

technology weakness   TCP/IP protocol weaknesses, operating system weaknesses, and network equipment weaknesses are listed by Cisco as the three technology weaknesses.

telco   A common abbreviation for the telephone company.

Telnet   The standard terminal emulation protocol within the TCP/IP protocol stack. It provides a method of remote terminal connection, enabling users to log in on remote networks and use those resources as if they were locally connected. Telnet is defined in RFC 854.

terminal adapter   A hardware interface between a computer without a native ISDN interface and an ISDN line. In effect, a device to connect a standard async interface to a non-native ISDN device, emulating a modem.

terminal emulation   The use of software, installed on a PC or LAN server, that allows the PC to function as if it were a "dumb" terminal directly attached to a particular type of mainframe.

TFTP   Trivial File Transfer Protocol: Conceptually, a stripped-down version of FTP, it's the protocol of choice if you know exactly what you want and where it's to be found. TFTP doesn't provide the abundance of functions that FTP does. In particular, it has no directory-browsing abilities; it can do nothing but send and receive files.

Thicknet Also called *10Base5*. Bus network that uses a thick cable and runs Ethernet up to 500 meters.

Thinnet Also called *10Base2*. Bus network that uses a thin coax cable and runs Ethernet media access up to 185 meters.

token A frame containing only control information. Possessing this control information gives a network device permission to transmit data onto the network. See also: *token passing*.

token bus LAN architecture that is the basis for the IEEE 802.4 LAN specification and employs token passing access over a bus topology. See also: *IEEE*.

token-card server Token cards are considered the most secure authentication solution available and are distributed by a token-card server. There are two kinds of token cards, synchronous and asynchronous. Currently, Cisco Secure Authentication Agent supports only the synchronous token card, which does not need a challenge from a token-card server to generate a token.

token cards/soft tokens Users receive token cards and a personal identification number (PIN). Token cards are typically small electronic devices about the size of a credit card-sized calculator. There are many token card vendors, and each has its own token card server. The PIN is entered into the card, which generates a secure password that the user can use to enter into the system for access. See also: *token-card server*.

token passing A method used by network devices to access the physical medium in a systematic way based on possession of a small frame called a token. See also: *token*.

Token Ring IBM's token-passing LAN technology. It runs at 4Mbps or 16Mbps over a ring topology. Defined formally by IEEE 802.5. See also: *ring topology* and *token passing*.

toll network WAN network that uses the public switched telephone network (PSTN) to send packets.

trace IP command used to trace the path a packet takes through an internetwork.

transform A transform describes a security protocol (AH or ESP) with its corresponding algorithms. ESP with the DES cipher algorithm and HMAC-SHA for authentication is an example of a transform. Another transform is the ESP protocol with the 56-bit DES encryption algorithm and the SHA-HMAC authentication algorithm.

transparent bridging The bridging scheme used in Ethernet and IEEE 802.3 networks, it passes frames along one hop at a time, using bridging information stored in tables that associate end-node MAC addresses within bridge ports. This type of bridging is considered transparent because the source node does not know it has been bridged, because the destination frames are sent directly to the end node. Contrast with: *SRB*.

Transport layer Layer 4 of the OSI reference model, used for reliable communication between end nodes over the network. The Transport layer provides mechanisms used for establishing, maintaining, and terminating virtual circuits, transport fault detection and recovery, and controlling the flow of information. See also: *Application layer*, *Data Link layer*, *Network layer*, *Physical layer*, *Presentation layer*, and *Session layer*.

transport mode   Term that can be used for discussing an encapsulation mode for AH/ESP. The transport mode encapsulates the upper-layer payload—either the TCP or UDP segment—of the original IP datagram. See also: *tunnel mode.*

trap   Used to send SNMP messages to SNMP managers.

TRIP   Token Ring Interface Processor: A high-speed interface processor used on Cisco 7000 series routers. The TRIP provides two or four ports for interconnection with IEEE 802.5 and IBM media with ports set to speeds of either 4Mbps or 16Mbps set independently of each other.

Triple DES (3DES)   A stronger and more secure version of DES that uses three different keys for encrypting data before it is sent to the peer.

Trojan horse   Software programs that appear to be benign or useful but actually cause problems once they are launched.

trunk link   Link used between switches and from some servers to the switches. Trunk links carry information about many VLANs. Access links are used to connect host devices to a switch and carry only VLAN information that the device is a member of.

trusted network   A network defined as an internal network, which would be on the "inside" of the DMZ.

TTL   Time To Live: A field in an IP header indicating the length of time a packet is valid.

TUD   Trunk up-down: A protocol used in ATM networks for the monitoring of trunks. Should a trunk miss a given number of test messages being sent by ATM switches to ensure trunk-line quality, TUD declares the trunk down. When a trunk reverses direction and comes back up, TUD recognizes that the trunk is up and returns the trunk to service.

tunneling   A method of avoiding protocol restrictions by wrapping packets from one protocol in another protocol's packet and transmitting this encapsulated packet over a network that supports the wrapper protocol. See also: *encapsulation.*

tunnel mode   Used in IPSec for encapsulating the complete IP datagram. Tunnel mode is used to protect datagrams that come from or are destined for non-IPSec systems. Tunnel mode can be used only when the peers are the endpoints of the communication.

U

U reference point   Reference point between a TE1 and an ISDN network. The U reference point understands ISDN signaling techniques and uses a two-wire connection.

UDP   User Datagram Protocol: A connectionless Transport-layer protocol in the TCP/IP protocol stack that simply allows datagrams to be exchanged without acknowledgments or delivery guarantees, requiring other protocols to handle error processing and retransmission. UDP is defined in RFC 768.

unicast Used for direct host-to-host communication. Communication is directed to only one destination and is originated from only one source.

unidirectional shared tree A method of shared-tree multicast forwarding. This method allows only multicast data to be forwarded from the RP.

unknown network A network that is defined as being neither outside of the DMZ nor inside of the DMZ.

unnumbered frames HDLC frames used for control-management purposes, such as link startup and shutdown or mode specification.

untrusted network A network that is outside of the DMZ. Hosts on this network cannot access the inside trusted network by default.

UTP Unshielded twisted-pair: Copper wiring used in small-to-large networks to connect host devices to hubs and switches. Also used to connect switch to switch or hub to hub.

V

VBR Variable bit rate: A QoS class, as defined by the ATM Forum, for use in ATM networks that is subdivided into real-time (RT) class and non–real time (NRT) class. RT is employed when connections have a fixed-time relationship between samples. Conversely, NRT is employed when connections do not have a fixed-time relationship between samples, but still need an assured QoS.

VCC Virtual channel connection: A logical circuit that is created by virtual channel links (VCLs). VCCs carry data between two endpoints in an ATM network. Sometimes called a *virtual circuit connection.*

VIP 1) Versatile Interface Processor: An interface card for Cisco 7000 and 7500 series routers providing multilayer switching and running the Cisco IOS software. The most recent version of VIP is VIP2. 2) Virtual IP: A function making it possible for logically separated switched IP workgroups to run virtual networking services across the switch ports of a Catalyst 5000.

virtual circuit (VC) A logical circuit devised to assure reliable communication between two devices on a network. Defined by a virtual path connection (VPC)/virtual path identifier (VCI) pair, a virtual circuit can be permanent (PVC) or switched (SVC). Virtual circuits are used in Frame Relay and X.25. Known as a *virtual channel* in ATM. See also: *PVC* and *SVC.*

virtual ring In an SRB network, a logical connection between physical rings, either local or remote.

VLAN Virtual LAN: A group of devices on one or more logically segmented LANs (configured by the use of management software), enabling devices to communicate as if they were attached to the same physical medium, when they are actually located on numerous different LAN segments. VLANs are based on logical instead of physical connections and thus are tremendously flexible.

VLAN ID Sometimes referred to as *VLAN color*, the VLAN ID is tagged onto a frame to tell a receiving switch which VLAN the frame is a member of.

VLSM Variable-length subnet mask: Helps optimize available address space and specify a different subnet mask for the same network number on various subnets. Also commonly referred to as *subnetting a subnet*.

VMPS VLAN management policy server: Used to dynamically assign VLANs to a switch port.

VPN Virtual private network: Provides secure communications across the Internet. A VPN tunnel encrypts data at the Network layer, which enables secure communications across a public network.

VTP VLAN Trunk Protocol: Used to update switches in a switch-fabric about VLANs configured on a VTP server. VTP devices can be a VTP server, client, or transparent device. Servers update clients. Transparent devices are only local devices and do not share information with VTP clients. VTPs send VLAN information down trunked links only.

W

WAN Wide area network: A designation used to connect LANs together across a DCE (data communications equipment) network. Typically, a WAN is a leased line or dial-up connection across a PSTN network. Examples of WAN protocols include Frame Relay, PPP, ISDN, and HDLC.

WareZ Refers to unauthorized distribution of software. It's not an actual attack on a corporate network or website; its motivation is to either sell someone else's software or distribute unlicensed versions of software for free on the Internet.

wildcard Used with access-list, supernetting, and OSPF configurations. Wildcards are designations used to identify a range of subnets.

windowing Flow-control method used with TCP at the Transport layer of the OSI model.

WINS Windows Internet Name Service: Name-resolution database for NetBIOS names to TCP/IP address.

WinSock Windows Socket Interface: A software interface that makes it possible for an assortment of applications to use and share an Internet connection. The WinSock software consists of a dynamic link library (DLL) with supporting programs such as a dialer program that initiates the connection.

workgroup switching A switching method that supplies high-speed (100Mbps) transparent bridging between Ethernet networks as well as high-speed translational bridging between Ethernet and CDDI or FDDI.

X

X.25 An ITU-T packet-relay standard that defines communication between DTE and DCE network devices. X.25 uses a reliable Data Link–layer protocol called LAPB. X.25 also uses PLP at the Network layer. X.25 has mostly been replaced by Frame Relay.

X Window System A distributed multitasking windowing and graphics system originally developed by MIT for communication between X terminals and Unix workstations.

Z

ZIP Zone Information Protocol: A Session-layer protocol used by AppleTalk to map network numbers to zone names. NBP uses ZIP in the determination of networks containing nodes that belong to a zone. See also: *ZIP storm* and *zone*.

ZIP storm A broadcast storm occurring when a router running AppleTalk reproduces or transmits a route for which there is no corresponding zone name at the time of execution. The route is then forwarded by other routers downstream, thus causing a ZIP storm. See also: *broadcast storm* and *ZIP*.

zone A logical grouping of network devices in AppleTalk. See also: *ZIP*.

Index

Note to the reader: Throughout this index boldfaced page numbers indicate primary discussions of a topic. *Italicized* page numbers indicate illustrations.

D

U

V

W

X

Z

The Official
Juniper™ Networks Certification Study Guides
From Sybex

The Juniper Networks Technical Certification Program offers a four-tiered certification program that validates knowledge and skills related to Juniper Networks technologies:

- JNCIA (Juniper Networks Certified Internet Associate)
- JNCIS (Juniper Networks Certified Internet Specialist)
- JNCIP (Juniper Networks Certified Internet Professional)
- JNCIE (Juniper Networks Certified Internet Expert)

The JNCIA and JNCIS certifications require candidates to pass written exams, while the JNCIP and JNCIE certifications require candidates to pass one-day hands-on laboratory exams.

The Only OFFICIAL Juniper Networks Study Guides Are From Sybex

Written and reviewed by Juniper employees, the Juniper Networks Study Guides are the only official Study Guides for the Juniper Networks Technical Certification Program. Each book provides in-depth coverage of all exam objectives and detailed perspectives and insights into working with Juniper Networks technologies in the real world.

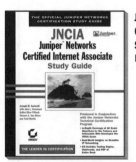

JNCIA: Juniper Networks Certified Internet Associate Study Guide
ISBN: 0-7821-4071-8

JNCIS: Juniper Networks Certified Internet Specialist Study Guide
ISBN: 0-7821-4072-6

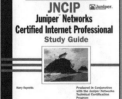

JNCIP: Juniper Networks Certified Internet Professional Study Guide
ISBN: 0-7821-4073-4

JNCIE: Juniper Networks Certified Internet Expert Study Guide
ISBN: 0-7821-4069-6

SYBEX®  **Juniper**™ NETWORKS

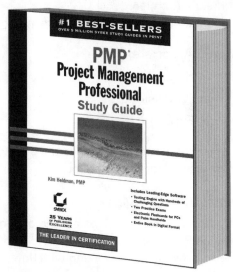

TELL US WHAT YOU THINK!

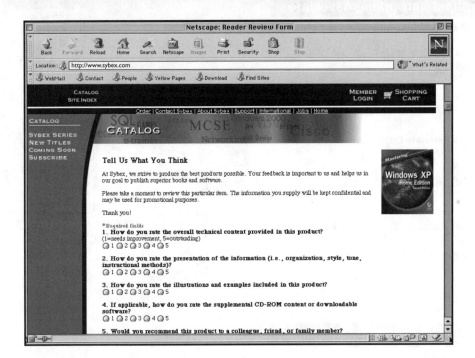

Your feedback is critical to our efforts to provide you with the best books and software on the market. Tell us what you think about the products you've purchased. It's simple:

1. Go to the Sybex website.
2. Find your book by typing the ISBN or title into the Search field.
3. Click on the book title when it appears.
4. Click **Submit a Review.**
5. Fill out the questionnaire and comments.
6. Click **Submit.**

With your feedback, we can continue to publish the highest quality computer books and software products that today's busy IT professionals deserve.

www.sybex.com

SYBEX Inc. • 1151 Marina Village Parkway, Alameda, CA 94501 • 510-523-8233

The Complete Cisco Certification Solution